Religion, Society, and Psychoanalysis

Religion, Society, and Psychoanalysis

Readings in Contemporary Theory

edited by

Janet Liebman Jacobs
University of Colorado

Donald Capps
Princeton Theological Seminary

Westview
PRESS
A Member of the Perseus Books Group

Copyright © 1997 by Westview Press, A Division of HarperCollins Publishers, Inc., except Chapter 1, Dan Merkur, "Freud and Hasidism," *The Psychoanalytic Study of Religion: Essays in Honor of George A. De Vos,* Vol. 19 (1994). Copyright © 1994 by The Analytic Press. Reprinted by permission.

Published in 1997 in the United States of America by Westview Press, 5500 Central Avenue, Boulder, Colorado 80301-2877, and in the United Kingdom by Westview Press, 12 Hid's Copse Road, Cumnor Hill, Oxford OX2 9JJ

Library of Congress Cataloging-in-Publication Data
Religion, society, and psychoanalysis : readings in contemporary
theory / edited by Janet L. Jacobs, Donald Capps.
      p.   cm.
   Includes bibliographical references and index.
   ISBN 0-8133-2647-8 (hardcover).—ISBN 0-8133-2648-6 (pbk.)
   1. Psychoanalysis and religion.   I. Jacobs, Janet Liebman.
II. Capps, Donald.
BF175.R44R438   1997
200´.1´9—dc21   97-573
                                                                                   CIP

10   9   8   7   6   5   4   3   2

Contents

Introduction ✍

The study of religion and psychoanalysis might naturally begin with Freud's varied writings on the illusional and delusional character of religious beliefs in Western society. Among the earliest of these writings is his 1922 essay, "A Seventeenth-Century Demonological Neurosis" (SE: 19). Complete with illustrations of a tormented artist encountering the Devil, this work lays out Freud's theories on God and Satan as father substitutes. Freud's analysis of the artist's religious redemption is in itself a fascinating case study. He based this work on a manuscript that, bearing a marked similarity to the story of Faust, told of a man who had made a pact with the Devil and was later redeemed through the intervention of the Virgin Mary. According to the manuscript, Christoph Haizmann, a painter, made a pilgrimage to the shrine of Mariazell in 1677. While at the church, he experienced convulsions and later told the priest that he had made a pact with the Devil nine years before when he had been despondent and unable to paint. Now, as the time approached for the Devil to claim Haizmann's body and soul, he sought the salvation of the Mother of God.

Freud was apparently intrigued by the manuscript and the psychosis that he believed to be at the heart of the painter's suffering. Twenty-five years earlier, Freud (1954) had written to his colleague Wilhelm Fliess on at least two occasions, suggesting that theologies of demonology originated out of psychoses that had found expression in the European witchcraze of the sixteenth and seventeenth centuries. With the essay on Haizmann and demonology, Freud returned to this hypothesis, clearly outlining his view that both God and the Devil were representations of the primal father. Through cultural evolution, these representations had become symbolized in images of divinity and supernatural evil. To support this theory, he drew on Haizmann's life. According to Freud, the painter's neurotic symptoms began soon after his father died. In a depressed and inactive state, he fantasized that the Devil had approached him nine times, offering to help him regain his art and livelihood. Finally, the painter agreed to the bond with the Devil. Freud believed that the Devil became the painter's father substitute when the painter "signed the pact."

That the Devil, as well as God, is an unconscious projection of the father is explained by Freud as the splitting off of the good parent from the feared and aggressive patriarch. In the essay on demonology, Freud described the psychic process as follows:

> We have here an example of the process with which we are familiar, by which an idea that has a contradictory—an ambivalent—content becomes divided into two sharply contrasted opposites. The contradictions in the original nature of God are, however, a reflection of ambivalence which governs the relation of the individual to his personal father. If the benevolent and righteous God is a substitute for his father, it is not to be wondered at that his hostile attitude to his father, too, which is one of hating and fearing him and of making complaints against him, should have come to expression in the creation of Satan. Thus, the father, it seems, is the individual prototype of both God and the Devil (SE: 19, 86).

Freud's theory of the primal father and the origins of demonology offers a backdrop against which to introduce this volume on the intersection of religion, society, and psychoanalysis. In Freud's 1922 essay, which he elaborated more fully in *The Future of an Illusion* (1927), he provided a theoretical foundation for examining the relationship between cultural constructions of good and evil and psychic desires and fears. At the same time, Freud's views challenge us to consider the nature of the divine and the reality principle out of which religious symbolism emerges and is given meaning. To fully understand Freud, however, and the significance of his theoretical contributions, one must first consider the cultural frame out of which his thoughts and insights emerged. What did it mean to be a Jewish scientist in predominantly Christian Europe and to develop a notion of God grounded in projection rather than faith? How do religious beliefs influence the construction of knowledge and the interpretation of psychic reality? In short, what is the connection between social forces and the production of scientific and religious thought? Questions such as these inspired the creation of this volume.

There are many ways to explore the interrelationship among social forces, religious systems, and the study of psychoanalysis. First, psychoanalytic theory helps us to explain diverse forms of religious experience, how symbols and the relationship to the divine are expressed through language and beliefs that are deeply embedded in the unconscious. Second, it is useful to consider the ways in which theological paradigms in turn influence the construction of psychoanalytic theories, how scientific inquiry is informed by the religious culture out of which knowledge is produced and disseminated. Finally, social and individual responses to trauma and significant life events can be given meaning through a psychoanalytic frame that, in many cases, cannot be separated from the religious values of the culture in which such events take place.

These diverse approaches to the study of psychoanalysis provide the context in which the chapters in this book have been assembled. In the diversity of essays and approaches represented here, the volume offers a contemporary discourse on such varied topics as psychoanalysis and mysticism, Freud and anti-Semitism, religious fundamentalism, object relations theory, ego psychology, child abuse, and the psychoanalytic construction of motherhood. Seeking to interrogate the complex ways in which religion, society, and psychoanalysis intersect, we have brought together the work of feminist thinkers, postmodern scholars, and traditional Freudian theorists.

Spanning three generations of psychoanalytic thought, the book is divided into three sections, each of which covers the significant theorists who have influenced the field of psychoanalysis. The first section of the book is devoted to a discussion of Freud. This discussion begins with an essay by Dan Merkur on Freud and Jewish mysticism, an area of study that was first explored by David Bakan in *Sigmund Freud and the Jewish Mystical Tradition* (1958). In that work, Bakan investigated the parallels between Kabbalistic writings and the psychoanalytic theories of Freud. Building on Bakan's groundbreaking study, Merkur provides a contemporary perspective on the relationship between Hasidism and Freudian theories of sexuality. Merkur's essay, which is reprinted from a volume in honor of George A. De Vos (1994), examines the extent to which Freud may have been exposed to Jewish mystical teachings. He then challenges the reader to consider the influence of Hasidic teachings on sexual fantasy and how these relate to Freud's views on sexual longing and repression.

The second chapter, by David Bakan, presents another facet of the ongoing interest in the interrelationship between Jewish theology and Freudian theory. Here, Bakan departs from his earlier work on mysticism to consider the writings of the twelfth-century Jewish thinker Maimonides as they relate to Freud's views on incest. Drawing on the aspects of Maimonides' philosophy that were influenced by the Greek intellectual tradition, Bakan discusses the parallels between Freud's understanding of incest as a natural inclination and the discourse on incest presented by Maimonides in *The Eight Chapters* (1912).

In comparison with the first two essays, Janet Liebman Jacobs's chapter provides a somewhat different view of Freud's relationship to his religious background. Her essay examines the impact of anti-Semitism on the construction of scientific thought, focusing on the effects of internalized racism on Freud's theories of femininity, incest, and the Oedipal father. Situating Freud within the cultural milieu of pre-Nazi Austria, Jacobs considers the influence of anti-Semitic ideologies on Freud's construction of the female personality. Through a feminist analysis of Freudian theory, her essay suggests that Freud projected his own self-hatred onto women, even as he longed for the idealized father figure of the Oedipal drama.

In the final chapter of this section on Freud, Ralph W. Hood Jr. brings together the feminist critique of Freud's abandonment of the seduction theory with a provocative discussion of psychoanalysis and fundamentalism. Here, he argues that Freud understood the limitations of treating fundamentalist beliefs as illusion and thus focused on the significance of the delusional nature of religion. Hood maintains that through the development of psychoanalysis, Freud created a theoretical foundation for considering the truth claims of fundamentalist beliefs. Thus, he concludes that in time fundamentalist religionists may develop a greater appreciation for classical Freudian theory.

The second section of the volume includes chapters on the second generation of psychoanalytic thinkers, including Karen Horney, Melanie Klein, Donald W. Winnicott, and Erik H. Erikson. This section begins with a discussion of Karen Horney by Marcia Westkott. In this essay, Westkott examines Horney's German upbringing, her disenchantment with conventional Christianity, her journey through psychoanalysis, and ultimately her interest and fascination with Zen Buddhism. Westkott offers a feminist perspective on Horney's critiques of Freud, which challenged the Freudian interpretation of female psychology. Toward the end of Horney's life, she became greatly influenced by the work of the Zen scholar Suzuki. Westkott's analysis focuses on the parallels that Horney found between her work and Zen teachings.

In Patricia Davis's essay on English-born Melanie Klein, the work of this theorist is analyzed through a discussion of motherhood in patriarchal culture. In particular, Davis considers the ways in which notions of maternal evil are constructed through religious paradigms, applying a Kleinian analysis of the good mother/bad mother split to the writings of the Christian fundamentalist James Dobson. Her essay concludes with an examination of the Susan Smith case and the culture's response to the young woman's murder of her two sons. Davis considers how Klein's theories can help us to understand both the idealization of Smith in contemporary society and the shock that her crime engendered once Smith's true role in the deaths of her children had been revealed.

The essay on the English psychoanalyst D. W. Winnicott, by James Jones, gives yet another perspective on the role of the mother in the unconscious. Drawing on the theoretical paradigm of object relations theory, Jones first considers the impact of Winnicott's familial attachments on his theoretical work, particularly as his relationship to his mother and father informed his ideas concerning maternal preoccupation and the development of the true and false selves. Jones then goes on to consider the ways in which Winnicott's ideas can be used to understand the creation of religion as a cultural construct. Here, he discusses the significance of the concept of "transitional space" as the source of religious symbols, myths, and beliefs.

Finally, the last essay in this section examines Erik Erikson's views on religion. In this chapter, Donald Capps focuses specifically on Erikson's *Young Man Luther* (1958) and explores connections between it and Erikson's essays on womanhood and the "inner space." In his work on Luther and his essays on womanhood, Erikson employed the clinical methodology developed in *Childhood and Society* (1950), which emphasized the interrelationship among body, ego, and the social-historical environment. Capps views Erikson's analysis of Luther through the lens of childhood fear and anxiety, concentrating on Luther's struggle in his later years to sustain some measure of ego integrity. He also suggests that the essays on womanhood and the "inner space" reveal Erikson's own adult anxieties regarding the maternal space from which he, like Luther, became estranged in early childhood.

The final section of the book focuses on what we have identified as the third and most contemporary generation of psychoanalytic theorists. Here, the works of Heinz Kohut, Ana-Maria Rizzuto, Alice Miller, Jacques Lacan, and Julia Kristeva are addressed. As the first chapter in this section, the essay on Kohut by Charles Strozier brings together an analysis of Kohut's views on religion with a discussion of the significance that Kohut's Jewish background had for his work. Strozier explores the religious themes of self psychology, first examining Kohut's critiques of Freud and then elaborating on Kohut's theories of idealization, mirroring, and twinship as each relates to a fundamental human need that religion satisfies. This discussion of self psychology is then contextualized by Strozier's analysis of Kohut's ambivalence about his Jewish roots, an ambivalence that became especially apparent in his views on empathy and Nazism.

Following Kohut, the next essay looks at the work of Argentine-born psychoanalyst Ana-Maria Rizzuto. In this analysis, John McDargh provides a biographical perspective on Rizzuto's development as a theorist and psychoanalyst, beginning with her work as a pastoral counselor in a multiclass Roman Catholic parish. He then describes the research that formed the basis for her significant work, *The Birth of the Living God* (1979). McDargh's discussion of Rizzuto highlights the value of her theories in bringing together the clinical and psychological perspectives. According to McDargh, Rizzuto's discourse on the interrelationship between religion and psychoanalysis provides an alternative understanding of God that links the concept of a transcendent entity with internal object representations.

Marion Goldman's chapter on Alice Miller offers yet another perspective on the relationship among religion, society, and psychoanalysis. Goldman introduces Miller as a German-born Swiss psychoanalyst whose theories are grounded in self psychology. She then elaborates on Miller's conceptualization of narcissism, a form of pathology that Miller attributes to destructive parenting within repressive religious cultures. In a further exploration of Miller's theoretical paradigm, Goldman analyzes religious seekership in contemporary society from the perspective of narcissistic transference, specifically examining the leader-follower dynamic among devotees of the late spiritual master Bhagwan Shree Rajneesh.

In the next two chapters, the work of preeminent French psychoanalyst Jacques Lacan is brought to bear on the discussion of religion and psychoanalysis. In a comparison of Lacan with Freud, William James Earle maintains that Lacan has a more complex and complicated view of the relationship among science, psychoanalysis, and religion than that embodied in Freud's work. Drawing specifically on a seminar given by Lacan in 1965, Earle interrogates Lacan's approach to the study of science, religion, and magic. Through this exploration into Lacan's writings, he concludes that Lacan, though approaching religion and science from a somewhat different place than Freud, nonetheless shares Freud's view that religion emerges out of the phenomenon of repression.

Carl Raschke further elaborates on Lacan's understanding of religion through an analysis of the relationship between the origins of language and the concept of God. In this essay, Raschke suggests that, in a departure from Freud, Lacan's theory on the structure of language provides new insight on the psychoanalytic meanings of religion and theological constructs. Thus, in contrast to Freud, semantic formation replaces instinct and repression as the source of the "religious unconscious." Within the Lacanian paradigm, religious consciousness is created through the acquisition of linguistic symbols that serve to fuse the imaginary with the real in the developing psyche of the child.

The final essay in the volume, by Diane Jonte-Pace, considers the work of Julia Kristeva as her theories are related to those of both Freud and Lacan. Beginning with a biographical sketch of Kristeva, Jonte-Pace situates this modern psychoanalyst within post–World War II Bulgaria, where she was educated both in Bulgarian and French schools before finishing her graduate training in France in the 1960s. Jonte-Pace describes the way in which Kristeva extends Freud's work through an analysis of how religion functions in both the individual psyche and in the larger culture. According to Jonte-Pace, Kristeva makes a unique theoretical contribution through a rethinking of Freud's major texts—*Totem and Taboo, The Future of an Illusion,* and *Civilization and Its Discontents.*

In examining the interaction between science and society, the authors of the varied essays in this volume expand the scope of scientific inquiry, bringing into focus the complex relationship between cultural forces and the production of knowledge. Topics such as Christian fundamentalism, Zen Buddhism, and anti-Semitism provide a cultural frame through which to consider the impact of religious beliefs and religious oppression on both the human psyche and the creation of scientific thought. In many cases, these essays depart from traditional approaches to the study of psychoanalysis. As such, this work challenges those paradigms that tend to exclude or ignore the social context from which science develops and human experience emerges. In bringing together the study of religion, society, and psychoanalysis, the collection offers an interdisciplinary perspective on psychoanalytic theory and practice in contemporary culture.

References

Bakan, D. 1958. *Sigmund Freud and the Jewish Mystical Tradition*. Boston: Beacon Press.

Boyer, B., R. Boyer, and H. Stein, eds. 1994. *Essays in Honor of George A. De Vos: The Psychoanalytic Study of Society*. Vol. 19. Hillsdale, N.J.: Analytic Press.

Erikson, E. H. 1950. *Childhood and Society*. New York: W. W. Norton.

———. 1958. *Young Man Luther: A Study in Psychoanalysis and History*. New York: W. W. Norton.

Freud, S. 1923. "A Seventeenth-Century Demonological Neurosis," SE: Vol. 19. Translated by J. Strachey. London: Hogarth Press.

———. 1954. *The Origins of Psychoanalysis: Letters to Wilhelm Fliess, Drafts and Notes: 1887–1902*. Edited by Marie Bonaparte, Anna Freud, and Ernst Kris, translated by E. Mosbacher and J. Strachey. New York: Basic Books.

———. 1955. *Totem and Taboo*. SE: Vol. 13. Translated by J. Strachey. London: Hogarth Press.

———. 1961. *The Future of an Illusion*. SE: Vol. 21. Translated by J. Strachey. London: Hogarth Press.

———. 1961. *Civilization and Its Discontents*. SE: Vol. 21. Translated by J. Strachey. London: Hogarth Press.

Maimonides. 1912. *The Eight Chapters*. Translated by J. I. Gorfinkle. New York: Columbia University Press.

Rizzuto, A.-M. 1979. *The Birth of the Living God: A Psychoanalytic Study*. Chicago: University of Chicago Press.

Part One

Freud

1

Freud and Hasidism

Dan Merkur

In rabbinical Judaism, the body was regarded as the vehicle of the intellect. The body was not in opposition to the spirit, as it was in Christianity, but it did not contribute to the intellect either (Roith, 1987). The body was "cared for, cleaned, maintained, without joy, without love, and without shame—like a machine" (Sartre, 1965, pp. 121–23). Women were viewed with contempt. The midrash, or rabbinical commentary on the narrative portions of the Bible, has God state:

> I will not create her [Eve] from the head, lest she be swelled-headed; nor from the eye, lest she be a coquette; nor from the ear, lest she be an eavesdropper; nor from the mouth, lest she be a gossip; nor from the heart, lest she be prone to jealousy; nor from the hand, lest she be lightfingered; nor from the foot, lest she be a gadabout; but from the modest part of man, for even when he stands naked, that part is covered [*Midrash Rabbah*, Genesis 18:2].

Romantic longing, which has its basis in the unavailability of the beloved, was avoided through the arrangement of early marriages (Roith, 1987). The religious obligation to procreate emphasized male ejaculation while discouraging forepleasure. The midrash similarly attributed a practical purpose to women's orgasms:

> If the woman issues seed first, she bears a male; if the man issues seed first, he sires a female.... R. Hiyya bar Abba said: Therefore, the male is dependent [for his procreation] upon the woman; and female, upon the man [*Midrash Buber Tanhuma*, Lev. 4:4].

The rabbinical "denial and suppression of the *erotic* as opposed to the *sexual*" (Roith, 1987, p. 130) was also consistent with the ritual practice of infantile circumcision, with its violent aggression against the penis and its implied threat to male sexual pleasure.

Freud's basic attitudes to sexuality were consistent with these traditional Jewish prejudices (Simon, 1957). "For all the candor about sexuality in his writing and culture critique, Freud personally practiced the most puritanical sexual morality" (Loewenberg, 1971, p. 364). He explained love as narcissistic identification, that is, as an unconscious self-interest (Freud, 1921). He never discussed the need to give pleasure to the loved one, and only rarely mentioned tenderness. He does not seem to have regarded either love or sex as ever involving fun. He chose to be completely celibate from the time he was 41 onward. On 31 October 1897, Freud (1954) wrote Fliess: "Also sexual excitation is of no more use to a person like me" (p. 227). In his view, sexuality was an irrational instinctual drive. His program of therapy aimed at the autonomy of reason and its acquisition of mastery over the passions (Roith, 1987).

A key question, then, is why Freud expanded the idea of sexuality to fill the entire category of natural impulses (Rieff, 1979). Since he sought the liberation of reason from sexuality, why did he expand rather than restrict the theoretical significance of sexuality? Other theoretical options were conceivable, as the object relations theories of W. R. Fairbairn (1952), Daniel Stern (1985), Christopher Bollas (1987), and others attest. Even if one holds, as I do, to the validity of libido theory, it is not enough to say that Freud, like Moses, saw the Promised Land but was unable to enter it. Since Freud had conventional Jewish attitudes about verbal candor and circumspect sexual behavior, how did he ever come by the idea of extending the concept of sexuality? It is easy to imagine a libertine arguing that sex underlies everything. But how are we to understand a prude like Freud?

In *Sigmund Freud and the Jewish Mystical Tradition* (1958), David Bakan argued that the sexual preoccupations of psychoanalysis had a historical forerunner in the Kabbalah. "Freud, consciously or unconsciously, secularized Jewish mysticism; and psychoanalysis can intelligently be viewed as such a secularization" (p. 25).

The Kabbalah ("tradition") is a distinctive school within Jewish mysticism that arose in the late 12th century as an esoteric concern of learned rabbinical Talmudists in Provence and Spain (Scholem, 1954). The Kabbalah rapidly eclipsed older forms of Jewish mysticism, and popularizations were developed. In the 17th and 18th centuries, the Kabbalah became the vehicle of mass revival movements. One movement, known as *Hasidut* ("Pietism"), grew into a conservative sect that eventually commanded the allegiance of most eastern European Jews. Freud acknowledged that his father had been raised as a Hasid (Roback, 1957). Like his father, his mother too hailed from Galicia, but whether of Hasidic or Orthodox stock is unknown.

Bakan (1958) noted that "there are two principal areas in which Kabbalah and psychoanalysis show striking similarity: techniques of interpretation and the importance and meaning attached to sexuality" (p. 245). Critics have rightly objected that the Jewish practice of dream interpretation has its basis in the Bible and was an integral component of the rabbinical tradition that all European Jews shared (Lorand, 1957; Handelman, 1981; Frieden, 1990). Dream interpretation was practiced by Kabbalists (Bilu, 1979), but it was not their exclusive possession. The same cannot be said, however, of their sexual doctrines and practices.

Although historians of the Kabbalah have only recently found the courage to acknowledge "the centrality of sexuality in the Kabbalah" (Tirosh-Roth-schild, 1991, p. 182), an extended concept of sexuality has been present in the Kabbalah throughout its history. The doctrine was given its classical formulation in the multivolume *Sefer Ha-Zohar* in the late 13th century, and Freud's library in Vienna contained a full set of the *Zohar* in French translation (Bakan, 1960).

The Talmud states that God created the world through 10 sayings. *Sefer Yetsirah*, "Book of Creation," introduced the term *sefirah* (pl. *Sefirot*) to approximate the idea of a hypostasis in Neoplatonism: a discrete rank or stage in the hierarchic emanation of being, which is simultaneously a modality of divine manifestation. In *Sefer Yetsirah*, the 10 *sefirot* are spirit, wind, water, and fire—the substances of Intellect, Soul, hylic matter, and form—and the six directions of space. Each derives from the *sefirah* preceding. The 10 hypostases are simultaneously 10 letters of the Hebrew alphabet; the further letters were each regarded as products of two primary letters—and two directions of space—taken together. The system of correspondences goes on to include the parts of the human body, the astronomical structure of the cosmos, the temporal divisions of the year, and so forth. Importantly, the *sefirot* are also 10 value criteria: "the value of life/death, the value of peace/evil, the value of wisdom/folly, the value of wealth/poverty, the value of fertility/desolation, the value of beauty/ugliness, the value of dominion/slavery" (*Yetsirah*, ed. Gruenwald, 1971, par. 37).

The Kabbalah built on these foundations. God was termed the 'Ein Sof ("Infinite") and regarded as wholly transcendent and ineffable. The ten *sefirot* of *Sefer Yetsirah* were harmonized with the Talmudic attributes of God and explained, in order of emanation, as the Supreme Crown (*Keter*), Wisdom (*Hokhmah*), Understanding (*Binah*), Loving kindness (*Hesed*), Judgment (*Din*), Mercy (*Rahamim*), Endurance (*Netsah*), Majesty (*Hod*), Righteous One (*Tsaddik*), and Sovereignty (*Malkhut*). Like the term 'Elohim ("God"), the godhood of the divine was often regarded as an attribute whose existence was contingent on the existence of humans for whom God is God. Godhood tended to be identified either with the first *sefirah*, *Keter*, or with the 10 *sefirot* as a group.

From its late 12th century beginnings in the anonymous *Sefer Ha-Bahir* ("Book of Luminescence"), the Kabbalah attributed sexuality to the *sefirot*. The doctrine was predicated on the Talmudic statement that Adam had been an androgyne prior to Eve's creation from his rib (Babylonian Talmud [BT], Hagigah 14a). Unimportant to rabbinical tradition, the motif became central to the Kabbalah, which referred to the *sefirot* collectively as *Adam Kadmon*, "primordial Adam," or "Adam [as he was] at first." This conception of an androgynous macroanthropic being was used to explain the scripture that "God created humankind in his image . . . male and female he created them" (Gen. 1:27). Kabbalists derived two inferences from the biblical verse: 1) God is both male and female; and 2) primordial Adam, who was similarly androgynous, was the image of God that the *'Ein Sof* had used as a model in creating humankind.

Different Kabbalists developed a great many variations on the basic theme of the androgyny of the macroanthropos. The androgyny of God in his totality extended to the *sefirot* in their individuality (Tirosh-Rothschild, 1991), and different passages in single texts might ascribe different sexual significances to single *sefirot*. Importantly, the archetypal significance that Kabbalists attributed to the *sefirot* did not extend to the names, terms, symbols, and images by which they referred to them. Kabbalists recognized and exploited the fact that terms and symbols may be applied in multivalent ways, meaning different things in different contexts. On the other hand, because the *sefirot* were regarded as the divine powers responsible for the creation, anything and everything could be interpreted in terms of the sexuality of the *sefirot*.

Because the Kabbalah postulates the latent sexuality of everything we know, it was only for the world of science that Freud (1905) was responsible for extending the concept of sexuality. Within the world of Judaism, Freud can instead be seen to have psychologized a concept of sexuality whose extent was already universal. A similar process of psychologizing—in Freud's (1901) phrase, of converting "mythology into metapsychology" (p. 259)—may be seen in his handling of German Romanticism (Merkur, 1993). Freud did not interpret sexuality Kabbalistically as the actual constitution of the universe. He located sexuality in its mental representation.

Bakan (1958) speculated that Wilhelm Fliess may have mediated Kabbalistic influences to Freud. "Fliess . . . combined three important Kabbalistic elements: the notion of bisexuality, the extensive use of numerology, and the doctrine of the predestination of the time of death—the doctrine of 'life portions'" (p. 62). Freud's theory of psychic bisexuality was definitely inspired by Fliess (McGrath, 1986). Unlike Fliess, however, Freud dispensed with the Kabbalah's traditional ascription of masculinity to the right side of the body and femininity to the left.

Donald Capps (1970) drew attention to the influence of Eduard von Hartmann, who was "not simply a German philosopher but an exponent of Jewish mysticism" (p. 175). In *Philosophy of the Unconscious* (Eng. tr., 1931), which Freud cited in *The Interpretation of Dreams* (1900), Hartmann outlined a technique for provoking unconscious creative insights that was intermediate between Kabbalistic meditative practices and Freud's free association. In the same book, Hartmann attributed mysticism to "the desire of the Ego for self-annihilation" (Vol. I, p. 364); the notion anticipated Freud's death instinct. In *The Sexes Compared* (1895), Hartmann expressed the Kabbalistic concept of sexuality in locating heterosexuality in both "the entire physical and spiritual life of Mankind" and "the teleological design of Nature" (pp. 1–2).

Freud's association with Fliess and his reading of Hartmann both occurred in the 1890s, on the eve of his development of psychoanalysis. Bakan (1958) suggested, however, that Freud first encountered the Kabbalah simply by being the son of his father. No systematic indoctrination is implied. Bakan speculated that Freud may have absorbed Kabbalistic ideas casually through "the kind of transmission which takes place when a parent or grandparent makes a comment on this or that problem of the day" (pp. VIII–IX). The comments do not have to have been statements of deep convictions. Kabbalistic lore could have been transmitted through remarks about prior beliefs that had since been abandoned, or about other people's superstitions.

Freud's biographers agree that Freud enjoyed a close and affectionate relationship with his father, Jacob (Jones, 1953; Schur, 1972; Clark, 1980; Krüll, 1986; Gay, 1987, 1988). Although Freud's parents were married in a Reform Jewish service, Jacob Freud seems to have abandoned Hasidic customs only some time after his migration to Germany. In *Interpretation of Dreams*, Freud (1900) related:

> I may have been ten or twelve years old, when my father began to take me with him on his walks and reveal to me in his talk his views upon things in the world we live in. Thus it was, on one such occasion, that he told me a story to show me how much better things were now than they had been in his days. "When I was a young man," he said, "I went for a walk one Saturday in the streets of your birthplace; I was well dressed, and had a new fur cap on my head. A Christian came up to me and with a single blow knocked off my cap into the mud and shouted: 'Jew! Get off the pavement!'" "And what did you do?" I asked. "I went into the roadway and picked up my cap," was his quiet reply. This struck me as unheroic conduct on the part of the big, strong man who was holding the little boy by the hand [p. 197].

Simon (1957) and Bergmann (1976) remarked that the "fur cap" was probably a *streimal*, a special hat that was obligatory for Orthodox Jews, then as now. For Jacob Freud to have been wearing a new one in Freiberg indicates that he did not leave Hasidism behind him when he left Eastern Europe. His Westernization was a more gradual process, and his second marriage, with Freud's mother, Amalia, continued to preserve a significant measure of tradition.

Freud acknowledged that his father taught him the Bible as a child, and hired a tutor to further his Jewish education. Freud remembered the tutor with affection. In a letter to Eduard Silberstein, dated 18 September 1874, Freud (1990) discussed the different festive foods that his "modestly pious family" ate on the Jewish New Year, the Day of Atonement, Purim, and Passover (pp. 62–63). In the spring of 1883, when Freud was still courting Martha Bernays, Martha's mother was a house guest of Freud's parents. Because Mrs. Bernays, an Orthodox rabbi's daughter, was herself strictly observant—for example, she wore a *sheitel,* or ritual wig—we may safely assume that Freud's parents kept a kosher house. Orthodox Jews will not so much as drink a glass of water in an unkosher home; the glass itself is a defilement (Rice, 1990).

Freud's niece, Judith Bernays Heller (1956), who lived for several years in her grandparents' home, remembered that Jacob was in the habit of studying the Talmud on his own, in its original Aramaic. She was also impressed at Passover when, during his conduct of the Seder ritual, Jacob recited the liturgy of the Haggadah by heart. Like the elegant command of the Hebrew language and biblical allusions that Jacob Freud exhibited in inscribing the family Bible to his son Sigmund (Rice, 1990), both Jacob's solitary Talmud study and his memorization of the Passover liturgy are notable achievements. The Talmud is not ordinarily studied alone; it is rehearsed alone, after classes with a teacher versed in its traditional exegesis. And unlike daily prayers, the Haggadah liturgy is not recited sufficiently frequently to be memorized without deliberate effort. At least in the Hasidic period of his youth, Jacob Freud must have been both highly observant and decently educated.

Although Bakan's thesis has its supporters, it has also met considerable resistance. Marthe Robert (1976) objected that "no parallel can be drawn between Freudian theory and any mystical tradition whatsoever unless we ignore everything Freud thought and said on the subject of such parallels" (p. 171). *Tant pis* for Freud. A series of studies have proved that he was much more profoundly schooled in Jewish culture than he publicly acknowledged (Simon, 1957; Loewenberg, 1971; Bergmann, 1976; Falk, 1978; Haymond, 1979; Klein, 1985; McGrath, 1986; Roith, 1987; Blatt, 1988; Rice, 1990; Yerushalmi, 1991). An example of Freud's behavior is instructive. After Abraham Roback (1929) had boasted of Freud in a book on *Jewish Influence in Modern Thought,* Freud wrote Roback, "I have never learned or spoken Yiddish" (Roback, 1957, pp. 30, 34). Freud's lie was as extravagant as it was gratuitous. Yiddish was his mother tongue. According to Theodor Reik,who visited her frequently, Freud's mother, Amalia, spoke a Galician Yiddish and never became fully competent in German (Rice, 1990).

When in the history of ideas it is possible to demonstrate both historical precedence and human contacts (i.e., Hasidism antedated psychoanalysis, and Freud was intimate with people, such as his father, who had once been Hasidic), it is not ordinarily considered necessary for the debtor to have acknowledged his indebtedness publicly, for the historicity of the debt to be established beyond reasonable question. People deny their debts for a variety of conscious and unconscious reasons.

We may sympathize with Freud's concern to protect psychoanalysis from "the danger of becoming a Jewish national affair" (Freud and Abraham, 1965, p. 34). By concealing the extent of his debts to Judaism, Freud sought to minimize his critics' recourse to *ad hominem* argumentation. Psychoanalysis was the creation of a Jew and, as such, Jewish cultural expression. It remains a target of anti-Semitism, even though its relation to Judaism has no more bearing on its scientific merits than the validity of Newton's physics is contingent on the apple that inspired him.

What is at stake is our understanding of the extent of Freud's originality. Did Freud truly stand outside time and space, uninfluenced by his parents' culture, as an utterly unprecedented genius, who independently discovered a series of crucial psychological insights that—coincidentally!—his culture-mates had painstakingly assembled over a period of millennia? Or shall we instead locate Freud within history and acknowledge his inspiration, among other influences, by selected aspects of Jewish culture?

Even if Freud had not misrepresented the extent of his Jewishness, it would remain a legitimate and responsible historiographic exercise to establish as fully as possible the extent of the parallels between the Kabbalah and psychoanalysis. Parallels do not exist by accident. If the parallels are not to be explained by an influence of the Kabbalah on Freud, they have to be explained another way. Appeal to coincidence may not be allowed, because the coincidences are too many in number. The parallels are present in the same culture, among blood relations, in the same era. We are not dealing with a parallel of Freud and tribal New Guinea, or Freud and the Apaches. We are talking about Freud and his Hasidic ancestors. If his father, Jacob, was not the link, who or what was? If, for the sake of argument, the Kabbalah did not influence Freud, it would be appropriate to search for a causal factor that the Kabbalah and Freud had in common.

I have elsewhere argued that Freud could have become familiar with some Kabbalistic ideas through the role played by the Christian Cabala in German Romanticism (Merkur, 1993). Here I would like to draw attention to two further parallels between psychoanalysis and the Kabbalah that cannot have been mediated by Romanticism but are instead distinctively Hasidic: 1) a regard for parapraxes as symbolic events that require interpretation; and 2) a regard for sexual fantasies not as shameful or sinful, but as symbolic motifs that can be made wholesome through interpretive insights.

In Hasidism the accidental happenings of everyday life may be treated as miracles whose symbolic interpretations disclose divine revelations. The following story (Buber, 1947) applies this general understanding of miracles to the specific circumstance of involuntary bodily actions.

> Once Rabbi Elimelekh was eating the sabbath meal with his disciples. The servant set the soup bowl down before him. Rabbi Elimelekh raised it and upset it, so that the soup poured over the table. . . . Some time after this, it became known that on that day an edict directed against the Jews of the whole country had been presented to the emperor for his signature . . . he signed the paper. Then he reached for the sand-container but took the inkwell instead and upset it on the document. Hereupon he tore it up and forbade them to put the edict before him again [p. 259; cf. p. 205].

From a Hasidic perspective, there is no difference in principle between a revelation and a miracle. In the one case, there is an original act of divine creation directly within the soul. In the other, it occurs in the external world perceptible to the soul. Both events proceed in nature or, more precisely, in creation.

Hasidic legend's close attention to minor involuntary actions definitely anticipated, and very possibly inspired, Freud's (1901, 1916–17) attention to the phenomena. He termed them "parapraxes." They are better known, of course, as "Freudian slips." In maintaining that parapraxes do not happen at random but are instead to be interpreted as dreams are, Freud was both perpetuating and revising the traditional Hasidic teaching. Freud's innovation consisted of psychologizing their explanation. Freud claimed that parapraxes are produced not by the miraculous interventions of a personal God, but as a natural function of the unconscious psyche.

How much influence did Hasidism have on Freud? To account for Freud's attention to parapraxes, we need to assume no more than that Freud once noticed a relative or other person giving heed to a parapraxis, and so became aware that involuntary bodily actions are not necessarily meaningless. The curiosity may have been forgotten for decades until Freud began to develop psychoanalysis.

Freud's study of parapraxes was important to his development and exposition of psychoanalysis, but his attitude toward sexual fantasies was scarcely less than pivotal. Here Freud was anticipated by one of the very few teachings that scholars trace with confidence to the founder of Hasidism, Rabbi Israel Baal Shem Tov (c. 1698–1760).

Among Hasidism's innovations was its rejection of the traditional Kabbalistic dualism of good spirit and evil matter. Because God was good, evil could have no true existence, and matter was necessarily good and holy. On the other hand, Hasidism retained the old gnostic idea of gathering fallen sparks of holiness and restoring them to the God. The paradox was resolved through the development of a monistic revision of the Kabbalistic creation myth. The primordial fall of divine light had occurred because the light was too severe to be endured in its full intensity. The light had to be weakened before existence of any kind could become possible. God had consequently contracted himself, diminishing his light to a lesser degree of power, in order to create an absence of light in which the world could exist. The diminished light that succeeded to reach and become the world could also be viewed, from man's perspective, as a revelation or flowing out of divine light from the *'Ein Sof* into the world (Dan, 1983).

The Hasidic doctrine of redeeming fallen sparks raised two logical problems. Because Hasidism abandoned the idea of an inner tension with the *'Ein Sof* it could not explain evil as something differing from God that could be destroyed once it was deprived of the holy sparks that were its sustenance. For Hasidism, evil traced directly to God. Evil was considered a temporary condition of the holy sparks themselves. Restoring fallen sparks to God was equivalent, in some cases, to restoring evil to God. In the process of restoration, the evil was changed, of course, into pure goodness. Still, the Hasidic doctrine did not permit the avoidance of evil. It required a direct confrontation with evil, in order to seize it and restore it to the *'Ein Sof.*

Unlike the Messianic movement of Sabbatai Sevi, Hasidism never went so far as to accept the doctrine of holy sins, the actual practice of evil in order to seize it and restore it. However, Hasidism did accept the necessity of thinking about evil in order to accomplish its restoration. The Baal Shem Tov's disciple, Rabbi Jacob Joseph of Polonoye, wrote (as cited in Ariel, 1988):

> I heard a convincing argument said in the name of my teacher [the Baal Shem Tov]. It concerned the strange thoughts (*mahshavot zarot*) which come to man in the midst of his prayer. . . . They appear in order to be repaired and elevated. The strange thought which appears one day is different from that of another day. [The Baal Shem Tov] taught that one must pay close attention to this matter. I learned from him how to repair the strange thoughts even if they are about women. One should elevate them and make them cleave to their source, the [*Sefirah*] *Hesed* [p. 179].

In meditation, a restoration (*tikkun*) may require no more than the overcoming of discordant thoughts by their linkage to the alternate state. For example, a person engaged in meditation might suddenly experience an unbidden sexual fantasy. To abandon the alternate state of consciousness and to pursue the fantasy was considered sinful. The Hasid's task was to reinterpret the fantasy, by allegorizing it. By treating the sexual fantasy as an allegory of the relation of God to the feminine *sefirah, Shekhinah* or *Malkhut,* the fantasy could be linked with the *sefirot.* In this manner, the evil would be transformed into good through its restoration to God. Simultaneously, the fantasy, which had threatened to interrupt the Hasid's ecstasy, would be made to further the alternate state. Scholem (1991) remarked:

One can virtually detoxify and transform sin and evil by contemplative absorption. By means of this contemplation one transforms ("sweetens") them at their very roots—albeit not by living them out in actuality, as was done by the Sabbatians, but by binding them to their root in holiness [p. 129].

Surely it was no coincidence that in the authentic teaching of the Baal Shem Tov we find the basic assumptions of Freud's technique of psychotherapy: that it is permissible to think wicked thoughts, that wicked fantasies cannot be helped, that the main thing to do is not to avoid the fantasies, but to defuse them by interpreting them and gaining insight into their proper meaning. Have we reason to doubt that Jacob Freud communicated the tolerant attitudes of Hasidic ethics in advising his son how to manage his fantasy life?

References

Ariel, D. S. (1988), *The Mystic Quest: An Introduction to Jewish Mysticism.* Northvale, NJ: Aronson.

Bakan, D. (1958), *Sigmund Freud and the Jewish Mystical Tradition.* Princeton, NJ: Van Nostrand.

_____. (1960), Freud and the Zohar: An incident. *Commentary,* 29:65–66.

Bergmann, M. S. (1976), Moses and the evolution of Freud's Jewish identity. *Israel Ann. Psychiat. Related Discipl.* 14:3–26.

Bilu, Y. (1979), Sigmund Freud and Rabbi Yehudah: On a Jewish mystical tradition of "psychoanalytic" dream interpretation. *J. Psychol. Anthropol.* 2(4):443–63.

Blatt, D. S. (1988), The development of the hero: Sigmund Freud and the reformation of the Jewish tradition. *Psychoanal. & Contemp. Thought,* 11:639–703.

Bollas, C. (1987), *The Shadow of the Object: Psychoanalysis of the Unthought Known.* New York: Columbia University Press.

Buber, M. (1947), *Tales of the Hasidim: The Early Masters,* trans. O. Marx. New York: Schocken Books.

Capps, D. (1970), Hartmann's relationship to Freud: A reappraisal. *J. Hist. Behav. Sciences,* 6:162–75.

Clark, R. W. (1980), *Freud—The Man and the Cause.* New York: Random House.

Dan, J. (1983), *The Teachings of Hasidism.* New York: Behrman House.

Fairbairn, W. R. (1952), *Psychoanalytic Studies of the Personality.* London: Routledge & Kegan Paul.

Falk, A. (1978), Freud and Herzl. *Contemp. Psychoanal.* 14(3):357–87.

Freud, S. (1900), The interpretation of dreams. *Standard Edition,* 4&5. London: Hogarth Press, 1953.

_____. (1901), The psychopathology of everyday life. *Standard Edition,* 6:1–279. London: Hogarth Press, 1960.

_____. (1905), Three essays on the theory of sexuality. *Standard Edition,* 7:130–243. London: Hogarth Press, 1953.

_____. (1916–17), Introductory lectures on psycho-analysis. *Standard Edition*, 15:15–82. London: Hogarth Press, 1961.

_____. (1921), Group psychology and the analysis of the ego. *Standard Edition*, 18:69–143. London: Hogarth Press, 1955.

_____. (1954), *The Origins of Psycho-Analysis: Letters to Wilhelm Fliess, Drafts and Notes: 1887–1902*, ed. Marie Bonaparte, Anna Freud & Ernst Kris. New York: Basic Books.

_____. (1990), *The Letters of Sigmund Freud to Eduard Silberstein, 1871–1881*, ed. W. Boehlich (trans. A. L. Pomerans). Cambridge, MA: Belknap-Harvard University Press.

_____. & Abraham, K. (1965), *Letters, 1907–1926*, ed. H. C. Abraham & E. L. Freud. New York: Basic Books.

Frieden, K. (1990), *Freud's Dream of Interpretation*. Albany, NY: State University of New York Press.

Gay, P. (1987), *A Godless Jew: Freud, Atheism, and the Making of Psychoanalysis*. New Haven, CT: Yale University Press.

_____. (1988), *Freud: A Life for Our Times*. New York: Norton.

Gruenwald, I. (1971), A preliminary critical edition of *Sefer Yezira. Israel Orient. Stud.* 1:132–75.

Handelman, S. (1981), Interpretation as devotion: Freud's relation to rabbinic hermeneutics. *Psychoanal. Rev.*, 68 (2):201–18.

Hartmann, E. von (1895), *The Sexes Compared*. New York: Macmillan.

_____. (1931), *Philosophy of the unconscious, Vols. I–III*. New York: Harcourt, Brace.

Haymond, R. (1979), Roots in the shtetl: Modern western thought and the case of Sigmund Freud. *J. Psychol. Judaism*, 3(4):235–367.

Heller, J. B. (1956), Freud's mother and father—A memoir. *Commentary*, 12:418–21.

Jones, E. (1953), *The Life and Work of Sigmund Freud. Vol. I: The Formative Years and Great Discoveries 1856–1900*. New York: Basic Books.

Klein, D. B. (1985), *Jewish Origins of the Psychoanalytic Movement*. Chicago: University of Chicago Press.

Krüll, M. (1986), *Freud and His Father*. New York: W. W. Norton.

Loewenberg, P. (1971), Sigmund Freud as a Jew: A study in ambivalence and courage. *J. Hist. Behav. Sciences*, 7:363–69.

Lorand, S. (1957), Dream interpretation in the Talmud (Babylonian and Graeco-Roman period). *Internat. J. Psycho-Anal.*, 38:92–7.

McGrath, W. J. (1986), *Freud's Discovery of Psychoanalysis: The Politics of Hysteria*. Ithaca, NY: Cornell University Press.

Merkur, D. (1993), Mythology into metapsychology: Freud's misappropriation of Romanticism. *The Psychoanalytic Study of Society* 18:345–360. Hillsdale, NJ: The Analytic Press.

Rice, E. (1990), *Freud and Moses: The Long Journey Home*. Albany, NY: State University of New York Press.

Rieff, P. (1979), *Freud: The Mind of the Moralist*, 3rd ed. Chicago: University of Chicago Press.

Roback, A. A. (1929), *Jewish Influence in Modern Thought.* Cambridge, MA: Sci-Art Publishers.

_____. (1957), *Freudiana.* Cambridge, MA: Sci-Art Publishers.

Robert, M. (1976), *From Oedipus to Moses: Freud's Jewish Identity,* trans. R. Manheim. Garden City, NY: Anchor Press/Doubleday.

Roith, E. (1987), *The Riddle of Freud: Jewish Influences on His Theory of Female Sexuality.* London: Tavistock Publications.

Sartre, J.-P. (1965), *Anti-Semite and Jew,* trans. G. J. Becker. New York: Schocken Books.

Scholem, G. G. (1954), *Major Trends in Jewish Mysticism,* 3rd ed. New York: Schocken Books.

_____. (1991), *On the Mystical Shape of the Godhead: Basic Concepts in the Kabbalah,* trans. J. Neugroschel. New York: Schocken Books.

Schur, M. (1972), *Freud: Living and Dying.* New York: International Universities Press.

Simon, E. (1957), Sigmund Freud, the Jew. *Leo Baeck Institute Year Book,* 2. London.

Stern, D. N. (1985), *The Interpersonal World of the Infant: A View from Psychoanalysis and Developmental Psychology.* New York: Basic Books.

Tirosh-Rothschild, H. (1991), Continuity and revision in the study of kabbalah. *AJS Rev.,* 16:161–92.

Yerushalmi, Y. H. (1991), *Freud's Moses: Judaism Terminable and Interminable.* New Haven, CT: Yale University Press.

2

Freud, Maimonides, and Incest

David Bakan

Incest was at the heart of Freud's theory. Freud maintained that the primordial sexual desire in human beings for close relatives was the major feature of the human mind. He maintained that civilization requires the suppression of this sexual desire aimed at relatives for its survival and that this suppression was the core feature of neurosis, the pathology of normal volition. And he developed a course of treatment for this malady based on the assumption that when the person becomes more fully aware of this suppressed desire, he or she would regain the volitional control lost in the neurosis.

Psychoanalysis, the system of thought developed by Freud, has also been a major topic in the intellectual history of the last century. It is interesting that Freud's ideas are still highly controversial. On the one hand, his ideas have a stubborn appeal for many. On the other hand, there is virtually an industry in Freud-bashing.

However, even those who are most receptive to Freud's thought characteristically circumscribe some of his notions on sex and incest and on the significance of insight for therapy and attempt to distance themselves from them.

I suggest that, even as Freud suggested, the rejection of these ideas is associated with some deep features of the culture. I believe we can open at least one path toward understanding these phenomena by considering psychoanalysis itself from a historical point of view. In particular, there may be some benefit in bringing some features of Jewish thought and history to bear. We may consider the possibility that a genuine clash of cultural ideas may be involved.

In this chapter, I will identify three things in Jewish history that may be informative in this respect. They correspond to three characteristics in

Freud's thought: the particular sensitivity to the significance of incestuous sexual desire in Freud, Freud's claim that the desire for incest is natural, and the assumption that there is therapeutic value in admitting the desire for incest.

Let me first make some observations about Freud's cultural background. His parents arrived in Vienna as part of the great migration of Jews from the small Jewish communities of eastern Europe into the major cities of Europe and the United States that took place in the late nineteenth and early twentieth centuries. From the dispersal of the Jews in ancient times until the French Revolution, the Jews lived in small self-governing communities in the various countries in which they resided. They had synagogues, schools, and rabbinical courts and married only within the Jewish community. The rabbis governed the communities in accordance with the laws written in Scripture, the Talmud, and records of rabbinical responses. Among other things, sexual conduct was very highly regulated by this law.

One has to note that although every society regulates sexual conduct, there was a special problem in connection with Jewish sexual and marital practices. For one of the major features of Jewish law was the prohibition against marriage with non-Jews. Thus, living in small communities, the number of people that any single person could rightfully consider as objects of desire was extraordinarily limited. On the one hand, non-Jews were not legitimate; on the other hand, close relatives, though not excluded for being non-Jews, could not rightfully be considered because of the possibility of incest. The marriage broker was an extremely important personage in the Jewish community. The marriage broker had not only to find persons suitable for each other but, perhaps even more important, also had to inquire diligently and discreetly to make sure that the match was not incestuous under Jewish law. Before a marriage, the community at large had to deal consciously with the question of incest, consider the possibility of it, and clear the couple intending to get married of the possibility of violating any of the laws against incest.

The most important ground of Jewish law in connection with incest is found in the relatively lengthy section on "uncovering nakedness" in the eighteenth chapter of Leviticus. That text uses two Hebrew words that are of particular significance, as I will indicate later. The text states: "You shall keep my *hukkim* and my *mishpatim*. . . . None of you shall approach to any that is near of kin to him to uncover their nakedness" (Lev. 18:5–6). This is then followed by a long list of specific incest injunctions, the first of which is against uncovering the nakedness of one's father or mother (Lev. 18:7), the main incestuous concern in Freud's thought. This passage from Scripture, enumerating the various forms of incest, is part of the Yom Kippur liturgy to the present day.

The historical situation of the Jews can then be presumed to have promoted a great sensitivity to incest, a sensitivity that we can recognize in Freud.

The significance of the Jewish context for the appreciation of Freud grows larger if we bring to bear the extraordinary interpretations of Maimonides in connection with incest.[1] Maimonides lived in the twelfth century. He is universally regarded as the single most significant figure in the history of Jewish thought after ancient times. However, to appreciate the significance of Maimonides, it is necessary to distinguish between two categories of his writing.

On the one hand, Maimonides wrote a systematic and comprehensive fourteen-volume compendium on Jewish law in Hebrew, called the *Mishneh Torah* (1974), which became the standard of law worldwide and over the centuries in the Jewish communities. It is still studied carefully in the rabbinical schools, and it remains the major standard work on Jewish law. With the development of modern Israel, in which great efforts have been made to integrate secular and religious law, it has acquired renewed significance in that country. On the other hand, Maimonides also wrote a number of works that were strongly influenced by Greek philosophy and the intellectual traditions that followed Greek philosophy. The former were embraced by the rabbinic leaders of the Jewish communities, but the latter were largely anathema to them.

However, there was a resurgence of interest during the nineteenth century in the second category of works by Maimonides, an interest associated with the development of liberal movements within Judaism such as the Jewish Enlightenment and the Reform movement. There is reason to believe that these liberal movements had an influence on Freud's father.

Among Maimonides' writings, there is a work on ethics in which he openly and clearly drew from the classical philosophers, especially from Aristotle and particularly from his work on ethics. It is a tract called *The Eight Chapters* (1912), and in it we find two notions that are central for Freud's psychoanalysis: that the desire for sexual relations with relatives is natural and that such desires should be openly admitted.

The aversion to incest is virtually universal. One of the main questions associated with incest is whether the aversion to it is natural or whether the desire for incest is natural but counteracted by a culturally induced aversion. Of the two views, the former is most commonly held. The latter, however, is the view maintained by Freud. Freud cited Edward Westermarck as believing that there is an innate aversion to sexual intercourse between persons who live closely together, due to the belief that inbreeding is detrimental to the species (1986: 122–123). At the time that Freud was writing *Totem and Taboo*, the former view had drawn support from the Darwinian theory that had become available, suggesting that the aversion to incest was the product of natural selection, based on the presumption that the offspring of incestuous relationships were inferior and therefore less likely to survive and reproduce.

Freud, in taking the second view, was joining Maimonides as he had indicated his position in *The Eight Chapters*. In doing so, Maimonides had actually taken a position opposed to the rabbis of the Talmud on this matter. Maimonides made the point by alluding to a distinction suggested by the text of Scripture. The text, as seen in the previous citation, uses two Hebrew words, *hukkim* and *mishpatim*. It is one of the great scriptural puzzles of history as to how to consider the list of incestuous prohibitions that follow with respect to these terms.

The classical interpretation of these words, as understood by the rabbis of the Talmud, was that commandments against such acts as murder and robbery were in the class of mishpatim. Mishpatim are commandments that aim to prevent wrongdoing of a kind that any reasonable person would know was wrong. However, things like the rules of the kosher code, purely religious or ceremonial things, were considered under the heading of hukkim. A person would not know that these were wrong had he or she not had the guidance of the Torah as given by Moses at Sinai. Without the help of the Torah, one would not know what foods were kosher and what foods were not and so on.

The rabbis of the Talmud classified the commandments against incest under the heading of mishpatim, together with murder and robbery (Epstein 1938:316). Maimonides, however, reclassified incest, placing it in the category of hukkim (1912:77–78). Thus, just as a person would have no reason not to eat meat and drink milk at the same meal, which is in violation of the kosher code, so would he or she have no reason not to engage in incestuous relationships, unless somehow instructed to the contrary. Thus, the desire for having sexual relations with close relatives is completely natural. Only through the law, the law that one has to be taught, does one know that engaging in sexual relations with relatives is wrong.

There is a common view that the mental act of desiring to do a wrongful act is itself a form of wrongdoing. This is expressed in Scripture in such things as the Tenth Commandment against "coveting" (Exod. 20:17) and in Jesus' statement that if a person desires to commit adultery, it is as though he had "already committed adultery . . . in his heart" (Matt. 5:28). This belief—that desire to engage in wrongdoing is itself wrongdoing—is a profound feature of Western culture.

Freud departed from this position radically. In all of his work, the distinction between desire and conduct is characteristically made. Desire for wrongdoing is not itself wrong. Rather, for Freud, the psychological repression of desire is responsible for pathology. His solution is not, however, acting out. To the contrary, the solution is not to remove the repression of the desire mentally. One of the fundamental working aims of psychoanalytic treatment is to bring the repressed desires out of the unconscious into consciousness. But that is not the same as bringing the desire to conduct.

We find this position stated explicitly by Maimonides. The desire to commit those things that fall under the heading of hukkim, including incest, should not be denied. Quite the contrary, they should be acknowledged. Maimonides, finding a rabbinical authority outside of the Talmud, different from those cited earlier, said that a "man should permit his soul to entertain the natural inclination for [the things forbidden by the hukkim such as] partaking of meat and milk together, wearing clothes made of both wool and linen, and incest ... the Law alone should restrain him from them" (1912:77). One should not say of these things that one does not want to do them. Quite the contrary, one should say, "I do indeed want to, yet I must not, for my father in heaven has forbidden it" (Maimonides 1912:76). In this way, Maimonides' position on desire and acknowledgment is reflected in Freud's views on the pathology of repression. Like Maimonides, Freud emphasized the conscious awareness of incestuous desire, which is distinguished from the actualization of such desire.

Notes

1. I have earlier indicated some relationships between Freud and Maimonides. See D. Bakan, *Maimonides on Prophecy,* Northvale, N.J.: Jason Aronson, 1991; D. Bakan, "Maimonides' Theology and Psychology," in B. R. Rubenstein and M. Berenbaum, eds., *What Kind of God? Essays in Honor of Richard L. Rubenstein,* Lanham, Md.: University Press of America, 1995, pp. 367–374.

References

Epstein, I., ed. 1938. *The Babylonian Talmud.* London: Soncino Press.

Freud, S. 1986. *Totem and Taboo.* SE: Vol. 13. Translated by J. Strachey. London: Hogarth Press.

Maimonides, M. 1912. *The Eight Chapters.* Translated by J. I. Gorfinkle. New York: Columbia University Press.

_____. 1974. *Mishneh Torah.* Translated by P. Birnbaum. New York: Hebrew Publishing.

3

Freud as Other

Anti-Semitism and the Development of Psychoanalysis

Janet Liebman Jacobs

The relationship between the development of psychoanalysis and Freud's Jewish background has been the subject of much debate and interest. Throughout the latter part of the twentieth century, numerous scholars have considered the influence of Jewish beliefs and culture on the creation of Freudian theory (Bakan 1958; Gilman 1993; Grollman 1965; Klein 1985; Robert 1976; Roith 1987). Although the study of Freud and Judaism is an important area of inquiry, the danger of such analyses is that they may become reductive. Freud was keenly aware of this possibility and of the anti-Semitism that informed the criticism of his work. Among the many critics of Freud, Carl Jung warned of the "corrosive nature" of the "Jewish gospel" and of the limitations of a theory that originated from "Jewish points of view" (Gilman 1993:31). In 1927, Jung stated that "it is a quite unpardonable mistake to accept the conclusions of a Jewish psychology as generally valid" (Gilman 1993:31).

The cultural and religious analyses of Freud that followed Jung's criticism, though not similarly anti-Semitic, have nonetheless contributed to the notion that psychoanalysis, if not exactly a "Jewish" science, has been greatly influenced by the religious culture of its founder. Such influences have ranged from the significance of mysticism on Freud (Bakan 1958; Merkur 1994) to the effects of Jewish patriarchal culture on psychoanalytic theory (Roith 1987). Without wishing to reinforce a reductive approach to the study of Freud and his Jewish background, in this chapter I will further elaborate on the culturally specific aspects of Freudian theory, particularly as they relate to the effects of anti-Semitism on Freud's views of personality development.

In her work on feminist epistemology, Sandra Harding (1987) maintains that scientific knowledge cannot be understood apart from the social context from which such knowledge is derived. Accordingly, Freud's work, like that of other scientists and scholars, has been informed by a diverse set of social factors, including religion, family culture, and the larger society in which he lived. These forces taken together created the social context out of which the science of psychoanalysis emerged and was given meaning.

The biographical data on Freud's family suggest that his parents and grandparents were deeply rooted in the culture and traditions of nineteenth-century Austrian Jewish life. Both Freud's father and mother were raised in Galicia, a region of the Austro-Hungarian Empire where, for centuries, Jews lived in isolated communities that formed the shtetl culture of eastern Europe. Within the sheltered world of rural ghetto life, Freud's paternal grandfather and great-grandfather were rabbis, as was a maternal great-grandfather (Grollman 1965). Thus, Freud was born into a family in which Orthodox Judaism had not only survived but had also found expression in the religious scholarship of his grandparents and great-grandparents.

In 1855, Freud's parents were married in Galicia. His mother, Amalia, was only sixteen years old when she wed Jacob Freud, a widower more than twice her age (Grollman 1965). Soon after they were married, Jacob and Amalia left Galicia, joining other rural Jews who were leaving the countryside for the more prosperous and progressive urban regions of Austria. They settled first in Freiburg, where Freud was born, and then moved to Vienna, where Freud was raised and educated and where he received his medical training (Robert 1976).

Much has been written about the household where Freud grew up, of a home in which Amalia's strong presence became legendary and where both husband and wife broke from the Orthodox and Hasidic culture of their past (Grollman 1965; Roith 1987). Seeking to assimilate into Viennese society, the Freuds were among the new class of urbanized Jews who rejected the dress, the ritualism, and the orthodoxy of shtetl life. As the first child in a newly acculturated Jewish family, Freud had an upbringing and secular education that was representative of a generation in transition, of a population of urban and educated Jews who saw their future in the intellectual rather than the religious traditions of their ancestors.

Although claiming little knowledge of Jewish tradition or religious training, Freud nonetheless identified as a Jew, an identification that informed his understanding of himself as a scientist. Freud maintained that it was his Jewish nature that had given him the intellectual freedom to create a revolutionary science and that had provided him with the personal strength to withstand the challenges and criticism that his work engendered. In 1926, on his seventieth birthday, Freud was honored by the Jewish organization of the B'nai B'rith in London. In an address to this group, he spoke directly of his ambivalent but deep connection to his Jewishness:

> Whenever I felt an inclination to national enthusiasm I strove to suppress it as being harmful and wrong, alarmed by the warning examples of the peoples among whom we Jews live. But plenty of other things remained over to make the attraction of Jewry and Jews irresistible—many obscure emotional forces, which were more powerful the less they could be expressed in words, as well as a clear consciousness of inner identity, the safe privacy of a common mental construction (SE 20:273–274).

The importance that Freud placed on his Jewish identity is a starting point from which to begin this chapter on the role that anti-Semitism played in the development of Freudian theory. Specifically, I will explore the effects of anti-Semitism on Freud's construction of the female persona and on the creation of a castration-centered theory of psychosexual development. Drawing on the work of, among others, Frantz Fanon (1967), Sander Gilman (1993), and Estelle Roith (1987), this work will situate Freud within the culture of nineteenth-century Viennese society, a culture in which the Jew clearly occupied the role of "other." During Freud's lifetime, anti-Semitic ideologies proliferated throughout Viennese society, finding their expression in the stereotype of the weak and effeminate Jewish male and the coarse and aggressive Jewish female (Gilman 1993; Roith 1987). The promulgation of these images, as well as others that portrayed the Jew as dirty and immoral, reinforced the notion that beneath the veneer of Christian gentility, which Jews like Freud had managed to cultivate, lay the real Semitic Jew whose shtetl origins could not be denied.

Freud experienced overt anti-Semitism while a student, and his intellectual development emerged within a scientific community that fostered notions of Semitic difference and racial inferiority, ideas that provided a scientific foundation for myths and beliefs that had for centuries stigmatized European Jewry. Thus, Freud's inner Jewish identity was shaped both by the history of Jewish oppression and by the anti-Semitism of the social and scientific communities of Vienna. The inner emotions to which Freud gave voice in his theory of the unconscious therefore bore the imprint of an internalized anti-Semitism that became symptomatic of the Jewish experience in prewar Europe.

Internalized Anti-Semitism and the Construction of the Self

In *Freud, Race and Gender*, Sander Gilman discussed the racialization of the Jew in late-nineteenth- and early-twentieth-century European culture:

For Jews, it was an age of intense insecurity, of anxiety about themselves and their world that was a response to the level of public defamation. This anxiety haunted Freud's dreams. . . . The Jews were eternal wanderers, according to the legend of the Wandering Jew, which had a remarkable efflorescence during this period, because of their denial of Christ, a denial caused by "blindness." Translated into racial parlance, they were marginalized in European society because of their innate biological and psychological differences. Freud's sense of the reality of anti-Semitism cannot be doubted (1993:13).

The racialization to which Gilman referred was manifested in ideologies that portrayed the Jew as physically dark and somehow diseased. Although such notions of racial impurity would find their strongest expression in the proliferation of Nazi ideology, the culture of nineteenth-century Vienna constructed the image of the Jew as different, weak in mind and in body. Within this framework of racial difference, the Jewish male became the antithesis of Christian masculinity, a feminized man whose circumcised body signified his racial inferiority.

The cultural designation of the Jew as different and inferior was further intensified by a Christian theological history in which the Jew was associated with evil and carnality. Like women, the Jews of sixteenth- and seventeenth-century Europe were accused by the church of consorting with the devil and of practicing witchcraft, their heresy a mark of their truly evil nature. Historian H. R. Trevor-Roper described the work of Pierre de l'Ancre, a French government official whose seventeenth-century tract on witches vilified the Jews:

A whole section of his [de l'Ancre's] work is devoted to the denunciation of the Jews; their absurd and indecent rites and beliefs, their cruelty and their greed, their poisoning of Christian wells, their forcible circumcision and ritual murder of Christian children. The Jews, says de l'Ancre, "by their filth and stink, by their sabbaths and synagogues", are so disgusting to God that he has not only withdrawn from them his grace and his promise: he has also condemned them to creep about the world "like poor snakes", deprived of every kind of office, dignity or public employment (1967:112–113).

That such beliefs survived the Renaissance and found their way into nineteenth- and twentieth-century European culture is evident in the continued association of racial difference with evil and immorality. Frantz Fanon made this point in his classic text *Black Skin: White Masks*: "*In Europe, the black man is the symbol of evil.* One must move softly, I know, but it is not easy. The torturer is the black man, Satan is black, one talks of shadows, when one is dirty one is black—whether one is thinking of physical dirtiness or of moral dirtiness" (1967:188–189, emphasis in original).

Although Fanon was referring primarily to the racialization of African-Europeans, he, like Gilman, recognizes that Jews and blacks occupy a similar space in the collective unconscious of the dominant society, a space in which fear of the other takes root in the social construction of racist and anti-Semitic ideologies:

> The Negro is the genital. Is this the whole story? Unfortunately not. The Negro is something else. Here again we find the Jew. He and I may be separated by the sexual question, but we have one point in common. Both of us stand for Evil. The black man more so, for the good reason that he is black. . . . The Jew, authentic or inauthentic, is struck down by the fist of the "*salaud.*" His situation is such that everything he does is bound to turn against him. For naturally the Jew prefers himself, and it happens that he forgets his Jewishness, or hides, hides himself from it. That is because he has then admitted the validity of the Aryan system. There are Good and Evil. Evil is Jewish. Everything Jewish is ugly (1967:180–182).

As such ideologies informed the cultural climate in which Freud lived and worked, his theories of psychosexual development reflect the internalization of such beliefs and stereotypes. Outwardly, Freud assumed the public persona of the acculturated Jew; his language, his dress, his assimilated lifestyle, and his nonreligious identification all worked to challenge the racial stereotype of the Jew as other. Yet, as Fanon explains through his own experience of racism in Europe, despite all attempts at acculturation, the trauma of otherness remains deeply ingrained in the unconscious of the stigmatized individual whose construction of the self is framed within the sociocultural belief systems of the dominant society. The effect of racist and anti-Semitic ideologies is to foster self-hatred and alienation among those who have been marginalized and negatively defined by the larger culture. Freud therefore became both the assimilated Austrian Jew as well as the racialized other whose knowledge of the human condition was filtered through his own internalized anti-Semitism. As the assimilated Jew, he spoke only German and opposed the founding of Israel; as the vilified Jew, Freud constructed a theory of psychoanalysis in which his sense of otherness was projected onto women and in which the development of the Oedipal complex fulfilled the desire for a heroic father figure.

The Emasculated Jewish Male and the Theory of Anatomical Deprivation

Freud's theory of female development is elaborated in two significant essays, "Some Psychical Consequences of the Anatomical Distinction Between the Sexes" (SE 19:1925) and "Femininity" (SE 22:1932). A reading of these essays, as well as other works by Freud, presents a view of women in which the female is portrayed as unalterably wounded by the effects of anatomical deprivation. Unable to recover from the psychic trauma of having been born without a penis, the girl child is destined to a life in which envy, inferiority, and shame underlie the development of the feminine personality. In the 1925 essay, Freud wrote:

> The psychical consequences of envy for the penis, in so far as it does not become absorbed in the reaction-formation of the masculinity complex, are various and far-reaching. After a woman has become aware of the wound to her narcissism, she develops, like a scar, a sense of her inferiority . . . she begins to share the contempt felt by men for a sex which is the lesser in so important a respect. . . . Of course, jealousy is not limited to one sex and has wider foundation than this, but I am of the opinion that it plays a far larger part in the mental life of women than of men and that that is because it is enormously reinforced from the direction of displaced penis-envy (SE 19:253–254).

In this essay, Freud further concluded that because of her lack of a penis, the girl child believes she has been castrated, and thus, unlike the boy, she is not motivated by fear of castration since the punishment has already taken place. The result is that girls develop a weaker superego, which leads to an inferior moral character:

> In girls the motive for the demolition of the Oedipus complex is lacking. Castration has already had its effect, which was to force the child into the situation of the Oedipus complex. Thus the Oedipus complex escapes the fate which it meets with in boys. . . . I cannot evade the notion (though I hesitate to give it expression) that for women the level of what is ethically normal is different from what it is in men. Their super-ego is never so inexorable, so impersonal, so independent of its emotional origins as we require it to be in men. Character-traits which critics of every epoch have brought up against women—that they show less sense of justice than men, that they are less ready to submit to the great exigencies of life, that they are more influenced in their judgements by feelings of affection or hostility—all these would be amply accounted for by the modification in the formation of their super-ego which we have inferred above (SE 19:257–258).

In his 1932 essay on femininity, Freud reiterated his understanding of the feminine personality, with an additional reference to the significance that shame plays in female development:

> Shame, which is considered to be a feminine characteristic *par excellence* but is far more a matter of convention than might be supposed, has as its purpose, we believe, concealment of genital deficiency. We are not forgetting that at a later time shame takes on other functions. It seems that women have made few contributions to the discoveries and inventions in the history of civilization; there is, however, one technique which they may have invented—that of plaiting and

weaving. If that is so, we should be tempted to guess the unconscious motive for the achievement. Nature herself would seem to have given the model which this achievement imitates by causing the growth at maturity of the pubic hair that conceals the genitals (SE 22:132).

Taken together, Freud's views on women, which he readily admitted did "not always sound friendly" (SE 22:133), have strong misogynistic undertones that have contributed to the continued denigration of women in contemporary Western society. Even as Freud was developing his theory of female personality, critics of this work were emerging. Among these critics was the psychoanalyst Karen Horney. In 1926, she published an essay on the masculinity complex in women in which she laid the foundation for future feminist analyses of Freudian theory. In this essay, Horney maintained that Freud's focus on castration anxiety and penis envy emerges out of a masculinist worldview in which male privilege is tied to male anatomy. Thus, for Freud, the absence of the penis signified a loss of privilege, status, and self-worth—a catastrophe he could only envision in the image of the female body. As such, Horney suggests that the association of female genitals with anatomical deprivation symbolized male fear of castration rather than the true nature of the female personality:

> Like all sciences and all valuations, the psychology of women has hitherto been considered only from the point of view of men. It is inevitable that the man's position of advantage should cause objective validity to be attributed to his subjective, affective relations to the woman, and according to Delius the psychology of women hitherto actually represents a deposit of the desires and disappointments of men. . . . In other words, how far has the evolution of women, as depicted to us today by analysis, been measured by masculine standards and how far therefore does this picture fail to present quite accurately the real nature of women (1967:56–57).

Although Horney's perspective is compelling, it focuses exclusively on Freud's masculine perspective and his identification with male privilege. What is missing from this important critique is the recognition of Freud's social location as a Jew within an anti-Semitic culture. As Gilman effectively argues, Freud's position as the Jewish other had its physical manifestation in his circumcised body, a biological trait that linked him to the image of the female as the castrated male:

> This is reflected in the popular fin de siècle Viennese view of the relationship between the body of the male Jew and the body of the woman. The clitoris was known in Viennese slang of the time simply as the "Jew" (Jud). The phrase for female masturbation was "playing with the Jew." The "small organ" of the

woman became the pars par toto for the Jew with his circumcised organ. This pejorative synthesis of both bodies because of their "defective" sexual organs reflected the fin de siècle Viennese definition of the essential male as the antithesis of the female and the Jewish male (1993:39).

In nineteenth-century Europe, the circumcised male body signified both physical and political emasculation. As the Jewish male was rendered powerless by the aggression and persecution of Christian Europe, his feminization was symbolized in a ritual act of genital alteration that linked him to both the integrity and the shame of his cultural heritage. Freud's construction of the physically mutilated and psychically wounded female can thus be understood as a reflection of both the physical and psychic wounds that were at the core of his own unconscious identity. The character traits that Freud attributes to the permanently scarred female—genital inferiority, weakness, passivity, and immorality—are precisely those traits that anti-Semitic ideologies attributed to the emasculated Jewish male. Thus, for Freud, the female gender becomes the personification of the anti-Semitic construction of flawed Jewish masculinity. This form of projection can help to explain the hatred and revulsion that characterized Freud's attitude toward female genitalia. In describing the significance of castration anxiety for the Oedipal stage in male development, Freud wrote:

> When a little boy first catches sight of a girl's genital region, he begins by showing irresolution and lack of interest; he sees nothing or disavows what he has seen. . . . It is not until later, when some threat of castration has obtained a hold upon him, that the observation becomes important to him: if he then recollects or repeats it, it arouses a terrible storm of emotion in him and forces him to believe in the reality of the threat which he has hitherto laughed at. This combination of circumstances leads to two reactions, which may become fixed and will in that case, whether separately or together or in conjunction with other factors, permanently determine the boy's relations to women: horror of the mutilated creature or triumphant contempt for her (SE 19:252).

That Freud used terms like *horror* and *contempt* to describe the boy's unconscious reaction to the sight of female genitalia would suggest that such deep emotional responses arose out of his own unconscious identification with the image of a mutilated body. Such identification would be consistent with the scientific writings of his day, as exemplified in the popular work of the Italian physician Paolo Mantegazza. Writing passionately on the practice of circumcision, Mantegazza concluded:

> Circumcision is a shame and an infamy; and I, who am not in the least anti-Semitic, who indeed have much esteem for the Israelites, I who demand of no liv-

ing soul a profession of religious faith, insisting only upon the brotherhood of soap and water and of honesty, I shout and shall continue to shout at the Hebrews, until my last breath: Cease mutilating yourselves: cease imprinting upon your flesh an odious brand to distinguish you from other men; until you do this, you cannot pretend to be our equal (as cited in Gilman 1993:57).

Perhaps more than any other of Freud's work, the case of Little Hans reveals the extent to which Freud understood the relationship between anti-Semitism and the Jewish male's identification with femaleness. In this case study, he explained how the small child Hans must have felt when he became aware of the female body, of the possibility that the threat of castration was real and that someone could take away his penis and "make him into a woman" (SE 10:36). In a significant footnote to this case, Freud argued that there was a strong relationship between the unconscious origins of anti-Semitism and the manifestation of the castration complex in the Christian psyche: "The castration complex is the deepest root of anti-Semitism; for even in the nursery little boys hear that a Jew has something cut off his penis—a piece of his penis, they think—and this gives them the right to despise Jews. And there is no stronger unconscious root for the sense of superiority over women" (SE 10:36).

Here, Freud located the shared roots of misogyny and anti-Semitism in the unconscious fear of castration that informs the psychosexual development of Christian masculinity. In linking Jewish men with women in the psyche of Christian males, he was moving closer to an understanding of the importance that anti-Semitism plays in psychological development. Yet Freud confined his observations only to Christian culture, failing to examine the effects that anti-Semitism has on the psyche of Jewish males as well— how images of mutilation and denigration inform the construction of the circumcised Jewish self. As a result, Freud's unconscious identification with the scarred and wounded female found its expression not in a contextualized theory of masculinity but in a universal theory of femininity that projected Freud's self-hatred and shame onto women.

If in theorizing about women Freud was actually providing insight into his own internalized anti-Semitism, then we may wish to rethink his work on the feminine personality from the perspective of Jew and Gentile rather than female and male. Within this framework, we might imagine how his writings would reflect this unconscious identification with Jewish male otherness. Taking, for example, a previously quoted passage from his writings on women, we can substitute the words *Jew* and *Gentile* for *women* and *sex*: "After a woman [Jew] has become aware of the wound to her [his] narcissism, she [he] develops, like a scar, a sense of her [his] inferiority. . . . She [the Jew] begins to share the contempt felt by men [Gentiles] for a sex [race] which is the lesser in so important a respect" (SE 19:253).

Engaging in this sort of speculative "rewriting" of the Freudian canon permits us to look inside the psyche of the marginalized male other, a process that helps to illuminate the internalized self-hatred that grows out of racist and sexist ideologies. In pathologizing the female, Freud shifts the identification of self as other to woman as other. With this shift, male superiority becomes the focal point for establishing a shared consciousness of masculinity between male Gentile and male Jew, an intrapsychic process that acts as a defense against the threat of anti-Semitism. Out of this shared consciousness of masculinity, Freud was able to universalize the male Oedipal crisis, thus creating a psychic drama in which the Jewish male, like his Christian counterpart, assumed his rightful place as moral authority in patriarchal culture. Through the development of psychoanalysis, Jewish fathers and sons became like their idealized Christian neighbors, exhibiting in the psychic arena the qualities of masculinity they had been denied in the real world of anti-Semitic European society.

Oedipus and the Jewish Father

In contrast to Freud's theory of women, his views on the psychoanalytic development of men focus on the relationship among impulse control, fear of male aggression, and paternal authority. His theory of the Oedipal crisis in boys describes an intrafamilial rivalry in which son and father vie for sexual dominance over the objectified figure of the sexualized mother:

> When a boy (from the age of two or three) has entered the phallic phase of his libidinal development, is feeling pleasurable sensations in his sexual organ and had learnt to procure these at will by manual stimulation, he becomes his mother's lover. He wishes to possess her physically in such ways as he has divined from his observations and intuitions about sexual life, and he tries to seduce her by showing her the male organ which he is proud to own. In a word, his early awakened masculinity seeks to take his father's place with her; his father has hitherto in any case been an envied model to the boy, owing to the physical strength he perceived in him and the authority with which he finds him clothed. His father now becomes a rival who stands in his way and whom he would like to get rid of. . . .
>
> The boy's mother has understood quite well that his sexual excitation relates to herself. Sooner or later she reflects that it is not right to allow it to continue. . . . At last his mother adopts the severest measures: she threatens to take away from him the things he is defying her with. Usually, in order to make the threat more frightening and more credible, she delegates its execution to the boy's father, saying that she will tell him and that he will cut his penis off (Freud 1949:71–72).

For Freud, sexual aggression becomes the defining impulse that structures his relationship both to his mother and father and that provides the critical psychic crisis that leads him into masculinity. Faced with the reality of threatened castration, he represses his desire for his mother while identifying with the authority of his father. This identification forms the core of the developing superego in males: "In normal, or it is better to say, in ideal cases, the Oedipus exists no longer, even in the unconscious; the super-ego has become its heir. . . . The catastrophe to the Oedipus complex (the abandonment of incest and the institution of conscience and morality) may be regarded as a victory of the race over the individual" (SE 19:257).

The relationship between male aggression and the ideal of patriarchy, as developed by Freud, can be linked to the wish fulfillment of the Jewish son whose real father falls far short of the ideal of Christian masculinity. This interpretation is supported especially by Freud's childhood memoir that appears in the *Interpretation of Dreams* (1950) as the famous "hat in the gutter" incident:

> I happened upon the youthful experience which even today still expressed its power in all these emotions and dreams. I might have been ten or twelve years old when my father began to take me with him on his walks, and in his conversation to reveal his views on the things of this world. Thus it was that he once told me the following incident, in order to show me that I had been born into happier times than he: "When I was a young man, I was walking one Saturday along the street in the village where you were born; I was well-dressed, with a new fur cap on my head. Up comes a Christian, who knocks my cap in the mud, and shouts, 'Jew, get off the pavement!'"—"And what did you do?"—"I went into the street and picked up the cap," he calmly replied. That did not seem heroic on the part of the big, strong man who was leading me, a little fellow, by the hand. I contrasted this situation, which did not please me, with another, more in harmony with my sentiments—the scene in which Hannibal's father, Hamilcar Barcas, made his son swear before the household altar to take vengeance on the Romans. Ever since then Hannibal has had a place in my phantasies" (1950:98–99).

Freud associated this memory with his youthful idealization of Hannibal, a hero of his childhood imagination whose Semitic origins had great significance for Freud. The hat in the gutter incident reveals that it is not only the ideal of the heroic Jewish son that appealed to the young Freud but also the image of the vengeful father, Hamilcar Barcas, a man who modeled bravery and courage in comparison with the passivity of Jacob Freud. The hat in the gutter incident thus informed Freud's unconscious desire for a strong and aggressive father figure. This longing was ultimately fulfilled through Freud's fantasy of the Oedipal father, a paternal male avenger who came to represent universal fatherhood in the mind of the disappointed and disillusioned Jewish son. Through the resolution of the Oedipal crisis, the passive Jewish father was transformed into the aggressive hero of Freud's childhood imagination.

Yet in contrast to the Hannibal saga, the Oedipal drama does not portray an aggressive father seeking revenge against a foreign enemy. Rather, Freud located the origins of male aggression and morality within the privatized world of family relations, a sphere in which Jewish male aggression had a basis in reality. Denied access to other avenues of male power and authority in Austrian society, Jewish men turned to the family as the primary arena in which they could act on and retain their masculinity. Thus, it is not surprising that struggles over the sexual possession of women became the lens through which Freud explored the meaning of aggression, desire, and fear. Although other aspects of aggression and impulse control may have influenced the psyche of the male child, Freud located the path to masculinity in fantasies of sexual domination that, for the Jewish male, bore some relationship to the reality principle.

As the domination of the father within the patriarchal Jewish family provided a cultural reference point from which to derive the drama of Oedipus, intrafamilial rivalry and sexual competitiveness among the males within the family became the context through which Freud constructed the fantasy of the idealized father. In this fantasy, the power of the father is turned not against a rival of equal stature and physique but against the defenseless child who represents no real threat to the adult Jewish male. Thus, the father of Freud's Oedipal drama is an aggressor whose power can only be imagined in the rivalry between father and young son. Within this psychoanalytic frame, the male child's control over sexual aggression, to the exclusion of other forms of impulse control, became for Freud the basis upon which male morality and civilization are established.

Conclusion

In this chapter, I have attempted to explore the relationship between social forces and the development of scientific thought. In examining the effects of anti-Semitism and racialization on Freud, we are better able to understand the misogyny embedded in his theories and the idealization of male aggression that informed his views of masculinity. I have argued that Freud's work was influenced by the internalization of anti-Semitic ideologies that led to his identification with the female as other and his desire for a masculine Jewish ideal. Such an interpretation is not meant to disregard the theory of infantile sexuality or to reduce Freud's views on women to mere projections of his own unconscious feelings. Given the social forces affecting female development in patriarchal Viennese society, characteristics such as shame and envy of maleness were undoubtedly present in the women that he treated, many of whom were struggling with the gender limitations of their social environment.

Perhaps Freud could recognize, at least in part, the "problem of femininity" precisely because the female experience of otherness resonated with his own innermost feelings of marginality. If, however, this were so, Freud either remained unaware of his identification with women or chose not to acknowledge this aspect of his own self-analysis within the larger context of psychoanalytic theory. Unlike Fanon, Freud did not engage in the kind of critical self-examination (at least not in the public sphere) that would link his scientific insights to his social location. As a result, psychoanalysis purports to present universal truths that have tended to idealize men while pathologizing women. Such "truths" have generally been elaborated without regard for the significance of social forces, such as anti-Semitism, racism, and sexism, that influence both the intellectual and the psychological development of marginalized members of society. An unfortunate legacy of Freud has thus been the perpetuation of scientific theories that fail to take into account the impact of the social environment on personality formation in contemporary society.

References

Bakan, D. 1958. *Sigmund Freud and the Jewish Mystical Tradition.* Boston: Beacon Press.

Fanon, F. 1967. *Black Skin: White Masks.* New York: Grove Weidenfeld.

Freud, S. 1911. SE: Vol. 10. Translated by J. Strachey. London: Hogarth Press and the Institute of Psychoanalysis.

_____. 1913. SE: Vol. 13. Translated by J. Strachey. London: Hogarth Press and the Institute of Psychoanalysis.

_____. 1923–1925. SE: Vol. 19. Translated by J. Strachey. London: Hogarth Press and the Institute of Psychoanalysis.

_____. 1925–1926. SE: Vol. 20. Translated by J. Strachey. London: Hogarth Press and the Institute of Psychoanalysis.

_____. 1932–1936. SE: Vol. 22. Translated by J. Strachey. London: Hogarth Press and the Institute of Psychoanalysis.

_____. 1949. *An Outline of Psycho-Analysis.* Translated by J. Strachey. New York: W. W. Norton.

_____. 1950. *The Interpretation of Dreams.* Translated by A. Brill. New York: Modern Library.

Gilman, S. L. 1993. *Freud, Race and Gender.* Princeton: Princeton University Press.

Grollman, E. A. 1965. *Judaism in Sigmund Freud's World.* New York: Bloch Publishing.

Harding, S. 1987. "The Instability of the Analytical Categories of Feminist Theory." In S. Harding and J. F. O'Barr, eds., *Sex and Scientific Inquiry.* Chicago: University of Chicago Press, pp. 283–302.

Horney, K. [1926] 1967. "The Flight from Womanhood: The Masculinity Complex in Women as Viewed by Men and by Women." In H. Kelman, ed., *Feminine Psychology.* New York: W. W. Norton, pp. 54–70.

Klein, D. 1985. *The Jewish Origins of the Psychoanalytic Movement.* Chicago: University of Chicago Press.

Mantegazza, P. 1938. *The Sexual Relations of Mankind*. Translated by S. Putnam. New York: Eugenics.

Merkur, D. 1994. "Freud and Hasidism." In L. Bryce Boyer, Ruth M. Boyer, and Howard F. Stein, eds., *Essays in Honor of George A. De Vos: The Psychoanalytic Study of Society*. Vol. 19. Hillsdale, N.J.: Analytic Press, pp. 336–347.

Robert, M. 1976. *From Oedipus to Moses*. Translated by R. Manheim. New York: Doubleday.

Roith, E. 1987. *The Riddle of Freud: Jewish Influences on His Theory of Female Sexuality*. London and New York: Tavistock Publications.

Roper, H. R. 1967. *The European Witchcraze of the Sixteenth and Seventeenth Centuries*. New York: Harper & Row.

4

Psychoanalysis and Fundamentalism

A Lesson from Feminist Critiques of Freud

Ralph W. Hood Jr.

The feminist critique of Freud's abandonment of the seduction theory has important lessons for psychoanalytic theories of religion. Despite Freud's insistence that religion is ultimately *delusion*, contemporary psychoanalytic theory and its offshoots confront religion primarily in terms of an expanded view of *illusion*. This avoids confrontation with the historical truth claims of religion, just as the abandonment of the seduction theory avoided confrontation with the historical reality of sexual abuse. Fundamentalists and feminists share a concern with the authenticity of historical narratives that contemporary psychoanalysis has attempted to minimize, if not ignore altogether.

I will explore this theme in three segments. First, I will present a feminist critique of Freud's abandonment of the seduction theory, along with current evidence supporting this critique. Second, I will argue that Freud recognized the insufficiency of treating fundamentalist religious claims as illusion.[1] He required that their delusional nature also be unmasked. Finally, I will emphasize that Freud's treatment of religion in both ontogenetic and phylogenetic terms produced its own historical narrative in which Oedipus became a dogma in contention with those of Moses and Christ that it hoped to explain.

Freud's Abandonment of the
Seduction Theory

It is instructive to note the tone in which two authorities express their divergent reactions to Freud's abandonment of the seduction theory. Peter Gay, the noted biographer of Freud, claimed, "The seduction theory in all its uncompromising sweep seems inherently implausible. . . . What is astonishing is not that Freud eventually abandoned the idea, but that he adopted it in the first place" (1988:91). By contrast, Elaine Westerlund critically reviewed the history of the seduction theory in Freud's private and public writings. She claimed, "Freud was seduced into and seduced others into protecting the sexual offender and thus betrayed the sexual victim" (Westerlund 1986:308). She also asserted that Freud never privately abandoned the seduction theory, which makes his disavowal of the theory a public betrayal of women. Her position is what I refer to as the feminist critique of Freud.

Regardless of gender, few authorities have failed to note that the abandonment of the seduction theory placed psychoanalysis upon a firm psychological footing. Ignoring historical authenticity in favor of internal psychodynamics is widely seen as the essential step for the emergence of the uniquely human science of psychoanalysis (Gay 1988:55–104). Yet in the clash between desire and reality, the feminist critique is more on the side of historical realities that are undesired than desires that are frustrated. Westerlund (1986:308) chided Freud for his loss of interest in validating the experiences of his female clients in favor of exploring the frustration of their desires. Freud's final theory of infantile sexuality (1905/1953) burdened the victims with the additional trauma that, even as infants, they may have desired that which was forced upon them. Feminists have taken the lead in insisting that infantile sexual abuse is factual and both undesirable and undesired. The most serious charge by feminists is that Freud's public abandonment of the seduction theory may have been indicative of a continuing male Weltanschauung in which exploitation of both women and children is acceptable.

Much ink continues to be spilled on Freud's initial seduction theory and the reasons it was abandoned. Three major theories have emerged, each of which has its powerful apologists.

Perhaps most controversial is Jeffrey Masson's claim surrounding Freud's first analytic patient, Emma Eckstein. As Masson (1984:55–106) reconstructed the history, Emma likely suffered from dysmenorrhea assumed by Wilhelm Fliess to be due to masturbation. The cure was nasal surgery followed by psychotherapy. Nasal surgery was recommended by Fliess based upon his dubious theory of a causal connection between the nose and the sexual organs. The surgery was botched, and Emma nearly hemorrhaged to death. Freud argued that the hemorrhage was due to psychological factors, shifting the burden away from Fliess to Emma's own psychodynamics. Whatever the historical merit of this claim, it did contribute to the critical turn in psychoanalytic theory from a focus upon externally imposed traumatic events to repressed endogenous desires. In a curious inversion, the claim to seduction became fantasy as fantasy became the reality of concern for psychoanalysis. In an ironic twist, Gay (1988:91) asserted that "only a fantasist like Fliess" could have supported the seduction theory.

The shift to fantasy as the crucial psychoanalytic concept has produced a rich theoretical edifice, but it replaces the repression of real traumatic events, unwanted and imposed from without, with the repression of desires found within. Masson marshaled a wide variety of evidence that Freud was intimately familiar with the reality of child sexual abuse, including the probability that he witnessed autopsies of victimized children at the Paris morgue (1984:14–54). Masson charged Freud with a failure of courage in abandoning the reality of infantile sexual abuse in an effort to defend his friend and colleague Fliess. If Masson is right, psychoanalysis was founded upon a denial of reality by the psychoanalysts rather than by their patients. To continue to minimize authentic historical realities in favor of a therapeutic approach focused upon repressed desires forces patients to the "needless repetition of their deepest and earliest sorrow" (Masson 1984:192).

Most compatible with what is now classical psychoanalytic theory is the almost universally accepted view that the abandonment of the seduction theory was and continues to be essential to psychoanalytic theory. Associated with this view is the claim that Freud's struggle with his own self-analysis was a major factor in his gradual awakening to the belief that fantasy, not historical reality, was the source of traumas sufficient to erect the psychoanalytic edifice (Ansieu 1986). Gay (1988), perhaps Freud's most apologetic biographer, argued that Freud's sustained self-analysis led to the discovery that the myth of Oedipus was the essential cornerstone upon which psychoanalysis could be built. Where Masson found a failure of courage and deceit at the heart of Freud's creation of psychoanalysis, Gay found courage and intellectual integrity in the discovery that a Greek myth was indeed a scientific fact. Yet the outcome is that the considerable trauma that results from actual childhood abuse fades into the background as psychoanalytic theories turn attention to the full range and scope of a desire-driven fantasy.

Finally, the third and perhaps most damaging attack on Freud has come from feminists. They have charged Freud with deliberate obfuscation of facts known even in his time. They have documented not only the actual sexual abuse of children, in Freud's day as now, but also the fact that Freud and other psychoanalysts protected peers who were known to sexually abuse their clients. For instance, Elaine Westerlund (1986:306) cited several sources to document Freud's tolerance of Sandor Ferenczi's sexual intimacy not only with his patients but also with his daughter. (Ferenczi was one of Freud's early psychoanalytic cohorts.) Likewise, she reminded us of evidence that Freud's earliest biographer, Ernest Jones, was sexually active with patients as well as young girls. Thus, feminist attacks on Freud's abandonment of the seduction theory, like Masson's critique, focus upon devious motivations. Both Masson and Westerlund identify protection of colleagues as a concern for Freud, but Westerlund elevates the charge to a general male preoccupation with protecting their own from responsibility for the actual exploitation of women and children, which continues within the psychoanalytic profession today. Although most scholars do not attribute direct sexual exploitation of women to Freud, he is accused of being complicitous with others known to have sexually abused women and children. Furthermore, authorities with varying degrees of sympathy for Freud have cited difficulties with his self-analysis as an additional reason for turning attention away from the reality of sexual abuse (Ansieu 1986; Gay 1988:96–100; Westerlund 1986: 310).

A general feminist critique has emerged, arguing that the conspiracy of silence surrounding even acknowledged abuse of women and children by male professionals is part of a general male pattern that continues today. Feminists argue that psychoanalysis as a profession must recognize this possibility, even while focusing upon internal psychodynamics rather than external reality.

Historical Versus Narrative Truth

The cultural importance of psychoanalysis can hardly be underestimated despite a well-documented "diminishing psychoanalytic realm" (Hale 1995: 322–344). Part of this diminishing realm is the extent to which classical Freudian theory claims to unmask myths held sacred within a culture. Freud insisted that every myth must contain at least some aspect of a historical truth. Yet cultural myths may so distort reality that an entire culture of believers may be deluded. Freud insisted on an external criterion by which individual and collective narrative claims to truth could be challenged. The criterion was history—but history unmasked as external to the social construction of the cultural myth. In what is surely his most controversial and least accepted work, *Moses and Monotheism*, Freud asserted:

> We have long understood that a portion of forgotten truth lies hidden in delusional ideas, that when this returns it has to put up with distortions and misunderstandings, and that the compulsive conviction which attaches to the delusion arises from this core of truth and spreads onto errors that wrap it round. We must grant an ingredient such as this of what may be called *historical* truth to the dogma of religion as well, which, it is true, bear the character of psychotic symptoms but which, as group phenomena, escape the curse of isolation (1939/1964:85, emphasis in original).

As I will show, Freud's claim to have discovered the historical truth of religious narratives is perhaps the most dubious claim within psychoanalysis.
However, the immediate concern is with the fact that narratives must link
with historical truths, religious or not. This is the lesson to be emphasized
from feminist critiques of Freud's abandonment of the seduction theory.
Feminists argue that Freud had firm knowledge of the historical authenticity
of child abuse. For instance, in his initial paper on the etiology of hysteria
(Freud 1896/1962), he was clear that actual sexual experiences in childhood
are ultimately at the basis of later hysterical symptoms. Furthermore, he argued that sexual activity on the part of children is not spontaneous. It is
elicited by a reaction to a previous seduction by an adult. Prior to the abandonment of the seduction theory, the term *seduction* referred to sexual
acts that were unwanted, unprovoked, and unwarranted (Westerlund
1986:297–298). Yet these claims were ignored or minimized when Freud
publicly abandoned the seduction theory.

Privately, Freud was admittedly protective of males known to be guilty. In
an early paper on hysteria (Freud 1895/1955), he modified the case histories
of both Katharina (case 4, pp. 125–134) and Rosalia (case 5, pp. 135–181) to
shift the burden of their seduction from their fathers to their uncles. In 1924,
Freud added footnotes to each case study admitting this fact (1895/1955, pp.
134 for Katharina and p. 170 for Rosalia). Both Masson (1984:232) and Westerlund (1986:298) denied that this distortion was a matter of professional
discretion. Both saw this as a deliberate distortion of historical reality,
rooted in Freud's own psychodynamics. Freud needed to absolve his father
from suspected abuse and in so doing created a theory that absolved all fathers from abuse. This is the explicit male Weltanschauung that feminists insist psychoanalysis as a profession fosters when it favors analysis of fantasy
over historical reality. Women sympathetic to psychoanalysis have, from day
one, focused upon, in Karen Horney's (1933) phrase, "the denial of the
vagina." The phallocentric biases of psychoanalysis continue to be criticized
by women committed to the general usefulness of psychoanalytic theory
(Mitchell 1975; Van Herik 1982).

At this juncture, it is important to make the case that the reality of infantile sexuality articulated by Freud (1905/1953), even if true, does not mitigate the reality of infantile sexual abuse. In fact, the evidence for infantile
sexual abuse, as I shall shortly document, is empirically stronger than that
for infantile sexuality as interpreted by psychoanalysts. The feminists,
though not necessarily denying the latter, demand that the former be acknowledged. It is this historical reality that psychoanalysis threatens to ignore. Consider the remarkable claim by Donald Spence (1982:21–22): "Although Freud would later argue that every effective interpretation must also
contain a piece of historical truth, it is by no means certain whether this is al-

ways the case; narrative truth by itself seems to have significant impact on the clinical process."

A narrative truth by itself finds historical facts irrelevant and purports to stand if not above then at least outside history. Whether true or not in a clinical sense, the feminist demand has been that when sexual assault is the issue, the reality of historical fact must be acknowledged; otherwise, therapy supports further denial and self-abrogation. Feminists have made historical fact central, at least in claims of seduction, and thus denied that narrative truth alone has healing power. To deny or ignore the authenticity of history does not heal; it continues the hurt.

The Reality of Sexual Abuse

To assume that sexual abuse is rare contributes to the likelihood that when claims of abuse are common, many must be false. It is assumed that sexual prohibitions against incest are as effective as they are common. As Lloyd Demause (1991) has documented, the incest taboo is perhaps the best candidate to fulfill the fascination with identifying universals among social scientists.

Although cultures vary in how they define incest, one would be hard put to defend the claim that there is or has been a culture lacking in incest prohibition, especially between immediate family members. Demause properly cited Kroeber (1939:446), who stated, "If ten anthropologists were asked to designate one universal institution, nine would likely name incest prohibition; some have expressly named it as the only universal one."

In *Totem and Taboo* (1913/1958), Freud most forcefully developed the view that prohibitions reflect desires. A universal incest prohibition affirms a universal human desire for incest. Consistent with the abandonment of the seduction theory in clinical psychoanalysis, theoretical psychoanalysis focusing upon cultural theory attributes incestuous desires, fulfilled or not, to psychodynamic forces within the individual. Furthermore, such desires are less repressed in primitive (meaning earlier in development) societies and individuals. Hence, incestuous fantasies are the proper domain of any primitive state of development, be it of individuals or cultures. Seduction shifts its meaning from the perpetuator offending the innocent to the victim soliciting the act, whether in fact successfully or not. Thus, children are forever victims not of sexual oppression from outside but of sexual desires erupting within. This is central to Freud's (1905/1953) justly contentious claim regarding the universality of infantile sexuality.

However profound such a theory may be, the facts remain that anthropological evidence parallels feminist claims that actual assault, not fantasized assault, is the historical reality. Rather than being a universal *desire*, largely unfulfilled, child sexual abuse, including incest, is a universal *act* commonly practiced. In Demause's extensively documented claim, the feminist critique of Freud was given a firm anthropological footing: *"It is incest itself—and not the absence of incest—that has been universal for most people in most places at most times. Furthermore, the earlier in history one searches, the more evidence there is of universal incest, just as there is more evidence of other forms of child abuse"* (1991:125, emphasis in original).

Demause's documentation of the universality of incestuous practices included not only direct assault on children by parents (typically father-daughter) but also indirect abuse, such as the forcing or permitting of sexual activity between children and others by one or both parents. In his sobering and critical review, Demause clarified that there is hardly any sexual abuse that has not been or does not continue to be fostered upon children in virtually all cultures. Sexual abuse, if not normal, is exceedingly common. Although the precise documentation of frequencies remains a matter of some dispute, it is not reasonable to argue that infantile sexual abuse is rare. This has been the feminist focus, and in this respect, feminists surely have not only won a debate but have also established the necessity for the historical reality of sexual trauma to be once again acknowledged within the parameters of psychoanalytic thought.

The Current Repressed Memory Debate

The fact that infantile sexual abuse is common need not be directly associated with current debates regarding repressed memories. Though there is little doubt that repression is a central concept in psychoanalytic theory, claims that the concept lacks empirical support (Holmes 1990) are best viewed as paradigm clashes. It is difficult to think of an experimental procedure that would be ethical and yet capable of establishing the reality of repressed memories, especially those of early infantile sexual trauma. Even the most critical reviews of repressed memories have failed to produce a single experimental study revealing cases of false traumatic memories recalled as true (Holmes 1990; Loftus 1993). False memories can be produced, but they most commonly involve nontraumatic events or essentially minor variations in the nature of the real trauma recalled, not the fact that a trauma occurred (Malmquist 1986). Psychoanalytic techniques, though admittedly nonexperimental, evolved precisely as a distinctly human psychology, confronting many issues that are not susceptible to direct experimental test or for which it would be ethically inappropriate to attempt experimental manipulation.

Within many forms of psychotherapy, repressed memories are widely acknowledged (Bruhn 1990), and they are axiomatic within psychoanalysis (Bower 1990). Accordingly, the issue I wish to confront is not whether repressed memories exist. Rather, I assume their existence and want to confront the issue of whether the memories repressed are true to actual historical events. The initial formulation of the seduction theory assumes they are; the abandonment of the seduction theory assumes that often they are not. However, whether such memories are veridical or not, psychoanalytic theory has evolved such that it largely ignores the relationship between repressed desires and actual traumatic events. Although the recent interest and investigation of false memories of early sexual seduction are important, they do not mitigate the conceptual concerns of this chapter—that the abandonment of the seduction theory fails to focus concern and theory upon genuine cases of sexual abuse. This is the basic thrust of what I identify as the feminist critique of Freud. It is also related to Freud's treatment of religion. However, in the case of religion, Freud continued to insist on the search for historical truth.

In an earlier invited paper for the *International Journal for the Psychology of Religion* (Hood 1992), I concentrated upon this claim to historical truth in denying the relevance of illusion-based theories of religion to explicate issues central to fundamentalist faiths. In a thoughtful critique of that paper, Jacob Belzen and Arnold Uleyn (1992) appropriately focused upon what they saw as implicit epistemological and theological issues; the first part of the title of their critique was "What Is Real?" I wish to return to some aspects of my paper to argue that feminists and fundamentalists can be seen as strange bed partners in answering precisely this question. I want to reemphasize that Freudian theory demands a confrontation with the historical reality claims of religion just as feminists demand a confrontation with the historical reality of sexual abuse. The emphasis in contemporary psychoanalysis treating religion as illusion in an expanded treatment of transitional phenomena places fundamentalist religious views in precisely the same position that feminists found themselves in with the abandonment of the seduction theory. Fundamentalists find no more validity in the use of illusion to confront religion than do feminists in the use of illusion to confront seduction.

Only in his analysis of religion was Freud keenly aware that treating religion merely as an illusion would not carry sufficient critical weight. If illusion was all psychoanalysis could use to analyze religion, it could be employed as efficiently by apologists to support religion. In Freud's words: "If the application of the psycho-analytic method makes it possible to find a new argument against religion, *tant pis* for religion; but defenders of religion will by the same right make use of psycho-analysis in order to give full value to the affective significance of religious doctrines" (1927/1961:37).

Freud's critical confrontation with religion assumes it to be not simply false but also a falsified history. As such, it is delusion. Despite the power of dogma, or perhaps because of it, the narrative truth of religion remains incomplete. To claim religion is delusion entails historical claims as to the reality of the content of religious beliefs. Fundamentalist beliefs make specific claims that Freud felt could be rejected out of hand. Psychoanalysis could contribute little new to the refutation of religious beliefs. What it uniquely offered was an explanation for the appeal of religion. Here are direct parallels to the debate over the seduction theory and parallels noted by others concerning the recollection of infantile abuse, deemed unlikely to have occurred. The burden shifts from a recognition of historical truth to a need to explain a false sense of history. Only the concept of delusion could carry this weight. This shift also burdens the theorists to defend a novel theory of history that is nevertheless true. The irony is that the Greek myth of Oedipus is proclaimed to be a scientific truth of psychoanalysis that can explain what fundamentalists proclaim as the truth of history.

Apologetics: Fundamentalist and Feminist

Scholars affirming the reality of sexual assaults as real historical events in the lives of women are often accused of being apologists for feminism. The response can only be that if women recollect authentic abuse, apologetics demands this recognition. The feminist critique is not that psychoanalytic views of desire are necessarily false but that those views ignore authentic historical trauma or find it largely irrelevant. At worst, psychoanalysis contributes to a falsification of history when authentic assault is treated merely as fantasy. Belzen and Uleyn suggested the same with my treatment of Freud's critique of religion. They noted, "Underneath this text there is an apologetic purpose, combined with an outdated epistemology concerning 'objective reality' and an erroneous understanding of recent developments within psychoanalytic theory" (Belzen and Uleyn 1992:168).

  Though I wrote then and now neither as a Christian nor as a fundamentalist, I do insist that fundamentalist religious claims are due a rational discussion within the psychology of religion. In so doing, I share with feminists an apologetic tone. Even fundamentalist religious beliefs should at least be introduced as legitimate truth claims, not dismissed out of hand. Again, this is precisely what feminists have demanded of psychoanalysis—that the reality of sexual abuse be admitted as a real possibility requiring theoretical confrontation, something that cannot be done with the abandonment of the seduction theory. To abandon a focus upon the authenticity of sexual assault in favor of the reality of sexual desire is to give desire an objectivity that history presumably lacks. Women as victimized within psychoanalytic theory presumably suffer from the delusion that they were assaulted. In terms of Freud's theory of infantile sexuality, fantasized assaults are illusions, often unconscious, of desire for the father that should be explored within the therapeutic setting. Yet in a curious twist, feminists have used what we might call a phylogenetic view of trauma, the commonality of sexual abuse of children now as throughout history (documented earlier), to suggest the probability that an ontogenetic view of trauma, sexual abuse within an individual developmental history, has a prima facie probability of being true.

In a parallel manner, the treatment of fundamentalist religion as delusion requires the phylogenetic dimension of Freud's theory of religion, which is rejected by many who accept his ontogenetic views. Accordingly, I shall shortly confront both these aspects of Freud's theory of religion. Freud's theory is linked with what I term the dogma of Oedipus. The value of this dogma is that it is a truth claim. The Oedipus dogma remains central to classical psychoanalysis (Rudnytsky 1987; Shafranske 1995:221–225). Yet it also has been seriously challenged as an outmoded orthodoxy by others (Deleuze and Guattari 1983).

The irony is that the challenge to Oedipus orthodoxy parallels the psychoanalytic challenge to religious orthodoxy. And, as I will shortly note, the movement to a conciliatory dialogue among modern psychoanalysts sympathetic to religion is based upon an expanded treatment of illusion incompatible with fundamentalist religious claims. These psychoanalysts have turned to a definition of religion that avoids claims to delusion as they abandon claims to truth. Yet fundamentalist religious claims are not within the transitional realm; they are claims to objective fact. Freud knew this and rejected such claims as delusion. It is important to understand Freud's rejection of the notion that one cannot confront the truth claims of religion for fear of being deluded into treating religion as if it were merely illusion.

The Rejection of Religion as Merely Illusion

Freud's phylogenetic and ontogenetic explanations of religion (to be discussed later) both exceed the parameters of illusion. Freud anticipated contemporary object relation theories of religion as transitional phenomena (discussed later) in his rejection of Hans Vaihinger's (1968) "as if" philosophy. John Bowker (1973:119) thought this a "fundamental mistake," much as contemporary psychoanalysts such as William Meissner (1984) and object relations theorists such as D. W. Winnicott (1971:1–25) find Freud's claim that religion can be challenged as delusion to be mistaken. They do this by restricting psychoanalytic analysis of religion to an expanded view of illusion that refuses to confront directly the reality claims of fundamentalist religious beliefs by treating them as transitional phenomena.

Yet within fundamentalisms, such symbolic transpositions are explicitly rejected. Doctrines such as transubstantiation or the resurrection of the dead run counter to established epistemologies. To attempt to salvage such doctrines by an appeal to their meaningfulness as transitional phenomena in the face of their contradiction to known reality claims is untenable. It is easy to make this charge stick to fundamentalist beliefs within Protestantism, from which many scholars and certainly most all psychoanalysts have a great distance (Hood 1983). But within Catholicism, there are psychoanalytic believers supporting precisely parallel claims (Godin 1985; Meissner 1984), as do Catholic theologians sympathetic to psychoanalysis (Küng 1979, 1984). In a terse response to the content of such belief associated with Reinhold Niebuhr's claim to a personal immortality in which the essential unity of mind and body are preserved eternally, Adolf Grünbaum (1987:186) noted, "Alas, this is literally nonsense!" In the same article, he challenged Meissner's views on transubstantiation with the same disdain. Freud viewed such religious beliefs in a similar way. He would side more with Grünbaum's rejection than with those who find a mystery in such beliefs that could salvage their obvious contradiction to more mundane epistemologies of what is real or possible. This is best illustrated by Freud's rejection of Vaihinger's philosophy of "as if."

Vaihinger's Philosophy of "As If"

Vaihinger ([1924] 1968) developed a systematic theory of fictions rooted largely in the work of Kant. In particular, Vaihinger's *fictionalisms* can be contrasted with pragmatism. Whereas pragmatism accepts as true ideas that prove to be useful in practice, fictionalism accepts the falsity of ideas that nevertheless prove useful in practice. The distinction is crucial, for fictionalism recognizes its useful ideas as false. Vaihinger ([1924] 1968:VIII) put it thus: "An idea whose theoretical untruth or incorrectness, and therewith its falsity, is admitted, is not for that reason practically valueless and useless; for such an idea, in spite of its theoretical nullity may have great practical importance." Fictionalism has many parallels with transitional phenomena. However, a crucial difference is that fictions are explicitly known to be false; their truth is in their utility.

Vaihinger's discussion of fictions ranged widely, encompassing fictions in mathematics, history, physics, biology, and the social sciences. It is important to emphasize that fictions, although false on the basis of reason alone, function in reality. A consciously falsified reality is the basis for effective practice in Vaihinger's theory insofar as this falsified reality is conceptualized "as if" it were real, despite the knowledge that, in fact, it is not real. As I shall shortly note, transitional objects are immune to reality claims in a way in which fictionalisms are not.

One aspect of Vaihinger's philosophy of "as if" is the "law of ideational shifts" ([1924] 1968:124–134). This is the tendency to treat fictions as hypotheses and to treat hypotheses as dogmas. The reverse process can also occur: Dogmas tend to become hypotheses, and hypotheses become fictions. With specific reference to religion, Vaihinger argued:

> Myths, similes, even the conscious fictions of the founders of religions either become dogmas to the founders themselves, or to their adherents among the people, and rarely pass through the stage of hypothesis. On the other hand, during the decline and break-up of a religion all three stages stand out very clearly. At first all religion consists in general dogmas (the dogma has itself developed from an hypothesis or even from a fiction). Then doubt appears and the idea becomes hypothesis. As doubt grows stronger, there are some who reject the idea entirely, while others maintain it either as a public or private fiction ([1924] 1968:129).

Here, Vaihinger painted a picture of religion compatible with the ideas of modern object relations theorists who treat religion as transitional. It is a comforting philosophy, removing religion from falsifying truth claims—or at least those truth claims falsified by science. Yet Freud's theory of religion, with the phylogenetic and ontogenetic aspects necessarily interlocked, mandates a rejection of Vaihinger, as Bowker correctly noted, since Freud demands that religion be treated in terms of its truth claims. If false, such beliefs must ultimately lose their social utility. Fundamentalists make the same claim. They hold their beliefs neither as public nor private fictions.

Freud's Rejection of Vaihinger

Freud's explicit reference to Vaihinger is a footnote in *The Future of an Illusion* (1927/1961:29). It is made with reference to a brief discussion of two possible defenses of dogmatic or fundamentalist religious beliefs.

The first discussion is of a well-known quote attributed to Tertullian, "Credo qua absurdum" ("I believe because it is absurd"). Freud ridiculed known absurdity held as belief. Dogmatic in his own commitment, he stated, "There is no appeal to a court above that of reason" (Freud 1927/1961:28). Even if beliefs are driven by desire, ultimately they must be tested by the court of reason. If found lacking there, continued adherence is delusion.

The second discussion relates closely to the contemporary redefinition of religious beliefs as transitional phenomena that Anthony Flew (1978) noted cannot escape philosophical criticism. The dismissal of Vaihinger's philosophy of "as if" is likely because Freud already had realized that illusion could not carry the weight of his devastating criticism of fundamentalist religions. Freud's terse rejection belied a firm understanding of Vaihinger, despite Bowker's claims to the contrary. To give illusion a central role in the truth claims independent of history is what Freud did in abandoning the seduction theory. With religion, however, this move was rejected. Freud alluded to illusion treated as immune from historical criticism as a view "not foreign to other thinkers" (1927/1961:29). His rejection was terse: "A man whose thinking is not influenced by the artifices of philosophy will never be able to accept it; in such a man's view the admission that something is absurd or contrary to reason leaves no more to be said" (Freud 1927/1961:29).

It is apparent that Freud had to reject Vaihinger precisely because Freud demanded that the conceptual referents in any theory of religion be judged according to their truth. Furthermore, truth for Freud required specific events that are developmental in the ontogenetic aspect of his theory and historical in the phylogenetic aspect of his theory. The events recalled must be true. If not, the truth of events must be uncovered in the content of what is recalled. This is what feminists demand of Freud's abandonment of the seduction theory. Yet Freud made this move only with respect to religion. The acceptance of beliefs "as if" they were true had no appeal to Freud. He accepted the literal claims of religion as a fundamentalist does: as claims to truth. As noted earlier, Freud rejected such claims and sought an explanation for their appeal. His own recollection concerning one of his children was offered as a rebuttal to Vaihinger's philosophy:

> I am reminded of one of my children who was distinguished at an early age by a peculiarly marked matter-of-factness. When the children were being told a fairy story and were listening to it with rapt attention, he would come up and ask: "Is that a true story?" When he was told it was not, he would turn away with a look of disdain. We may expect that people will soon behave in the same way towards the fairy tales of religion in spite of the advocacy of "As if" (Freud 1927/1961:29).

Freud's understanding of Vaihinger allowed him to reject the holding of fictional beliefs "as if" they were true, as psychologically functional. They will necessarily fail for one who knows their historical untruth, and they cannot function "as if" for those who delusionally accept their historical truth. Religion as transitional is a religion ignored by both fundamentalists and Freud. The issue for Freud's theory of religion was to set his claim to the historical origins of religion against those of classic religious dogma. They were competing claims to truth to be adjudicated in the court of reason. Fundamentalist religious claims cannot function for the believer nor for Freud "as if," and hence, their illusory base is not at issue. However, their delusional base is. Freud's religion of the heart is both driven and pulled by illusion great enough to distort the truth it necessarily reveals, if only darkly. His religion is no "as if" but rather "is," and it is a distortion of a reality dimly remembered. Repetition and the return of the repressed maintain the gods, if not God, and allow, indeed demand, a psychoanalytic illumination (Badcock 1980; Marcuse 1955; Ricoeur 1970).

Illusion and Transitional Phenomena

Although Freud cannot be said to have explicitly developed a theory of illusion, his entire corpus is, in a sense, a theory of illusion. The context here is obviously the extent to which desire is the driving force behind all human cognition and action. For Freud, the test for truth was always some reality correspondence that emerged developmentally, whether conceptualized in terms of instinct or of object relations. Successful development requires an "education to reality" (Freud 1927/1961:49), although Freud accepted the fact that artistic expression is divorced from the reality principle. He even postulated an evolutionary principle whereby imagination was exempt from reality testing, producing illusions formulated as fantasy and providing satisfaction to creative artists and their public (Freud 1930/1961). Ironically, contemporary object relations theorists have attempted to treat not only all of culture but also specifically religion and art as if they were similar in being illusion (Meissner 1984; Pruyser 1976, 1987; Winnicott 1971:1–25).

This treatment of illusion, when unpacked critically, contains two issues of concern to contemporary psychoanalytic treatments of illusion and transitional phenomena. First, illusions, offering "consolation in life," belie a recognition, if not a negation, of reality. Art, to the extent it is not *merely* realistic, transcends reality and, in so doing, provides both pleasure and consolation (Badcock 1985:135–171). But it makes no claims to truth in the process.

Second, the truth in illusion is that of human desire—desire unfulfilled to be sure but desire recognized as such in what Grünbaum (1987) called Freud's commonsense hypothesis. Illusion, orthogonal to objective reality, is veridical to the subjective reality of desire. Like Marx, Freud theorized that religious suffering was always real suffering, a true recognition of unfulfilled desire. However, the crux of the matter, for both Freud and Marx, is why the fantasized fulfillment of subjective religious truth is not in terms of an objective historical truth. Ultimately, the question is why religious consolation cannot, like art, be a real consolation. The answer is that only religion is delusion as well as illusion. Insofar as it makes no reality claims, art can only be illusion. Contemporary psychoanalysts would attempt to claim the same for religion as for art, something that Freud explicitly denounced and fundamentalists find abhorrent. Art, not religion, remains divorced from reality. Freud saw no alternative to art. However, religion was another matter, claiming to engage reality and be its spokesperson. Freud rejected the voice of religion and purported to unmask its hidden truth. As illusion, he said, it was less than pure; it was a desire-driven distortion of reality—in a word, delusion.

Among current psychoanalysts, probably no theorist has coined concepts to extend Freud's treatment of illusion more effectively than Winnicott. Yet as I will show, the contemporary salvaging of religion by an expanded treatment of illusion fails to engage fundamentalist religion, much as Freud's abandonment of the seduction theory failed to engage the concerns of contemporary feminists.

Winnicott's Influence

Heavily influenced by the thought of Winnicott, the treatment of illusion in the expanded sense of transitional phenomena marks an intermediate world, neither subjective nor objective. As such, reality and illusion cannot be contradictory terms. Yet this misses what is crucial in Freud's theory of religion. The question is whether *religion* contradicts reality, not whether illusion does. Only by equating religion with illusion is the issue of contradiction bypassed.

The treatment of religion as a transitional phenomenon has been developed extensively for images of God by Ana-Maria Rizzuto (1979), in a sketchy fashion for faith and prayer by Meissner (1984:160–184), and in a "three world" model of thinking in which religion occupies an illusionist world by Paul Pruyser (1983, 1985, 1987). All these theorists have utilized Winnicott's (1971) notions of transitional objects and phenomena as appropriate descriptions of religion. Here, religion remains merely illusion and avoids the clash with objective reality claims. Illusion becomes the very matrix of culture. However, Winnicott's illusion makes no claim to the reality testing of either fundamentalist or feminist concerns. The veridicality of what he terms illusory experience avoids epistemologies that some see as outmoded. The test of one's reality is ultimately intersubjective:

> It *is* usual to refer to "reality testing," . . . I am here staking a claim for an intermediate state between a baby's inability and his growing ability to recognize and accept reality. I am therefore studying the substance of *illusion,* that which is allowed to the infant, and which in adult life is inherent in art and religion, and yet becomes the hallmark of madness when an adult puts too powerful a claim on the credulity of others, forcing them to acknowledge a sharing of illusion that *is* not their own. We can share a respect for *illusory experience,* and if we wish we may collect together and form a group on the basis of the similarity of our illusory experiences. This is a natural root of grouping among human beings (Winnicott 1971:3, emphases in original).

Winnicott's expanded view of illusion identifies that which is distinctly human. It is the basis for culture insofar as it provides the realm of intersubjectivity that is, to use the title of the classic text by Peter Berger and Thomas Luckmann (1967), *The Social Construction of Reality.* The basis for this construction is shared meaning, psychologically rooted for Winnicott in transitional objects and phenomena that begin to emerge around four months of age, "between the thumb and the teddy bear" (1971:2). Some of the defining characteristics of transitional objects are obvious in the willingness of a sympathetic other not to challenge the infant's assumptive rights over the object, the prerogative of only the infant to change the object, and the gradual "decathecting" of the object as it is relegated to limbo (Winnicott 1971:5).

As Flew (1978:490) noted, the key word is not *object* but *transitional*. Winnicott permitted transitional phenomena without transitional objects. For instance, he allowed that the mother herself can be a transitional object. It is fundamental, however, that there is an object, a physical thing that can be possessed. This differentiates Winnicott's position from Melanie Klein's "internal objects" (Winnicott 1971:9). Whatever the transitional object, its use is such that the transition is "between a baby's inability and his growing ability to recognize and accept reality" (Winnicott 1971: 3). Yet for Winnicott, unlike Freud, there is no perspective beyond culture by which religion could be delusional. Indeed, transitional phenomena become "diffused over the whole cultural field" (Winnicott 1971:5). No criteria of delusion are possible since there is no criterion outside the cultural group by which reality is judged.

Winnicott (1971:86–94) distinguishes between object relations and object use. Only in object use does the object have an independent existence. As such, it cannot be the repository of omnipotent control as in object relations. The infant must develop a capacity to use the object in terms of adjusting to the reality principle. Here is both paradox and acceptance of paradox in an object both created and discovered by the infant (Winnicott 1971:89). Much of this process is guided by the mother.[2] She brings the infant into her world and reproduces the cultural reality that is the matrix for their existence. No delusion is possible in a reality that is intersubjectively shared and ultimately illusion.[3] To claim objectivity for that illusory experience is now the delusion. Only a shared subjectivity, which Berger and Luckmann (1967) called *intersubjectivity,* identifies cultures and traditions. There is no Archimedean point from which to make a judgment. As Winnicott put it:

> Should an adult make claims on us for our acceptance of the objectivity of his subjective phenomena we discern and diagnose madness. If, however, the adult can manage to enjoy the personal intermediate area without making claims, then we can acknowledge our own corresponding intermediate areas, and are pleased to find a degree of overlapping, that is to say common experiences between members of a group in art or religion or philosophy (1971:14).

To stop at this point is to emphasize the impasse in current thought, well articulated in the sociology of knowledge insofar as one shifts from an individual to a cultural solipsism (Berger and Luckmann 1967). Purely social constructionist perspectives can postulate no criteria external to culture by which to judge claims to truth. They are part of postmodern views of the so-

cial sciences (Roseneau 1992). However, the point is well taken, as A. McIntyre (1988) and others have stressed, that even if culture is socially constructed, judgments as to truth can be made. It takes more than declaration
to see epistemologies opposed to postmodern views as "outdated concerning
the 'objectivity of reality'" (Belzen and Uleyn 1992:168). Fundamentalist beliefs demand acceptance in terms of historical claims to truth. Their opposition to modernism continues in terms of an opposition to postmodernism as
well. Freud not only rejected fundamentalist truth claims out of hand but
also had an alternative to explain the truth of religious history as he knew it.
Thus, he could claim fundamentalist beliefs to be delusions. Even should
they be the normative view of an entire culture, they would remain delusions
nevertheless.

One suspects that contemporary psychoanalysts are as distant from sympathy for religious fundamentalism as was Freud. Some, such as Hans Küng,
Meissner, and Rizzuto, are sympathetic to religion treated as transitional
phenomena. Yet to treat all religion as demanding no agreement with historical truth claims is to adopt a view of religion that is likely compatible with
the symbolic treatment of sacred texts. However, this approach eliminates
fundamentalism by definition. It is decidedly a liberal philosophical treatment of religion that Freud opposed. As he noted:

> Philosophers stretch the meaning of words until they retain scarcely anything
> of their original sense. They give the name "God" to some vague abstraction
> which they have created for themselves; having done so they can pose before all
> the world as deists, as believers in God, and they can even boast that they have
> recognized a higher, purer concept of God, notwithstanding that their God is
> now nothing more than an insubstantial shadow and no longer the mighty per-
> sonality of religious doctrines (Freud 1927/1961:32).

Thus, with Winnicott's notion of transitional objects and phenomena, one
is likely to miss the crucial historical reality claims to truth that Freud recognized and critiqued. With Freud, there are more than merely transitional objects to consider. There is the claim that fundamentalists demand that some
truth may come from God. As Bowker (1973) noted in his critique of social
scientific theories of religion, part of our sense of God may come from God,
a thesis not seriously entertained by social scientists who construct methodological barriers against this possibility. By presenting an alternative to this
thesis, Freud gave the thesis more serious possibility than modern psychoanalysts do by their refusal to treat religion as anything other than illusion.

Freud was part of the Enlightenment project common to early social scientists who felt they could provide an exhaustive secular explanation for religion (Preus 1987). This assumes religion is in some sense "wrong," something Freud surely acknowledged. It also curiously respects more literal
beliefs as at least claims to truth. Fundamentalist religious beliefs are among

such claims. It must seem apologetic to insist that such beliefs be challenged in terms of their literalness and not redefined so as to make no reality claims that can be challenged. Similar demands have been made by feminists on behalf of reinstating the seduction theory, as I have already noted. It is a curious twist of fate that places feminists and fundamentalists on the same side in demanding that their own narratives be treated in terms of literal, not symbolic or fictive, truth claims. If either are deluded, so be it. The point is that their beliefs must be expressed so that the possibility of delusion is there. Ironically, in so doing, the possibility of their truth is also thereby admitted. Freud rose to that occasion, but with the hindsight of history, the limits of Oedipus as a counter to Christ are more than apparent.

Oedipus as Dogma

It is widely accepted that, like Marx, Freud was indebted to Ludwig Feuerbach (Grünbaum 1987; Küng 1980; Pruyser 1973) for his firm belief in the ability of a purely natural scientific explanation to illuminate both the process and the content of religious beliefs. After Feuerbach, critical theology became anthropology. Theological discourse upon the nature of ultimate reality became fodder for more proximate psychological explanations. The discussion of gods seems suspiciously like an anthropology projected onto nonexistent beings and nonexistent realms of existence. In Feuerbach's words, knowledge has "dissolved the Christian *Weltanschauung* in nitric acid" (quoted in Küng 1980:261). The rejection of classical dogmatic religious claims is the nonargumentative backdrop Freud assumed for his discussion of religion. Contemporary analyses of religion as a transitional phenomenon, however provocative and useful, are analyses of a religion that both Freud and fundamentalists refuse to label as such. The Oedipal resolution also has proven not so soluble as Feuerbach thought.

The Ontogenetic Perspective

Freud's ontogenetic perspective on religion remains widely acceptable within psychoanalytic circles. Authoritative summaries of this developmental view are readily available (Grünbaum 1987; Küng 1980:262–339; Meissner 1984:57–72; Pruyser 1973:252–258; Shafranske 1995:214–221). However, most authorities emphasize the many links between Freud's ontogenetic and phylogenetic perspectives. Typically, psychoanalysts with personal religious commitments emphasize the neutrality of Freudian theory about the truth claims of religious beliefs (Godin 1985; Meissner 1984), as do those theologians sympathetic to psychoanalytic theory (Küng 1979, 1984). Quotes from Freud to this effect are easy to marshal, particularly when references are restricted to *The Future of an Illusion*. It is true that Freud classified religions among the illusions of humankind, meaning only that wish fulfillment is the primary motivation for belief. Indeed, as Grünbaum (1987) suggested, this claim of Freud's is amenable to empirical testing within common measurement paradigms.

Freud's claim that religious beliefs are one type of illusion suggests a preliminary developmental view that foreshadows his phylogenetic concerns. Illusion points to desire, and desire has a dual history. Its ontogenetic development parallels ("recapitulates") its even more primordial phylogenetic past. Just as individual compulsions contain and cater to powerful illusions rooted in infantile desire for which there are at least vague recollections, so, too, does fundamentalist religious belief appeal to historical and developmental truths rooted in the genetic heart of humans. Freud affirmed this in one of his last works on religion:

> I have never doubted that religious phenomena are only to be understood on the pattern of the individual neurotic systems familiar to us—as the return of long since forgotten, important events in the primeval history of the human family—and that they have to thank precisely this origin for their compulsive character and that, accordingly, they are effective in human beings by force of the *historical truth of their content* (1939/1964:58, emphasis added).

Given this assertion, it is crucial to acknowledge that Freud's theory of religion cannot stand on its ontogenetic claims alone. Essential to Freud's theory is not simply religion as an illusion but also religion as a delusion. Religions become mass delusions insofar as Freudian theory insists that all religious claims should be assessed both on psychological grounds and with respect to their truth claims (Grünbaum 1987:154). Freud knew that the psychological ax cut both ways—psychological motivations for beliefs of any kind cannot be used to affirm or deny the truth claims of such beliefs. Religion can be delusion only if it can be shown to contain beliefs that contradict reality. Freud respected religion enough to challenge it on its own grounds, through its actual dogmatic claims that hold sway in the hearts, if not the minds, of the masses. Powerful desires, often unconscious, distort reality, and as such, illusion has its contribution to make to the theory of religion as delusion.

The Phylogenetic Theory

Even among those who look favorably on Freud's ontogenetic treatment of religion, Freud's phylogenetic view is resoundingly rejected (Küng 1979; Meissner 1984). Until recently, few have been willing to consider seriously, even as a viable hypothesis, that Freud's treatment of the primal horde is but one possibility, valuable for Freud even as a "just so" story (Freeman 1967). Freud's phylogenetic speculation can be readily summarized.

Freud accepted Darwin's speculation that the immediate forerunners of human culture were animals that lived in hordes. In hordes, a dominant male maintains control over all females while driving maturing males from the horde to eliminate any competition for sexual pleasure. Freud speculated that the decisive step toward human culture occurred when ousted males united in a cooperative slaying of the dominant male. However, the psychologically ambivalent attachment to the slain father produced remorse, resulting in the dual taboos of prohibiting the killing of any father in the future and demanding that sexually mature males seek satisfaction outside their family group. As a result, the horde was broken into individual families, each dominated by a male who internalized the prohibitions of the slain horde leader. Freud combined Darwin's horde speculations with anthropological descriptions of the totemic feast in which members of a given totem periodically slay and eat the totem animal in a sacrificial meal. The identification of totems, typically animals, as symbolic father figures allowed Freud to speculate that the totemic structure of early society was a cultural resolution of the Oedipal drama documented in clinical casework for individuals. The slain father of the primal horde scenario was thus linked to the totemic structure of primitive cultures. Consequently, Freud was able to postulate a parallel between cultural and individual development, both of which require resolution of the Oedipal complex. Although presented as an admittedly speculative theory, the crucial point is that the events associated with the cultural resolution are declared to be historical facts.

Criticism of Freud's theory abounds, from the near universal complaint that the monotraumatic origin of culture assumes a Lamarckian basis to evolution to the near universal rejection of Freud's acceptance of anthropological summaries of assumed essential features of totemism. However, supporters of Freud's basic claims are not unknown. For instance, Margaret Mead (1963) argued that if Freud's Oedipal drama occurred later in individual development, during preadolescence, then robust and strong males could easily attack an aged and weakened father. The constant repetition of this delayed Oedipal drama over many generations would allow it to be an evolutionary factor in survival. In a similar fashion, Geza Róheim (1950), an anthropologist sympathetic to Freud, argued that the constancy of the dilemmas of individual development are sufficient warrant to provide selection considerations consistent with modern evolutionary theory and supportive of the dual tenets of the Oedipal drama: obedience to the father and taboos on incestuous activity. More recent empirically grounded work seeking verification of Darwin's primal horde concept has raised once again the reasonableness of this hypothesis and marshaled relevant empirical evidence (Badcock 1980:1–37; Endleman 1981:115–127; Holmstrom 1991).

Freud's acceptance of Darwin's primal horde scenario is not important. It was crucial for him that the content of classical Jewish and Christian dogma be a disguised or distorted truth and that what was disguised was itself historical and factual—in a word, real. Other historical truths would work as well, although Darwin's speculation was the best available hypothesis for Freud's critical work. To emphasize the necessity of the phylogenetic dimension to Freud's theory of religion removes it forever from a transitional realm. It raises the possibility of delusion as a scientific claim countering religious claims to truth. Of course, this assumes that fundamentalist and scientific claims clash within similar worlds where their contradictory claims can be acknowledged and adjudicated. One cannot protect religion from possible reductionist scientific explanations by faintly praising it into a transitional realm. That is a realm where fundamentalists refuse to go and one in which Freud had the good sense not to place them.

It is essential to Freud's developmental view that religion infantilizes mankind. It does so in a pejorative sense, not because one affirms one's dependency on some other but because the other on whom one is dependent does not exist. The other once did exist but only as parent when one was an infant. Freud's Oedipal drama and its resolution are too well known to recap here. What is important is its central role in religious development individually and collectively. If the argument is made that religious beliefs are effectively maintained insofar as their illusory nature appeals to what is most developmentally fundamental in humankind, then argument and proof recede in the face of those who hope too hard and who suffer too much. The ontogenetic basis of this is enhanced by possible phylogenetic proclivities in which our deepest hurts are repetitive precisely in that they confront the continued crushing of our most profound desires. Freud explained his view thus:

> [Religions] are illusions, fulfillments of the oldest, strongest and most urgent wishes of mankind. The secret of their strength lies in the strength of those wishes. As we already know, the terrifying impression of helplessness in childhood aroused the need for protection—for protection through love—which was provided by the father; and the recognition that this helplessness lasts throughout life made it necessary to cling to the existence of a father, but this time a more powerful one. Thus the benevolent rule of a divine Providence allays our fear of the dangers of life; the establishment of a moral world-order ensures the fulfillment of the demands of justice, which have so often remained unfulfilled in human civilization; and the prolongation of earthly existence in a future life provides the local and temporal framework in which these wish-fulfillments shall take place. . . . It is an enormous relief to the individual psyche if the conflict of its childhood arising from the father complex—conflicts which it has never wholly overcome—are removed from it and brought to a solution which is universally accepted (1927/1961:30).

If part of the tremendous affective appeal of religious dogma is linked to childhood states, repetition and recollection are crucial to understanding

Freudian religious dynamics. Each circumstance of helplessness triggers recollections of past states, and ultimately, they all link to dependency in childhood and its various Oedipal resolutions (Badcock 1980). Yet in purely theoretical terms, Freud recognized that this was not sufficient to account for the overwhelming appeal of religious dogma. The Christian Weltanschauung suggested a repetition rooted in a phylogenetic base. As Paul Ricoeur put it: "The Oedipus complex of the individual is too brief and too indistinct to engender the gods; without an ancestral crime as part of our phylogenetic past, the longing for the father is unintelligible; *the* father is not my father"(1970:537).

The linkage in religious dogma to a god that is father to all must be a distortion of some other fact, and Freud sought that fact in history. But few accept the way in which he found it in a phylogenetic and historical history. The controversy surrounding that history is well known and summarized effectively and critically in many recent works (Badcock 1980:1–37, 248–252; Meissner 1984:104–133; Pruyser 1973; Ricoeur 1970:159–343; Shafranske 1995:209–214). Oedipus is less firm in its scientific base than the dogma it supports. The important point is that only if Freud was correct in certain aspects of his own historical claims can he have refuted contrary claims within religious traditions. The particularities of this debate are not germane; only the conceptual claim that Freud made applies. Religions become delusions when illusionary beliefs are held contrary to reality claims. Freud had no problem with the social support for religion because mass delusions are common and perhaps essential as stages in the development of civilization. It is sufficient to note that only within his historical phylogenetic model could Freud claim that dogmatic religious truths are delusions rather than illusions. The claim is empirical, both on the part of fundamental religious claims and on the part of Freud's Oedipal rejection of them. To take away what is most essential to Freudian theory under the guise of a more narrowly defined empiricism interested only in transitional phenomena alters Freud's theory of religion in a direction he anticipated and rejected. Fundamentalists can at least respect Freud's understanding of their faith as much as they can oppose his rejection of it. The Freudian claim to have illuminated delusional religious beliefs allows Christopher Badcock (1980) to claim that psychoanalysis is the triumph of the rational and the proper heir to a thoroughly secularized Protestantism—something fundamentalists within all faiths have understood and opposed.

Conclusion

Armed with his Oedipus, Freud felt he could explain the historical errors of fundamentalist religion while illuminating the truth they masked. One suspects that as contemporary psychoanalysts find a safe haven in the transitional realm for a dialogue with religion, the more fundamental religionists will increasingly come to appreciate classical Freudian theory. Granted, the distance between fundamentalists and social scientists who study religion is great (Hood 1983). Most would admit that the rejection of a fundamentalist, literal reading of history and the commitment to epistemologically trouble-some religious doctrines demands a better evidential basis than Freud, armed with Oedipus, provided. Yet Freud had the courage to claim what has be-come the dogma of Oedipus as an empirical truth in opposition to religious dogmas, themselves believed to be empirically grounded in real history. With religion treated as a transitional phenomenon, fundamentalists are denied their narrative, as were the feminists. Now, both demand that not simply the truth of desire but also the truth of history be acknowledged. That funda-mentalists may be deluded as to this truth is a possibility appreciated only if their faith claims are taken seriously as truth claims. Freud did this for reli-gion even as he ignored it for women in the abandonment of the seduction theory. Ironically, contemporary psychoanalysts compounded this error by treating the fundamentalist faith claims as Freud treated claims of seduction. These statements may sound apologetic, but perhaps they will serve to awaken others to the seriousness with which fundamentalists and feminists defend historical narratives. To both, truth still matters. The risk of defend-ing fundamentalists among their "cultured despisers" (with due apology to Schleiermacher) admittedly forces me to skate on thin ice. But as I write, the news speaks of a cold winter to come, and it may be no mere illusion to think the ground will firm with time.

Notes

1. I use fundamentalist religious claims to cover religious assertions deemed likely to be incompatible with other accepted commonsense assertions, most likely scientif-ically based. Such claims are most common within fundamentalist religions. In this sense, fundamentalist claims cut across all religious traditions insofar as they demand a more literal acceptance of claims apparently opposed to commonsense reality claims based upon science (see Marty and Appleby 1991). Freud decidedly opposed a more symbolic treatment of such assertions. They had to stand or fall as claims to concrete fact. Freud, of course, dismissed such claims out of hand as obviously non-sense.

2. Portions of this chapter restate my original argument with specific reference to the parallels between fundamentalists' and feminists' concerns.

3. An argument in favor of theism can be constructed from this claim if one as-sumes a superior intentionality guiding adults in terms of a world of object use paral-lel to that with which mothers guide children. The argument is beyond the scope of this chapter, but it does serve to remind the reader that fundamentalist religious claims continue to have merit if only their ontological claims are not rejected out of

hand. There is what Di Censo (1991) called a "transformative dimension" not only of Freud's treatment of illusion but, I would argue, also of transitional phenomena.

References

Ansieu, D. 1986. *Freud's self analysis.* Translated by P. Graham Madison. New York: International Universities Press.

Badcock, C. D. 1980. *Psychoanalysis of culture.* Oxford: Basil Blackwell.

_____. 1985. *Madness and modernity.* Oxford: Basil Blackwell.

Belzen, J. A., and A. J. R. Uleyn. 1992. What is real? Speculations on Hood's implicit epistemology and theology. *International Journal for the Psychology of Religion,* 2, 161–169.

Berger, P., and T. Luckmann. 1967. *The social construction of reality.* New York: Anchor.

Bower, G. H. 1990. Awareness, the unconscious, and repression: An experimental psychologist's perspective. In J. Singer, ed., *Repression and dissociation: Implications for personality theory, psychopathology, and health.* Chicago: University of Chicago Press, pp. 209–231.

Bowker, J. 1973. *The sense of God: Sociological, anthropological, and psychological approaches to the origin of the sense of God.* London: Oxford University Press.

Bruhn, A. R. 1990. *Earliest childhood memories.* Vol. 1, *Theory and application to clinical practice.* New York: Praeger.

Deleuze, G., and F. Guattari. 1983. *Anti-Oedipus: Capitalism and schizophrenia.* Translated by R. Hurley, M. Seem, and H. R. Lane. Minneapolis: University of Minnesota Press.

Demause, L. 1991. The universality of incest. *Journal of Psychohistory,* 19, 123–164.

Di Censo, J. 1991. Religion as illusion: Reversing the Freudian hermeneutic. *Journal of Religion,* 71, 167–179.

Endleman, R. 1981. *Psyche and society: Explorations in psychoanalytic sociology.* New York: Columbia University Press.

Flew, A. 1978. Transitional objects and transitional phenomena: Comments and interpretations. In A. Grolinick, L. Barkin, and W. Muensterberger, eds., *Between reality and fantasy.* New York: Aronson, pp. 485–501.

Freeman, D. 1967. "Totem and Taboo": A reappraisal. In W. Muensterberger and S. Axelrad, eds., *The psychoanalytic study of society.* Vol. 4. New York: International Universities Press, pp. 9–33.

Freud, S. [1955-1974]. The standard edition of the complete psychological works. Edited and translated by J. Strachey. Hogarth Press and Institute of Psychoanalysis.

_____. 1895/1955. *Case 4: Katharina.* Vol. 2, pp. 125–134, and *Case 5: Fräulein Elisabeth von R.,* Vol. 2, pp. 135–181.

_____. 1896/1962. *The aetiology of hysteria.* Vol. 3, pp. 187–222.

_____. 1905/1953. *Three essays on the theory of sexuality.* Vol. 7, pp. 123–243.

_____. 1913/1958. *Totem and taboo.* Vol. 13, pp. 1–162.

_____. 1927/1961. *The future of an illusion.* Vol. 21, pp. 1–56.

_____. 1930/1961. *Civilization and its discontents.* Vol. 21, pp. 57–145.

_____. 1939/1964. *Moses and monotheism*. Vol. 23, pp. 3–137.

Gay, P. 1988. *Freud: A life for our time*. New York: Doubleday.

Godin, A. 1985. *The psychological dynamics of religious experience*. Birmingham, Ala.: Religious Education Press.

Grünbaum, A. 1987. Psychoanalysis and theism. *The Monist*, 70, 152–192.

Hale, N. G. 1995. *The rise and crisis of psychoanalysis in the United States: Freud and the Americans, 1917–1985*. New York: Oxford University Press.

Holmes, D. 1990. The evidence for repression: An examination of sixty years of research. In J. Singer, ed., *Repression and dissociation: Implications for personality theory, psychopathology, and health*. Chicago: University of Chicago Press, pp. 85–102.

Holmstrom, R. 1991. On the phylogeny of the Oedipus complex: Psychoanalytic aspects of the anthropoid apes. *Psychoanalysis and Contemporary Thought*, 14, 271–316.

Hood, R. W., Jr. 1983. The social psychology of religious fundamentalism. In A. W. Childs and G. W. Melton, eds., *Rural psychology*. New York: Plenum, pp. 169–198.

_____. 1992. Mysticism, reality, illusion, and the Freudian critique of religion. *International Journal for the Psychology of Religion*, 2, 141–164.

Horney, K. 1933. The denial of the vagina. *International Journal of Psychoanalysis*, 14, 57–70.

Kroeber, A. 1939. *Totem and Taboo* in retrospect. *American Journal of Sociology*, 55, 446–451.

Küng, H. 1979. *Freud and the problem of God*. Translated by E. Quinn. New Haven: Yale University Press.

_____. 1980. *Does God exist?* New York: Doubleday.

_____. 1984. *Eternal life?* Translated by E. Quinn. Garden City, N.Y.: Doubleday.

Loftus, E. F. 1993. The reality of repressed memories. *American Psychologist*, 44, 518–537.

Malmquist, C. P. 1986. Children who witness parental murder: Post-traumatic aspects. *Journal of the American Academy of Child Psychiatry*, 25, 320–325.

Marcuse, H. 1955. *Eros and civilization*. Boston: Beacon.

Marty, M. E., and R. S. Appleby, eds. 1991. *Fundamentalism observed*. Chicago: University of Chicago Press.

Masson, J. 1984. *The assault on the truth: Freud's suppression of the seduction theory*. New York: Farrar, Straus and Giroux.

McIntyre, A. 1988. *Whose justice? Which rationality?* Notre Dame, Ind.: University of Notre Dame Press.

Mead, M. 1963. "Totem and Taboo" reconsidered with respect. *Bulletin of the Menninger Clinic*, 27, 185–199.

Meissner, W. W. 1984. *Psychoanalysis and religious experience*. New Haven: Yale University Press.

Mitchell, J. 1975. *Psychoanalysis and feminism: Freud, Reich, Laing, and women*. New York: Vintage.

Preus, J. S. 1987. *Explaining religion*. New Haven: Yale University Press.

Pruyser, P. 1973. Sigmund Freud and his legacy. In C. Y. Glock and P. E. Hammond, eds., *Beyond the classics?* New York: Harper & Row, pp. 243–290.

_____. 1976. Lessons from art theory for the psychology of religion. *Journal for the Scientific Study of Religion*, 15, 1–14.

_____. 1983. *The play of the imagination: Toward a psychoanalysis of culture*. New York: International Universities Press.

_____. 1985. Forms and functions of the imagination in religion. *Bulletin of the Menninger Clinic*, 49, 353–370.

_____. 1987. The tutored imagination in religion. In P. W. Pruyser, ed., *Changing views of the human condition*. Macon, Ga.: Mercer University Press, pp. 101–117.

Ricoeur, P. 1970. *Freud and philosophy*. Translated by D. Savage. New Haven: Yale University Press.

Rizzuto, A.-M. 1979. *The birth of the living god: A psychoanalytic study*. Chicago: University of Chicago Press.

Róheim, G. 1950. *Psychoanalysis and anthropology*. New York: International Universities Press.

Roseneau, P. 1992. *Post-modernism and the social sciences*. Princeton: Princeton University Press.

Rudnytsky, P. L. 1987. *Freud and Oedipus*. New York: Columbia University Press.

Shafranske, E. 1995. Freudian theory and religious experience. In R. W. Hood Jr., ed., *Handbook of religious experience*. Birmingham, Ala.: Religious Education Press, pp. 200–230.

Spence, D. P. 1982. *Narrative truth and historical truth: Meaning and interpretation in psychoanalysis*. New York: W. W. Norton.

Vaihinger, H. [1924] 1968. *The philosophy of "as if."* Translated by C. K. Odgen. New York: Barnes and Noble.

Van Herik, J. 1982. *Freud on femininity and faith*. Berkeley: University of California Press.

Westerlund, E. 1986. Freud on sexual trauma: An historical review of seduction and betrayal. *Psychology of Women Quarterly*, 10, 297–310.

Winnicott, D. W. 1971. *Playing and reality*. New York: Basic Books.

Part Two

Psychoanalysis and the
Second-Generation Theorists

5 ∽

Karen Horney's Encounter with Zen

Marcia Westkott

In the summer of 1952, the German-born psychoanalyst Karen Horney traveled from her home in New York City to Japan to tour the major Zen monasteries in the company of her host D. T. Suzuki, the renowned interpreter of Zen Buddhism to the West. A pilgrimage of sorts, Horney's trip was the culmination of her deepening interest in Buddhism. She had cited Suzuki in her last two books and had met with him in the winter of 1950–1951 while he was on a lecture tour in New York. Unfortunately, Horney never had the opportunity to develop fully her encounter with Buddhism. Soon after her return, she was diagnosed with cancer; two months later, at the age of sixty-seven, she died.

Horney's interest in Buddhism at the end of her life was not idle curiosity but the discovery of a philosophy that resonated with her own life's work. Through her writing, teaching, and clinical practice, Horney committed herself to understanding the self as a means to deconstructing the inner conflicts that cause psychological suffering. The earliest stirrings of this quest led her away from conventional Christianity to Freudian psychoanalysis and then, more self-consciously, away from Freud's theories to her own creative work. In Suzuki's writings, Horney discovered ideas that validated her own theories and challenged her to think about the self in new ways. Although we shall never know what might have come of Horney's encounter with Zen had she had more time to pursue it, we can—by examining her spiritual and intellectual search—consider the ways in which Zen Buddhism began to change her thinking.

Family Conflict and Religious Doubts

Horney was born Karen Clementine Danielsen in 1885 near Hamburg, Germany. As a girl, she was caught in the cross fire of her parents' conflicted marriage. Her mother, Clothilde (nicknamed "Sonni") van Ronzelen, came from aristocratic origins and was beautiful, self-absorbed, and often depressed. She demanded unconditional obedience from her daughter and used her as a sounding board for her own unhappy thoughts and feelings. Horney's father, Berndt Wackels Danielsen, was stern, authoritarian, and conventional. He espoused the biblical justification for female subservience and followed the conservative teachings of his friend and pastor Nikoli von Ruckteschell. From the earliest entries in her *Adolescent Diaries* (1980), Horney sided with her mother. Between the ages of fourteen and sixteen, she wrote frequently about her "ill and unhappy" mother whom she wanted desperately to help (p. 19). She also recorded the anger and contempt she felt for her father, echoing her mother's judgments: "I can't respect that man who makes us all unhappy with his dreadful hypocrisy, selfishness, crudeness, and ill-breeding, etc." (p. 19).

In her first diary entry at age thirteen, Horney recorded her stirring religious doubts: "In spiritual matters I still feel *very unworthy*, for although I am steadily growing up, I do not yet feel the true need for religion. A sermon can overwhelm me and at times I can act accordingly, but prayer. . . . The need—a spiritual poverty—in a word: the thoughts . . . May God kindly help me" (Horney 1980:4, emphasis in original). Although she wrote of lacking a "true need for religion," her subsequent entries recorded another yearning: for a faith that she could reconcile with her probing intelligence and empirical bent. In the face of religious teaching that contradicted her own observations and experiences, she turned for guidance to others, including her brother, a friend, and a teacher. However, affirmations of these helpers concerning issues such as miracles and the reality of the Holy Ghost only served to underscore Horney's sense of failure in matters of faith (pp. 23–33).

Horney's questioning of Christianity was not confined to those teachings that she could not directly experience. It was also inextricably linked to her conflict with her father. When she was fifteen, she recorded several New Year's resolutions, including the following: "to try to fulfill the 4th Commandment at least outwardly. Today I read in a book that one should honor one's father not for his personal characteristics but to honor the authority that God has vested in him. But it is awfully difficult" (Horney 1980:22). The difficulty stemmed both from supporting her mother's marital grievances and from her father's lack of encouragement and support. At the time, she was trying to convince her father to support her advanced schooling at the gymnasium. Doggedly adhering to conventional definitions of femininity, Danielsen was not disposed to spend money on his daughter's education. To his bright and intellectually curious daughter, for whom school was a "joy" as well as a respite from parental strife, the idea of not continuing her education was a curse (p. 26). The issue was finally resolved when Horney agreed to sign a document stating that if her father would pay for her education, "he need do nothing for me" after graduation (p. 27).

Danielsen's conventional religious faith gained support from the teachings of Pastor von Ruckteschell, a Lutheran minister known for his pious sermons designed to lure the working class away from socialism and for his conservative attitudes toward sexual behavior (Quinn 1987:31–33). The pastor was a frequent visitor to the Danielsen household, often intervening in the marital disputes on the side of his friend. It is not surprising that when Horney was required to attend the pastor's confirmation class, she resisted his teachings and turned instead to the more accessible liberal lessons of her religion teacher, Herr Schultz: "My religion is in a desperately sad state at the moment. Was and is Christ God? What is God? Is there resurrection? Is God personal? Is he a God of love? Confirmation lessons don't make it any clearer for me. I say this now with deep disappointment. Only the religion lessons with Herr Schultz, my idolized teacher, bring me some light" (Horney 1980:18).

Even Schultz, however, could not withstand the persistence of young Horney's doubt. In his class, she suggested that when Paul saw the vision of Christ, he might have been in "an overwrought nervous condition" and that there was "really no proof of Christ's resurrection" (Horney 1980:25); Schultz's subsequent rebuke stung her. Although she continued to prefer his classes to those of the more dogmatic von Ruckteschell, her efforts to profess a belief continued to erode. Religious doubt, combined with her increasing anger at her father (by this time, she referred to him in her diary as "that man" or "the master of the house"), deepened her sense of guilt for lacking Christian faith and love. At the time of her confirmation in 1901, Horney wrote: "My day of confirmation was not a day of blessing for me.—On the contrary, it was a great piece of hypocrisy, for I professed belief in the teachings of Christ, the doctrine of love, with hatred in my heart (and for my nearest, at that). I feel too weak to follow Christ. Yet I long for the faith, firm as a rock, that makes oneself *and others* happy" (pp. 37–38, emphasis in original).

The adolescent Karen Danielsen never found in Christianity the unshakable faith for which she longed. As a young woman, she continued to struggle against the patriarchal authority that she encountered there, both in the conservatively interpreted religious teachings and in the flesh-and-blood reality of her own father. After entering the gymnasium, Horney became even more disaffected from both religious practice and her father. She turned increasingly to her education: "I live altogether for school . . . it gives me joy, inexpressible joy" (Horney 1980:47). Eventually, it was in psychoanalysis that she searched—not for faith in the traditional sense but for knowledge that could substitute for "faith, firm as a rock, that makes oneself *and others* happy."

Psychoanalysis and Therapy

Although Karen Horney would write five books and numerous articles addressing theoretical issues in psychoanalysis, her primary concern was with applying theoretical constructs to therapeutic ends in order to help people who were suffering from psychological conflict. Her path to this purpose wound inextricably through her own struggles and inner conflicts.[1]

After graduating from the gymnasium in 1906, Karen Danielsen entered medical school, and while completing her education, she married a business lawyer, Oscar Horney, in 1909. She gave birth to three daughters (between 1911 and 1915) and practiced psychoanalysis in Berlin. During this period in the 1910s and in the early 1920s, Karen Horney was struggling with her own conflicts. She was in analysis with Freud's protégé Karl Abraham, an experience that led her to become aware of her own struggles as a daughter, sister, wife, and mother. The analysis also brought her into conflict with her newly adopted profession; she was disappointed with the lack of therapeutic progress with Abraham, and, relatedly, she began to question the Freudian explanation of women's psychology. Not surprisingly, her first public address before the international psychoanalytic community in 1922 challenged Abraham's thesis that penis envy is a fixed and universal characteristic of women (Horney [1924] 1967). Horney's subsequent criticism of Freud's theories on women became increasingly bold and daring, and they drew from her own experience as a mother caring for and observing her growing daughters (Moulton 1975) and as a wife struggling in a deteriorating marriage (the Horneys separated in 1926 and later divorced). By the time she was invited to teach at the University of Chicago in 1932, Karen Horney had once again challenged a patriarchal authority and had been admonished for doing so. Freud had isolated and then ignored Horney's attempts to reform the official psychoanalytic interpretation of feminine psychology. This left her marginalized within her chosen profession just as she was beginning to formulate her own views. Thus, Horney's move to the United States—first to Chicago and then, two years later, to New York—gave her the opportunity for a fresh start both professionally and personally.

Horney's break with Freudian psychoanalysis was not simply ideological; it was fundamentally practical and ethical. Simply put, Freudian theory did not help her to help her patients. Her second book, *New Ways in Psychoanalysis* (Horney 1939b), is instructive for understanding this break and thus for understanding the primacy she gave to ameliorating suffering. (For Horney, human suffering, inner conflict, and neurosis were parallel concepts.) The book's first sentence left no doubt about her position on the subject: "My desire to make a critical re-evaluation of psychoanalytic theories had its origin in a dissatisfaction with therapeutic results" (p. 7). Freud's theoretical emphasis on instinct was the most fundamental stumbling block for Horney. Instinct theory posited an inevitable conflict between instinctual drive (id), reality (ego), and moral strictures (superego). According to the Freudian theory, these categories form the structure of the mature psyche, where inner conflict remains a permanent fact of life; the task of therapy is simply to learn how to manage the conflict more efficiently through strengthening the ego (47–78).

Horney rejected the moralism of Freud's science and compared it to "the Christian ideology of a conflict between good and evil, between moral and immoral, and between man's animal nature and his reason" (Horney 1939b:191). More significantly, she also rejected the fatalism inherent in the resignation to the idea that psychological conflict—among id, ego, and superego—is the inevitable and permanent human condition. Inner conflict, she argued, is not an unalterable fact of life but the result of a developing child's adaptive responses to unsupportive and even dangerous environments. The subsequent neurotic character structure is formed by the anxious and hostile responses that the developing self creates as defenses. "Man does not collide with his environment as inevitably as Freud assumes; if there is such a collision it is not because of instinct but because the environment inspires fears and hostilities. The neurotic trends which he develops as a consequence, though in some ways they provide a means of coping with the environment, in other ways enhance his conflicts with it" (p. 191). These "neurotic trends"—which are tenaciously held defenses—create suffering through inner conflict, which serves to exacerbate conflict with others.

Horney was especially critical of the therapeutic implications of Freud's concept of the ego. "It will be seen the 'ego' approximating Freud's description is not inherent in human nature but is a specifically neurotic phenomenon" (Horney 1939b:189). She believed that people who are psychoanalyzed will, in effect, simply become more alienated from themselves. Allocating energy to the id and moral judgment to the superego, Freud had created a tripartite, fragmented self: The mediating ego is a superficial, cynical manager of competing demands, and the adaptive ego is devoid of both passion and morality. And in Horney's opinion, this meant "that theoretically there is no liking or disliking of people, no sympathy; no generosity, no feeling of justice, no devotion to a cause which is not in the last analysis essentially determined by libidinal or destructive drives" (p. 187). Moreover, this idea of the ego, whose function is to manage instinctually derived drives, creates destructive consequences for therapy. The managerial ego promotes a somewhat superficial, fragmented, and resigned sense of self. Thus, "although an analyzed individual is better adapted he has become 'less of a person' or as one might say, less alive" (p. 188).

To strengthen the ego, then, is to resign oneself to the neurotic—that is, conflicted—character structure. It is to foster an adaptive alignment with the external world as a bulwark against the tensions of the inner struggle. But for that approach to work, the external world must provide an orderly, predictable, and methodical structure. In an effort to stifle the inner conflict, neurotics "cling to the belief that life is calculable and controllable." They cannot accept that "life is to some extent like an adventure or like a gamble, subject to good and ill luck, full of unpredictable perplexities" (Horney 1939b:243). When the exigencies of life do not proceed as planned, the beleaguered ego is reproachful of others and searches for alternative external supports.

Horney's rejection of Freud's concept of the tripartite psyche, with its attendant acceptance of the inevitability of inner conflict, derived from her more therapeutically oriented approach to psychoanalysis. Although not immune to his patients' pain, Freud was primarily a theoretician who used analytic sessions to develop, expand, and amend his theoretical models (Rieff 1959:9–11). Horney, by contrast, was primarily a clinician, who used or discarded theory to the extent that it helped her patients (Westkott 1986:60). She discarded instinct theory because, among other reasons, it fostered an acceptance of a conflicted self and thus, unwittingly, a dependence on external circumstances for finding happiness. She turned instead to a holistic concept of self and a therapeutic approach, one that "helps the patient to realize gradually that he is following the wrong path in expecting happiness to come to him from without, that the enjoyment of happiness is a faculty to be acquired from within" (Horney 1939b:290). It was this therapeutic emphasis that led her to formulate her concept of the "real self," a concept that she eventually found to be compatible with Zen.

The Real Self

Karen Horney's concept of the real self embodies the promise of healthy development and the hope of the therapeutic process. If a child is raised in a loving and respectful environment by caretakers who are able to convey positive cultural values through which human beings are cherished and encouraged to grow, the real self can emerge.

> Only the individual can develop his potentialities. But, like any other living organism, the human individual needs favorable conditions for growth "from acorn into oak tree"; he needs an atmosphere of warmth to give him a feeling of inner security and inner freedom enabling him to have his own feelings and thoughts and to express himself. He needs the good will of others, not only to

help him in his many needs but to guide and encourage him to become a mature and fulfilled individual. He also needs healthy friction with the wishes and wills of others. If he can thus grow with others, in love and in friction, he will grow in accordance with his real self (Horney 1950a:18).

A child who is thus nurtured will become spontaneous and self-directed, developing "the clarity and depth of his own feelings, thoughts, wishes, interests; the ability to tap his own resources, the strength of his will power; the special capacities or gifts he may have; the faculty to express himself, and to relate himself to others with his spontaneous feelings" (Horney 1950a:17). A person whose real self has been fostered will feel free "to love and to feel concern for other people" (p. 16), not due to some externally imposed commandment but from the wellspring of genuine compassion. The expressing of the real self allows one to be wholehearted: "to be without pretense, to be emotionally sincere, to be able to put the whole of oneself into one's feelings, one's work, one's beliefs" (Horney 1945:242). Thus, the concept of the real self refers to the seamlessly whole psyche where judgment, desire, and reasoning are not splintered off from one another into different functions (as in the superego, id, and ego) but are integrated into a whole discerning, feeling, and thinking person.

Horney developed her concept of the real self from William James's idea of the spiritual self, elaborated in his *Principles of Psychology* (James [1890] 1950:296–305; Horney 1939a:130). For James, the spiritual self was the "inner subjective being," which could be tapped through "abandoning the outward-looking point of view, and of our having become able to think subjectively as such, *to think ourselves as thinkers*" ([1890] 1950:296, emphasis in original). James acknowledged that although such an awareness is a "momentous" and "rather mysterious operation," it involves a primary "distinction between thought as such, and what it is 'of' or 'about'" (pp. 296–297). Consciousness of the spiritual self is consciousness of an "active element of all consciousness" that is part of a broader "stream" or "unity." Thus, "whatever qualities a man's feelings may possess, or whatever content his thought may include, there is a spiritual something in him which seems to *go out* to meet those qualities and contents, whilst they seem to *come in* to be received by it. . . . It is the home of interest,—not the pleasant or the painful, not even pleasure or pain, as such, but that within us to which pleasure and pain, the pleasant and the painful, speak" (pp. 297–298, emphasis in original).

James drew from personal experience to convey "*the feeling of this central active self*" ([1890] 1950:229, emphasis in original).

I am aware of a constant play of furtherances and hindrances . . . tendencies which run with desire, and tendencies which run the other way. The mutual inconsistencies and agreements, reinforcements and obstructions . . . reverberate backwards and produce what seem to be incessant reactions of my spontaneity upon them, welcoming or opposing, appropriating or disowning, striving with or against, saying yes or no. This palpitating inward life is, in me, that central nucleus (James [1890] 1950:299).

According to James, this feeling of *"spiritual activity . . . is really a feeling of bodily activities whose exact nature is by most men overlooked"* ([1890] 1950:301–302, emphasis in original). The experience of these body sensations is fluid, moving back and forth between body and brain, and then also constantly moving within the body. "My brain appears to me as if all shot across with lines of direction, of which I have become conscious as my attention has shifted from one sense organ to another, in passing to successive outer things, or in following trains of varying sense-ideas" (p. 300). In moving among these constantly shifting sensations, James noted, one becomes aware of the reality that "*all* that is experienced is, strictly considered *objective;* that this Objective falls asunder into two contrasted parts, one realized as 'Self,' the other as 'not-Self'; and that over and above these parts there is nothing save the fact that they are known, the fact of the stream of thought being there as the indispensable subjective condition of their being experienced at all" (p. 300, emphasis in original). It is this stream of knowing, the subjectivity, that directly experiences the self in relationship to the not-self, the me and the not-me, "as objects which work out their drama together"(p. 304). James implied that the thinker is, in effect, the activity of thinking itself and that experience of this activity is awareness of "a stream of consciousness, pure and simple" through which self and world are connected: "Between the Postulated Matter and the Postulated Thinker, the sheet of phenomena would then swing, some of them (the 'realities') pertaining more to matter, the others (the fictions, opinions, and errors) pertaining more to the Thinker. But *who* the Thinker would be, or how many distinct Thinkers we ought to suppose in the universe, would all be subjects for an ulterior metaphysical inquiry" (p. 304, emphasis in original).

As early as 1939, Horney (1939a) began to draw on James's concept of the spiritual self to explain what she meant by the real self. In her last book, *Neurosis and Human Growth* (1950a), she gave her most detailed description: "To present more fully its propensities in the terms of William James: it provides the 'palpitating inward life'; it engenders the spontaneity of feelings. . . . It produces the 'reactions of spontaneity' to our feelings or thoughts, 'welcoming or opposing, appropriating or disowning, striving with or against, saying yes or no'" (Horney 1950a:157). Horney's emphasis on the clinical and therapeutic, however, led her to focus more on the ethical and intrapsychic implications than on the phenomenological components of James's work.

All this indicates that our real self, when strong and active, enables us to make decisions and assume responsibility for them. It therefore leads to genuine integration and a sound sense of wholeness, oneness. Not merely are body and mind, deed and thought and feeling, consonant and harmonious, they also function without serious inner conflict. In contrast to those artificial means of holding ourselves together, which gain in importance as the real self is weakened, there is little or no attendant strain (Horney 1950a:157).

These "artificial means of holding ourselves together" are the "crippling shackles of neurosis" that block the expression of spontaneity and keep one linked to a compulsively pursued, "idealized self" (Horney 1950a:158). The idealized self is a defensive strategy, which a child develops in response to devaluing or dangerous behaviors from parents or other caretakers. Horney interpreted these dangers of family life as cultural constructions and not extensions of the "healthy frictions," inevitable for individual growth. In Western industrialized society, pervasive competitiveness forms a cultural pattern, which infuses social relations and promotes attaining an image of success. People are thus valued for "what they appear to be [rather] than for what they are" (Horney 1942:98), and this fosters a superficial cultivation of a grandiose image of superiority. If parents are insecure and vulnerable to these pressures for self-aggrandizement and an other-directed image of success, they will be self-absorbed and in need of social admiration, thus interfering with their capacity to respond fully to the developing needs of their children. In the extreme, this inability may be manifested in physical or sexual abuse, but it also is seen in the more pervasive, less obvious lack of genuine concern for the child:

> People in the environment are too wrapped up in their own neuroses to be able to love the child, or even to conceive of him as the particular individual he is; their attitudes toward him are determined by their own neurotic needs and responses. In simple words, they may be dominating, overprotective, intimidating, irritable, overexacting, overindulgent, erratic, partial to other siblings, hypocritical, indifferent, etc. It is never a matter of just a single factor; but always the whole constellation that exerts the untoward influence on a child's growth (Horney 1950a:18).

Such behaviors foster treating a child as a narcissistic extension of the parent's own idealized self. A child who is used in this way comes "to feel that his right to existence lies solely in . . . living up to the parent's expectations— measuring up to their standards or ambitions for him, enhancing their prestige, giving them blind devotion; in other words he may be prevented from realizing that he is an individual" (Horney 1942:44). Whether it be blatant abuse or these more subtle forms of disregard, neglect, and narcissistic use, the various forms of childhood danger create, according to Horney, a normal

pattern of childhood experience in modern society. A child's protest against
the behavior, however, is too dangerous, for it serves to criticize parents who
cannot tolerate anything less than blind admiration. The child is forced,
then, to repress her or his true feelings. Out of fear of reprisal or further loss
of "love," the child represses legitimate anger: The feared and resented parent becomes admired, and the child turns her or his hostility inward. This
"shift from true rebellion to untrue admiration" (Horney 1942:51) is the reaction formation, which creates a defense against the interpersonal danger.
By admiring the powerful parent and accepting her or his abusive or neglectful behavior as normal or deserved, the child eliminates interpersonal conflict and diffuses danger. Through this defensive strategy, the child loses
touch with and, indeed, comes to fear and hate her or his real self. Horney
described this effect in her patient Clare: "By admiring what in reality she
resented, she became alienated from her own feelings. She no longer knew
what she herself liked or wished or feared or resented" (p. 51). Instead of responding to the now hated and feared real self (which may become so fully
repressed that it is no longer experienced), a child develops "basic anxiety,"
protectively adopts the behaviors that the neglectful or abusive parent requires, and develops related defensive survival strategies to navigate through
the interpersonal world. These behaviors and strategies come to form an
"idealized self" or "proud self," an internalized definition of what the self
should be in order to be safe in, or acceptable to, the rest of the world.

The conflicted, that is, neurotic, character structure is thus formed. Hatred of one's real self—experienced as contempt for one's body, genuine feelings, and unique qualities—is perpetuated in the internalized false ideal,
which incorporates externally defined expectations for behavior and feelings. The idealized self is not the locus of moral regulation but instead a
complex of stereotypical and superficial "shoulds" that creates an arrestment
in moral development, an alienation from the true self, and "the neurotic
counterfeit of normal moral strivings" (Horney 1950a:73). The idealized self
is the locus of false pride and the perpetuator of inner criticism. It promotes
a compulsive need to live up to imagined and impossible ideals, an anxious
attention to the judgments of others, and hatred of and alienation from the
real self.

Horney described the alienation from the real self as a silent and invisible—a spiritual—death:

> The loss of self, says Kierkegaard, is "sickness unto death"; it is despair—de-
> spair at not being conscious of having a self, or despair at not being willing to be
> ourselves. But it is a despair (still following Kierkegaard) which does not clamor
> or scream. People go on living as if they were still in immediate contact with
> this alive center. Any other loss—that of a job, say, or a leg—arouses far more
> concern. . . . Patients coming in for consultation complaining about headaches,
> sexual disturbances, inhibitions in work, or other symptoms; as a rule, they do

not complain about having lost touch with the core of their psychic existence (Horney 1950a:158; see also Kierkegaard 1941).

The therapeutic task is to begin with the presenting symptoms—what the patient actually experiences—and to create the delicate balance between safety and challenge through which the patient and therapist work to deconstruct the false, idealized self and discover/create the real self. The therapeutic process invites the release from the compulsive dictates of pride and fear and the recovery of the alive center of spontaneity, authentic feeling, and choice. The "road of analytical therapy ... is the *road to reorientation through self knowledge*" (Horney 1950a:341, emphasis in original); it is the journey to recovering that "palpitating inward life," of spiritual being, the real self.

The Turn to Zen

Horney's first published reference to D. T. Suzuki appeared in *Our Inner Conflicts* (1945), where she cited *Zen Buddhism and Its Influence on Japanese Culture* (Suzuki [1938] 1959). According to Richard DeMartino, who was Suzuki's assistant at the time, there is good evidence to suggest that Horney was aware of Suzuki's work as early as 1938 through her patient Cornelius Crane. Crane's uncle, Charles Crane, was ambassador to China and the recipient of Suzuki's dedication in his 1938 book (DeMartino 1991). It was, in fact, Cornelius Crane's ex-wife, Cathalene Crane Bernatschke, who first introduced Horney and Suzuki in the winter of 1950–1951; the two "struck up, almost from the outset, a warm, close friendship that was to grow progressively deeper right up to her death on December 4, 1952" (p. 268).

At the time of their meeting, eighty-year-old Suzuki had published many of his nearly thirty books in English and was in temporary residence at Columbia University (Quinn 1987:402). Born in 1870 in the Japanese province of Kaga, Suzuki was introduced early in life to multiple religious influences. His father was a Confucian, his mother Buddhist. The family belonged to the Rinzai sect of Zen, which was rare in Kaga where the Soto sect predominated. As an adolescent, Suzuki demonstrated the strong determination and persistent curiosity that characterized his later life. He questioned Christian missionaries and his Zen teacher alike and traveled alone to a monastery to ask a Zen master about the meaning of Hakuin Zenshi's *Ortegama* (Suzuki 1986:4). He entered Tokyo University in 1890, but his real passion was studying and practicing Zen, first with Imagita Kosen, then with his successor Shaku Soen in Kamakura. As a teacher and student of both Zen and English, Suzuki assisted Paul Carus in the translations and publications of Buddhist texts and accompanied Carus to the United States, where he continued to assist in these publishing efforts for the next ten years (Humphreys 1986:85). When he returned to Japan, Suzuki began writing about Zen in English in an effort to help Westerners understand its precepts. His influential first volume of *Essays in Zen Buddhism* was published in London in 1927, followed by many others. When he died in 1966 at the age of ninety-five, he had served as a university professor in Japan and in the United States, had written and translated prolifically, was an active participant in the World Congress of Faiths, had founded a depository of ancient and modern texts on world Buddhism, and had traveled and lectured throughout the world (Abe 1986).

When Horney met him in 1951, Suzuki was already well established internationally as the leading scholar and teacher of Zen. It is not surprising that Horney took to Suzuki and to Zen. She would have been attracted to Suzuki's empirical mind, his unstinting curiosity, his lack of pretense, his concentration, and his kindness. Horney would have resonated with Suzuki's ability to navigate between cultures and languages. Having deliberately shifted her therapeutic focus from the conventional analytic concern with a patient's past to the dynamics of existing psychological struggles, Horney would have been attracted to the Buddhist attention to the present. Similarly, she would have found Zen's pragmatism and attention to everyday life compelling. Having rebelled against both Christian and psychoanalytic dogma, she would have liked Zen's abjuring systematic philosophy and external authority. Additionally, she would have found the Zen focus on direct experience to echo her own approach to working with people. And having turned increasingly to spiritual—especially mystical—questions in her later life (Quinn 1987:403), Horney would have found the spiritual dimension of Zen interesting, at the very least.

Once she began to engage in conversations with Suzuki and others, Horney started to draw similarities between Zen and her own work. For example, she saw in the Buddhist concept of *dukkha* (suffering) a parallel to her formulation of "basic anxiety." However, as DeMartino observed (1991: 269), these parallels skimmed over some profound differences. In Buddhism, for example, dukkha refers to a human condition that can be transcended through spiritual liberation; basic anxiety refers to a socially constructed condition emerging from inadequate parenting. Nevertheless, Horney saw in the Buddhist teachings an opportunity to expand her understanding of the human psyche and her ability to help heal its conflicts. In the fall of 1952, after her return from Japan, she gave a course on psychoanalytic technique for other experienced analysts as well as candidates in training through the American Institute for Psychoanalysis. Although cancer prevented her from completing the course, the five essays that she did present—posthumously published as *Final Lectures* (1987)—provide a window into the ways in which she was rethinking both therapeutic techniques and the real self.

Most obvious to the reader of the *Final Lectures* is the admiration that Horney held for the Zen quality of being wholeheartedly in the moment. Not only did she continue to hold that as a therapeutic goal for the patient, she also identified it as an essential attitude of the therapist.

> That attention should be wholehearted may seem banal, trite, and self-evident. Yet in the sense that I mean wholehearted attention, I think it rather difficult to attain. I am referring to a power of concentration. . . . This is a faculty for which the Orientals have a much deeper feeling than we do. . . . Wholeheartedness of attention means being there altogether in the service of the patient, yet with a kind of self-forgetfulness . . . self-forget, but be there with all your feelings. . . . The best advice that I can give is that [let] everything come up, emerge, and at the proper time, be observed (Horney 1987:19–21).

In the second lecture, Horney cited a passage describing a man's behavior that she thought embodied this quality:

> The guests who sat at the long table were about two hundred in number and it seems almost incredible when I say that nearly the whole of the attendance was performed by the headwaiter, since he put on and took off all the dishes while the other waiters only handed them to him and received them from him. During all these proceedings nothing was spilled, no one was inconvenienced, but all went off lightly and nimbly as if by the operation of a spirit. Thus, thousands of plates and dishes flew from his hands to the table and, again, from his hands to the attendants behind him. Quite absorbed in his vocation, the whole man was nothing but eyes and hands (1987:33–34).

What struck Horney about the headwaiter's behavior was his ability to be "entirely absorbed in what he was doing—operating with all his facilities while remaining at the same time quite oblivious to himself." She argued that this capacity to have "the highest presence and the highest absence" is a way of being that is difficult for Westerners to grasp but is "the very essence of Zen" (Horney 1987:34). Horney admired someone who had a capacity for unself-consciously and effortlessly being in the world, the kind of person whom Suzuki described as an "artist of life" (Suzuki 1960:15). "To such a person, his life reflects every image he creates out of his inexhaustive source of the unconscious. To such, his every deed expresses originality, creativity, his living personality. There is in it no conventionality, no conformity, no inhibitory motivation. He moves as he pleases. His behavior is like the wind which bloweth as it listeth" (p. 16).

When Horney defined wholeheartedness as "self-forget but [being] there with all your feelings," she gave a new slant to her earlier formulations (e.g.,

Horney 1945:242). In her earlier work, wholeheartedness referred to a kind of enthusiasm, a capacity for joy, energy, and wholeness without the self-criticism of the proud, false self (e.g., Horney 1950a:157). In her last formulation, wholeheartedness also included a capacity for mindful detachment—"not just cold detached observation"—but unlimited, nonjudgmental receptivity (Horney 1987:20), the kind of matter-of-fact acceptance of ordinary experiences and the feelings they produce that Suzuki had frequently described: "Zen just feels fire warm and ice cold, because when it freezes we shiver and welcome fire. The feeling is all in all . . . all our theorization fails to touch reality" (Suzuki 1964:41).

Horney echoed Suzuki's distrust of theorization in her description of the second category of the therapist's attentiveness: comprehensiveness. To be comprehensive means to pay attention to every possible observation. "DON'T SELECT TOO EARLY," Horney admonished, and she repeated Freud's instruction to leave nothing out in the process of observing free associations (Horney 1987:21). Here again, Horney was referring not only to the patient's process but also to the therapist's. Introducing interpretations may close off the patient's feeling her way into the experience. But it may also affect the therapist's capacity to be attentive. "If you need to know and understand everything quickly, you may not see anything" (p. 23).

Finally, Horney advised, the therapist should not bring personal judgments into the process. "THERE IS NO PERSONAL AXE TO GRIND," she emphasized (Horney 1987:31). The closest Westerners can come to understanding this perspective is through the idea of objectivity. "But that is different from what is usually meant by the expression 'objective observer' when used to describe the scientific approach. As a therapist, I don't see how cold objectivity is possible." Instead, Horney counseled, it is more like what the Zen masters might speak of as "nonattachment"(p. 31). Whatever words she may have chosen to describe it, in these final lectures Horney was attempting to teach her students how to bring to the therapeutic setting the meditative attitude of mindfulness and receptivity. This is the nonjudgmental openness to feeling about which Suzuki often spoke and the relaxed attentiveness recommended by a contemporary analyst who is influenced by his own Buddhist practice. "When a therapist can sit with a patient without an agenda, without trying to force an experience, without thinking that she knows what is going to happen or who this person is, then the therapist is infusing the therapy with the lessons of meditation. The patient can feel such a posture" (Epstein 1995:187).

The meditative posture thus invites the emergence of the real self. When a patient is caught in the inner conflict between her or his false, proud self and feelings of self-contempt, the real self is not safe to develop. The proud, false self is the inner critic that condemns actual behavior and reminds oneself of a fundamental underlying worthlessness. It is always looking outward toward the opinion of others. One thus becomes caught on the seesaw of pride and shame. When one momentarily achieves perfectionist dictates, she or he feels a transitory moment of pride. But when a single infraction or flaw appears, feelings of worthlessness resurge. One who is caught between these extremes of pride and shame, self-congratulation and self-contempt, cannot find a middle ground of self-acceptance. The real self is thus quashed between the dictates of a defensive pride and the abyss of self-hatred (Horney 1945:151–152).

Perhaps not so coincidentally, Suzuki spoke of this conflict in terms reminiscent of Horney's at a conference on Zen Buddhism and psychoanalysis, held in Mexico City in 1957:

> Individuality . . . is always conscious of others and to that extent controlled by them. Where individualism is emphasized, the mutually restrictive feeling of tension prevails. There is no freedom here, no spontaneity, but a deep, heavy atmosphere or inhibition, suppression, and suppression overpowers one. . . . When this aspect of the Self grows up to become too prominent and overbearing, the real self is pushed back and is frequently reduced to a non-entity, which means it is suppressed (Suzuki 1960:31).

Before meeting Suzuki, Horney spoke about the release from the conflict between pride and self-contempt and the emergence of the real self in mechanistic terms. The first stage involved a "disillusioning process" (Horney 1950a:347). In the therapeutic relationship, patients gradually realize that the proud attributes they think they possess—and that they *should* possess—are merely fictions, illusions, internally imposed dictates that create inner coercion. Once this realization is achieved, a second process of tapping the "constructive forces," that is, the desire and capacity for authenticity often manifested in dreams, can be encouraged to develop. Although Horney acknowledged an overlapping and mutual influence in these two stages, she nevertheless thought about them sequentially, as if the seed of the real self lay dormant, waiting for the cloud of pride to recede before it could blossom (e.g., Horney 1950a:348–365).

As Horney began to study Zen, her ideas about the recovery of the real self shifted (see Kondo 1991). From an earlier structural definition of the real self as a spatially defined entity, Horney began to move toward a more temporal concept of the real self as a process, resembling something akin to Suzuki's "state of utmost fluidity or mobility" (Suzuki [1938] 1959:14). Horney appeared to initiate this shift by reexamining her 1949 publication "Finding the Real Self," an unusual article—consisting of a letter from a patient with an introduction by Horney—published in the *American Journal of Psychoanalysis*. According to Richard DeMartino, as Horney was about to take leave of Suzuki after their first meeting in 1951, she asked DeMartino to comment on the piece (DeMartino 1991:268). In the section containing the letter, the patient described a process of finding the real self by giving up her false, idealized self and allowing herself to feel the pain: "How well I knew pain—every pore of me clogged with inward rage, self-pity, self-contempt, and despair" (Horney 1949:5). In the therapeutic process, the patient came to see that in the absence of these reactive feelings that constituted her pain, "there was nothing. There just was nothing." The patient described this sense of absence as "not being a self. Not-being" (p. 5). She interpreted this experience of not being a self as the consequence of having her real self "stifled by the neurosis, the Frankenstein monster [the false, proud self] originally designed for protection" (p. 6). The letting go of the false self and the concomitant feeling of the pain that the false self created marked this patient's release into life. "Oh, the million things you discover with the first touch of life! Almost before you've turned the key all the separate fragments of existence rush to fall into place. How can you see, think, speak, remember fast enough to keep pace? Is there nothing which doesn't fit here, even dying and terror and broken things? There is nothing of it unknown to you" (pp. 6–7).

There are two aspects to the real self suggested in this letter that Horney developed after her conversations with Suzuki. The first is the notion of the real self's discovery through experiencing fully one's pain. In her *Final Lectures*, she began to emphasize just being with the feelings as they arise, without judgment and without categorizing or explaining. Being attentive to experience, however pleasurable or painful, "can be therapeutically valuable only if it is without condemnation, without justification, without embellishment, and without any interest in the reasons for the feeling—just the experience of the emotion itself." This is the experience of "accepting oneself as one is and not just with one's intellect, but of accepting oneself feelingly at the time; 'This is me!'" Horney described the sense of peace that accompanies such an acceptance, calling it also a feeling of liberation, "an experience of what we call the 'real self'" (1987:98–99). She called upon the analysts in the audience to stop judging and categorizing and to just allow the feelings to emerge with quiet attentiveness. This attitude of accepting experience "without embellishment and condemnation" is a release from directiveness and moralizing that allows for "liberation" (p. 104).

Horney described her own experience of "liberation" through simultaneously giving up a fictive claim of the proud self and feeling deeply the effects of this claim. She was returning from Mexico City during World War II, was bumped from her reserved seat on an airplane, and had to return from Texas to New York by train. During the night on the train, she gradually allowed herself to feel the rage she was experiencing as the result of a claim she had maintained, "That shouldn't happen to me!" After she made the connection between these feelings and her claim for something special, "I had an enormous feeling of liberation. Rarely in my life have I been so happy. . . . What happened was not the deliberate and conscious relinquishing of this claim. Apparently, it just fell away. . . . You could also interpret this experience as surrender, of my having relinquished or surrendered certain neurotic factors and therefore feeling more at one with myself" (Horney 1987:94–95).

Horney's description echoes the Zen idea of *Satori*, or liberation. Indeed, for her to use the term *liberation* to describe the emergence of the real self is itself a change. Similarly, her speaking of surrendering into the feelings of the moment as the passage to liberation suggests Suzuki's description of Satori. "When the freezing point is reached, water suddenly turns into ice. . . . Satori comes upon a man unawares, when he feels that he has exhausted his whole being." The consequence of such liberation is a "new birth" and a "new viewpoint" that creates a new way of being in the world. "All your mental activities will now be working to a different key, which will be more satisfying, more peaceful, and fuller of joy than anything you ever experienced before. The tone of life will be altered" (Suzuki 1964:95–97).

The second shift in Horney's approach to the real self is more subtle. In the letter mentioned earlier, Horney's former patient described experiencing her real self in terms that explicitly drew on James's more fluid notion (probably thanks to Horney's reference) as that which both "welcomes and rejects" (Horney 1949:6). The patient was suggesting a capacity to embrace the fluidity of experience and its dualities—the good and the bad, the pleasure and the pain—as a fluctuating continuum. In contrast, Horney had earlier described the real self in spatial terms as a positive solidity (albeit at times merely a seed), characterized by an essential healthiness, responsibility, and set of constructive forces (e.g., Horney 1950a). In her *Final Lectures*, where she counseled "the taking seriously of fleeting and abortive feelings" (1987:103), Horney appeared to be shifting to a more fluid concept of the real self. Concomitantly, she also began to shift her attention as a therapist from the *content* of the patient's concerns (the object of her feelings) to the patient's *relationship* to those feelings. Horney described her conscious choice to make this shift while working with a patient who interjected that she was worried about something. Instead of focusing on the content—on the object of the patient's concern, which she implied she would have done in the past—Horney instead explicitly encouraged her patient to stay with her relationship to the feeling itself (pp. 103–104).

One can recognize a Zen influence in these subtle changes in Horney's therapeutic practices and concept of the real self. She seemed to be moving toward the idea that the self is "ever moving or becoming" (Suzuki 1960:25). And she appeared to be incorporating in her therapeutic practice the meaning of Suzuki's counsel: "Unless the mind that avails itself of the technical skill somehow attunes itself to a state of the utmost fluidity or mobility, anything acquired or superimposed lacks spontaneity of natural growth" (Suzuki [1938] 1959:14). Yet, there is much in Zen that Horney never had the chance to explore. How would she have responded to what Suzuki described as the "irrational" aspect of Zen, to the spiritual experience of Satori, to the radically antitheoretical position? Would she have returned to James (who had also been influenced by Buddhism) to ground her understanding of the fluid sense of self in more familiar terms? Or would she have pursued her study of Buddhism further, perhaps following other strands?[2] Although we shall never know what course Horney would have taken, we do know that Zen deepened her sense that experience is the key to self-knowledge. For the woman who began her journey into psychoanalysis with a desire to understand herself, it is somehow fitting that she should have discovered Zen. To have pursued it more fully, she would have had to have lived it.

> Taking it all in all, Zen is emphatically a matter of personal experience; if anything can be called radically empirical, it is Zen. No amount of reading, no amount of teaching, no amount of contemplation will ever make one a Zen master. Life itself must be grasped in the midst of its flow(Suzuki 1964:132).

> Nothing becomes as real to us as that which we directly experience (Horney 1987:91).

Notes

1. In the most recent book on Karen Horney's life and work, Bernard Paris (1994) persuasively developed the thesis that Horney's personal struggles motivated her to seek self-understanding, a quest that inspired her to develop a new psychoanalytic paradigm.
2. In his recent book, Mark Epstein (1995) explored many rich connections between Buddhism and psychotherapy, some of which Horney anticipated and others that she probably would have found most compelling.

References

Abe, M. 1986. The Influence of D. T. Suzuki in the West. In M. Abe, ed., *A Zen Life: D. T. Suzuki Remembered*. New York: Weatherhill, pp. 109–120.

DeMartino, R. J. 1991. Karen Horney, Daisetz T. Suzuki, and Zen Buddhism. *American Journal of Psychoanalysis* 51, pp. 267–283.

Epstein, M. 1995. *Thoughts Without a Thinker: Psychotherapy from a Buddhist Perspective*. New York: Basic Books.

Horney, K. [1924] 1967. On the Genesis of the Castration Complex in Women. In H. Kelman, ed., *Feminine Psychology*. New York: W. W. Norton, pp. 37–53.

_____. 1939a. Can you take a stand? *Journal of Adult Education* 11, pp. 129–132.

_____. 1939b. *New Ways in Psychoanalysis*. New York: W. W. Norton.

_____. 1942. *Self Analysis*. New York: W. W. Norton.

_____. 1945. *Our Inner Conflicts: A Constructive Theory of Neurosis*. New York: W. W. Norton.

_____. 1949. Finding the real self: Forward to a letter. *American Journal of Psycho-analysis* 9, pp. 3–7.

_____. 1950a. *Neurosis and Human Growth.* New York: W. W. Norton.

_____. 1950b. Psychoanalysis and moral values: A symposium. *American Journal of Psychoanalysis* 10, pp. 64–65.

_____. 1980. *The Adolescent Diaries of Karen Horney.* New York: Basic Books.

_____. 1987. *Final Lectures.* Edited by D. Ingram. New York: W. W. Norton.

Humphreys, C. 1986. Dr. D. T. Suzuki and Zen Buddhism in Europe. In M. Abe, ed., *A Zen Life: D. T. Suzuki Remembered.* New York: Weatherhill, pp. 81–89.

James, W. [1890] 1950. *The Principles of Psychology.* Vols. 1–2. New York: Dover Press.

Kierkegaard, S. 1941. *The Sickness unto Death.* Translated by W. Lowrie. Princeton: Princeton University Press.

Kondo, A. 1991. Recollections of Dr. Horney. *American Journal of Psychoanalysis* 51, pp. 255–266.

Moulton, R. 1975. Early papers on women: Horney to Thompson. *American Journal of Psychoanalysis* 35, pp. 207–223.

Paris, B. J. 1994. *Karen Horney: A Psychoanalyst's Search for Self-Understanding.* New Haven: Yale University Press.

Quinn, S. 1987. *A Mind of Her Own: The Life of Karen Horney.* New York: Summit Books.

Rieff, P. 1959. *Freud: The Mind of the Moralist.* Garden City, N.Y.: Anchor Press–Doubleday.

Suzuki, D. [1938] 1959. *Zen and Japanese Culture.* Princeton: Princeton University Press. (Originally published as *Zen Buddhism and Its Influence on Japanese Culture.*)

_____. 1960. Lectures on Zen Buddhism. In D. T. Suzuki et al., *Zen Buddhism & Psychoanalysis.* New York: Harper & Row.

_____. 1964. *An Introduction to Zen Buddhism.* New York: Grove.

_____. 1986. Early Memoirs. In M. Abe, ed., *A Zen Life: D. T. Suzuki Remembered.* New York: Weatherhill, pp. 3–12.

Westkott, M. 1986. *The Feminist Legacy of Karen Horney.* New Haven: Yale University Press.

6

Melanie Klein, Motherhood, and the "Heart of the Heart of Darkness"

Patricia H. Davis

Mother love, we believe, is profoundly sacred. Mother is the one who would walk through fire to save us.

—editorial, *MS Magazine*

For what is that which we call evil but the absence of good?

—Saint Augustine

The social construction of motherhood is a major part of the foundation upon which the rest of a culture is built. The social and religious meanings attached to motherhood resonate with and inform meanings for life and death, sexuality, gender relationships, power and ownership, generativity, creativity, nurture, the continuance of the tribe, race, culture, and a culture's proper relationship to ultimate beings and meanings. A breakdown in a culture's shared meanings about motherhood, therefore, is a cause for great anxiety, as it threatens the foundation of other values and of the culture itself. Symptoms of the breakdown of meanings about motherhood in our own culture are abundant: conflict over sex education in schools, the abortion struggle, political warfare over issues of contraception and "planned parenthood," religious and political right-wing groups demanding a return to "family values," attacks against lesbian and gay people, and debates over welfare, working mothers, and feminist/womanist agendas. Motherhood is clearly a battleground in Western culture today.

Melanie Klein's psychoanalytic theories are extremely useful in understanding the social construction of motherhood and the ways in which Western patriarchal culture needs motherhood (and mothers) to function to protect itself from perceived threats of disintegration and annihilation. Klein's work, for the most part, describes the development of the infant in relationship with the mother and her body (especially her breasts). Although it is clear that Klein's major interests lay with the infant—she spent very little time describing mothers—her theories of infantile fantasies and anxieties also have clear parallels with Western culture's anxieties about its own survival.

This chapter is divided into three sections. The first describes Klein's theory of infantile psychic development very briefly. The second uses Klein's theory as a tool to understand religious valuations of motherhood in Western culture. Finally, the third part analyzes the well-known case of Susan Smith, a mother who murdered her two small children; Smith is instructive because she refused to be a "good mother" and because she became the target of intense cultural attacks. Through Smith, an understanding of the meaning of the religious valuation "evil" when it is attached to "mother" will be developed.

Melanie Klein's Theory

Melanie Klein was born in Vienna in 1882 into an unorthodox family, in terms of both its lifestyle and its religious choices. Her father, an unambitious but intellectual physician (turned dentist), rejected his Jewish family heritage. Her mother was a shopkeeper (unusual for a physician's wife) who sold exotic plants and animals, including reptiles. Klein was the youngest of four children in the family and was extremely close to her next oldest brother and sister, Emanuel (five years older) and Sidonie (four years older). Both of these siblings died early, and it has been suggested that both instilled in her a sense of mission to achieve on their behalf.

During her adolescence, Klein developed a strong desire to study medicine, but an early marriage in 1903 to one of Emanuel's friends, Arthur Klein, and the births of her three children put an end to those plans. Arthur's vocation as an engineer required the couple to move to small towns in Slovakia and Silesia during the first few years of their marriage. During this time, Klein developed severe depression relating to her brother's recent death, her unhappy marriage, her tempestuous relationship with her mother, and the births of her children (Gross-Kurth 1986).

In 1911, Klein and her husband moved to Budapest, where she first became acquainted with Sigmund Freud's work (on dreams) and began an analysis with Sandor Ferenczi. It was under the guidance of Ferenczi that she began her own work analyzing children. She later thought of this analysis as incomplete, however, because Ferenczi did not analyze her negative transferences and because he was not a sufficiently orthodox Freudian for her tastes—he used educative techniques rather than pure analyst-neutral analysis.

In 1921, she moved to Berlin, where she established a psychoanalytic practice for both adults and children and began an analysis with Karl Abraham, whom she judged to be the most important of her psychoanalytic mentors. He encouraged her in her work on child analysis, and it was under his tutelage that she began to develop her ideas on perhaps her most important contribution to psychoanalytic method: play therapy. For Klein, play was the *work* of children, parallel to dreams in adults:

> The brick, the little figure, the car, not only represent things which interest the child in themselves, but in his play with them they always have a variety of symbolical meanings as well which are bound up with his phantasies, wishes, and experiences. This archaic mode of expression is also the language with which we are familiar in dreams, and it was by approaching the play of the child in a way similar to Freud's interpretation of dreams that I found I could get access to the child's unconscious (1955a:55).

In 1927, after the death of Abraham and with the encouragement of Ernest Jones, she left Berlin, her husband, her two oldest children, and the Berlin Psychoanalytic Society (which had become increasingly intolerant of her work) to go to London. Her clinical practice with children was leading her in directions that she saw as compatible with Sigmund Freud's work but that were seen by the Berlin Society and especially by Anna Freud as being too innovative and unfaithful to Freud's original vision and thought. The Berlin Society was especially critical of her innovations in psychoanalytic method, including her explorations into the possibilities of transference relationships between the analyst and young children. Klein's work in London also led to many disputes within the psychoanalytic community there (especially after Anna Freud immigrated to London during the war) and finally caused a long-standing split in the British Psychoanalytical Society.

Based on her knowledge (acquired through analysis of children, including her own) of the existence of the primitive superego and the importance of aggression and anxiety in the infant, Klein had begun to reformulate the Freudian vision of the internal world and development of the child. In 1933, with the publication of "The Early Development of Conscience in the Child," Klein posited that the child's principle anxiety arises out of a persecutory fear based on the child's projection of its own aggressiveness onto the mother. Where Freud had posited *libidinal energies* that propelled the child toward attachment to objects for satisfaction, Klein made a decisive shift in positing that the child establishes relationships to objects on the basis of a *psychological* phenomenon—the anxiety arising out of the child's aggressive impulses. For Freud, the Oedipal period was the culmination of infantile sexuality out of which the superego developed; for Klein, Oedipal issues began emerging in the first year of a child's life, based on a persecuting superego that was already primitively developed.

In "Notes on Some Schizoid Mechanisms" (1946), one of the later and most comprehensive formulations of her thought, Klein summarized her work and described the three elements for which she is most widely known: *the paranoid-schizoid position, projective identification*, and *the depressive position.*

In her summary, she reiterated that object relations exist from the beginning of life, with the first object being the mother's breast. The breast becomes split in the child's mind into two parts—a good and gratifying breast onto which the child projects good elements of himself or herself and the bad or frustrating breast onto which the child projects his or her aggressiveness. This split is the important signifier of the paranoid-schizoid position of very earliest infancy.[1]

The aggressiveness aimed toward the bad breast protects the child from his or her own primary anxiety originating from the death instinct (the "fear of annihilation" [Klein 1946:179]), the birth experience, and the experience of privation, which are all felt to be caused by objects. The destructive/aggressive impulse is partially attached to the bad breast through projective identification (the projection of, in this case, hated "parts of the self" onto the object) and is turned against the breast from the very beginning. Aggression is expressed in sadistic (oral and, later, anal and urethral) fantasies; these fantasies include the child's wish to rob the mother's body of its good contents (sucking the breast dry, scooping the breast out) and to enter the mother's body, to fill the mother with the child's own excrement, and to control her (Klein 1955b:310). Aggression, however, is never totally projected onto objects, and it remains a potent force within the child's ego; the child always experiences his or her self as potentially being destroyed from within.

The child introjects goodness from the good breast and also projects goodness (also through projective identification—in this instance of the "loved parts" of the self) onto it. This projective identification with the good breast is essential for building up the ego and for future object relations. If, however, too much of the good self is projected, the ego is depleted, resulting in too much dependence on the idealized mother.

The young child's ego lacks cohesion, and therefore a "tendency towards integration alternates with a tendency towards disintegration" (Klein 1946: 179). In the interaction between the processes of introjection and projection, the child forms an ego and a superego. In the processes of splitting objects into good and bad (in the child's fantasy), the ego is also split. The more the object is felt to be "in pieces," the weaker the ego is. For Klein, the disintegration of the ego at this point—its "falling to pieces"—underlies states of disintegration in schizoid processes.

Two defense mechanisms that are closely connected with splitting, introjection, and projection and that also help protect the child from primary anxiety are the "hallucinatory gratifications": idealization and denial. In idealization, the good aspects of the object (breast) are exaggerated to ameliorate the threat of the bad object. The idealized breast also "springs from the power of the instinctual desires which aim at unlimited gratification" (Klein 1946:182). Denial serves to reduce the threat of the bad object by refusing to accept that the bad object exists, along with the consequent anxiety and pain it causes. But with the idealization and denial come the dissolution of the object relation, and with the denial of the situation and object relation, a part of the ego is denied as well.

For Klein, the infant makes a substantial leap during the second quarter of the first year and becomes able to introject the complete object (the mother's whole body instead of the breast only). The good (loved) and bad (hated) aspects of the mother are now brought together, resolving the schizoid aspects of the ego but, for the first time, introducing both the idea of potential loss and feelings of guilt "because the aggressive impulses are felt to be directed against the loved object" (Klein 1946:189). This ushers in the depressive position. This position serves to strengthen and integrate the ego because it "makes for an increased understanding of psychic reality and better perception of the external world, as well as for a greater synthesis between inner and outer situations" (p. 189). The feelings of loss and guilt result in a drive to make reparation to the object and prepare the way for more satisfactory future object relations.

If a child successfully works through the paranoid-schizoid (persecutory) and depressive positions in the first two years of life, then the primary anxiety will lose its strength (along with the other anxieties attached to the introjections and projections), object idealization will become less powerful, and bad objects will become less threatening. During all of this working through, the ego develops strength and unity. Inability to work through the paranoid-schizoid and depressive positions can result in the "violent splitting off and destroying of one part of the personality under the pressure of anxiety and guilt" (Klein 1946:195).

Thus, for Klein, the infant is in a constant state of flux—splitting and integrating, introjecting and projecting parts of itself onto good and bad objects that are also always being transformed and shaped by the infant's fantasies. The infant's ego is always in danger of being overwhelmed by primary anxieties, and it uses fantasies that are both loving and destructive to protect itself. The destructive fantasies that Klein described, including those with oral-, anal-, urethral-, and genital-sadistic/sexual elements, were quite shocking to those accustomed to viewing the infant as dwelling in a state of primary happiness, innocence, and bliss. It must be remembered, however, that Klein posits this sadistic infant/creature as responding to threats to its own existence by mobilizing all that it can bring to bear—a very weak and unstable ego structure. Klein is not providing an early-twentieth-century description of Calvinist "total depravity," however; the infant's primary motivation or drive is to survive the onslaught of destructive impulses that threaten to annihilate it.

A question that intrigues many of Klein's critics concerns the child's relationship to the larger social reality: How do the child's fantasies distort the mother and the social world even as they are also constructing it? What is the "real world" that the infant seems to strive to approximate in his or her own representations? Klein provides few answers to these questions. Anthony Elliott pointed out that, in Kleinian theory, fantasy "is correctly seen as the crucial psychic underpinning of all social activity, [but] it is not recognized as being inseparably bound up with the material conditions of its making. . . . Klein's privileging of the internal realm of fantasy leads to a crucial neglect of the role of social and cultural factors in the structuring of human relationships" (1994:85). Ironically, the exploration of relationships with the mother (as a real person), others in the infant's social realm, and the influence of the social structure itself is the glaring gap in Klein's theory.

Motherhood/Culture

But one might ask, What about the mother (and the mother's culture)—the "stuff" of the child's fantasies, projections, and introjections? One of the major and consistent critiques of Klein's work has been that the mother, the primal object, remains for all purposes hidden from view—positive or negative, good or bad, her actual personality and relationship with the infant seem to have little or no effect on her infant's development. Introjections, projections, and projective identifications are made upon the mother and her body, but she has relatively little to do as an active player in the infant's drama. Klein's underdeveloped, hidden, or "blank slate" mother is remarkable, given that Klein's intentions were to portray the earliest development of the infant as dependent upon a changing (but real) relationship with the mother and given the rich and detailed analysis of the effects of infantile psychopathologies and conflicts on the adult that Klein provided in her work (Greenberg and Mitchell 1983:146–147).

In her book *Banished Knowledge: Facing Childhood Injuries*, Alice Miller accused Klein of developing her theories of the "cruel child" (meaning, one supposes, Klein's description of the infant with sadistic impulses) without analyzing herself as a mother—including her own cultural and personal ambivalence about children. Miller argued that Klein observed children in her practice "against the background of her own upbringing, and apparently couldn't see beyond what she had learned in her own youth from her mother" (1990:45). For Miller, the signs of sadistic impulses, such as the screams of newborn infants, are the expression of psychic distress in the infant and are avoidable if infants are properly cared for and not abused. Children, Miller asserted, learn cruelty and sadism from their parents and teachers, and they behave "just as cruelly as they are treated by others" (1990:46). According to Miller, in a loving environment, an infant would not need to develop sadistic impulses.

A reader does not have to go as far as Miller does—rejecting Klein's work entirely—to see that she raises interesting questions: What about the analyst/observer's cultural and family biases and ambivalence? What about the mother? What part does the mother play in the development of the infant's ego? And might the mother—normally the first and most powerful object of the infant's ambivalence (love and hate)—have similar kinds of ambivalence toward the infant?

It is clear that Miller is at least partially correct when she implies that Klein had a very ambivalent view toward children and motherhood in her own personal life. Klein's biography is full of suggestive (and some quite clear) material in this regard. She married young and began to have children immediately, thus frustrating her desires to attend medical school and become a physician. In an undated autobiographical story, "Life Calls," Klein wrote about her experience of her wedding night and sexuality with shock: "And does it therefore have to be like this, that motherhood begins with disgust?" (quoted in Gross-Kurth 1986:40–41). In addition, Klein's husband began to have affairs with other women during the first year of their marriage.

Her pregnancy experiences were not pleasant; she was nauseous for much of the time. According to her autobiography, after the birth of her first child, Melitta, in 1904, she felt trapped and was torn between what she felt she *should* be feeling and what she actually felt: "I threw myself as much as I could into motherhood and interest in my child. I knew all the time that I was not happy, but saw no way out" (quoted in Gross-Kurth 1986:42). During her pregnancy with her second child, Hans, she sank into deep depression, which lasted for years.

When her son was less than a year old and her daughter was four, she began taking long vacations and trips away from the family, ostensibly to find a cure for depression and unspecified "nervous disorders." For two years, she was away from home as much as she was there, leaving her own mother to care for her children. During this period, she felt guilt and worried about the children's welfare but justified her absence as being necessary to restore her health. In 1909, she panicked when she thought (incorrectly) that she might be pregnant again; she would have her third child, Erich, in 1914, when she was thirty-two years old. It was at this time that she first encountered Freud's work and sought analysis with Ferenczi.

Her later relationships with her children have become infamous, especially her relationship with Melitta (Schmideberg), who also became a psychoanalyst. Their animosity toward each other was well known and has even been chronicled in a play that depicts vicious arguments and often public disagreements between them. Melitta apparently waged a war against her mother in the British Society, comparing Kleinian analysis to religious brainwashing: "Analysis is regarded as an atonement, as a cleansing process, as a religious exercise; getting on in analysis means doing one's duty, obeying one's parents, learning one's prayers, defecating" (quoted in Gross-Kurth 1986:229).

But if Klein's experience of motherhood might be judged worse than most, it should not be thought of as idiosyncratically balanced on the negative side of ambivalence. Many mothers in Western culture complain of remarkably similar feelings, although most are not willing or economically and physically able to act on them as Klein did by leaving home for extended periods to seek her own health.

Adrienne Rich, for instance, began her acclaimed volume on motherhood, *Of Woman Born*, with a copy of an entry from her own journal that is an exceptionally honest display of ambivalence toward her young children:

> My children cause me the most exquisite suffering of which I have any experience. It is the suffering of ambivalence: the murderous alternation between bitter resentment and raw-edged nerves, and blissful gratification and tenderness. Sometimes I seem to myself, in my feelings toward these tiny guiltless beings, a monster of selfishness and intolerance. Their voices wear away at my nerves, their constant needs, above all their need for simplicity and patience, fill me with despair at my own failure, despair too at my fate, which is to serve a function for which I was not fitted.
>
> And yet at other times I am melted with the sense of their helpless, charming and quite irresistible beauty—their ability to go on loving and trusting—their staunchness and decency and unself-consciousness. *I love them*. But it's in the enormity and inevitability of this love that the sufferings lie (Rich 1986:21–22, emphasis in original).

In terms of Klein's theory, Rich's ambivalence toward her children does not seem to be of the schizoid (ego-splitting) kind. She does not see her children as both good and bad objects; they are not portrayed as devilish at some points and angelic at others. They appear to be unified in her mind; her ego is not in danger of shattering or splitting.

Her ambivalence comes from the depressive and more "realistic" position: Although she is sometimes a monster, they are guiltless. They need and deserve something from her—patience and simplicity—that she can rarely offer. Rich portrayed a deep ambivalence, a palpable love, along with a feeling that "motherhood" was something that might destroy her. She continued her journal entry: "I am weak sometimes from held-in rage. There are times when I feel only death will free us from one another, when I envy the barren woman who has the luxury of her regrets but lives a life of privacy and freedom" (Rich 1986:21). Death alone was capable of freeing her from her children and the burdens of motherhood.

As Rich and others have pointed out, mothers in Western culture have reason to be ambivalent about children and motherhood. Many women conceive children through forced sex; pregnancy is an experience that is often devastating to their bodies; childbirth is painful beyond words and too often dehumanized by the medical industry; young children bring immobility, constraints on time, energy, ambition, and creativity, and changes in marriage relationships; and then, as a crowning indignity, mothers are often blamed for their children's pathologies and problems.

Yet the positive pole of the mother's ambivalence is the only side culturally and religiously endorsed. Women are to be "Madonnas," blessed by their children, blissfully in love with them and their husbands, content to remain in the private arena caring for their families and nurturing relationships. They are to forswear public power in favor of the nursery and are promised that, in the end, as the ones who "rock the cradle," they will (along with the other meek) inherit (rule) the earth.

Although rhetoric about the positive pole of the mother's ambivalence is not confined to the religious right, it is most pronounced there. Leaders of the religious right seem to focus much of their energies on shoring up the so-called traditional family and "family values" against the family's perceived enemies: the liberal mainstream media, radical feminists, and homosexuals.

James Dobson, president of Focus on the Family, an organization "dedicated to the preservation of the home," has spent his career promoting conservative values and idealizing traditional patriarchal ideas of femininity and motherhood—the positive "Madonna" side of mothers' ambivalence. His books are full of language about the importance of "good" mothering for the stability and survival of the culture: "Countless times each day a mother does what no one else can do quite as well. She wipes away a tear, whispers a word of hope, eases a child's fear. She teaches, ministers, loves, and nurtures the next generation of citizens. And she challenges and cajoles her kids to do their best and be the best" (Dobson and Bauer 1990:164). He contends:

> Female sex-role identity has become a major target for change by those who wish to revolutionize the relationship between men and women . . . every element of the traditional concept of femininity has been discredited and scorned, especially those responsibilities associated with homemaking and motherhood.

... We can make no greater mistake as a nation than to continue this pervasive disrespect shown to women who have devoted their lives to the welfare of their families" (Dobson 1982:351).

Dobson cautioned his readers about women who do not wish to become mothers with a note about the tremendous power of women and a warning about potential calamitous results if that power is misused: "There's something ambiguous [sic] about insisting on a 'right' [not to bear children] which would mean the end of the human race if universally applied! If women wearied of childbearing for a mere thirty-five years on earth, the last generation of mortals would grow old and die, leaving no offspring to reproduce. What god-like power is possessed by the female of the species!" (Dobson and Bauer 1990:354).

His word to mothers when they complain of being bored or depressed warned them against indulging in negative feelings: "You will not always be saddled with the responsibility you now hold. ... Enjoy every moment of these days—even the difficult times—and indulge yourself in the satisfaction of having done an essential job right!" (Dobson and Bauer 1990:355).

His admonition to enjoy even the "difficult times" glosses over (denies) the powerful negative aspects of motherhood, and it refuses permission for mothers to feel the negative pole of their natural ambivalence: hatred, rage, deep depression, and suicidal despair—natural results of idealized motherhood in Western, patriarchal culture.

A Kleinian analysis of Dobson reveals a psychic picture much different than that provided by Adrienne Rich; Dobson's is replete with clearly schizoid features. For Dobson, there is a definite splitting of the ego; there are two kinds of women: good women, who follow the biblical mandates to have children, stay at home with them, hold the family together, and live in submission to their husbands, and bad women, who, in his mind, oppose God and the family. Good mothers are those who can overcome depression and boredom (their own ambivalence) to "wipe the tear" and "cajole" the child to the kinds of achievements they are not able to attain themselves. Bad women are those who have no faith, hate the family, refuse to have children, despise those women who do, and may, at their will, kill off the human race.

The schizoid idealized mother is built up to protect against the bad woman who would destroy the family, God's intentions, and the patriarchy. In one of Dobson's most recent books written for young adults, he spoke of a young woman who complained to him that the system that "saddles" a mother with dressing, feeding, transporting, retrieving, nurturing, bathing, helping, disciplining, and tucking in the children without her husband's help is not fair. To this, Dobson replied: "But that's the way the system [patriarchy] works" (1995:75–76). He is unambiguous that the woman, according to nature and God's law, is assigned primary responsibility for these tasks and should "indulge herself" in the satisfaction of having done an essential, if culturally undervalued, job well.

The defense mechanism of choice of the disintegrating paranoid-schizoid position is to separate the idealized breast as far as possible from the bad breast, to protect it and the psyche from danger. The bad woman is so bad and so threatening ("god-like" in her power) that she would destroy the human race for her own pleasure. She has sex outside of marriage, enjoys it, and lures unsuspecting men into it; she aborts/kills her babies; she is a lesbian; she is allied with powerful liberal cultural forces such as the media; she tries to influence good women to follow in her ways; and she hates men and wants to destroy them and their institutions. The bad woman is a threat to men and to God. According to a Kleinian analysis, the bad woman is also obviously a projection of Dobson's and his followers' primal fears of annihilation, based in their own unresolved anxieties and feelings of uncontrollable aggression.

Dobson's schizoid and persecutory fears about women and motherhood, however clear and almost humorous in their alarmist tone and paranoia, are not unique to him or to the religious right, however. There are undertones of splitting and persecutory fear even in the most liberal of individuals and institutions. Recent discussions of sexual harassment in the mainline churches, for instance, have brought forth warnings for clergy about illusory (fantasy) persecutory/predatory/bad women who are reputedly searching out clergy targets for lawsuits. These bad women reportedly attempt to seduce clergy into sexual involvement in order to bring lawsuits against the ministers. The lawsuits will, according to the stories, produce such huge monetary rewards for the women that they will bring clergymen and their churches (and even, potentially, their denominations) to ruin.

One interpretation of these stories of bad/greedy/sadistic women (none of whom has ever actually materialized) may be that they are persecutory projections of men's fears of their own powerful and uncontrollable drives to harass and be sadistic toward women.

Susan Smith and the "Heart of Darkness"

Cultural reaction to the tragic story of Susan Smith and her sons is a good example of the playing out of such schizoid thinking about women and mothers. Feelings of shock and horror reverberated throughout the United States when Susan Smith, a symbolic representative of one its most important objects—the idealized side of the split mother—refused to act out the ideal role and revealed herself to be a "bad woman."

Smith, a twenty-three-year-old white South Carolina wife and mother, held a responsible position at a prestigious local firm and was from a well-respected family (her stepfather was a member of the Christian Coalition). She seemed to have adopted the traditional and conservative values of her family and community and appeared to be free of obvious mental illness. Yet on the evening of October 25, 1994, she bundled her two small boys into her maroon car, drove them all to a lake on the outskirts of her town, positioned the car on a boat ramp, started it rolling, jumped out, and then stood by and watched as the car and her children sank in the deep and muddy water.

For nine days, she held the nation captive as she told and retold the untruthful story that she and her children had been the victims of a black man who had carjacked her car at a deserted intersection outside of town and kidnapped the boys. When she finally confessed to the murders and the car was recovered with the boys' bodies hanging upside down, still buckled into their car seats, the nation virtually disintegrated with shock and bewilderment. How could such a seemingly good mother perform such a heinous act? How could a traditional mother kill her children? It was not long before the tabloid newspapers, prosecutors, people on the streets, and even the *New York Times* proclaimed her "evil."

The June 4, 1995, *New York Times Magazine,* issued a month before the beginning of Smith's trial, featured an article entitled "Staring into the Heart of the Heart of Darkness" in which the author, Ron Rosenbaum, proclaimed Smith's story to be a great one because it raised profound "theological issues." "What was going through Susan Smith's mind in committing the EVIL DEED (as the tabloid STAR called it)—and what went through God's mind in permitting it?" (Rosenbaum 1995:36).

Rosenbaum interviewed Susan's pastor, the Reverend Mark Long, for some insight into her motivations that evening. Long explained his Methodist/Arminian understanding of the situation: that Susan was a moral agent who had a choice between God and the devil and that she had chosen evil. Rosenbaum went to the lake, stood on the shore, and wondered to himself what could have been so compelling about the devil's presentation to Smith that night to convince her to murder her own children. Rosenbaum's underlying question is the philosophical one, "Can evil be done for evil's sake?" Did Susan Smith commit evil for its own sake, or was she duped? Was her act "malignant wickedness?" (Rosenbaum 1995:43).

From a Kleinian perspective, however, a question must be asked of Rosenbaum: Why did he (and seemingly most of the rest of the Western Hemisphere) choose Susan Smith to be a representation of evil, when the murder of children by their parents is a tragically commonplace occurrence? Most parent-murderers do not receive either the notoriety or the religious/moral label "evil." In the well-publicized case, for example, of the murder of six-year-old Elisa Izqioerdo by her mother, Awilda Lopez (an emotionally unstable, crack-addicted woman of color), New York's Child Welfare Agency received as much or more condemnation than Lopez. Even in the funeral sermon, Elisa's minister seemed almost to absolve the murderer: "Elisa was not killed only by the hand of a sick individual, but by the impotence of silence of many, by the neglect of child-welfare institutions and the moral mediocrity that has intoxicated our neighborhoods" (Epperson and Rivera 1995:36).

The answer to the question "Why is Susan Smith considered *evil* but not Awilda Lopez?" lies, again, in the paranoid-schizoid position of Western culture toward motherhood. When the idealized mother commits a heinous crime against her children, she shakes religious and cultural foundations. The good breast, which is introjected into the infant (culture), cannot also be the bad one, or the infant (culture) will also be found tainted. In the same way, the good breast, which receives the projected good parts of the infant, corrupts those parts when it shows itself to be bad. By contrast, the woman whom society labels as bad (Lopez) is expected to be hostile and sadistic to her offspring. When she murders her child, the culture blames itself for failing to protect the child.

According to Klein's theory, if the culture had progressed to a more realistic (reparative) position regarding motherhood, the deeds of Susan Smith (a woman who appeared to be good and yet committed bad acts) would not have been such a shock. Only an object like the idealized mother that is initially split off and held apart from the split bad object would have the power to disrupt as Susan Smith did when she forced the splits together by her actions. Only a mother who breaks the bounds of cultural splits and projections could be accused of reinventing "EVIL" or representing the "heart of darkness." Awilda Lopez is not considered evil or even blameworthy because she is, for all her heinous acts, merely playing out her projected role as the "bad woman"—she is not white, she is drug-addicted, she is emotionally unstable. She can shock the culture by the sadistic nature of her abuse but not by the fact that she abuses or kills.

Reaction to Susan Smith's confession was very swift; immediate attempts were made by the media, by those who knew her, and by the church to again separate the good from the bad. She was portrayed either as a bad woman masquerading as a good one or as a good woman so victimized that she was not responsible for her actions.

Her family members were some of the most important witnesses who tried to portray her (or parts of her) as evil. Her brother testified that he could not believe that the Susan he knew "was at that lake," implying that another "evil" Susan must have been there. Her husband, David, wrote a book, *Beyond All Reason*, detailing his and Susan's life together and especially recounting Susan's sins: vanity ("She was fearful about what another pregnancy would do to the shape of her body" [1995:120]); selfishness ("If there's one thing I can fault Susan for—it was that she had this tendency to leave the boys at other people's houses while she went about her business" [p. 143]); lying; being sexually aloof; and finally, being unfaithful to him sexually with the man for whom she would sacrifice her children (according to David's interpretation) when he threatened to break up with her.

All of these "sins" are indicative of Susan's deep feelings of ambivalence about being a mother. According to her husband, her children had ruined her body—her main source of self-esteem—and had restricted her life financially, emotionally, and physically. Nevertheless, both the sheriff to whom she confessed and the FBI agent who interviewed her found her to be extremely remorseful, guilt-ridden, and depressed to the point of suicide about her acts. She undoubtedly had deep grief about her sons' deaths. The FBI agent, in fact, testified that she held Smith on her lap because Smith needed reassurance that she was not a "bad mother" (Bragg 1995a).

Other people—her defense attorney, media commentators, and townspeople—chose another tactic to reseparate the ideal mother from the evil one. They portrayed Smith as a victim; for them, she was a good but terribly damaged woman. Her defense attorney rejected an insanity plea (which might have brought some sense of resolution) and instead chose to depict her as a good mother who "snapped" because of her history of abuse. He brought in testimony about her stepfather, who admitted to molesting her when she was a young adolescent, and about the effects on her of her father's suicide when she was five years old. A sociologist for the defense testified that she was a young woman who led "two lives": Her surface life was that of "a quiet person with a sweet personality"; her deeper life was full of "chaos and confusion" (Bragg 1995c). A psychiatrist for the defense portrayed Susan as a woman suffering from depression who had fallen into a "destructive cycle of sexual relationships to ease her loneliness" (Bragg 1995b). And essayist Barbara Ehrenreich, in a piece for *Time,* blamed a culture that promotes romantic love as salvation to girls and women with little self-esteem: "In the Susan Smith case, the female dilemma [is] at its starkest: Not the pallid 'family-vs.-career' predicament, but a zero-sum choice between romantic love and mother love, with guaranteed misery no matter which you choose" (Ehrenreich 1995).

A culture that understood the powerful ambivalence of motherhood would not have had to conduct the intensive search of Smith's soul and its own to understand her actions. The psyche that has at least attained the depressive position is able to relate to its objects "whole" and not split and understands Susan Smith as a woman who, for whatever reasons, *acted* when her negative feelings about motherhood overpowered the positive. When "motherhood" threatened to destroy other parts of her self, parts that she deemed essential for her own survival, she destroyed "motherhood" by destroying her children. A culture that had worked through its own persecutory anxiety would understand that when Susan Smith justified the murders of her sons by saying, "We [couldn't] go on living like this," she meant that when she sent her boys (back) to the watery womb of the lake, she had killed a projected part of herself along with them.

In the end, the jury convicted Susan Smith, but the jurors were not willing to sentence her to death. Perhaps the life sentence (and not the death sentence) was a recognition (or at least a sense) on the jurors' part that they were not completely blameless in this crime, that their projection of the "good mother" onto Smith was a factor in the deaths of her children. Her defense attorney seemed to imply that the community bore some of the responsibility for her actions when he challenged the jury to reflect on the biblical admonition: "He that is without sin among you, let him first cast a stone at her." Finally, Susan's husband brought the question of "why" full circle in the final chapter of his book by suggesting that there is no rational reason for her actions and by warning that other seemingly normal people (even other good mothers) may be capable of committing similar evil acts: "People look for some magic formula to tell them 'why.' . . . That there's no explanation bothers them. It means that *they* could be living with someone with a dark side who could one day do something unspeakable. It's a hard thought to handle" (Smith and Calef 1995:256).

Conclusion

In her life and in her theory, Melanie Klein made it clear that she was an atheist, interested in individual psychology and especially in the psychic development of children. Her theories, however, have profound implications for understanding the ways in which cultures and religious communities construct such important and foundational ideas as motherhood and evil. Her theories of the paranoid-schizoid and depressive positions, especially, illuminate the powerful cultural/religious anxiety surrounding such issues as feminism, abortion, contraception, and changing gender roles. In addition, they are useful in analyzing somewhat mysterious and seemingly inconsistent cultural responses to events and experiences that seem equally horrible.

Klein's theories would suggest that it will be a better day for mothers, for infants, and for Western culture when the political barriers to moving beyond the persecutory paranoid-schizoid position are removed and when critical discourse, especially by women and mothers, about patriarchal constructions and expectations of motherhood can become widespread. This kind of discourse is necessary to reduce the anxiety of the culture and of individuals about the potential destructiveness of change. Hopefully, it will lead to a valuing of the actual (not the idealized) experiences of motherhood and will enrich, and possibly even save, the lives of many mothers and children.

Notes

1. Klein referred to the depressive and paranoid-schizoid "positions" rather than stages because she wanted to signify "a state of organization of the ego and characteristically conjoint phenomena" (Segal 1979:125–136) and not a chronological progression. The paranoid-schizoid position does initially precede the depressive position in the infant's life, but after the initial sequence, the positions fluctuate throughout life.

References

Bragg, R. 1995a. Mother Was Remorseful, Witness Says. *New York Times*, July 21, p. A10.

_____. 1995b. Psychiatrist for Susan Smith's Defense Tells of a Woman Desperate to Be Liked. *New York Times,* July 22, p. 16.

_____. 1995c. Smith Defense Portrays a Life of 'Chaos.' *New York Times*, July 27, p. A14.

Dobson, James. 1982. *Dr. Dobson Answers Your Questions.* Wheaton, Ill.: Tyndale House Publishers.

_____. 1995. *Life on the Edge: A Young Adult's Guide to a Meaningful Future.* Dallas: Word Publishing.

Dobson, James, and Gary L. Bauer. 1990. *Children at Risk: The Battle for the Hearts and Minds of Our Kids.* Dallas: Word Publishing.

Ehrenreich, Barbara. 1995. Susan Smith: Corrupted by Love? *Time,* August 7, p. 78.

Elliott, Anthony. 1994. *Psychoanalytic Theory.* Oxford: Blackwell Publishers.

Epperson, S. E., and E. Rivera. 1995. An Abandoned Child. *Time,* December 11, pp. 32–36.

Greenberg, J. R., and S. A. Mitchell. 1983. *Object Relations in Psychoanalytic Theory.* Cambridge, Mass.: Harvard University Press.

Gross-Kurth, Phyllis. 1986. *Melanie Klein: Her World and Her Work.* New York: Alfred A. Knopf.

Klein, Melanie. 1946. Notes on Some Schizoid Mechanisms. In J. Mitchell, ed., *The Selected Melanie Klein.* New York: Free Press, 1986, pp. 176–200.

_____ 1955a. The Psycho-Analytic Play Technique: Its History and Significance. In J. Mitchell, ed., *The Selected Melanie Klein.* New York: Free Press, 1986, pp. 34–54.

_____. 1955b. On Identification. In M. Klein, P. Heimann, and R. E. Money-Kyrle, eds., *New Directions in Psycho-Analysis: The Significance of Infant Conflict in the Pattern of Adult Behavior.* London: Tavistock Publications, pp. 309–345.

Miller, Alice. 1990. *Banished Knowledge: Facing Childhood Injuries.* Translated by Leila Vennewitz. New York: Anchor Books. (Originally published in 1988.)

Rich, Adrienne. 1986. *Of Woman Born: Motherhood as Experience and Institution.* New York: W. W. Norton. (Originally published in 1976.)

Rosenbaum, Ron. 1995. Staring into the Heart of the Heart of Darkness. *New York Times Magazine,* June 4, pp. 36–44.

Segal, Hannah. 1979. *Melanie Klein.* New York: Viking Press.

Smith, David, and Carol Calef. 1995. *Beyond All Reason: My Life with Susan Smith.* New York: Kensington Books.

7

Playing and Believing
The Uses of D. W. Winnicott in the Psychology of Religion

James W. Jones

I have been drawn to the writings of the British psychoanalyst Donald W. Winnicott (1896–1971) since I first read them as part of my own training many years ago. His straightforward and concrete descriptions of his patients' struggles (as well as his own) were a welcome relief from the metapsychological scholasticism of Ronald Fairbairn and Heinz Kohut. His willingness to be real in his interactions with patients and write frankly of his failures as often as of his successes, rather than hiding behind the austere analytic demeanor that was constantly modeled for me, helped me hold on to my own humanity in the course of my studies. The fact that he began as a pediatrician and clearly loved children seemed to parallel something in my own internship as a child psychologist. His courage in working with juvenile delinquents and other "antisocial personalities" (as he called them) seemed to resonate with my experiences working as a psychologist in a maximum-security prison and as part of the family court, as well as with some early episodes of my own on the other side of the juvenile justice system. And in many of his writings, Winnicott sounded as if he was struggling to get beyond the dichotomy of objectivity and subjectivity that has done so much mischief in modernity—the same struggle that has consumed much of my own intellectual energy.

Wait just a minute! you are probably thinking right now. What kind of introduction can this be to a scholarly essay?

Implicit in the way Winnicott worked and wrote was the insistence that knowledge and knowers, thoughts and thinkers, cannot be separated. Every theory is the product of some theoretician, and that must never be forgotten.

Winnicott never wrote an essay in which he was not explicitly as well as implicitly present in and through his text. His willingness to speak personally, to come clean on where he himself was in relation to what he was writing about, endeared me to him personally and also, paradoxically, theoretically. To write abstractly about his ideas and my ideas about him would be to do him a great injustice; it would also miss what I think is his most important *theoretical* contribution to the psychology of religion.

Winnicott's Life and Thought

The place to start, then, must be with the relation of Winnicott's ideas to Winnicott's own life. What led him to focus his formidable intellectual abilities on concepts such as "transitional objects," "true and false selves," "maternal preoccupation," "regression in the transference," and "the capacity to be alone"? In his discussions of psychoanalytic technique, Winnicott suggests that the task of interpretation is to supply the patient an experience that could repair some fundamental deficiency in the patient's early experience. What deficiency in his own early experience is D. W. Winnicott seeking to repair through his interpretation of psychoanalysis?

During his final years, Winnicott began work on an autobiography to be titled "Not Less Than Everything." He started with a quote from T. S. Elliot—"costing not less than everything"—and a "prayer" of his own—"Oh God, may I be alive when I die." Later, he wrote a bit of fantasy about being alive when he died, watching everything as a spectator (C. Winnicott 1989:4). What he feared was not the physical aspects of death, which he said he "knew all about" from his medical training, but rather not being there to *experience* it. This insatiable drive for immediate experience runs through his life and work. Curiosity and its offshoot creativity are for him the core of human life.

Winnicott tended to describe his early life in almost utopian terms, a tendency carried over in the biographical essay by his second wife who noted that his early life "sounds too good to be true. But the truth is that it *was* good, and try as I will I cannot present it any other light" (C. Winnicott 1989:9). But ironically, the incidents Clare Winnicott reported from her late husband's autobiographical notes regarding his relationship with his father and mother were far from happy.

Winnicott apparently found his father unapproachable and feared disappointing him. His father wanted his son to go into the family business, but Winnicott wanted to be a physician. He wrote that he tried to make the idea of medicine repulsive and to learn to love the idea of business in order to please his father. It was only when a boarding school chum confronted him and said, "What are you doing, you're absolutely mad. Do what you want to do" that he realized how important medicine was and replied, "How wonderful. Do you think I really can?" (C. Winnicott 1991:184). But he had a friend broach the subject with his father because he could not bring it up himself.

The impression of Winnicott's father that emerged from his autobiographical reflections was of a stern and distant figure, removed from his son's life. This impression was confirmed when Winnicott wrote, "Now my sisters were older than I, five and six years; so in a sense I was an only child with multiple mothers, and with a father extremely preoccupied in my younger years with town as well as business matters" (C. Winnicott 1989:8). Looking back on his life, Winnicott later wrote, "It is probably true that in my early years [my father] left me too much to all my mothers. Things never quite righted themselves" (p. 8). Mirroring his own early experience, Winnicott would produce a theory that was noteworthy for the absence of the father and that focused exclusively on the impact of the mother.

This did not, however, mean that Donald had no feelings about his father. In addition to whatever resentment he felt about being "left too much to all my mothers," Winnicott also recorded the following incident:

> I took my own private croquet mallet (handle about a foot long because I was only three years old) and I bashed flat the nose of the wax doll that belonged to my sisters and that had become a source of irritation in my life because it was over that doll that my father used to tease me. She was called Rosie. Parodying some popular song he used to say (taunting me by the voice he used)
>
> > *Rosie said to Donald*
> > *I love you*
> > *Donald said to Rosie*
> > *I don't believe you do*
>
> . . . so I knew the doll had to be altered for the worse, and much of my life has been founded on the undoubted fact that I actually *did* this deed, not merely wished it and planned it (C. Winnicott 1989:7).

Besides the taunting, there appears to have been a rather punitive side to his father. For example, in his notes, Winnicott recorded an early encounter with his father as follows: "When (at twelve years) I one day came home to midday dinner and said 'drat' my father looked pained as only he could look, blamed my mother for not seeing to it that I had decent friends, and from that moment he prepared himself to send me away to boarding school" (C. Winnicott 1989:8). Although Winnicott called his father "good tempered," the picture that emerges from these vignettes is of a more distant and punitive, if not sadistic, man. Throughout his biographical notes, Winnicott seemed to deny any ambivalence about his parents and to insist that "my home is a beautiful home and I only wish I could live up to it. However, I will do my best and work hard" (p. 9). But these vignettes reveal the basis for a great deal of anger at his father.

An idealizing tendency may have been at work there. In his theorizing, Winnicott wrote of anger in a way that, as I will discuss, made anger something positive. Aggression was seen as the necessary catalyst for the crucial determination of objective, as opposed to subjective, reality. Perhaps this tendency to make aggression positive was rooted in Winnicott's need to either deny or to put a good face on his anger at his father.

Thus, Adam Phillips commented that Winnicott's portrait of his father was "suspiciously cheerful" and "determinedly benign" (1988:26, 27). In analyzing this aspect of Winnicott's life, Jeffrey Rubin (n.d.) suggested that Winnicott adopted what Fairbairn called the "moral defense" against bad object relations in which children (in this case Winnicott) blame themselves and their moral failings for the rejection they receive in order to maintain the fantasy of their parents' goodness. There may also be a collusive element in this defense in that the children collude with their parents' needs to maintain an overly idealized and grandiose view of themselves.

Clare Winnicott wrote that "freeing himself from the family" and "establishing his own separate life and identity" was a major problem for Donald, and she attributed that to the "quality" and "richness" of his early life. Other, less benign dynamics may also have played a part in creating that problem. And given the paternal punitive rigidity revealed in the family episodes, it is no wonder that Winnicott made the need to safeguard and develop a "true self" a central tenet in his theory.

If Winnicott's father was absent, what were the multiple mothers like, those women in whose company Donald spent his early years? Phillips recorded a poem that Winnicott wrote when he was seventy and sent to his brother-in-law with the question "do you mind seeing this hurt coming out of me?" The poem is called "the tree."

> *Mother below is weeping*
> *weeping*
> *weeping*
> *Thus I knew her*
> *Once, stretched out on her*
> *as now on dead tree*
> *I learned to make her smile*
> *to stem her tears*
> *to undo her guilt*
> *to cure her inward death*
> *To enliven her was my living* (Phillips 1988:29)

The poem speaks of what becomes, in Winnicott's theorizing, the most crucial aspect of infantile development—the way in which the mother holds the child. But the poem evokes young Donald's experience of being held with an image of a child stretched out on his mother's lap like Christ crucified on the cross. By making "maternal preoccupation," in which the mother is temporarily totally responsive to her infant's needs, the heart of his developmental psychology, Winnicott restores in the domain of theory an experience that was absent from his own early life.

As Phillips noted, the poem also touches on one of Winnicott's central clinical concerns—how the infant responds to the maternal absence. In Winnicott's terms, maternal absence is not primarily a physical lack but rather an emotional deficiency in which the mother is not emotionally in tune with her infant. This may happen because the mother is so preoccupied with her own issues that she is unable to give her undivided attention to her infant. It may also happen because the mother is depressed. In a later theoretical paper, Winnicott described maternal depression in words that eerily echoed his poem: "In certain cases, however, the mother's central internal object is dead at the critical time in her child's early infancy, and her mood is one of depression. Here the infant has to fit in with a role of dead object, or else has to be lively to counteract the mother's preoccupation with the idea of the child's deadness. . . . The task of the infant in such a case is to be alive and to look alive and to communicate being alive" (1965:191–192). And so Winnicott "learned to make her smile, to stem her tears, to undo her guilt, to cure her inward death." And later, he became a man who was often the life of the party, who rented a piano for his college room and "played it unceasingly," turning his room into "a popular meeting place." One of his patients, remembering him from his service in a wartime hospital, recounted that Winnicott "liked to sing a comic song on Saturday evenings in the ward—and sang 'Apple Dumplings' and cheered us all up" (C. Winnicott 1989:11). And even later, he would write many times (perhaps from his own experience) of how a forced and compliant cheerfulness would serve to hide the individual's "true self."

Winnicott's Contribution to Psychoanalytic Theory

I have already introduced many of Winnicott's chief theoretical concerns—the true and false self, maternal preoccupation, holding, aggression, and objectivity (which became the basis for his ideas about object relating and object use)—through an exploration of Winnicott's own life. Now these concepts must be elaborated in their own right.

I agree with Frank Summers (1994) that, although Winnicott's writings are not systematic, a coherent, developmental system undergirds all that Winnicott wrote. His task, as he himself articulated it, was to counterbalance the Freudian concentration on internal dynamics with an equal emphasis on what he called "the environmental factor" (Winnicott 1965:251). Winnicott refused to replace intrapsychic dynamics with interpersonal ones but rather sought to keep them in balance. By environmental factors, Winnicott really meant maternal ones and later the influence of the analyst who, in Winnicott's view, continues the work of the mother. Thus, he often called mental illness "an environmental deficiency disease" (p. 256), by which he meant it is caused by a deficiency in maternal care.

The infant begins in a state of what Winnicott called "absolute dependence." At this stage, there is no separation, hence Winnicott's famous epigram, "There is no such thing as a baby" but only the "nursing couple." The maternal side of this reciprocal unit is (or should be) in a state that Winnicott called "primary maternal preoccupation." This state of perfect (or near perfect) attunement of mother to infant begins even before birth. By knowing intuitively what her infant needs and providing it consistently, the mother protects the infant from any experience of separation and preserves the infant's sense of omnipotence through which its every wish is magically fulfilled. This was the most radical of Winnicott's theoretical innovations: He shifted psychoanalytic attention from the vicissitudes of drives to the quality of early interpersonal relationships.

Winnicott's contemporary, Fairbairn, was making a similar innovation, and so both can be regarded as forefathers of what Stephen Mitchell (1988) called "the paradigm shift in psychoanalysis" from drive theory to relational theory. But there is an important difference between Winnicott and Fairbairn on precisely this point about the developmental meaning and function of early object relations. For Fairbairn, early relationships are crucial because their internalization provides the material out of which the developing sense of self is constructed. Winnicott rarely has recourse to the concept of internalization. Rather, he begins from an inherent tendency toward self-development, which is either facilitated or thwarted by the child's interpersonal (primarily maternal) environment. Early object relations are crucial not because they are internalized but because they facilitate or distort development.

The mother performs two sorts of functions for the infant, functions that Winnicott called "the object mother" and "the environmental mother." The object mother meets the infant's biological needs for food, changing, and so forth. This is necessary but not sufficient. Winnicott felt that Freud concentrated so much on the satisfaction or frustration of biological needs that he ignored the interpersonal provisions necessary for ego development. The function of the environmental mother Winnicott called "holding," which denotes "not only the actual physical holding of the infant but also the total environmental provision" (1965:43). The environmental mother meets the infant's "ego needs" for consistency, stimulation, and, most important, freedom from "impingement" on the developing true self, for "the holding environment has as its main function the reduction to a minimum of impingements to which the infant must react with resultant annihilation of personal being" (p 47).

Understanding and treating the "personal being" is the core of a psychoanalysis whose ultimate goal is to enable the patient to "feel real," which is "more than existing; it is finding a way to exist as oneself, and to relate to objects as oneself" (Winnicott 1971:137). The biggest barrier to feeling real is an identification with the false self. In his paper on "Ego Distortion in Terms of True and False Self" (1965:140–152), Winnicott made it clear that the primary responsibility for creating such a false self lies with the mother, for "where the mother cannot adapt well enough, the infant gets seduced into compliance" (p. 146). Rather than establishing that "primary maternal preoccupation" whereby the mother "achieves a high degree of identification with her infant" (p. 147), this mother forces her infant to identify with her needs as a condition of the mother-child relationship.

The false self is the compliant self who puts aside its natural and spontaneous desires in order to comply with the mother's desires. Though appearing to undermine the true self, in reality the false self saves the true self and protects it from being annihilated by overwhelming maternal demands. But this protective compliance exacts a price. Being forced to attend to its mother's needs, the infant (and later the patient) "lacks something, and that something is the essential central element of creative originality" (Winnicott 1965:152). Without access to that essential creative originality, the patient cannot feel real, for "only the True Self can be creative and only the True Self can feel real" (Winnicott quoted in Phillips 1988:135).

The concept of the false self has clear clinical content (the lack of spontaneity and creativity, the inability to feel alive), but of its opposite—the true self—Winnicott wrote, "There is but little point in formulating a True Self idea except for the purpose of trying to understand the False Self, because it does no more than collect together the details of the experience of aliveness" (1965:148). The true self has two sources. One is "the spontaneous gesture" in which the infant acts freely, without any impingement. The other is "the aliveness of the body tissues and the working of body-functions" (Winnicott 1965:148).

Bodily sensations play a significant role in Winnicott's developmental schema. Psyche and soma are two sides of the same coin. In a paper entitled "Mind and Its Relation to the Psyche-Soma" (1958:243–254), Winnicott argued that there is originally no distinction between mind and body and that too great a separation of mind and body is a sign of psychopathology. Given the unity of psyche and soma, disturbances in early interpersonal relations get expressed somatically or psychologically. If the mother is too distant or erratic in her caretaking, mentation must take over the care of the psychological organism and provide the satisfactions and nurturance lacking in the environment. Thus, the intellectual processes become overdeveloped, and the mind feels itself over and against the body; as a result, "there can develop an opposition between the mind and the psyche-soma" (Winnicott

1958:246). Thus begins the split between mental and physical in which we "find mental functioning becoming a thing in itself. . . . The psyche of the individual gets seduced away into this mind from the intimate relationship which the psyche originally had with the soma. The result is a mind-psyche which is pathological" (pp. 246–247). Consequently, a breakdown of the relationship between the mother and the infant gets transformed into a breakdown of the relationship between the mind and the body; the mother's being out of touch with her baby results in a mind out of touch with its body.

One characteristic of the true self, Winnicott wrote, is "the capacity for the use of symbols" (1965:150). In this context, Winnicott referred to his discussion of transitional phenomena and so linked the true self with the infant's creativity, first manifest in the use of transitional objects. And since, as I shall discuss shortly, transitional processes are the foundations of culture (including religion), Winnicott said that where there is a high degree of false self organization, "there is found a poor capacity for using symbols, and a poverty of cultural living" (p. 150). Such an inability to appreciate the symbolic world, derived from too great an identification with the false self, will obviously inhibit a person's appreciation of religious language as well as that of art and literature.

Around six months of age, the infant begins to become aware of its separation from the surrounding environment—an awareness it has been protected from if the mother's attunement has been "good enough." With the awareness of its mother's separateness (and later the separateness of other objects in the world), the infant loses its feeling of omnipotent control over its environment. This loss does not occur at once but rather gradually. To comfort the infant for this loss of maternal attunement and to aid in the movement from illusory omnipotence to objective reality, the infant has recourse to "transitional objects" (the proverbial blanket or teddy bear) that come from the outside world but over which he or she can exercise a remnant of omnipotent control.

Transitional objects cushion the move from subjectivity to acknowledging the independence of the external world. They exist in the external world and are also given their meaning and special status by the child's imagination. Thus, they stand midway between the omnipotent world of the infant's experience and the reality-based world of the adult.

Children play with transitional objects, and therefore play is an essential part of the transitional process, for playing stands at the interface of the physical world and the world of inner psychological process. The experience of play (even by oneself) carries echoes of the baby's earliest interactional experiences because "the playground is a potential space between the mother and the baby or joining mother and baby" (Winnicott 1971:47). Even when the baby plays alone, he or she is still operating interpersonally. Thus, Winnicott's theory is not primarily about certain kinds of objects—teddy bears and blankets—but rather about certain kinds of relational experiences (Jones 1991b).

Encompassing inner and outer reality, the transitional experience of play transcends the dichotomy of objectivity and subjectivity, for it is "an inter-mediate area of *experiencing,* to which inner reality and external life both contribute" (Winnicott 1971:2, emphasis in original). Because it is neither subjective nor objective but contains elements of both, this transitional realm was called paradoxical by Winnicott. In stating this paradox, he was seeking to move beyond the dichotomy of objectivity and subjectivity by proposing "a third area of human living, one neither inside the individual nor outside in the world of shared reality" (p. 110). Between inner and outer lies *interaction.* Neither the objective environment nor the isolated individ-ual but rather the interaction between them defines this third domain, for it "is a product of the *experiences of the individual . . .* in the environment" (p. 107, emphasis in original). This intermediate reality is interpersonal from its inception. Beginning in the interactional space between the mother and in-fant, it *remains an interpersonal experience* as it gradually spreads out from the relation to the mother to "the whole cultural field," for "the place where cultural experience is located is in the *potential space* between the individual and the environment (originally the object)" (p. 100, emphasis in original).

The infusion of meaning from the inner world into actions and objects in the public sphere and/or the expression of inner-generated truths by means of external physical and verbal forms describes not only children playing with teddy bears and empty boxes but also the creation of symphonies, sculptures, novels, and scientific theories. In discussing transitional objects, Winnicott was not just talking about "child's play" but was also proposing nothing less than a psychoanalytic theory of culture that begins from the in-terpersonal matrix of infant and parent, moves to the development of cre-ativity through play and the use of transitional objects, and ends with the symphonies of Beethoven, the paintings of Rembrandt, and the theories of Einstein. Winnicott's theory is not primarily about teddy bears and blankets but about how certain kinds of interpersonal experiences give rise to culture, for "cultural experience [is] an extension of the idea of transitional phenom-ena and of play" (Winnicott 1971:99).

Culture, science, religion, and art are thus normal extensions of the transi-tional realm. For Freud, cultural institutions are defenses against fratricide, foreign structures heteronomously imposed on the individual in the service of instinctual control. By contrast, Winnicott does not theorize an inevitable conflict between the individual and culture because cultural forms develop naturally from the pleasures of the intermediate experience (Flax 1990).

Winnicott is proposing an independent line of development for the sym-bolic process that starts from the play of children and eventuates in the theo-ries of high-energy physics, the complex melodies of Mozart, and the evocative symbols of the world's major faiths. Winnicott suggests that the symbolic order (which is really all of culture) cannot be reduced to the vicissitudes of drives but rather has its own line of development. The symbolic process is not derived from instinctual dissatisfaction, and it does not exist only to serve biological needs. Rather, the symbolic process arises naturally out of spontaneous, true-self creativity, first on the part of the child and later for the adult as well. The transitional sphere derives from the impulse of the true self toward creativity and self-expression. Here, Winnicott presents a strong argument for the integrity of the symbolic world, which obviously appeals to those for whom the symbols of religion or art play an important role (for more on Winnicott's theory of symbolism in relation to religion, see Jones 1996).

The recognition of objects outside the boundary of the infant's self makes the objects possible targets of aggression. Actually, for Winnicott, the reverse is closer to the truth: By being targets of aggression, objects come to exist outside the boundary of the infant's omnipotent control. In what he called "object relating," the object remains primarily an expression of the infant's fantasies and wishes. But "the object, if it is to be *used*, must necessarily be real in the sense of being a part of shared reality, not a bundle of projections" (Winnicott 1989:221, emphasis in original).

To move from object relating to object usage, from fantasized omnipotent control to the recognition of independent reality, "the subject destroys the object" (Winnicott 1989:222). Or rather, the child thinks it has destroyed the object by his or her aggressive attack. But the object does not remain destroyed, and so the child learns that it exists outside of his or her omnipotent fantasies and "because of the survival of the object, the subject may now have started to live a life in a world of objects" (p. 223). This capacity to "use objects," that is, to recognize objective reality, cannot, according to Winnicott, "be said to be inborn, nor can its development be taken for granted. The development of a capacity to use an object is another example of the maturational process" (p. 222).

Refusing to take what Freud called "the reality principle" for granted, Winnicott analyzes the psychological origin of the experience of objectivity. He finds its source in aggression and destructiveness. Thus, he transforms aggression and destructiveness from intrinsically antisocial instincts or necessary evils to positive impulses that serve as the source of our sense of reality. "Destruction turns up and becomes a central feature so far as the object is objectively perceived, has autonomy, and belongs to shared reality ... destruction plays its part in making the reality, placing the object outside the self" (Winnicott 1989:223).

Feminist philosophers have drawn attention to the historical connections between masculine aggression and the ideals and practices of objectivity enshrined in modern science and rationalistic philosophy (Keller 1985, 1992;

Flax 1990; Merchant 1980). In a different way, Winnicott is making a similar connection. Objectivity results from the deployment of aggression and (Winnicott does not notice this) therefore carries aggression and destruction within itself. For Winnicott, such ruthless objectivity is a positive step because it makes possible science, reason, and a certain kind of sanity. But Winnicott also insists on the importance of creativity and intuition and that we cannot live by objective rationality alone. However, shorn of intuition and spontaneous creativity, bare objectivity may well prove dangerous and destructive, in part because of the aggression that lies at its heart.

The Use of Winnicott in the Psychology of Religion

One of the first to apply Winnicott's ideas to understanding religion was the psychologist Paul Pruyser. Like Winnicott, Pruyser senses that the modern dichotomy of objectivity and subjectivity is too rigid. Too much of reality is left unaccounted for; there must be "a third, transcendent sphere, a special level of thought and action which combines strands of premises and meanings into a kind of experience that has its own validity, *its own 'consensual validation'*" (Pruyser 1974:217, emphasis in original).

Like Winnicott, Pruyser uses Freud's term *illusion* for this alternative reality, but he wants to redeem the term from the negative connotations Freud gave it. This "illusionistic world" stands midway (literally, on the chart that Pruyser drew to illustrate his point) between the "autistic world" of pure, unconstrained fantasy and the "realistic world" of "hard, undeniable facts" (Malony and Spilka 1991:177). This illusionistic world is characterized by "tutored fantasy, adventurous thinking, orderly imagination, inspired connections, imaginative entities or events, symbols, playing, [and the] transcendent object prefigured by the child's transitional object" (p. 177).

For Pruyser, the psychological roots of religion lie in the illusionistic sphere. From the play of the imagination comes forth the beliefs, rituals, and stories that become the core of a religion. More specifically, Pruyser suggests that the image of a transcendental reality grows from the child's experience with transitional objects. Pruyser directly asserts that the "transitional object is the transcendent" (Malony and Spilka 1991:163) in that it exists "beyond the ordinary division we make between the mental image produced by the mind itself and the objective perceptual image produced by the real word impinging upon the sensory system" (p. 163). But he does not lay out in any detail the stages of development by which the blanket and the teddy bear are transformed into the idea of God.

Although beginning from the desire to go beyond the dichotomy of fact and fantasy, Pruyser's solution is simply to slip a third area between these two. They remain opposing domains. This third area is introduced in a way that does not impact on or transform our conceptions of either objectivity or subjectivity. Unfortunately, the dichotomy between subjectivity and objectivity, fantasy and factuality cannot be overcome by simply adding a third category. A more radical restructuring of our understanding of human knowledge is called for, one that does not leave the old positivistic image of the "realistic world" intact but rather transforms our thinking about the physical world. Rather than segregating religious knowing into a third type of knowledge, such a transformation needs to underscore the imaginative and "illusionistic" nature of all forms of human understanding.

Winnicott himself points to such an epistemological transformation. To him, illusion is not an error but a source of truth. The creative intuition fostered in the transitional space is a crucial human mode of knowing. Along similar lines, a major transformation has occurred in our understanding of science since Freud (a discussion of these changes can be found in Jones 1981). Instead of the usual empiricist model of reason as a set of universal rules, a more nuanced account of scientific methodology (and by extension knowledge in general) reveals that it involves "imagination, interpretation, the weighing of alternatives, and application of criteria that are essentially open" (Bernstein 1983:56). Our knowledge of reality is shaped by categories, cognitive schemas, and metaphors through which experience is mediated, and so it is no exaggeration to say that these schemas and metaphors "create realities" (Lakoff and Johnson 1980:156). Such categories and metaphors stand conceptually between objectivity and subjectivity, involving discursive reason and creative expression. They are "transitional" phenomena. Even the most rule-governed activities, such as the experimental method, depend on such metaphors, which "unite reason and imagination" (Lakoff and Johnson 1980:193). George Lakoff and Mark Johnson suggest that this mixture of reason and imagination is true of natural and social science, critical philosophy, and religious thought, for all "human conceptual systems are metaphorical in nature and involve an imaginative understanding" (1980:194).

Knowledge arises neither from the external world impressing itself on our passive minds nor from the projection of our subjective ideas onto a blank screen. Rather, "understanding emerges from interaction, from constant negotiation with the environment and other people" (Lakoff and Johnson 1980:230). Or, in Winnicott's more vivid language, truth is both "created and found." Like Winnicott's "transitional process," such a philosophy is neither subjective nor objective but is rather a third alternative.

Contemporary philosophy of science, as summarized in a book authored jointly by a cognitive psychologist and a philosopher of science, converges with Winnicott's concern to transcend the dualism of subjectivity and objectivity and reinstate imaginative interaction as a source of knowledge. As Michael Arbib and Mary Hesse wrote:

> Scientific models are a prototype . . . for imaginative creations or schemas. . . . Symbolic worlds all share with scientific models the function of describing and redescribing the world; and for all of them it is inappropriate to ask for literal truth as direct correspondence with the world. . . . We do not suddenly put on a different hat with regard to "truth" when we speak of the good or God from that we wear for natural science (Arbib and Hesse 1986:161).

Contemporary philosophy of science concurs that all knowledge is transitional and interactional in Winnicott's sense. *Discursive reason and imaginative creation interpenetrate.* Pragmatic realities constrain imaginative reconstructions while creative reinterpretations reframe empirical experience. *No hard and fast line can be drawn between objective and subjective spheres or between the products of reason and of imagination.* (I have made this point repeatedly in earlier discussions [Jones 1992 and 1996], which should be consulted for more elaboration of the epistemological implications of Winnicott's discussion of transitional processes.)

William Meissner and Ana-Maria Rizzuto follow Pruyser's example in calling upon Winnicott's concept of transitional objects in order to develop a psychoanalytically informed understanding of religion. Meissner (1984) emphasizes the location of transitional phenomena on the border between objectivity and subjectivity. Neither subjective nor objective, religious symbols are transitional phenomena because they belong neither to the objective domain of physical things nor to the subjective world of hallucination and daydream.

The crucifix, the Star of David, ritual gestures and vestments, sacred texts and phrases, and holy shrines all involve objects in the world of space and time, but they are, for the believer, not only physical and temporal. For Meissner, religious symbolization is "transitional" because "the objects as religious symbols are neither exclusively perceived in real and objective terms, nor simply produced by subjective creation. Rather, they evolve from the amalgamation of what is real, material, and objective as it is experienced, penetrated, and creatively reshaped by the subjective belief and patterns of meaning attributed to the object by the believer" (1984:181). As transitional objects, religious symbols stand at the interface of subjective and objective worlds, using physical, artistic, and linguistic objects to convey a spiritual or moral meaning.

In her research into the origin and transformations of the individual's "God representation," Ana-Maria Rizzuto (1979) explicitly locates the individual's God-representation in the "transitional space," halfway between sheer hallucination and physical reality. In this realm of imagination, the child creates a private but real world of transitional objects—teddy bears, imaginary friends, security blankets, personal games, and magical beliefs. The individual's personal God representation lives among them as "a special transitional object . . . created from representational materials whose sources are the representations of primary objects" (Rizzuto 1979:178) Throughout life, this private representation is continually reworked as it is brought in contact with the official God representation of the child's culture and religious community and as it confronts the vicissitudes of life. If, in the course of the life cycle, the individual's God representation can be reworked to accommodate new experiences, it can then be "used for belief" (p. 200). But if the developing self cannot use his or her God representation to make sense of his or her experience, it is discarded, at least temporarily. At a later time, it may be brought out and dusted off if new experiences call for it. Regardless of its vicissitudes, the God representation remains forever a transitional object.

> Throughout life God remains a transitional object at the service of gaining leverage with oneself, with others, and with life itself. This is so, not because God is God, but because, like the teddy bear, he has obtained a good half of his stuffing from the primary objects the child has 'found' in his life. The other half of his stuffing comes from the child's capacity to 'create' a God according to his needs (Rizzuto 1979:179).

Following Winnicott's phraseology, Rizzuto wrote that the individual's private God "is a psychically created object who is also 'found'" (1979:87): It is created by the child's imaginative capacities from pieces of the child's internalized parental representations and found embedded in the institutions of culture.

Pruyser, Meissner, and Rizzuto find in Winnicott's work a psychological location for religious phenomena. They believe that Winnicott provides a nonreductive understanding of religious symbols by positioning such symbols in an intellectual territory intermediate between objectivity and subjectivity.

This currently popular Winnicottian approach to religion assimilates religious phenomena to transitional objects. Previously, I noted two rather different referents to the term *transitional*: (1) certain objects like blankets and teddy bears that are, as Winnicott said, "neither inside nor outside," and (2) a state of consciousness or mode of experience, a "transitional space," that transcends the dualism of inner and outer, subjective and objective. Elsewhere, I have argued extensively that Meissner and Rizzuto focus too much on the first referent and much less on the second (Jones 1991a, 1991b).

Meissner and Rizzuto downplay Winnicott's focus on the interpersonal world and emphasize instead the interplay of "subjective" and "objective" factors in the constellation of transitional objects. This yields a viable location for religious symbols that belong neither to the totally objective domain of physical objects nor to the purely subjective world of hallucination and daydream.

However, when writing about transitional objects, Winnicott was calling attention to a certain capacity for *experience*. Although teddy bears and security blankets are left behind, this capacity to transcend the dichotomies of inner and outer, subjective and objective continues to mature and becomes the basis for human creativity in the arts, sciences, and throughout culture, becoming "diffused . . . spread out over the whole cultural field" (Winnicott 1979:14). Watching a child play with a teddy bear, Winnicott saw a child developing the capacity to write a novel or invent a machine or propose a theory.

The significance of Winnicott's work for the study of religion lies here. Sacred moments are "transitional" because they allow entrance again and again into that transforming psychological space from which renewal and creativity emerge. Through rituals, words, stories, or introspective disciplines, religion evokes those transitional psychological spaces, which continually reverberate with the affects of past object relations and are pregnant with the possibility of future forms of intuition and transformation.

Winnicott's discussion of transitional space resembles Victor Turner's use of the term *liminality*, which refers to "that which is neither this nor that, and yet is both" (Turner 1967:99). Turner focuses on the social functions of "liminality," especially the creation of community. Those who enter the liminal state, where social and intellectual distinctions vanish, are bound together by the experience.

For Turner, ritual is especially important in the creation of liminality. In an article published shortly after his death, Turner (1986) specifically connected play and ritual in ways that bring his thesis close to Winnicott's. Turner called ritual a "transforming performance" (1986:158). He specifically linked the culture-creating power of ritual to its evocation of a liminal (or "transitional") state since "through its liminal processes [ritual] holds the generating source of culture" (p. 158). Play, too, "is for me a liminal or limoid mode essentially interstitial, betwixt-and-between all standard taxonomic modes, essentially elusive" (p. 169). The link of play and ritual explains their creative potential, for both "can be said perhaps to play a similar role in the social construction of reality as mutation and variation in organic evolution" (p. 171).

Turner and Winnicott point to the transforming power of entering a liminal or transitional state of consciousness, where the usual distinctions of inner and outer, subjective and objective temporarily fade. Such states are a central part of religious practice. Winnicott's reflections on the transitional process provide the student of religion with a way to ground such practices in the psychology of human development and to move beyond Freud in understanding and respecting the psychological integrity of transitional and liminal experiences.

Critique of Winnicott

This is not the place for an extended critique of Winnicott's theorizing (critiques can be found in Flax 1990; Summers 1994; Greenberg and Mitchell 1983). However, the following deficiencies in his work should be noted.

In Winnicott's writings, the developmental saga is told only from the child's perspective. The child's mother, who plays the central role in the early months, is theorized only in terms of her maternal role. Her subjectivity is discussed only in its problematic aspects, that is, when her preoccupations or depression interfere with her primary and undivided attunement with her infant. This theoretical oversight may reflect a tendency in Winnicott to idealize woman in her role as mother. The picture found in his article on "Primary Maternal Preoccupation" (Winnicott 1958:300–305) is of the mother who sacrifices her own desires for her infant, a sacrifice that is continued in Winnicott's theorizing in which maternal subjectivity is lost in favor of that of the infant.

Reversing Freud's focus on the Oedipal father, Winnicott makes the mother the significant figure in the psychological development of the child. This maternal centrality is exaggerated by the lack of any paternal role. This theorizing is congruent with Winnicott's own experience of being abandoned by his father and left too much in the care of mothers. To the extent that he saw his work as only a supplement to Freud's, Winnicott could rightly claim that Freud had already thoroughly covered the role of the father. But as Winnicott's work comes to stand on it own (or as part of a "relational paradigm" à la Mitchell), the father and his law fail to find any constructive place (Moi [1989] criticizes all object relations theorizing on this score). In this sense, Winnicott's theory represents an idealized view of his early childhood—a child surrounded by empathic mothers with no intrusion from the father.

Although Winnicott insisted that psychoanalysis must pay more attention to environmental factors, the only environmental factor he discusses is the mother's capacity to bond. He pays no attention to the wider social context in which the mother-infant bonding takes place.

Winnicott does not overtly repudiate Freud's instinct theory as, for example, Fairbairn does. As a matter of fact, in part because of the tutelage of Melanie Klein, Freud's aggressive instinct is retained and transformed by Winnicott. However, the Freudian emphasis on erotic satisfaction is virtually lost. The dynamic significance of bodily drives and sensations is highlighted, but little if any role is given to sexuality in Winnicott's theory. Again, this may reflect, in part, an idealization of the woman as mother, in which the erotic aspect of femininity is lost to the maternal.

The Language of Self-Involvement

I have already noted the self-involving quality of Winnicott's writing, wherein no separation is attempted between the writer and his ideas. This is clearly an extension of the psychoanalytic task in which the patient's words are always returned to the patient's lived experience. But Winnicott is extending this to his own presentation of case material and even theoretical speculation. Unlike some relational theorists who stress the interaction of analyst and patient at the theoretical level but still present their cases only in terms of the patient's subjectivity and not their own, Winnicott is clearly as present in and through his clinical presentation as he is in his clinical interventions.

This refusal to absent himself or take the stance of the uninvolved spectator makes an important epistemological point, which is captured by Michael Polanyi's term *personal knowledge* (Jones 1981). What we claim to know is always an extension of who we are: the commitments we made, the skills we learned, the passions that hold us captive. Human knowledge is never separate from human knowers. In psychoanalysis, this means that interpretations are never simply reflections of the patient's subjectivity by a neutral analyst but rather are expressions of the interaction of the two subjectivities of analyst and patient. In the same way, the psychology (or sociology or anthropology or philosophy) of religion is never simply the result of a neutral process of rational reflection or data collection.

The empathic interrogation that Winnicott displays as the essence of psychoanalytic understanding can serve, I think, as a fruitful model of all human understanding (this is argued in more detail in Jones [in press]). Envisioning understanding as a relational activity gets us beyond the dichotomy of objectivity and subjectivity that has so bedeviled modern epistemology. All knowing is relational knowing in which there is neither isolating objectivity nor unrelieved subjectivity but rather interaction. In addition, Winnicott refuses to dichotomize thought and feeling, reason and intuition. Every heuristic activity is transitional in that it involves the interaction between the researcher and her or his subject, the fusion in some measure of subjectivity and objectivity, and reliance on both reason and intuition.

My claim that the open-ended, interactive, relational practice of psychoanalysis, exemplified by Winnicott, is a cogent model for all human understanding has two implications for the psychology of religion.

First, relational psychoanalysis undercuts the dichotomous empiricism whose hegemony has characterized so much of modern thought. This epistemological transformation has ramifications beyond psychoanalysis into philosophy and even our understanding of natural science. In an epistemic framework that refuses to dichotomize thought and feeling, reason and intuition and that insists on remaining open to both, the conflict between religion and science loses much of its force.

Second, a heuristic process built around interaction, dialogue, open interpretation, and the importance of affect and intuition is potentially able to approach religious material openly and empathically as well as critically and analytically. Rather than necessarily pathologizing the forms in which religious experience is embodied (ritual, meditation, ecstatic states, moral reflection), such a hermeneutic impels psychoanalysis into dialogue with the kinds of knowing found in humanity's religious and spiritual traditions.

Conclusion

Winnicott's work contributes to the psychological understanding of religion in the following ways:

1. His idea of transitional objects provides a viable way of understanding the nature of religious objects and symbols (Rizzuto 1979; Meissner 1984, 1990). In contrast to classical analysis, Winnicott provides a nonreductive account of the origin of the symbolic world by offering an independent line for its development (Jones 1996).
2. His discussion of transitional space provides a model for understanding religious experience (Jones 1991a, 1991b).
3. His emphasis on the importance of imagination and creativity and the articulation of an "intermediate area" of experience calls into question the modern dichotomizing of objectivity and subjectivity and permits a more open-textured epistemology in which religious knowledge can find a place (Pruyser 1974; Jones 1992, 1996, and in press).
4. His advocacy of a relational model of human nature can form the basis for a renewed theological anthropology (McDargh 1983; Jones 1991a, 1996).

Notes

While thinking about the relationship of Winnicott's life experiences to his theorizing, Jeffrey Rubin shared with me an insightful paper of his entitled "The Wish to Be Seen and the Dread of Being Found: A Psychobiographical Study of D. W. Winnicott." Although focusing on slightly different issues than I have here, his paper and subsequent conversations were a great help to me in thinking about this topic.

References

Arbib, M., and M. Hesse. 1986. *The Construction of Reality.* Cambridge: Cambridge University Press.

Bernstein, R. J. 1983. *Beyond Objectivism and Relativism.* Philadelphia: University of Pennsylvania Press.

Brennan, T. 1989. *Between Feminism and Psychoanalysis.* New York: Routledge.

Chodorow, N. 1989. *Feminism and Psychoanalytic Theory.* New Haven: Yale University Press.

Flax, J. 1993. *Disputed Subjects: Essays on Psychoanalysis, Politics and Philosophy.* New York: Routledge.

_____. 1990. *Thinking Fragments: Psychoanalysis, Feminism, and Postmodernism in the Contemporary West.* Berkeley: University of California Press.

Gay, V. 1983. "Winnicott's Contribution to Religious Studies: The Resurrection of a Cultural Hero." *Journal of the American Academy of Religion* 51: 371–392.

Gilligan, C. 1982. *In a Different Voice.* Cambridge, Mass.: Harvard University Press.

Goldenberg, N. 1990. *Returning Words to Flesh.* Boston: Beacon Press.

_____. 1979. *Changing of the Gods: Feminism and the End of Traditional Religions.* Boston: Beacon Press.

Greenberg, J., and S. Mitchell. 1983. *Object Relations in Psychoanalytic Theory.* Cambridge, Mass.: Harvard University Press.

Hare-Mustin, R., and J. Marecek. 1990. *Making a Difference: Psychology and the Construction of Gender.* New Haven: Yale University Press.

Jones, J. In press. "The Real Is the Relational: Psychoanalysis as a Model of Human Understanding." In J. A. van Belzen, ed., *Hermeneutical Approaches to the Psychology of Religion.* Amsterdam and Atlanta: Rodopi.

_____. 1996. *Toward a Relational Psychoanalysis of Religion.* New Haven: Yale University Press.

_____. 1992. "Knowledge in Transition: Towards a Winnicottian Epistemology." *Psychoanalytic Review* 79, no. 2: 223–237.

_____. 1991a. *Contemporary Psychoanalysis and Religion: Transference and Transcendence.* New Haven: Yale University Press.

_____. 1991b. "The Relational Self: Contemporary Psychoanalysis Reconsiders Religion." *Journal of the American Academy of Religion* 59, no. 4: 501–517.

_____. 1982. "The Delicate Dialectic: Religion and Psychology in the Modern World." *Cross Currents* 32, no. 2: 143–153.

_____. 1981. *The Texture of Knowledge: An Essay on Religion and Science.* Lanham, Md.: University Press of America.

Jones, J., and N. Goldenberg. 1992. *Transforming Psychoanalysis: Feminism and Religion. Journal of Pastoral Psychology* 40, no. 6: 343–406.

Jonte-Pace, D. 1985. "Religion: A Rorschachian Projection Theory." *American Imago* 42, no. 2: 199–234.

Keller, E. F. 1992. *Secrets of Life, Secrets of Death: Essays on Language, Gender, and Science.* New York: Routledge.

_____. 1985. *Reflections on Gender and Science.* New Haven: Yale University Press.

Keller, E. F., and J. Flax. 1988. "Missing Relations in Psychoanalysis: A Feminist Critique." In S. Messer, L. Sass, and R. Woolfolk, eds., *Hermeneutics and Psychological Theory.* New Brunswick, N.J.: Rutgers University Press.

Lakoff, G., and M. Johnson. 1980. *Metaphors We Live By.* Chicago: University of Chicago Press.

Malony, N., and B. Spilka. 1991. *Religion in Psychodynamic Perspective: The Contributions of Paul W. Pruyser.* New York: Oxford University Press.

McDargh, J. 1993. "Concluding Clinical Postscript: On Developing a Psychotheological Perspective." In M. L. Randour, ed., *Exploring Sacred Landscapes: Religious and Spiritual Experiences in Psychotherapy.* New York: Columbia University Press.

_____. 1988. "Beyond God as Transitional Object." Paper presented to the College Theology Society meeting, Los Angeles, California.

_____. 1983. *Psychoanalytic Object Relations Theory and the Study of Religion.* Lanham, Md.: University Press of America.

Meissner, W. 1990. "The Role of Transitional Conceptualizations in Religious Thought." In J. Smith and S. Handelman, eds., *Psychoanalysis and Religion.* Baltimore: Johns Hopkins University Press.

_____. 1984. *Psychoanalysis and Religious Experience.* New Haven: Yale University Press.

Merchant, C. 1980. *The Death of Nature.* San Francisco: Harper & Row.

Miller, J. B. 1976. *Toward a New Psychology of Women.* Boston: Beacon Press.

Mitchell, S. 1993. *Hope and Dread in Psychoanalysis.* New York: Basic Books.

_____. 1988. *Relational Concepts in Psychoanalysis.* Cambridge, Mass.: Harvard University Press.

Moi, T. 1989. "Patriarchal Thought and the Drive for Knowledge." In T. Brennan, ed., *Between Feminism and Psychoanalysis.* New York: Routledge.

Phillips, A. 1988. *Winnicott.* Cambridge, Mass.: Harvard University Press.

Pruyser, P. 1974. *Between Belief and Unbelief.* New York: Harper & Row.

_____. 1968. *A Dynamic Psychology of Religion.* New York: Harper & Row.

Rizzuto, A.-M. 1979. *The Birth of the Living God.* Chicago: University of Chicago Press.

Rubin, J. n.d. "The Wish to Be Seen and the Dread of Being Found: A Psychobiographical Study of D. W. Winnicott." Manuscript.

Saur, M., and W. Saur. 1993. "Transitional Phenomena as Evidenced in Prayer." *Journal of Religion and Health* 32, no. 1: 1–15.

Smith, J., and S. Handelman. 1990. *Psychoanalysis and Religion.* Baltimore: Johns Hopkins University Press.

Summers, F. 1994. *Object Relations Theories and Psychopathology.* Hillsdale, N.J.: Analytic Press.

Turner, V. 1986. "Body, Brain and Culture." *Cross Currents* 36: 156–178.

_____. 1967. *The Forest of Symbols.* Ithaca: Cornell University Press.

Winnicott, C. 1991. "An Interview with Clare Winnicott." In P. Rudnytsky, ed., *The Psychoanalytic Vocation: Rank, Winnicott, and the Legacy of Freud.* New Haven: Yale University Press.

_____. 1989. "D.W.W.: A Reflection." In D. W. Winnicott, *Psychoanalytic Explorations*, edited by C. Winnicott, R. Shepherd, and M. Davis. Cambridge, Mass.: Harvard University Press.

Winnicott, D. W. 1989. *Psychoanalytic Explorations.* Edited by C. Winnicott, R. Shepherd, and M. Davis. Cambridge, Mass.: Harvard University Press.

_____. 1988. *Human Nature.* New York: Schocken Books.

_____. 1971. *Playing and Reality.* New York: Routledge.

_____. 1965. *The Maturational Process and the Facilitating Environment.* London: Hogarth.

_____. 1958. *Through Paediatrics to Psychoanalysis.* New York: Brunner-Mazel.

8

Childhood Fears, Adult Anxieties, and the Longing for Inner Peace

Erik H. Erikson's Psychoanalytic Psychology of Religion

Donald Capps

Erik H. Erikson was certainly the most widely known psychoanalyst in the United States during his lifetime, and his death on May 12, 1994, at the age of ninety-one, has prompted many of his former colleagues, students, and admirers to speak and write about the influence of his work on their professional and personal lives. In time, we are likely to see more systematic efforts to assess his contribution to psychoanalytic thought. Such efforts will certainly give some attention to his contribution to the psychoanalytic study of religion, as religion was a topic that he frequently wrote upon throughout his career.

Of course, there were many assessments of his writings on religion while he was still alive. The most systematic treatment of his contribution to the psychoanalytic study of religion is Hetty Zock's *A Psychology of Ultimate Concern* (1990), which includes a chronological reconstruction of Erikson's psychological approach to religion, focusing on the following key texts in the Erikson corpus: *Childhood and Society* (1950, revised in 1963), *Young*

Man Luther (1958), *Insight and Responsibility* (1964), *Gandhi's Truth* (1969), and *Dimensions of a New Identity* (1974). Zock explored such Eriksonian themes as nostalgia for the mother and religion as affirmation of the sense of basic trust (*Childhood and Society*); religion as ideology, the nostalgia for the father, and the existential identity (*Young Man Luther*); religion as reaffirmation of hope and faith (*Insight and Responsibility*); religion as a special kind of ideology, religious actuality, and the immortal identity (*Gandhi's Truth*); and the distinction between religious and nonreligious worldviews (*Dimensions of a New Identity*). Zock also gave much attention to Erikson's psychohistorical method as reflected in his two major texts on religious leaders (*homo religiosus*), *Young Man Luther* and *Gandhi's Truth*. Given her systematic treatment of Erikson's writings on religion and the fact that she focused on Erikson's own commitment to explore the central role that religion plays at the nexus of individual development and social-historical processes, Zock's work is unlikely to be surpassed as a critical introduction to Erikson's contribution to the psychoanalytic study of religion.

However, the very fact that her book provides a chronological reconstruction of Erikson's writings on religion frees the rest of us to limit ourselves to a specific text or basic theme in his writings on religion and to explore that text or theme in somewhat greater detail. By the same token, it also allows us to venture beyond those writings that are clearly recognized as concerned with religion and to see connections or continuities between these and some of the other writings that are not ostensibly concerned with religious subjects or themes. For this chapter, I will try to do both of these things at once, focusing initially on Erikson's major text on religion, *Young Man Luther*, and then venturing beyond this text to make connections between it and his essays on womanhood and the "inner space" (1968, 1975b). Although at first glance there may seem to be little connection between a text on Martin Luther, the sixteenth-century religious reformer, and essays intended to address the situation of contemporary women, I believe that there are deep links between them and that by juxtaposing these texts, we gain significant new insights into Erikson's own understanding of religion. If this project results in exposing the "limits" as well as the "power" of Erikson's vision of religion (see Roazen 1976), I hope that it will also show that the "limits" thereby exposed are quite different from those that have already been ascribed to these texts, that is, by church historians in the case of *Young Man Luther* and by feminist authors in the case of the womanhood and the inner space essays. It goes without saying that any author, however perspicacious, has a "limited" vision and sees the world with blunted sight (cf. Trevor-Roper 1988). This is certainly true of Erikson. But the question that concerns me here is not whether his views on religion are limited but whether we have accurately understood what these limitations are and, mutatis mutandis, whether we have also misperceived the "power" of his vision.

Erikson's Personal and Professional Background

Before I begin discussion of the texts in question, I want to provide a brief account of Erikson's personal and professional life, as this has a direct bearing on my investigations into his texts. He was born on June 15, 1902, near Frankfurt, Germany. In his intellectual biography of Erikson, Robert Coles noted: "Before Erikson was born his parents had separated, and his mother left Denmark for Germany to be near friends. Eventually, with Erik, she stopped to rest at Karlsruhe, where she knew a number of people" (1970:13). The vagueness of this account of Erikson's birth should raise our suspicions, and Erikson's autobiographical account of his birth and infant years is also notable for its imprecision:

> I grew up in Karlsruhe in southern Germany as the son of a pediatrician, Dr. Theodor Homburger, and his wife Karla, née Abrahamsen, a native of Copenhagen, Denmark. All through my earlier childhood, they kept secret from me the fact that my mother had been married previously; and that I was the son of a Dane who had abandoned her before my birth. They apparently thought that such secretiveness was not only workable (because children then were not held to know what they had not been told) but also advisable, so that I would feel thoroughly at home in their home (1975a:27).

What goes unsaid is that his mother conceived him outside of wedlock and that his mother's husband, from whom she became separated prior to Erik's birth, was not his birth father. Erikson's *New York Times* obituary explained: "The cover story was that his mother and father had separated before his birth, but the closely guarded fact was that he was his mother's child from an extramarital union. He never saw his birth father or his mother's first husband" (May 13, 1994).

My purpose in drawing attention to the circumstances of Erikson's conception is not to make a moral point but to set the context for my exploration into the texts that I will focus upon in this chapter. In his autobiographical essay, Erikson noted that he "played in with" his parents' subterfuge "and more or less forgot the period before the age of three, when mother and I had lived alone" (1975a:27). He added that his "sense of being 'different' took refuge (as it is apt to do even in children without such acute life problems) in fantasies of how I, the son of much better parents, had been altogether a foundling" (p. 27). Then, lest there be any misunderstanding, he assured his reader that "my adoptive father was anything but the proverbial stepfather. He had given me his last name (which I have retained as a middle name) and expected me to become a doctor like himself" (p. 27). Reared as Erik Homburger, he changed his surname to Erikson shortly after immigrating to the United States in 1933.

Erikson's birth father was a Danish Gentile, and his mother was Jewish, as was his stepfather. He used the word *identity*, unquestionably his most famous contribution to the psychoanalytic (and even popular psychology) lexicon, to describe the dilemma that his mixed ethnic background created for him as an adolescent:

> Identity problems sharpen with that turn in puberty when images of future roles become inescapable. My stepfather was the only professional man (and a highly respected one) in an intensely Jewish small bourgeois family, while I (coming from a racially mixed Scandinavian background) was blond and blue-eyed, and grew flagrantly tall. Before long, then, I was referred to as "goy" in my stepfather's temple; while to my schoolmates I was a "Jew." Although during World War I, I tried desperately to be a good German chauvinist, I became a "Dane" when Denmark remained neutral (Erikson 1975a:27–28).

The fact that he was reared in an Orthodox Jewish family context accounts, in part, for his lifelong interest in ritual, as reflected in his early studies of Native American rituals in *Childhood and Society*, in his essay on the ontogeny of ritualization (1987), in his Godkin lectures published under the title *Toys and Reasons: Stages in the Ritualization of Experience* (1977), and in his last published essay on religion, "The Galilean Sayings and the Sense of 'I'" (1981). Though not disagreeing in principle with Freud's insight that obsessive-compulsive behavior has a remarkable similarity to religious rituals (Freud 1963a), Erikson also noted a major dissimilarity between them—the meanings of obsessive-compulsive behavior are private, whereas the meanings of religious rituals are communally shared and understood. The fact that religious rituals reflect a shared worldview led him to study how they manifest group tensions, compromises, and aspirations and also how they reenact the ritual engagements of mother and infant as the two of them "mutually activate" one another in the early months of the child's life. In his later writings, especially *Toys and Reasons*, he wondered whether his own celebrated life cycle theory was itself a sort of ritual construct designed to offer "ceremonial reassurances" that the individual life has a formfulness about it and is not therefore a random and chaotic thing. In "The Galilean Sayings and the Sense of 'I,'" he identified the three major ritual forms in first-century Judaism: those of the temple centered around the great yearly holidays of national renewal; those of the synagogue, reflecting textual preoccupation with the wording of Scriptures and demonstrations of righteous behavior; and the ritualization in everyday life, focused around rituals of the table presided over by the Jewish mother, "a most down-to-earth goddess of the hearth" (Erikson 1981:340). He suggested that Jesus focused on the latter as he flaunted traditional dietary laws and the established rules of table fellowship.

But if Erikson's early years in the Homburger household disposed him toward a lifelong interest in ritual, his later adolescence and early adulthood reawakened an interest in the visual arts. He noted in his autobiographical essay that during the years he and his mother lived alone, "her friends had been artists working in the folk style of Hans Thoma of the Black Forest. They, I believe, provided my first male imprinting before I had to come to terms with that intruder, the bearded doctor, with his healing love and mysterious instruments. Later, I enjoyed going back and forth between the painters' studios and our house, the first floor of which, in the afternoons, was filled with tense and trusting mothers and children" (Erikson 1975a:27). Electing not to attend university after completing gymnasium, he embarked on the life of a "wandering artist" and acknowledged that in choosing the occupational identity of "artist," he was choosing more "a way of life" than a specific occupation, a way of life that was ostensibly "anti-establishment," though one, ironically, that the establishment had created for youths with "idiosyncratic needs" (p. 25). However, at the time, he was only aware of his "intense alienation" from everything his "bourgeois family stood for." For several years, he wandered the forests, attended art schools in his home town of Karlsruhe and in Munich, worked on drawings, etchings, and woodcuts, and eventually came to reside in Florence, where he gave up sketching altogether and simply wandered through the streets and over the hills, "trying to come to grips with himself" (Coles 1970:5).

In 1927, having returned to his hometown of Karlsruhe, ostensibly for good, he was invited by his childhood friend Peter Blos to go to Vienna to assist him in a school that had been founded by Dorothy Burlingham, an American who had gone to Vienna to be psychoanalyzed. It was a school for American and English children, many of whom, along with their parents, were in analysis. Thus began Erikson's sudden and most unexpected introduction to Freud's circle. As he continued his work as a teacher, he was befriended by Freud's daughter Anna, who was deeply interested in the psychoanalysis of children and who in time became Erikson's personal analyst. He recalled having told her that "no matter how much he had learned about himself, psychoanalysis was not for him" and that he intended to return to his work as an artist, to which she replied that psychoanalysis needed people "who can make others see" (Coles 1970:22). Thus, in his late twenties and early thirties, he continued to teach at Dorothy Burlingham's school but also attended seminars in clinical psychoanalysis. He became part of a new generation of psychoanalysts who emphasized the adaptive functions of the ego. Erikson believed that he first heard the term *identity* mentioned in one of its earlier usages at a seminar taught by Paul Federn on the boundaries of the ego (1975a:37).

In 1929, two years after Erikson arrived in Vienna, he met Joan Serson, a young woman of mixed Canadian and American background who had come to Vienna to do research on German dance; while there, she had decided to enter analysis. They were married several months later, and by the time he graduated from the Vienna Psychoanalytic Society in 1933, they had two sons. (Their third child, a daughter, was born in 1938.) For several years, it had been evident that the psychoanalytic institute could not survive both the U.S. depression, which made it more difficult for well-to-do Americans to seek psychoanalysis, and the European economic and political upheavals. So in 1933, the family emigrated to the United States, and Erikson became a child analyst in Boston and also became associated with the Harvard Psychological Clinic.

In 1936, Erikson moved to New Haven to take a position at Yale Medical School, and, while in that post, he carried out the field research at Pine Ridge Reservation in South Dakota that he reported on in *Childhood and Society*. In 1939, he moved to California, where he remained for over a decade, dividing his time between San Francisco, where he worked as a psychiatrist with veterans of World War II, and Berkeley, where he became connected with the Institute of Child Welfare. These proved to be extremely important professional involvements for Erikson because it was in working with war veterans that he came to formulate his basic concepts of identity and identity diffusion, and it was as a member of the research team at Berkeley that he became involved in a longitudinal study of children that not only contributed to his interests in developmental theory but also resulted in the research study that he discussed in the womanhood and the inner space essays. The life cycle theory for which he became famous was formulated in the late 1940s and was presented in his first major book, *Childhood and Society*, in a chapter entitled "The Eight Ages of Man" (Erikson [1950] 1963:247–274). This book catapulted Erikson to instant popularity. Robert Coles wrote of *Childhood and Society* in 1970: "I doubt that any other book by a student of Freud is as well known over the world," and he noted that it is one of a handful of texts that is universally used in psychiatric training centers (1970:118).

Young Man Luther, the text that I will focus on in this chapter, never found such a permanent niche in educational curricula, though it did energize interdisciplinary work in psychology and history or in what came to be called psychohistory. In spite of vigorous attacks in the 1960s and 1970s by historians who condemned it as poor science, this scholarly enterprise has flourished to this day. However, Erikson's own unique and even idiosyncratic manner of working between the boundaries of history and psychoanalysis has given way, for the most part, to efforts to place the enterprise on a more methodologically rigorous foundation. This has meant, among other things, that his tendency to work with three, not just two, disciplines simultaneously—history, psychology, *and religion*—has been replaced by a more modest wedding of psychology and history (see Capps 1978).

From *Childhood and Society* to *Young Man Luther*

Erikson did not originally plan to write a book-length study of Martin Luther. His initial intention was to include a chapter on Luther in what would have been his second book, *Identity and the Life Cycle* (1959), following a procedure he had used effectively in *Childhood and Society*, which includes historical chapters on Adolf Hitler and Maxim Gorky. But as he became involved in research on the Luther chapter, he realized that he could not contain Luther within the space of a single chapter. As he explained in the preface to *Young Man Luther*: "This study of Martin Luther as a young man was planned as a chapter in a book on emotional crises in late adolescence and early adulthood. But Luther proved too bulky a man to be merely a chapter. His young manhood is one of the most radical on record: whatever he became part of, whatever became part of him, was eventually destroyed or rejuvenated. The clinical chapter became a historical book" (Erikson 1958:7). Considering that it was not planned as such, the fact that *Young Man Luther* is his most carefully crafted text is something of an irony. Although *Childhood and Society* drew on several earlier published papers and was expanded when republished in 1963, *Young Man Luther* was written in the interval between the original publication of *Childhood and Society* and 1958. Most of Erikson's later books, including *Identity and the Life Cycle* (1959), *Insight and Responsibility* (1964), *Identity: Youth and Crisis* (1968), and *Life History and the Historical Moment* (1975), are, like *Childhood and Society*, compilations of essays previously published in various journals. Two other books, *Dimensions of a New Identity* (1974) and *Toys and Reasons* (1977), are based on public lectures. His only subsequent work that may be said to be more a book than a collection of essays on related themes is *Gandhi's Truth* (1969), which is modeled after *Young Man Luther*. Yet even *Gandhi's Truth* was preceded by the publication of articles on Gandhi. Thus, *Young Man Luther* stands out in Erikson's corpus as a text that was not prefigured in his earlier writings and that was, uniquely for him, a self-contained text. It has also been acclaimed as the single most important text in the psychology of religion since William James's *Varieties of Religious Experience* (Pruyser 1963).

By focusing on *Young Man Luther*, I recognize that I will not do justice to various topics and themes on religion emphasized in other Erikson texts. However, *Young Man Luther* is a book that, much like a magnet, draws many of these other topics and themes to it, so that even if, for example, Erikson wrote quite extensively about religious rituals prior and subsequent to this work, his basic understanding of ritual may be discerned in *Young Man Luther*, especially in his sympathy toward Luther's impatience with formulaic religion and search for religious forms that more genuinely express the shared anxieties and longings of the human community. Although it focuses on the leader of what has become a denomination within Protestant Christianity, *Young Man Luther* is neither partisan nor parochial. That many who are avid readers of other Erikson texts have been disinclined to read *Young Man Luther* is certainly understandable, given that its subject is a historical figure in whom they may have little interest. Yet what those who *do* read *Young Man Luther* often comment upon is not that it provided valuable new insights into Luther's personality or character but that it taught them how a good clinician approaches the life of a troubled patient, especially one for whom religion is a chief preoccupation. And this, I believe, is how Erikson himself wanted his book to be understood and appropriated. As he commented in the preface, "The clinical chapter became a historical book. But . . . clinical work is integral to its orientation" (Erikson 1958:7). *Young Man Luther* is one of the most impressive psychoanalytic clinical case studies extant, rivaling Freud's own clinical case studies of "Wolf Man," "Rat Man," and "Dr. Schreber" (Freud 1963b), and it is especially valuable as a clinical study of an individual whose psychopathology was both precipitated and ameliorated by religion.

Young Man Luther has been viewed as the catalyst for psychohistorical studies, and this is also what Erikson perceived himself to be about. After all, its subtitle is "A Study in Psychoanalysis and History." As Erikson pointed out in the first chapter, he

> could have avoided those methodological uncertainties and impurities which will undoubtedly occur by sticking to my accustomed job of writing a case history, and leaving the historical event to those who, in turn, would consider the case a mere accessory to the event. But we clinicians have learned in recent years that we cannot lift a case history out of history, even as we suspect that historians, when they try to separate the logic of the historic event from that of the life histories which intersect in it, leave a number of vital historical problems unattended. So we may have to risk that bit of impurity which is inherent in the hyphen of the psycho-historical as well as of all other hyphenated approaches. They are the compost heap of today's interdisciplinary efforts, which may help to fertilize new fields, and to produce future flowers of new methodological clarity (1958:15–16).

But *Young Man Luther* is also valuable for the way it goes about exploring the relations between psychology and religion. The historical context is extremely important, as Erikson explored the convergence of Luther's psychological conflicts with the large-scale social and political events of the day. But equally important is the interrelationship between psychology and religion, and even as the risks of methodological impurity here are just as great, so are the prospects of producing "future flowers of new methodological clarity." In the final analysis, one must take full account of the complex interrelationships of psychology, history, *and* religion, viewing them "configurationally" and not "linearly" (or in terms of one-way causalities) (see Erikson 1982:96–97). But for those of us who identify ourselves as psychologists of religion, there is much to be gained by using *Young Man Luther* to study specifically the relationships between psychology and religion.

Religion as Ideology

In the first chapter of *Young Man Luther*, entitled "The Fit in the Choir," Erikson took four biographical studies of Luther as representative. He noted that those written by theologians tended either to "spiritualize" him (as though everything he did was an act of God for which he was merely an open vessel) or to "demonize" him (as though the same process was involved, only it was Satan and not God who was in control); those studies written by psychiatrists or lay analysts tended to treat Luther as a textbook case of psychopathology, thus neglecting the fact that he was not only a man of extraordinary gifts but also a man who reconfigured the very pathologies that these authors ascribed to him through his personal struggle to a new religious ideology. In his own interpretation of Luther, Erikson explored the complex interrelationships between Luther's religious predispositions and his psychological vulnerabilities (which were major and chronic). He also showed that Luther was not the helpless victim of his pathologies but rather that he used these pathologies in a deeply innovative way toward the construction of a new religious worldview—one that spoke to the needs and aspirations of members of his own generation (or those younger) who were no less endangered psychologically than he was. By viewing this new religious worldview as an ideology, Erikson wanted to avoid arguments for the ultimate truth (or falsity) of Luther's theological views. Instead, he argued that Luther, in his own historical and social location, "presented in his words and in his bearing the image of man in whom men of all walks of life were able to recognize in decisive clarity something that seemed right, something they wanted, they needed to be" (1958:223–224).[1] Thus, his sympathies were with Luther and against the establishment to which Luther tried but failed to conform. But this is not because he had a "Lutheran" bias against "the Catholic Church" but because he sided with religious innovators or "actualists" wherever they may be found, individuals who are trying to breathe new ideological life into old and tired social institutions and cultural forms (see also Erikson 1969:399).

Psychoanalytic Ego Psychology

As a psychoanalyst, Erikson does have some firm commitments on the other side of the psychology-religion equation. At the time he wrote *Young Man Luther,* he personally identified with the "ego psychology" school or movement in psychoanalysis, and this orientation informed his approach to all clinical cases, Luther's included. In his initial chapter in *Childhood and Society,* entitled "Relevance and Relativity in the Case History," he set forth his manner of "seeing" any clinical case in which he was directly (or indirectly) involved, for example, the cases of a young boy who had developed phobic reactions following his grandmother's death and of a combat marine who had been discharged from the armed forces as a "psychoneurotic casualty." In discussing these cases, he suggested that there are essentially three processes to which the clinician needs to be attentive: the *somatic process* (i.e., physiological processes inherent in the organism); the *ego process* (i.e., the individual's own "sense of coherent individuation and identity"); and the *social process* (i.e., family, class, community, and national factors that precipitate, sustain, and alleviate the illness). A human being "is at all times an organism, an ego, and a member of a society and is involved in all three processes of organization. His body is exposed to pain and tension; his ego, to anxiety; and as a member of a society, he is susceptible to the panic emanating from his group" (Erikson [1950] 1963:36). The clinician's task and responsibility is to observe all three processes and to be especially attentive to the ways they influence one another.

Guided by the clinical model set forth in *Childhood and Society,* he explored in *Young Man Luther* the interrelationships between Luther's somatic processes (e.g., his struggles with bodily diseases; his physical changes over the course of his life, especially the fact that his body weight increased considerably from his young adulthood to middle adulthood, resulting in the "bulky" Luther of popular memory; his bouts with constipation and urine retention; and his unusual sensitivities to the organs of hearing and speaking); his ego processes, especially as expressed in his struggle to find his true identity in terms of both his social role as monk turned reformer and, existentially, as a redeemed child of God; and social processes, especially as reflected in fundamental ideological changes that were occurring in sixteenth-century Europe as the medieval worldview that had held sway for several centuries was being challenged and replaced by the new renaissance in political theory, in the arts and sciences, and in views of human nature. Of the last, Erikson suggested that Luther "did the dirty work of the Renaissance, by applying some of the individualistic principles immanent in the Renaissance to the Church's still highly fortified home ground—the conscience of ordinary man" and that he "accepted for his life work the unconquered frontier of tragic conscience" (1958:195). By conscience, Erikson meant that inner ground where we and God have to learn to live with each other as man and wife. Psychologically speaking, it is where the ego meets the superego; that is, where our self can either live in wedded harmony with a positive conscience or is estranged from a negative one. Luther comes nowhere closer to formulating the auditory threat, the voice of wrath, which is internalized in a negative conscience than when he speaks of the "false Christ" as one whom we hear expostulate "*Hoc non fecisti,*" "Again, you have not done what I told you"—a statement of the kind which identifies negatively, and burns itself into the soul as a black and hopeless mark (1958:195).

As Luther saw it, this false Christ "becomes more formidable a tyrant and a judge than was Moses" (p. 195).

Erikson's inclusion of "ego processes" in his clinical model was to become the hallmark of his way of adapting psychoanalysis to the needs of his own era. From the very outset of his career as a psychoanalyst, he identified with the ego psychology movement in psychoanalysis, and by the time *Childhood and Society* was initially published in 1950, he had already written several essays on ego psychology. In his work with U.S. veterans of World War II, he began to describe their difficulties in readjusting to civilian life as "ego identity" problems, mainly because they perceived little continuity between the self that they had been prior to combat service and the self that they had become as a result of their war experience. This led him to focus on the need for a sense of continuity or coherence across the whole lifespan, and his theory of the human life cycle (with its eight psychosocial crises) sets forth the typical impediments that individuals will confront at various junctures in life as they attempt to keep themselves together and maintain a sense of continuity in spite of all the circumstances of life that threaten to undermine it. It is no accident that the process culminates in an "integrity vs. despair" crisis, for "integrity" implies that one has in fact succeeded in maintaining a sense of continuity and sameness through the course of one's life and "despair" signifies that one has failed in this regard and that there is no longer time to alter this tragic fact of one's life. This life cycle construct figures quite prominently in *Young Man Luther* as Erikson used it to inform his assessment of Luther's own struggle to realize "a sense of coherent individuation and identity" ([1950] 1963:36).

Childhood Fears and Adult Anxieties

The chapter in *Childhood and Society* that is most relevant to *Young Man Luther* because it addresses the underlying reasons why this sense of continuity is so problematic and difficult to realize is the concluding chapter, entitled "Beyond Anxiety" (Erikson [1950] 1963:403–424). Here, Erikson focused on what he considered the major impediment to adults' inner sense of personal integration or integrity—the fact that their childhood fears continue to manifest themselves in adulthood, now in the form of inexplicable anxieties. If the child was justified in having fears (after all, the child *was* vulnerable), the adult's anxieties are less explicable, as they are typically experienced even when there is little or no real external threat. If there *is* such a threat, the adult reacts, as did the child, with fear. But almost by definition, anxieties involve a sense of being threatened that has no clear justification and thus no identifiable solution in the external world. The difference between fears and anxieties is that "fears are states of apprehension which focus on isolated and recognizable dangers so that they may be judiciously appraised and realistically countered," whereas "anxieties are diffuse states of tension (caused by a loss of mutual regulation and a consequent upset in libidinal and aggressive controls) which magnify and even cause the illusion of an outer danger, without pointing to appropriate avenues of defense or mastery" (Erikson [1950] 1963: 406–407). To be sure, "these two forms of apprehension obviously often occur together, and we can insist on a strict separation only for the sake of the present argument" (p. 407). Still, there *is* a difference between fear and anxiety, for it is not "the fear of a danger (which we might be well able to meet with judicious action) but the fear of the associated state of aimless anxiety which drives us into irrational *action*, irrational *flight*—or, indeed, irrational *denial* of danger. When threatened with such anxiety we either magnify a danger which we have no reason to fear excessively—or we ignore a danger which we have every reason to fear" (p. 407).

Erikson argued that adult anxieties often have their origins in childhood fears that were never adequately resolved and that therefore left the child with a lasting sense of being under threat. Such childhood fears fuel and exacerbate adult anxieties, and as a result, everyone will carry into adulthood a deep sense of once having been small and vulnerable: "A sense of smallness forms a substratum in his mind, ineradicably. His triumphs will be measured against this smallness, his defeats will substantiate it" (Erikson [1950] 1963:404). He identified the most prominent fears that occur with regularity in childhood, such as the fear of sudden changes, of exposure, of being immobilized, and of being abandoned, but the fear that has greatest relevance to Luther is *the fear of being attacked from the rear*, which Erikson attributed to adult sadism (p.410).

Like other childhood fears, this fear involves a configuration of somatic, ego, and social processes, as the adult's attack on the child's buttocks (somatic) is a threat to the child's personal sense of well-being (ego) and reflects a particular understanding of how children are to become socialized to a particular worldview (social). Regarding the last, Erikson noted that Native Americans expressed bewilderment when they saw Caucasian American parents beating their children and surmised that this was their way of communicating to their offspring that earth is a living hell and of inculcating in their children a desire for the paradise that awaits them after death (1958:69).

He also noted that being struck from behind, the locus of Luther's fears, is forever associated with a guilty conscience, which was the focus of Luther's lifelong anxiety, as exhibited in his struggle with the "false Christ" who verbally condemned him: "You have not done what I told you."

Thus, Erikson's psychoreligious analysis of Luther is prefigured in the final chapter of *Childhood and Society,* where he argued that the neurotic anxieties of adults not only have their roots in childhood but are also the consequence of the fact that *our child self survives into adulthood,* forming an ineradicable substratum in our minds, permanently affecting our way of seeing things. This means that the child self cannot but form a significant part of the adult's "ego," especially in its role as the source of anxieties that are otherwise inexplicable because these have little or nothing to do with current threats to the adult's sense of personal well-being. Especially interesting to Erikson was the role played by a society's ideologies, which are often unexamined and merely taken for granted, in its attitudes toward and treatment of its children. Among psychoanalysts of his era, he was perhaps the most outspoken critic of traditional psychoanalysis's failure to explore the relationships between the psychological and the social. And he was especially interested in the ways that societies influence parents to rear their children so as to prepare them to assume a traditional "image" or "model" of adulthood that has not been subjected to careful examination and whose legitimacy is merely taken for granted. However, in this regard, he did not spare psychoanalysis itself. Although he remained quite loyal to psychoanalytic ego psychology throughout his life, he nevertheless included ego psychology in his general criticism of psychoanalysis, due to its tendency to focus on the "inner world" to the neglect of the "outer world."

In a 1961 address to the American Psychoanalytic Association, published in *Insight and Responsibility* under the title "Psychological Reality and Historical Actuality" (Erikson 1964:161–215), he took psychoanalysis to task for paying so little attention in its theoretical formulations to the role "the outside world" plays in the patient's regaining of psychic health. To be sure, ego psychologists Heinz Hartmann and Hans Leowald had written about "the world of things really existing in the outer world," but even this reference to the human environment as an "outer world" attested "to the fact that the world of that intuitive and active participation which constitutes most of our waking life is still foreign territory to our theory" (Erikson 1964:163). What was needed was a word like *actuality,* connoting "the world of participation" that individuals share with other individuals. In turn, these actualities are codetermined by an individual's stage of development, personal circumstances, and historical and political processes.

Although this essay was written several years after the publication of *Young Man Luther,* it reflects a long-standing concern of Erikson's, one he articulated as early as 1954 in an essay on Freud's method of dream interpretation. What concerned him in this earlier essay was the fact that Freud was so interested in penetrating the unconscious "depths" of a dream that he neglected its more manifest surface, the seemingly obvious or taken for granted external, social, or historical "actualities" that have significant bearing on the dream. So many psychoanalysts "mistake attention to surface for superficiality, and a concern with form for lack of depth," but "like good surveyors, we must be at home on the geological surface as well as in the descending shafts" (Erikson 1987:246). He stopped short of accusing Freud of neglecting the manifest features of the dream for self-serving reasons, but in his assessments of Freud's cases of Irma, Count Thun, and especially Dora, he showed that there were social circumstances in the lives of these patients that Freud's "depth" analyses systematically ignored. For example, Dora was a girl in late adolescence who had accused her parents of having known that a male friend of her father's had been trying to seduce her and done nothing about this, mainly, she suspected, because her father was having an affair with his friend's wife. In Erikson's view, Freud's complaint that Dora was ignoring her own psychic, unconscious depths (i.e., the "fact" that she unconsciously "wanted" to be seduced by her father's friend) neglected the actualities of the case—specifically the fact that Dora was deeply concerned about matters of fidelity and truth, including Freud's own fidelity to her, which she felt was violated by his refusal to support her in her effort to get the truth of the matter out into the open (1964:166–174). In her recent study of the Dora case, Hannah S. Decker quoted Erikson's view that "to call the older generation's infidelities by their name may have been a necessity before she might have been able to commit herself to her own kind of fidelity"; she added, "Dora's adult life was to prove him right" (1991:113).

Erikson's concern to hold "psychological reality" and "social actuality" in tension, not permitting them to be viewed separately from one another, played a very prominent role in *Young Man Luther* as he worked throughout the book to discern continuities between Luther's psychic life (i.e., the neurotic anxieties that loomed so large in his struggles with the contents of his own mind) and the social world in which he was an active participant. One question this posed for Erikson was whether Luther could have been a better, more effective leader, especially in his middle to late adulthood, if he had not become so bedeviled by his anxious thoughts, which reflected the continuing power of the fearful child that would not be eradicated. Erikson believed that Luther's fixation on these childhood fears "absorbed energy which otherwise might have helped the old Luther to reaffirm with continued creativity the ideological gains of his youth; and if this energy had been available to him, he might have played a more constructive role in the mastery of his passions, as well of the compulsions, which he had evoked in others" (1958:249).

In short, Erikson was a psychoanalytic ego psychologist, but he wanted to take the ego's "environment" more seriously than his predecessors had done.

Furthermore, he recognized that religion is a very significant feature of that environment, especially as an ideology that underwrites certain child-rearing practices, which in turn result in the creation of childhood fears that continue to manifest themselves in adult anxieties. In a paradoxical sort of way, religion produces fears that result in the anxieties that religion then seeks either to eliminate or assuage.

The Boyhood Beatings of Martin Luther

What, in Erikson's view, was the actual basis for Luther's childhood fears? What was their primary source? In his chapter in *Young Man Luther* entitled "Obedience—To Whom?" Erikson discussed at length the fact that Luther was severely beaten by his father, his mother, and his teachers. In emphasizing that Luther was beaten as a child, he anticipated the objection that Luther's experiences could not have been unique in this regard, for child beating was a very common, perhaps universal, practice. Against the views of one of Luther's biographers, Erikson argued that "the professor's statistical approach to a given effect—the assertion that the cause was too common to have an uncommon effect on one individual—is neither clinically nor biographically valid. We must try to ascertain the relationship of caner and caned, and see if a unique element may have given the common event a specific meaning" (1958:64). What mattered most both clinically and biographically was the effect of the beatings on the relationship involved. That the "caner" was father, or mother, or teacher and that the caned was "little Martin" and not one of the other Luther children made an important difference. Erikson noted that the clinician needs a "framework" within which to evaluate the beatings inflicted on "little Martin," and this framework includes, among other things, a very careful listening to what the individual sufferer has to say about the beatings that he endured as a child:

> Many authorities on Luther, making no attempt at psychological thinking, judge this matter of punishment either to be of no importance, or on the contrary, to have made an emotional cripple of Martin. It seems best, however, to outline a framework within which we may try to evaluate these data. In my profession one learns to listen to exactly what people are saying; and Luther's utterances, even when they are reported secondhand, are often surprises in naive clarification (1958:64).

Erikson first took up the fact that some of the beatings were inflicted by Luther's father. What interested him here was Luther's later observation that once when his father beat him, "I fled him and I became sadly resentful toward him, until he gradually got me accustomed (or habituated) to him again" (Erikson 1958:64). Erikson suggested that the "meaning" the beating had for Luther was that even when he was mortally afraid of his father, he could not really hate him but could only feel sadness. Conversely, though his father could not let the boy come close and was murderously angry at times, he could not let him go for long: "They had a mutual and deep investment in each other which neither of them could or would abandon, although neither of them was able to bring it to any kind of fruition" (p. 65). Erikson saw Martin as the child who had been selected to justify his father, and thus a great premium was placed on what Martin was—or was not—accomplishing and what he had—or had not—done for his father.

There were also the beatings inflicted by Luther's mother. Erikson focused here on Luther's account of the time that his mother beat him "until the blood flowed" over his theft of a single nut. Luther had told this story to illustrate the importance in parent-child relations of ensuring that the punishment truly fits the offense. Erikson believed that Luther's father was the predominant parent in Luther's life, guarding the father-son relationship so jealously "that the mother was eclipsed far more than can be accounted for by the mere pattern of German housewifeliness." However, the fact that Luther's mother also severely beat him must not, Erikson cautioned, be ignored. Does this mean that she failed to stand between the father and the son to whom she had given birth? Was she acting as his father's agent when she beat him, or was she acting on her own initiative? To get at the "meaning" of her beatings of Martin, Erikson related them to Luther's comment that his mother bore and lost many of her children (who "cried themselves to death") and that she attributed their deaths to having been "bewitched" by a neighbor woman. Erikson admitted that he did not know what to make of this, largely because he did not know what Luther himself made of it. But he noted that biographers have surmised that Luther's mother suffered under his father's personality and gradually became embittered and that the sad isolation that characterized young Martin was also characteristic of his mother. Given the lack of evidence in support of these biographers' surmises, Erikson wrote that

> A big gap exists here, which only conjecture could fill. But instead of conjecturing half-heartedly, I will state, as a clinician's judgment, that nobody could speak and sing as Luther later did if his mother's voice had not sung to him of some heaven; that nobody could be as torn between his masculine and his feminine sides, nor have such a range of both, who did not at one time feel that he was like his mother; but also, that nobody would discuss women and marriage in the way he often did who had not been deeply disappointed by his mother— and had become loath to succumb the way she did to the father, to fate (1958:72–73).

I will return later to this exercise of Erikson's "clinician's judgment," as I believe it was formed by his own experiences as a boy—that he, too, had shared his mother's deep sense of personal isolation, had also identified her as the source of his own giftedness, and yet, by the same token, had been "deeply disappointed by his mother."

Then there were the beatings inflicted by Luther's schoolteachers. At age seven, Luther was sent to Latin school, where

> halfway-qualified teachers were available to schools like these only when they could get no other work—while they were still young, or when they were no longer employable. In either case they were apt to express their impatience with life in their treatment of the children, which was very similar to the treatment that the town miller's men gave their donkeys. The teachers rarely relied, and therefore could not rely, on conscience, ego, or cognition; instead they used the old and universal method of *Pauken*, "drumming" facts and habits into the growing minds by relentless mechanical repetition. They also drummed the children themselves *mit Ruten in die Aefftern*, on the behind, other body parts being exempt (Erikson 1958:78).

Erikson noted that Luther's biographers radically differ on the long-term effects of these beatings by the teachers, depending on whether they consider the adult Luther to have been seriously neurotic. One suggested that a "lusty caning" did not harm Martin any more than it did the other children. However, others made "the most of Luther's statement, made in middle age, that the hell of school years can make a child fearful for life" (Erikson 1958:78). Erikson believed that an adult's assertion that "I was beaten, but it didn't do any permanent damage" only indicates that speaker's capacity to make the best of what cannot be undone; "whether or not it did them any harm is another question, to answer which may call for more information about the role they have come to play in adult human affairs" (pp. 68–69). In Luther's case, what Erikson found significant was the fact that the boys at Latin school were beaten for speaking German, for swearing, or for speaking impulsively or out of turn. Beatings were therefore associated with an injunction against "verbal freedom" (p. 79).

In light of these injunctions against "verbal freedom," Erikson's decision to introduce Luther to his readers by recounting the story of Luther's "fit in the choir" is quite significant. This episode reportedly occurred when Luther was training to become a monk. The Scripture text read in the monastery chapel that day was Mark 9:17–29, the story of the man who brought his son to Jesus because he had a "dumb spirit." When he heard the story, Luther is reported to have roared like a bull, "It isn't me!" Of course, the very fact that he denied identity with the son who could not speak by speaking out himself and disrupting the mass confirmed, paradoxically, his identity with the son in the biblical story. But the feature of the story that especially interested Erikson was that "verbal freedom" was precisely what was at issue for young Luther. Would he ever find a way truly to speak his mind, and if he ever did, how might he assure himself that his words were divinely sanctioned?

In his chapter entitled "The Meaning of 'Meaning It,'" which focuses on Luther's emergence as a religious reformer, Erikson contended that Luther found a way to speak—truly—by engaging first in intense prayer, stimulated by his personal identification with the biblical psalms that expressed the trustworthiness of God. He suggested that Luther's praying was introspective (a focused process of self-observation), and he compared it to Freud's use of introspection in the psychoanalytic hour. For a few brief years, Luther spoke as a man whose voice was free, who said what he meant and meant what he said. But then his childhood fears returned, taking the form of neurotic anxieties, and the last two decades of his life (until his death at age sixty-three) were ones of considerable torment, of battling various psychosomatic illnesses, and of having it out with deep and chronic melancholic moods. He was a man beset with neurotic anxieties, phobic and paranoid. Erikson explored this last period of Luther's life in his chapter entitled "Faith and Wrath."

Luther's symptoms were not unique in his times, and his gift of language enabled him to embellish them with a melodramatic and even histrionic flair. Nonetheless, Erikson sought to discern beneath all the rhetorical bombast what meaning these symptoms had for Luther. What impressed him in this regard were two features of Luther's symptomatology. The first was that Luther talked frequently and freely about matters best described as "anal." He often spoke of his buttocks, of his problems with constipation and urine retention, of his "diets" (which included gorging himself so that he might force the eliminative process to work), and of his farts and feces, and he once described himself as a "ripe turd" about to cut itself loose from the world, that "gigantic asshole." The second feature was that Luther was very much given to explosively uncouth invectives hurled at his enemies and at the devil himself (whose "face" was Luther's "ass"). Though such verbal expletives might be explained as the "manic" aspect of Luther's manic-depressive disorder, the actual form they took is religiously significant, for it was as though the only way he *could* continue to pray and thus sustain his trust in God was to allow himself to give voice as well to all this invective and cursing. The fact that he suffered in later life with a chronic middle-ear infection was also significant because the resultant constant buzzing in his ears "became the mediator between his physical and his mental torments, the weapon of his inner voice" (Erikson 1958:244).[2]

Luther's obsessive preoccupation with his backside and the endless vocal competition between divine supplication and demonic invective revealed, in Erikson's judgment, "the active remnants of his childhood repressions" (1958:245). There are obvious somatic symptoms here, as well as social circumstances owing to Luther's controversial public position, for, after all, he *did* have many powerful enemies. But Erikson took special interest in the ego processes involved—a man's desperate struggle to hold himself together, to maintain a sense of continuity and sameness in spite of enormous internal pressures toward losing the sense of identity he achieved as an articulate young reformer who had truthfully meant what he said and fearlessly said what he meant. Childhood fears that were held at bay throughout his career as a revolutionary force for change had returned with a vengeance, fueling severely neurotic anxieties and threatening his ego identity to its core.

This middle-age Luther interested Erikson as much as young man Luther. At the very least, the middle-age Luther enabled him to view Luther as a tragic figure, a man who, for reasons that were at least in part beyond his control, discovered that the personal solutions that had worked so well in his young adulthood were failing him now. These solutions, discussed in detail in the chapter on "The Meaning of 'Meaning It,'" had essentially involved a new understanding of Christ, one that entailed no longer seeing Christ as "an ideal figure to be imitated, or abjectly venerated, or ceremonially re-membered as an event in the past [but as] today, here, in me, [as] what works in us [and hence] the core of the Christian's identity" (Erikson 1958:212). "For a little while," said Erikson, "Luther, this first revolutionary individu-alist, saved the Savior from the tiaras and the ceremonies, the hierarchies and the thought-police, and put him back where he arose: in each man's soul" (p. 213). In this reinterpretation of Christ, Luther addressed his problems of *ego identity*. For Luther, Christ was now recognized as the one who both vouchsafed and vouched for his essential identity. As Erikson put it, "The artist closest to Luther in spirit was Dürer, who etched his own face into Christ's countenance" (p. 213).

However, in his subsequent chapter on "Faith and Wrath," Erikson fo-cused on how Luther was no longer so confident that Christ was indeed "today, here, in me," that Christ was in fact "working in him," that Christ was indeed "the core of his identity." As his childhood fears returned, so did his original—and false—view of Christ as tyrant and judge, as provocateur of a guilty conscience, as once again making this accusation against him: "Again, you have not done what I told you." And indeed, Luther's support for the German princes against the peasant revolt that his own earlier revolu-tionary actions had helped to release gave considerable cause for such a guilty conscience and for the profound anxieties he experienced as a man whose Christ had turned against him. Thus, concomitant with his guilty conscience was a deep and pervasive sense of self-pity, itself reflecting an anxiety that Erikson, in *Childhood and Society*, traced back to childhood fears of being left empty or, more simply, of being left, abandoned ([1950] 1963:410–411).

The Child in the Midst Is Your Self

So what was Luther to do? To lose his Christ was to lose his sense of having an identity, for he had staked everything that he was or hoped to become on the assurance that Christ was and ever would be the guarantor of his identity and without whom he was absolutely, abjectly nothing. In the epilogue to *Young Man Luther,* Erikson implied that Luther turned the tables on his anxieties and doubts by the same method of introspection with which he had secured his ego identity back in his young adulthood. But this time, the insight his self-observation yielded was that for a man of heightened religious sensibilities, the issue of ego identity—the ability to experience one's sense of self as having continuity and sameness over time—is an inevitably chronic problem, one that can never be resolved once and for all in a lifetime. As Erikson put it, "the integrity crisis" that comes last in the lives of ordinary persons is "a life-long and chronic crisis in a *homo religiosus*" (1958:161). So, on the one hand, the *homo religiosus* is one who "can permit himself to face as permanent the trust problem which drives others in whom it remains or becomes dominant into denial, despair, and psychosis" (p. 262); on the other hand, the *homo religiosus* is "always older, or in early years suddenly becomes older, than his playmates or even his parents and teachers and focuses in a precocious way on what it takes others a lifetime to gain a mere inkling of: the questions of how to escape corruption in living and how in death to give meaning to life" (p. 261). Hence, *homo religiosus* experiences *discontinuity* as the deepest reality of all because he is an "adult" in his childhood years and very much a "child" in his adult years.[3]

As *homo religiosus,* Luther must have realized that he could not but be an endangered self, that he could never take for granted his claim on his ego identity, his desire to have an intact, invulnerable, inviolable sense of self. Yet it was precisely his acceptance, in his later years, of his profound vulnerability to discontinuity, dissociation, and fragmentation that became, as it were, his real meaning to himself and to others so afflicted. Or to put it somewhat more clinically, the one anxiety to which Luther was chronically subject was the anxiety of losing himself. And yet, in this very regard, his childhood fears were, ironically enough, rather supportive, for even in his most desperate moments, their survival in the unconscious substratum of his mind was living proof that he was somehow continuous with the young boy whose father could not let him go for long and whose mother sang to him of some sure heaven.

This does not mean that the abuses he suffered as a child may be excused or pardoned, for, as Erikson noted, "the most deadly of all possible sins is the mutilation of a child's spirit, for such mutilation undercuts the life principle of trust" (1958:70). But it does mean that through the very *survival* of our childhood fears, we recover whatever "continuity and sameness" we may confidently affirm as our own. The felt "smallness" that is an ineradicable substratum of our adult minds may be the only assurance we have (or need?) that we have not and cannot entirely lose our fundamental identity. Strangely enough, the fearful child becomes the ineradicable core of this very identity.

Alluding in the epilogue to Jesus' invitation to a child to stand in the midst of his disciples (Matt. 18:1–4), Erikson concluded that what Luther and Freud did, each in his own way, was to place the child at the very center of adult life. Thus:

> In this book, I have described how Luther, once a sorely frightened child, recovered through the study of Christ's Passion the central meaning of the Nativity; and I have indicated in what way Freud's method of introspection brought human conflict under a potentially more secure control by revealing the boundness of man in the loves and rages of his childhood. Thus both Luther and Freud came to acknowledge that "the child is in the midst." Both men perfected introspective techniques permitting isolated man to recognize his individual patienthood (Erikson 1958:253).

Although Erikson celebrated the "healthy" young man Luther, he had profound sympathy for the older Luther, that is, the Luther who understood himself all too well ever to imagine that he could shake off his patienthood no matter how long he lived or how hard he tried, for how could he eradicate the *fearful child* who was deeply imprinted in the recesses of his mind? Nor, Erikson seemed to say, should he want to. Thus, the logic of Erikson's psychoanalysis of old man Luther points beyond Christ, Luther's savior in his young adulthood, to Luther's own child-self as savior, as that that "works inside" him and becomes the core of his identity.

To say this is, of course, to accept that there were limits to Luther's own self-observations, for he never consciously made this transfer from the saving Christ to the saving child who was the core of his identity as *homo religiosus*. But the biblical story to which Erikson alluded is clear on this very point: Jesus does not bid his disciples to attend to him but rather to the child—the child who is their very own self. If we agree with William James that our beliefs are reflected in what we choose to attend to (1950, vol. 2:295), then it follows that Jesus means for his disciples to believe in the child self who is the sole guarantor of their sense of continuity as they undergo the inevitable disintegrative effects of aging. Erikson indirectly supported this conclusion when he described, in the epilogue, the "three objects [that] awaken dim nostalgias" in the adult self. One is the simple and fervent wish for a hallucinatory sense of unity with the maternal matrix; another centers on the paternal voice of guiding conscience; and the third, the most primordial of all, concerns "the pure self itself, the unborn core of creation, the—as it were, pre-parental—center where God is pure nothing: *ein lauter Nichts*, in the words of Angelus Silesius" (Erikson 1958:264). If this "pure self" is the core of one's ego identity, access to this pure self occurs when we admit our childhood fears into our adult consciousness. When these fears are not raised to consciousness, they continue to manifest themselves in adult anxieties, which, in turn, jeopardize "the pure self itself."

Adult Anxieties and Social Panic

I am quite aware that one cannot do justice to Erikson's *Young Man Luther* in the course of a single chapter. The attempt to capture in a few pages the core meanings of a text so rich and nuanced, so clinically astute and yet so poetically allusive will inevitably fall far short of a reading of the text itself. Yet one service that such an interpretive essay may provide is to highlight certain issues or themes that otherwise may lie embedded, even obscured, by the sheer bulk of the original text. I have focused here on the matter of childhood fears and adult anxieties in part because this is a major theme of *Young Man Luther* but also because it plays a central role in the psychology of religion. One reason that James's *Varieties of Religious Experience* (1982) and Erikson's *Young Man Luther* have established themselves as "classic" texts in the psychology of religion is that both focus on the issue of fear. James cast his lot with the mind-curers of his day because for them, fear was the central religious issue. As he stated in *Varieties*: "Whereas Christian theology has always considered *forwardness* [or willfulness] to be the essential vice of this part of human nature, the mind-curers say that the mark of the beast in it is *fear*; and this is what gives such an entirely new religious turn to their persuasion" (James 1982:98). He recounted his own experience of the worst form of "panic fear," an episode in his mid-twenties in which he suddenly felt as though he were losing his mind, and he concluded that he had always felt that this experience had a "religious bearing" in that "the fear was so invasive and powerful that if I had not clung to scripture-texts like 'The eternal God is my refuge,' etc., 'Come unto me, all ye that labor and are heavy-laden,' etc., 'I am the resurrection and the life,' etc., I think I should have grown really insane" (pp. 159–161).

In turn, Erikson used James's *Varieties* to support his case that behind the "willfulness" of a child lies a deeper, more primordial will—the will to live, the struggle to have and to be a self, a will generated by the child's "sense" that our grip on life is ever so tenuous and that our chance to be a self in the earliest years of life depends on the succor and goodwill of our adult caretakers (1958:120–122). Thus, though the beating of children is ostensibly designed to curb or break the child's willfulness, to make the child *want* to be obedient, its effect is to heighten the child's fears for its ultimate existence and to provoke the child to ever more desperate acts of will, ones that reach down to and activate the child's innate intention to survive at whatever cost to self and others.

Erikson's *Young Man Luther* suggests that religion may come down on one side or the other. It may see itself in the role of making the child obedient by curbing, curtailing, or even attempting to break the child's will until conscience forms. Or it may envision itself as the assuager of the child's fears, so that the child may grow into an adult who is not overwhelmed by debilitating anxieties. When *Young Man Luther* is read as the sequel to *Childhood and Society* and especially as continuous with its final chapter, "Beyond Anxiety," it challenges adults to recognize that assuaging children's fears is far more important for their future well-being than controlling their errant wills. Against those adults who believe that failing to curb the will of the child will result in future disasters, Erikson knew that the greater danger is that childhood fears will foster adult anxieties that, aided by unscrupulous political leaders, may coalesce in widespread group panic, as happened twice in the land of his birth within his own lifetime.

This brings us in turn to the final issue with which this exploration of *Young Man Luther* is concerned, namely, why Erikson decided to write a book in the mid-1950s on Martin Luther. Of course, we have his wry comment that he did not intend to write a *book* about Luther but that Luther proved too "bulky" a subject for a book chapter. But this does not explain why he wanted to write about Luther in the first place. In his preface to *Young Man Luther,* he tried to explain his decision to write this book in a few brief paragraphs concerning his desire to take "account of recent thinking about the ego's adaptive as well as its defensive functions." He noted that his study of Luther would enable him to "concentrate on the powers of recovery inherent in the young ego" (Erikson 1958:8). If a deeply troubled youth like Luther could be salvaged, so, Erikson believed, might equally endangered contemporary youths. But then he acknowledged that he doubted whether "the impetus for writing anything but a textbook can ever be rationalized" and noted that his choice of subject forced him to deal with problems of faith and of Germany—"two enigmas which I could have avoided by writing about some other young great man. But it seems that I did not wish to avoid them" (p. 9).

This suggests that he had deeply rooted reasons for writing *Young Man Luther*, a point to which I will return in discussing his essays on womanhood and inner space. At the same time, his own argument in behalf of the "more manifest surface" invites us, especially in light of the theme of this chapter, to consider his 1951 resignation as a professor of psychiatry at the University of California and to see this experience as a powerful catalyst for writing *Young Man Luther*. Though *Childhood and Society* was still in press at that time, Erikson became involved in a political struggle between the faculty and the board of regents. The board had established a new requirement that every faculty member sign a special loyalty oath and a declaration that he or she was not a member of the Communist Party and did not support any party or organization that advocated the violent overthrow of the U.S. government. Erikson refused to sign the oath and instead resigned in protest. In his written statement explaining his decision, he emphasized that he was not a Communist and that his refusal to sign was based on other reasons. Like all other employees of the university, he had already signed a constitutional oath that admirably and fully covered his obligations to country, state, and job. He greatly resented being asked to "affirm that I meant what I said when I signed the constitutional oath," adding, "To me, this contract is an empty gesture" (Erikson 1987:619).

Then why did he not sign it? Why did he not acquiesce in an empty gesture if it "save[d] the faces of very important personages, help[ed] to allay public hysteria, and [hurt] nobody?" His response was "that of a psychologist. I do believe that this gesture which now saves face for some important people will, in the long run, hurt people who are much more important: the students" (Erikson 1987:619). For many students, then and now, their years of study represent their only contact with adults who teach them how to see two sides of a question and yet to be decisive in their conclusions, "how to understand and yet act with conviction" (p. 619). Older people may shrug off these empty gestures, but when younger persons who put their trust in these older adults see what is going on, a "dangerous rift" may well occur between the "official truth" and "those deep and often radical doubts which are the necessary condition for the development of thought" (p. 619). Moreover, this empty gesture played into the social panic pervasive in the country. If not the professors, Erikson asked, "who will represent, in quiet work and in forceful words, the absolute necessity of meeting the future (now full of worse than dynamite) with a conviction born of judiciousness? If the universities themselves become the puppets of public hysteria, if their own regents are expressly suspicious of their faculties, if the professors themselves tacitly admit that they need to deny perjury, year after year—will that allay public hysteria?" (p. 620).

Being a psychologist, Erikson studied "hysteria," private and public, in personality and in culture and also "the tremendous waste in human energy which proceeds from irrational fear and from the irrational gestures which are part of what we call 'history'" (1987:620). How then could he ask his students to work with him "if I were to participate without protest in a vague, fearful, and somewhat vindictive gesture devised to ban an evil in some magic way—an evil which must be met with much more searching and concerted effort" (p. 620). He concluded: "I may say that my conscience did not permit me to sign the contract after having sworn that I would do my job to the best of my ability" (p. 620).

Seven years intervened between his resignation and the publication of *Young Man Luther*, the writing of which took up at least four of these intervening years. In my judgment, his resignation had considerable influence on his decision to write about Luther. Such an influence is most evident in the chapter entitled "The Meaning of 'Meaning It,'" which focuses on the period in Luther's life that culminated in his famous refusal to recant his writings before the Diet of Worms ("Here I stand, I can do not other") as one in which Luther was "affectively and intellectually alive." During this period of his life, Luther "made the verbal work of his whole profession more genuine in the face of a tradition of scholastic virtuosity. His style indicates his conviction that a thing said less elegantly and meant more truly is better work, and better craftsmanship in communication" (Erikson 1958:220). Erikson concluded: "Man never lives entirely in his time, even though he can never live outside it; sometimes his identity gets along with his time's ideology, and sometimes it has to fight for its life" (p. 221).

I believe that Erikson saw in Luther a kindred soul and that his personal identification with the adult Luther was especially strong as he considered the costs of his own decision to take a personal stand and refuse to say what he did not and could not mean. That the issue was whether he would participate in the exploitation of a society's susceptibility to panic made it all the more imperative that he represent his profession with all the personal integrity that he could summon from his own struggle with the first of what he called the two major religious questions in life: how to escape corruption in living and how in death to give meaning to life (Erikson 1958:261).

From *Young Man Luther* to "Womanhood and the Inner Space"

In the epilogue of *Young Man Luther,* Erikson offered a defense of what he had written and made his first reference to "the inner space," which he contrasted with "outer space":

> I have implied that the original faith which Luther tried to restore goes back to the basic trust of early infancy. In doing so, I have not, I believe, diminished the wonder of what Luther calls God's disguise. If I assume that it is the smiling face and the guiding voice of infantile parent images which religion projects onto the benevolent sky, I have no apologies to render to an age which thinks of painting the moon red. *Peace comes from the inner space* (1958:265–266, emphasis added).

Exactly ten years later, he published his essay entitled "Womanhood and the Inner Space" (Erikson 1968:261–294). Because this essay engendered much controversy and criticism, he wrote a second essay entitled "Once More the Inner Space" (Erikson 1975b:225–247). I view these two essays as writings on religion, inviting connections between them and *Young Man Luther.*

If Erikson was ill prepared for the controversy that followed the publication of *Young Man Luther,* he seemed even more startled by the negative responses to his first essay on womanhood, for women had been among his most enthusiastic readers and most stalwart supporters, in part because his writings and personal demeanor reflected an identification with women that was patently missing in the writings of other male psychoanalysts. The negative response, led by Kate Millett's quite devastating critique (1969), had a kind of domino effect, leading to feminist critiques of his life cycle theory as male biased (Gilligan 1982; but see Capps 1993:134–136) and to objections to his portrayal of the American "Mom" in his essay on "Reflections on the American Identity" (Erikson [1950] 1963:285–325). His efforts to dissociate himself from Freud's views on women, as in his critique of Freud's treatment of Dora, were overwhelmed by this wave of negative response, and even to this day, there is a prevailing reluctance to reconsider his essays on womanhood in light of changes in feminist ideology. In contemporary literature on women's issues, his first essay is usually summarized (and rejected) with a brief, cryptic sentence, and the second essay is completely ignored.

I suggest that the earlier controversy may be fruitfully recontextualized by viewing the two essays as contributions to the psychology of religion and thus as extensions of the same approach to psychology and religion that Erikson developed in *Young Man Luther*. In the original "womanhood" essay, Erikson indicated that he was very much aware of embarking on a subject that "always retains an intense actuality" both for himself, the author, and for the reader (1968:265). Invoking the Vermont farmer's response to a driver who asked him for directions—"Well, now, if I wanted to go where you want to go, I wouldn't start from here"—he acknowledged that his professional identity as a psychoanalyst was a liability, for he decidedly did *not* want to begin his analysis of womanhood with Freud's own theories of penis envy and the like. But he suggested that this identity might also be a strength, as psychoanalysis always alerts us to the danger that new insights into matters of identity may produce new repressions.

The essay centers on Erikson's own contribution in the 1940s to the large research study conducted by the Institute of Child Welfare at Berkeley. Over a two-year span, he saw 150 boys and 150 girls three times each, presenting them each time with the task of using toys to construct an "exciting scene" from an imaginary movie and then verbalizing the "plot" of the story. Gender differences were not the initial focus of his interest, but as the study progressed, he

> soon realized that in evaluating a child's play construction, I had to take into consideration the fact that girls and boys used space differently, and that certain configurations occurred strikingly often in the constructions of one sex and rarely in those of the other. The differences themselves were so simple that at first they seemed a matter of course. History in the meantime has offered a slogan for it: the girls emphasized *inner* and the boys *outer* space (Erikson 1968:270, emphasis in original).

This, at least, was true for two-thirds of the girls and two-thirds of the boys. A typical girl's scene was depicted:

> [It] is a house *interior*, represented either as a configuration of furniture without any surrounding walls or by a simple *enclosure* built with blocks. In the girl's

scene, people and animals are mostly *within* such an interior or enclosure, and they are primarily people or animals in a *static* (sitting or standing) position. Girls' enclosures consist of low walls, i.e. only one block high, except for an occasional *elaborate doorway*. These interiors of houses with or without walls were, for the most part, expressly *peaceful*. Often, a little girl was playing the piano. In a number of cases, however, the interior was *intruded* by animals or dangerous men. Yet the idea of an intruding creature did not necessarily lead to the defensive erection of walls or the closing of doors. Rather the majority of these intrusions have an element of humor and pleasurable excitement (Erikson 1968:270–271, emphasis in original).

After describing the boys' typical scenes (high towers that collapse, people and animals *outside* enclosures, elaborate automotive accidents, etc.), Erikson indicated that various interpretations have been offered for these differences in play constructions, some based on psychoanalytic psychosocial theory, others based on social role theory. However, he argued for "an altogether more inclusive interpretation, according to which a profound difference exists between the sexes in the experience of the ground plan of the human body" (Erikson 1968:273). Unlike men, women have "a productive interior" that not only affords "a sense of vital inner potential" but also "exposes women early to a specific sense of loneliness, to a fear of being left empty or deprived of treasure, or remaining unfulfilled and of drying up" (p. 277). This theme of "emptiness," reminiscent of the "Beyond Anxiety" chapter of *Childhood and Society* (Erikson [1950] 1963:410–411), is especially associated with women because "emptiness is the female form of perdition—known at times to men of the inner life . . . but standard experience for all women" (Erikson 1968:278). He found support for his view of women being identified with "inner space" and men with "exterior" or "outer space" in a motion picture produced in Africa—"visual data" he called it—showing that in a wandering troop of baboons, the males protectively surrounded the females. He was especially impressed that the body structure, posture, and behavior of the males and females fit into "an ecology of divided function," each sex adapted "to their respective tasks of harboring and defending the concentric circles, from the procreative womb to the limits of the defensible territory" (p. 280).

Erikson noted that *human* society and technology has transcended this early evolutionary arrangement, making room for "cultural triumphs of adaptation." Yet "when we speak of biologically given strengths and weaknesses in the human female, we may yet have to accept as one measure of all difference the biological rock-bottom of sexual differentiation. In this, the woman's productive inner space may well remain an inescapable criterion, whether conditions permit her to build her life partially or wholly around it or not" (Erikson 1968:281). However, he also commented on the tendency of the *young* woman to become "free from the tyranny of the inner space" as she ventures "into 'outer space' with a bearing and a curiosity which often appears hermaphroditic if not outright 'masculine.' A special ambulatory dimension is thus added to the inventory of her spatial behavior, which many societies counteract with special rules of virginal restraint" (p. 282).

He concluded that "only a total configurational approach—somatic, historical, individual—can help us to see the differences of functioning and experiencing in context, rather than in isolated and senseless comparison" (Erikson 1968:284). If the somatic has a vital role to play, so does history and so does the individuality of each woman (and man). He noted that psychoanalytic ego psychology has emphasized the importance of the ego as mediator between the somatic, historical, and personal, "for the ego is the guardian of the indivisibility of the person" (p. 289). Thus, his emphasis on the "somatic" was not a "renewed male attempt" to argue that woman's procreative endowment "dooms" every woman to perpetual motherhood or as warrant for denying her "full equivalence of individuality" and "full equality of citizenship." However, he worried about a "militant individualism and equalitarianism" that had "inflated this core of individuality to the point where it seems altogether free of somatic and social differences" (p. 290). The real question "is how these three areas of life reach into each other—certainly never without conflict and tension and yet with some continuity of purpose" (p. 291). He expressed the hope that as women break out of the "confinements that have been their historical fate," they may bring to their own explorations of "outer space"—their "ambulatory" venturesomeness now no longer confined to the "moratorium" of young womanhood but expanded to include women of every age—the special concerns of their biological "innerness," especially their exposure "to a specific sense of loneliness" and "fear of being left empty" or more simply of "being left" (Erikson 1968:278, [1950] 1963:410).

The essay concluded with reference to his last conversation with theologian Paul Tillich, who worried that the psychoanalytic emphasis on the ego and its adaptation to the world might make individuals poorly adapted to face "ultimate concerns." He thought Tillich agreed with his reply that only when ego adaptation is achieved is one free to face and recognize these "ultimate concerns": "One may add that man's Ultimate has too often been visualized as an infinity which begins where the male conquest of outer space ends, and a domain where an 'even more' omnipotent and omniscient Being must be submissively acknowledged. The Ultimate, however, may well be found also to reside in the Immediate, which has so largely been the domain of woman and of the inward mind" (Erikson 1968:293–294).

In "Once More the Inner Space" (1975b), published seven years later, Erikson began with an artistic allusion that reminds us of his comment at the close of *Young Man Luther*—that he made no apologies to a militant age that insisted on painting the moon red. He asked his reader to turn with him to his earlier paper: "Let us see how some sentences, when used for political rhetoric, lost their theoretical half tones and, instead, took on one (inflammable) color" (p. 228). The critic who made Erikson see "red" was Kate Millett, author of *Sexual Politics* (1969). Her primary criticism of Erikson was that in viewing anatomy as one of the three "defining" features of sexual differentiation, he merely repeated and reinforced "psychoanalysis' persistent error of mistaking learned behavior for biology. . . . Anatomy is only destiny insofar as it determines cultural conditioning" (Millett 1969:215, quoted in Erikson 1975b:228).

If his critics were saying that anatomy did "determine cultural conditioning" to some extent, Erikson believed there was then no real argument between them. But he worried that this admittedly ironic agreement between them would obscure his basic point that the somatic, the historical, and the individual—"the three aspects of human fate"—are *relative* to one another, for each "co-determines" the others: "Such 'systematic going around in circles' (as I have called it, so as not to overdo the word 'relativity') takes some thought which is indispensable to the study of human facts" (Erikson 1975b:228). Thus, he claimed to be thinking "configurationally" or in circular fashion, while his critics were imputing to him, and perhaps employing themselves, a way of thinking that was basically linear, involving one-way causalities. He also reminded his reader that if Freud the medical doctor made his famous "biology is destiny" statement to challenge the hubris of Napoleon's well-known assertion that "history is destiny," then Erikson, "an heir of ego psychology," had dared to ask "rather modestly whether we ourselves are not also part of our destiny. I find myself in a body that exists in a particular social place and historical period, and I must attempt to make the most and the best of that. . . . A freer choice nobody can claim or grant to anybody" (Erikson 1975b:229).

As for his emphasis on the "inner space," he noted that one publication (approvingly) took him to mean that men are "penetrators," women are "enclosers," men are "outer-directed," and women "inner-directed." Another author (disapprovingly) took him to say that men are active, women intuitive; men are interested in things and ideas, women in people and feelings. Another critic (Millett) understood him to be saying that a woman who has not experienced childbirth will forever feel unfulfilled and that with each menses, a woman cries to heaven over a child not conceived.[4] These, he contended, were all misreadings of the original essay, due in part to his own writing style, which, in addition to some vagueness of language, also included a "few imprudent words and phrases as well as some ambivalently poetic ones" that he would want to change. But the misreadings were also due to the fact that in the United States, the dominant discourse is the social one, so that whatever a psychologist might write about "womanhood" (or "manhood," for that matter) is immediately scrutinized for its "social role" implications. Though not averse to having his views scrutinized in this way, he thought it important then to differentiate "the role concepts which emerge in a given country (such as Talcott Parsons' in this country) and the role ideology dominant in it" (Erikson 1975b:236). If in the United States, "the emphasis on *choice* in all social roles has become an ideological faith" (witness America's emphasis on the "self-made man"), the danger is that this ideology will obscure what "no true role *concept* would ignore," namely, "the fact that functioning roles . . . are tied to certain conditions: a role can only provide leeway within the limits of what bodily constitution can sustain, social structure can make workable, and personality formation can integrate" (p. 236).

Concerned that women may be "taken in" by the same ideology that had men believing they could be whatever they "chose" to be (i.e., the "self-made man"), he nonetheless discussed, in the last half of the article, ways in which the sociocultural meanings traditionally ascribed to the somatic dimension of the overall configuration of human life may themselves be reconfigured so that the traditionally negative view of the "inner space" as a metaphor of confinement and passivity (and, in more extreme cases, of masochistic suffering, with its "secondary gains of devious dominance") may be replaced with a more positive view. Here, he supported those who argue for the right of a woman to exercise personal autonomy over and within the "inner space," defining *autonomy* in this instance not as "separateness" (as Carol Gilligan defined it in her *In a Different Voice*) but as "self-governance." He *was* "pro-choice"—a woman's "inner space" *was* her own—but he hoped that this was a genuinely free choice, "when it can be made with a minimum of denial and of guilt and with a maximum of insight and conviction" (Erikson 1975b:243).

Equally important as this self-empowering view of the "inner space" is the need to review the fact that young women have been forced in the past to restrain their "ambulatory" modes of somatic being in favor of a certain "inner-directedness." Their "self-centered strength and peace" was bought at the price of abandonment of "much of the early locomotor vigor and the social and intellectual initiative and intrusiveness which, potentially, girls share with boys" (Erikson 1975b:242). Thus, he saw the necessity for women (and men) to develop those potentials that in the past were not developed because "each sex overdeveloped what was given" and then "compensated for what it had to deny." Each received "special approbation for a divided self-image" (p. 242). This essay concludes much as the original one did with the observation that males have traditionally sought the ultimate in the far reaches of "outer space" while women have traditionally experienced it in the innermost core of their being. He said we need a new "guiding vision" wherein men withdraw their "commitment from a variety of overextended fighting fronts" and engage in "a new search for anchor in that inner space which we all share," while women bring "the special modes of [their] experience" to "the overall planning and governing so far monopolized by men" (p. 247). That the "inner space" has a religious—*numinous*—quality for Erikson was inescapable, and precisely for this reason he said that he would not withdraw or apologize for what he said in the conclusion of the earlier essay "in somewhat creedal terms about the Ultimate residing in the Immediate" (p. 247). This statement, of course, recalls his poetic reflections on the "inner cosmos" in the concluding paragraphs of *Young Man Luther*, especially his reference to the "pure self itself, the unborn core of creation." He was not speaking here of woman's child but of the child self who lives in the inner space of each and every one of us.

One obvious feature of Erikson's womanhood and the inner space essays is that he used the same clinical framework introduced in *Childhood and Society* and employed in *Young Man Luther*, in which the somatic, ego, and social (or historical) processes are viewed together—configurationally—and special attention is paid to the ways they enhance and delimit one another. Also, as in *Young Man Luther*, he was especially attentive to the integrative and empowering role of the ego. In this way, he affirmed, as he did in *Young Man Luther*, that *individuality* is destiny too. But given my interest in recontextualizing these essays, locating them within the ambiance of the psychology of religion, I am more concerned here with his view of the "inner space" as the place in which the "Ultimate" resides, together with his observation that men have been oriented toward the conquest of "outer space" while the "inner space" has "so largely been the domain of women." Rare is the man who makes the "inner space" his focus of interest, and even when a man does, it often happens that he addresses it as something alien, something to be feared, and thus the provocateur of fantasies of flight or of conquest.

To explain men's prevailing attitude toward the "inner space," we may turn to Freud's essay on "The Uncanny" (1958) in which he discussed the sense of "the uncanny" ("unheimlich") as "nothing else than a hidden, familiar thing that has undergone repression and then emerged from it" (p. 153). When "uncanniness" is experienced, this is always the effect of the resurfacing of earlier memories, and the locus of greatest uncanniness is the mother's body. This unusually heightened sense of the uncanny among men persists into adulthood in the form of fears of the female genital organs, this "unheimlich place" that is "the entrance to the former *heim* [home] of all human beings, to the place where everyone dwelt once upon a time and in the beginning" (pp. 152–153). Thus, "the *unheimlich* is what was once *heimisch*, home-like, familiar; the prefix 'un' is the token of repression" (p. 153).

Commenting on Freud's essay, Norman Bryson suggested that the boy is made aware that "the persistence of his desire to remain within the maternal orbit represents a menace to the very center of his being, a possibility of engulfment and immersion that threatens his entire development and viability as a subject" (1990:172). He must escape, and "he can do so by no other means than by claiming as his another kind of space, . . . a space that is definitely and assuredly *outside*, . . . a space where the process of identification with the masculine can begin and can succeed" (p. 172). But such escape creates its own problems as he continues to bear the marks of a "double-edged exclusion and nostalgia," an "irresolvable ambivalence which gives to feminine space a power of attraction" even as he "apprehends feminine space as alien, as a space which also menaces the masculine subject to the core of his identity as male" (pp. 172–173).

Bryson's interpretation of Freud's essay affords a new way of viewing Erikson's essays on womanhood and the inner space: These essays may be seen as a man's effort to apprehend the "inner space" as a means to address the very existential problem of men's "divided self-image," thereby laying the foundations for a more elaborate vision of self-reconciliation or wholeness. But if so, Erikson's "ambivalently poetic" phrases also reveal just how "alien" and "exclusive" this space appears to men. In contrast to *Young Man Luther*, where Erikson wrote with a certain surefootedness and with clinical self-confidence, the two essays on womanhood and the inner space were written with a fair amount of awkwardness, even defensiveness, as though he were writing about a subject that bore all the marks of a "double-edged exclusion and nostalgia." His confession in the second essay that he had written "a few imprudent words" in the first implies that he was aware he was writing about something that was "alien"; his suggestion that he would now want to withdraw certain "ambivalently poetic" words and phrases indicates that he had written out of deep nostalgia for that which was once familiar but had since been de-familiarized. For all his efforts at clarification, at addressing both positive and negative readings (and misreadings) of his earlier text, the essays come across as ambivalent, revealing the author's own sense of estrangement and nostalgia for the subject of his essay, for "the inner space" itself. He seems awkward and ill at ease, as though the clinician's confidence in his interpretative framework is somehow being undermined by deeply rooted feelings of nostalgia and hurt.

Millett, too, observed the "awkwardness" reflected in Erikson's original essay, which she attributed to the fact that "no matter how he tries to brighten the picture, Erikson is incapable of stopping at the right moment, but must always go on to exhibit his own distaste or misgiving for the situation he is trying to reinterpret in such positive terms" (1969:218). In her view, the reason for "the uneasy, even contradictory, tone of the essay is due to the fact that Erikson vacillates between two versions of woman, Freud's chauvinism and a chivalry of his own" (p. 212). Rather, I would attribute its "uneasy" tone to something much deeper, to his sense of being an outside observer of what he experienced earlier as an infant, as a certified insider. Hence, he was ambivalently alienated and nostalgic. At issue is not "women in general" but Erikson's (and perhaps every other man's) experience of his mother and the "space" that she embodied as "de-familiarized." Millett also noted that "maternity is something of a preoccupation with him" (p. 211). Here again, I agree, but this, too, has a highly personalized connotation for him because, as noted earlier, he was conceived out of wedlock and described himself as "the son of a Dane *who had abandoned [my mother] before my birth*" (Erikson 1975a:27, emphasis added). As the son of an abandoned mother, Erikson no doubt believed that he could well have suffered the fate of all those children who, like Luther's siblings, died in childhood from adverse circumstances or even maternal neglect. Was it for him, then, that she married the doctor to whom she took young Erik for medical care? If so, he did not feel at home "in their home," but he did not rebel (*that* came much later), choosing instead to "play in" with the myth that his stepfather was his real father, and he "more or less forgot [repressed?] the period before the age of three, *when mother and I had lived alone*" (p. 27, emphasis added). His sense of loss—of the "inner space" as inclusive of himself and exclusive of all others—was revealed in an understated sort of way in his reference to his stepfather as "*that intruder*" (p. 27, emphasis added).

Thus, his references in his first essay on womanhood and the inner space to the woman's fear of "being left" (abandoned) and his suggestion that men are essentially "intruders" into the inner space are deeply autobiographical. As for himself, the essays reveal the child self and its fears and hurts as *this* self, a certified insider in the maternal orbit, found itself from the time of his mother's remarriage on the outside looking in, estranged from the "inner space" with which he had been on the most familiar of terms. In light of this autobiographical subtext to the womanhood and the inner space essays, we can see that his comments about Luther's ambivalent feelings toward *his* mother were not simply a "clinician's judgment" but were reminiscent of his own personal experiences. He identified with Luther's sense that he and his mother shared a certain "sad isolation"; at the same time, he identified with Luther's sense of having been "deeply disappointed by his mother," vowing that he would not "succumb the way she did to the father, to fate" (Erikson 1958:73). But if Luther's mother sang to her son of "some heaven," Erikson shared Luther's desire for a taste of that distant heaven in the here and now, in the "inner space," where a man may at least be at peace with himself.

Conclusion

I suggest that for Erikson, religion is the primary means by which the inner space, originally associated with the mother, is internalized and in the process becomes the locus of the pure self itself. Although the mother-child relationship continues to provide powerful religious images of trust, nurturance, and care, the deeper relationship that is virtually beyond imagining is the relationship of the self to itself, and herein lies the most fundamental source of religious visions of reconciliation and wholeness. Adult anxieties are the measure of the degree to which such reconciliation eludes us, whereas openness to our childhood self, especially to its fears and its sense of endangerment, is a measure of the degree to which such reconciliation is coming to pass. If Jesus placed the child in the midst of his disciples, thus subverting traditional social hierarchies in which children are the second-class citizens of this world and of the next, and if Freud placed the child in the midst of his psychoanalytic theory and practice, Erikson placed the child in the midst of the inner space itself, declaring the child to be once again a certified insider. This, I suggest, is the core of Erikson's psychoanalytic psychology of religion and of his own religious vision.

Notes

1. The reader will note that Erikson did not use gender-inclusive language here. His earlier writings were published before this became the accepted norm. His later writings are more reflective of these norms.

2. Ironically, Erikson himself suffered from hearing difficulties as he got older. In *Young Man Luther*, he emphasized the importance of the sense organs to our mental functioning, quoting with approval Leonardo da Vinci's observation that "mental things which have not gone through the senses are vain and bring forth no truth except detrimental" (Erikson 1958:192).

3. Though Erikson did not make a correlation between his claim that some children are older than their years and child abuse, Carolyn Steedman did (1994: 165–166), though she emphasized that such early "knowingness" is far more likely in the case of sexual abuse than of physical abuse only.

4. Erikson took particular offense at Kate Millett's rather jeering reaction to this passage in the original essay: "How a woman thus can be hurt in depth is a wonder to many a man, and it can arouse both his empathic horror and his refusal to understand. Such hurt can be re-experienced in each menstruation; it is a crying to heaven in the mourning over a child; and it becomes a permanent scar in the menopause" (Erikson 1968:278). He noted that Millett read the word "it" in the phrase "it is a crying to heaven in the mourning over a child" to mean "mourning over each menstrual loss, wherefore she undertook to count how many periods women average in a lifetime and how often, therefore, Erikson thinks, they are crying to heaven over a child not conceived" (1968:234). Erikson partially blamed himself for this misunderstanding, suggesting that if he had italicized the word "it," one would surely know that he was referring to the "hurt" that registers so deeply when a woman mourns her child's death: "To older people like myself, the loss of a child by death was once a more expectable experience in family life, whereas in past generations all living children represented a triumph of survival" (1975b:234).

References

Bryson, N. 1990. *Looking at the Overlooked: Four Essays on Still Life Painting.* Cambridge, Mass.: Harvard University Press.

Capps, D. 1978. "Psychohistory and Historical Genres: The Plight and Promise of Eriksonian Biography." In P. Homans, ed., *Childhood and Selfhood: Essays on Tradition, Religion, and Modernity in the Psychology of Erik H. Erikson*. Lewisburg, Pa.: Bucknell University Press, pp. 189–228.

_____. 1993. *The Depleted Self: Sin in a Narcissistic Age*. Minneapolis: Fortress Press.

Coles, R. 1970. *Erik H. Erikson: The Growth of His Work*. Boston: Little, Brown.

Decker, H. S. 1991. *Freud, Dora, and Vienna 1900*. New York: Free Press.

Erikson, E. H. [1950] 1963. *Childhood and Society*. New York: W. W. Norton.

_____. 1958. *Young Man Luther: A Study in Psychoanalysis and History*. New York: W. W. Norton.

_____. 1959. *Identity and the Life Cycle*. New York: International Universities Press. Republished in 1961 by W. W. Norton.

_____. 1964. *Insight and Responsibility: Lectures on the Ethical Implications of Psychoanalytic Insight*. New York: W. W. Norton.

_____. 1968. "Womanhood and the Inner Space." In *Identity: Youth and Crisis*. New York: W. W. Norton, pp. 261–294.

_____. 1969. *Gandhi's Truth: On the Origins of Militant Nonviolence*. New York: W. W. Norton.

_____. 1974. *Dimensions of a New Identity*. New York: W. W. Norton.

_____. 1975a. "'Identity Crisis' in Autobiographic Perspective." In *Life History and the Historical Perspective*. New York: W. W. Norton, pp. 17–47.

_____. 1975b. "Once More the Inner Space." In *Life History and the Historical Moment*. New York: W. W. Norton, pp. 225–247.

_____. 1977. *Toys and Reasons: Stages in the Ritualization of Experience*. New York: W. W. Norton.

_____. 1981. "The Galilean Sayings and the Sense of 'I.'" *Yale Review* 70: 321–362.

_____. 1982. *The Life Cycle Completed: A Review*. New York: W. W. Norton.

_____. 1987. *A Way of Looking at Things: Selected Papers from 1930 to 1980*. Edited by S. Schlein. New York: W. W. Norton.

Freud, S. 1958. "The Uncanny." In B. Nelson, ed., *On Creativity and the Unconscious*. New York: Harper & Row, pp. 122–161. First published in 1919.

_____. 1963a. "Obsessive Acts and Religious Practices." In P. Rieff, ed., *Character and Culture*. New York: Collier Books, pp. 17–26. First published in 1907.

_____. 1963b. *Three Case Histories*. Edited by P. Rieff. New York: Collier Books. Previously published in 1909, 1911, and 1918.

Gilligan, C. 1982. *In a Different Voice: Psychological Theory and Women's Development*. Cambridge, Mass.: Harvard University Press.

James, W. 1950. *The Principles of Psychology*. 2 vols. New York: Dover Publications. First published in 1890.

_____. 1982. *The Varieties of Religious Experience*. Edited by M. Marty. New York: Penguin Books. First published in 1902.

Millett, K. 1969. *Sexual Politics*. New York: Simon and Schuster.

Obituary for Erik H. Erikson. *New York Times,* May 13, 1994.

Pruyser, P. 1963. "Erikson's *Young Man Luther*: A New Chapter in the Psychology of Religion." *Journal for the Scientific Study of Religion* 2: 238–242.

Roazen, P. 1976. *Erik H. Erikson: The Power and Limits of a Vision*. New York: Free Press.

Steedman, C. 1994. *Strange Dislocations: Childhood and the Idea of Human Interiority 1780–1930*. Cambridge, Mass.: Harvard University Press.

Trevor-Roper, P. 1988. *The World Through Blunted Sight*. London: Penguin Press.

Zock, H. 1990. *A Psychology of Ultimate Concern: Erik H. Erikson's Contribution to the Psychology of Religion*. Amsterdam: Rodopi.

Part Three

Contemporary Psychoanalytic
Perspectives

9

Heinz Kohut's Struggles with Religion, Ethnicity, and God

Charles B. Strozier

There are few figures in the psychoanalytic community since Freud's time as personally alive, intellectually brilliant, and multifaceted as Heinz Kohut. After a lonely childhood in Vienna, where he was born in 1913 and which he left in 1939 to escape the Nazis, he would become a leading figure in mainstream psychoanalysis in the 1950s and 1960s. He was the consummate insider in those two decades—"Mr. Psychoanalysis," as he later joked—on all the powerful committees, friend of all the right people from Anna Freud to Kurt Eissler, and the author of articles that seldom questioned the assumptions of the field. He even served a stint as president of the American Psychoanalytic Association. He became quietly noteworthy at the Chicago Institute, where he built his thriving practice and indulged his interests in music, literature, history, and the arts. He made a wide range of friends, though some felt he might have worn his vast knowledge and refined cultural sensibilities a little more lightly.

Two early essays by Kohut attracted attention within psychoanalysis, one on Thomas Mann's *Death in Venice* and a second on empathy, but few people were really prepared for the significance of his 1971 book, *The Analysis of the Self*. Even he seems to have been taken aback at the response, which included effusive praise from all those he most cared about (and many others), as well as the first hints of the kind of criticism that was to haunt him. By marshaling the help of Anna Freud and Joseph Sandler, he fended off (and prevented the publication of) a gratuitous charge of plagiarism by an English analyst who was an overly enthusiastic student of D. W. Winnicott.[1]

That was the worst of numerous charges; others suggested that he was "ruin-
ing analysis," that he was "insufferably vain," and that, in gathering younger
colleagues around him, he was "fostering adulation."² But he pushed on in
his original work on narcissism and the self, writing another book in 1977,
Restoration of the Self, many essays that have since been collected in the four
volumes of *Search for the Self*, and two posthumously published books,
How Does Analysis Cure? and *Self Psychology and the Humanities*.³

One important theme in Kohut's work was religion, though he never
wrote a book or even a paper specifically on the subject. "I don't think I
could honestly say that religion is one of my foremost preoccupations," he
once said, "[but since] I'm interested in human beings and *their* preoccupations, in what makes them tick, what's important to them, and what's on
their minds, obviously religion is a powerful force in life. It has been an essential aspect of human existence as long as there has been any knowledge of
human activity at all. So, naturally, I'm interested in it as a student of people."⁴ At a personal level, Kohut regularly attended the Unitarian Church in
Hyde Park, near the University of Chicago. He became a friend of its minister and even at times spoke to the congregation. He read *Christian Century*
for years and seemed particularly concerned with the application of his ideas
to what is generally called pastoral counseling.⁵ Certainly, many theologians
and practitioners sensed in Kohut a kindred spirit striving to define a meaningful relation to God.

Kohut had a restlessly inquisitive mind. He easily breached disciplinary
boundaries and refused to be constrained by academic conventions. But
Kohut also recognized the limits of his own knowledge. For all his soaring
intellect, he was in fact quite modest about what he could really know and
understand. Nowhere was this clearer than in his 1981 comments about religion in his conversations with Robert L. Randall. He made it quite clear to
Randall, then a young theologian, that it was "your baby" to provide the
more complete explanation of the links between self psychology and religion. He was in no way attempting a kind of self psychological *Future of an
Illusion*. He was only providing a framework for such a task, the barest outline that needed fleshing out to be really meaningful. It was not, I think, a
falsely modest position. For one thing, he often took such a stance on the relation of self psychological ideas to other realms of human experience.⁶ But
more important, he outlined for Randall just that: a framework and not a
completely developed set of ideas. It does not make his thoughts less interesting, but it does require us to take them with some caution and to grant
them the tentativeness that Kohut himself intended. In talking with Randall,
Kohut certainly never meant to hand down self psychological dicta that
would become dogma.

In his work on religion, Kohut draws his baseline with Freud, especially
The Future of an Illusion. Freud's error in this work, Kohut feels, was in ap-

plying the "yardstick of scientific values to religion." By such criteria, religion seems foolish indeed. The story of the "humanoid god" who created the world in a week is ridiculous as physics. It is pure fairy tale, "abominably poor science," he states. Such tales of origins cannot hope to compete with scientific explorations of the world and its beginnings and the workings of the natural world. To consider another example, take the "gimmick" of the afterlife, a place where the virtuous go. That fits beautifully with all the superficial needs of what Kohut derisively calls "Guilty Man" or the self Freud imagines. Freud's whole purpose is to unmask (or, as we might now say, deconstruct) the completely irrational, fantastical, illusionary nature of religious beliefs that in their deeper understanding are merely projections from our own early experience of infantile helplessness.

But, Kohut suggests, in that very rationalism lies Freud's profound misperception of the true purpose of religion, which is simply in another realm from science. There are three great cultural enterprises for Kohut: science, art, and religion. "Science deals with cognitive issues, with explanations. Art deals with beauty, creating beautiful things, pleasing things. And religion is neither the one nor the other." Its unique function is to "shore up, to hold together, sustain, to make harmonious, to strengthen, man's self." For many in the twentieth century, psychoanalysis has robbed religion of those functions and become a substitute religion.[7] Certainly, that has profoundly influenced religion, but it has also placed a terrific burden on psychoanalysis itself, corrupting its true mission—to search for psychological truth. The key to the religiosity of psychoanalysis lies in the adoration of and excessive loyalty toward the founder by its followers. No physicist in his right mind would ever place Newton on such a level. We have discovered all kinds of new laws since Newton, and yet no one would claim that that represents a rebellion against him. Things move forward, and new giants appear who enhance our understanding of the world and our capacity to explain it.

But there is more to Kohut's thinking on religion than a critique of Freud. He also seeks to outline more precisely the "human needs" religion meets. He addresses this general topic in terms of the self-selfobject experience of idealization, mirroring, and twinship. All these terms need definition and clarification but none more so than *selfobject*, which lies at the heart of his theory. In devising the term *selfobject*, he sought to capture the way in which we establish and maintain our psychological wholeness through our narcissistic relationship with primary caretakers and later their symbolized substitutes. This relationship is not one of identification or introjection or any of the more familiar concepts used in psychoanalysis to describe the more primitive connections between self and objects. Kohut wants to stress that, initially, objects as such (and as seen by external observers) are not felt as separate by the self. We take in their functions, indeed their very beings, in the making of our selves. We respond to the caretaking, the feeding, the holding, the touching of the mother as though she were part of us. We experience her soothing as indistinguishable from our own. The boundaries between self and other are completely permeable; the baby, in fact, is psychologically whole if seen in the context of the maternal matrix. A normal baby is never a baby alone because the baby "includes the caretakings and responses of [the] selfobject that is empathically fitted with him."[8] In time, of course, there is a gradually increasing awareness of separateness of the self from the caretaking figure(s), but we never stop turning to the functions of others to meet our deepest self needs. We are never fully apart, independent, autonomous. Equally significant, selfobject functions, which are never actual people or objects in any event, in time get abstracted and symbolized into various cultural forms. That is where an institution like religion enters.

Issues of idealization lie at the heart of any effort to understand religion from a self psychological point of view. Kohut would never fall prey to simple reductionism. "I would have no doubt that anything as encompassing and broad and basic as religion is to man . . . could not possibly relate to just one dimension of the self." That said, he recognizes the centrality of idealization in his reflections about religion and returns to them often—and for good reason. Idealizing needs are perhaps the most conspicuous aspects of religion. We can hardly dispense with a concept of God "because there must be something idealizeable, something that nears perfection or that is perfect, something that one wants to live up to, something that lifts one up." The fragmenting self, he notes, is weak, chaotic, and disharmonious. In religion, one searches for and often finds a sense of uplift and healing from that fragmentation. This may come from a particularly inspiring sermon, which lifts one out of the humdrum of everyday existence and gives meaning where there had been emptiness. The service itself, with its familiar rituals and words and song, may inspire and soothe. Even the rhythms of the church year can be significant in this regard. "The mere unrolling of specific holidays in the course of a twelve month period . . . the gradual decline with winter, and the rebirth with Easter spring, appeals to something deep in all of us."

Such experiences touch the psychological core of the child's first encounters with the majestic mother who uplifted it as a baby and held it close to her. That baby alone is "frightened, disheveled, fragmented." The mother, on the other hand, is "calm, big, powerful." Uplifted, the child merged into the mother's greatness and calmness. Later, Kohut says, we all suffer various kinds of narcissistic blows, which can be powerfully disorienting. Some find they are soothed by going into a church and sitting there. Others might experience a similar kind of healing in a more abstracted spiritual form, such as climbing to the top of a mountain or looking down into the Grand Canyon or walking in the woods. Still others find uplift in listening to great and beautiful music. But whatever the form, such spiritual uplift is a central part of how we understand the role of religion in our lives. And this sense we have of God's purpose evokes our earliest encounter with the maternal self-object matrix. Kohut here offers no simplistic causal relation between God and mother. We do not merely seek uplift from God because our mothers once picked us up to hold and feed and soothe us. Religion is not, as it was basically for Freud, a rather mundane human institution but rather a complex interplay of human psychological needs and the deeper workings of the Divine. Unlike Freud, one might say, Kohut grants a God and then tries to understand our psychological relation to her.

In the Randall interviews, one of the more interesting themes Kohut pursues about idealization and uplift (a theme he also took up in his contemporaneous interviews with me[9]) is the issue of death. (At the time of the conversation, he was in fact dying, which he knew and talked about to intimates, and he was in increasing pain.) Kohut's key idea is that a healthy individual is not afraid of death. It is too natural a part of the curve of life, "of being born, of growing, of reaching some flowering of the program that's laid down in us early in life," which inevitably involves death as part of its course. It is the same with a rose.

> There is a seed, there is a flowering, there is a wilting, there is a death and the next generation of roses takes over. I think that one isn't really fully alive if one doesn't somehow down deep in one's bones feel this eternal rhythm of life, this coming and going of which one is only a link in a chain. To me this is an uplifting thought, not a discouraging thought. It goes beyond my individuality to something broader and more enduring than this little me that is common, hasn't been here during Plato's time and will not be here in a thousand years when there's another Plato or maybe nothing. Who knows? Why do I have to be around and have been around? I wasn't and I won't. That doesn't disturb me.

Yet in death there are certain experiences and conditions that need to be met. The first is that in the actual process of dying, selfobjects are vital. People tend to withdraw from the dying person. If someone can connect at that stage and convey genuine feelings—"you're dying, and I will also cross that threshold one of these days," "the way you handle this is an inspiration to me," "I will get a great deal of strength from watching how you do this"— that dying person will feel confirmed.

Religion, too, supports the dying person in a myriad of idealizing selfobject ways quite aside from the foolishness of the hope for an afterlife. There are enduring issues in the world, Kohut says, like the great mystery of creation, both of the world and of the complexity and beauty of human culture. None of that is accidental, but it will in some way endure, whether or not we observe it. That is precisely what is meant by eternal life. The fairy tale of heaven with winged angels singing hallelujah, he adds, "doesn't particularly send me." It sounds rather "boring." In fact, "the greatness of an experience is timeless." It has intrinsic value, even should the human race become extinct some day. That is what the God concept is all about at its most idealized and philosophical level. "There is something about this world in our experience that does lift us up beyond the simplicity of an individual existence, that lifts us into something higher, enduring, or, as I would rather say, timeless."

The second self need that religion meets has to do with what Kohut called *mirroring*. We all have a need for "responsiveness to our own vitality," as well as powerful ambitions and a "sense of innate greatness." One of Kohut's favorite examples to illustrate these self needs and how they are best met by the selfobject is the young child first starting to walk. He struggles to his feet (to use the example of a little boy) and totters off very precariously across the room. He feels buoyed and excited by his own accomplishment and yet terribly insecure that he might fall and lose it all. He looks back at the mother and sees her smiling with confidence and joy at what he is doing. That "gleam in the mother's eye" in turn firms his own faltering confidence and steadies his step. The gleam is himself reflected or mirrored back. Neither she nor that smile is experienced, for the most part, as at all separate from himself. Through the gleam, he knows at the deepest level her trust and presence and that as a result he can trust himself to be capable of making it to the table and from there to almost any other challenge he will face in life.[10]

Such mirroring needs, Kohut says, are met in religion through what is usually called grace or the idea that "there is something given to you, some innate perception of your right to be here and to assert yourself, and that somebody will smile at you and will respond to you and will be in turn with your worthwhileness." In the Old Testament, a crucial text that defines the idea of grace is Psalm 84:11: "For the Lord God *is* a sun and shield; the Lord will give grace and glory. No good *thing* will He withhold from them that walk uprightly." That basic idea runs through the Christian sacred texts, though it is added, of course, that Jesus becomes the medium through which the grace of God flows. Acts 20:24, for example, states: "But none of these things move me, neither count I my life dear unto myself, so that I might finish my course with joy, and the ministry, which I have received of the Lord Jesus, to testify the gospel of the grace of God." Kohut's favorite text on grace is secular—the line from Eugene O'Neill's *Great God Brown*: "Man is born broken. He lives by mending. The grace of God is glue." The psychological point is that God's grace is available for us to heal our wounds and to mirror our needs simply for the asking, in the same way the protective, secure mother, especially the gleam in her eye, provided cohesion for our selves through all the vagaries of development. But if that mother, as in *Long Day's Journey into Night*, is drug-addicted, there is no grace, and the family degenerates into drunken brawling.

Life and creativity in general, Kohut feels, emerge out of this fall from grace. At best, we have a glimmer of the mother's gleam. But we are spurred on by the very "shortcomings of that early grace," which in religious terms is the perfect mirroring and calmness of God. The therapeutic process here is what he elsewhere calls *optimal frustration* and *transmuting internalization*, but in the Randall interviews, his example is culture. To elaborate his point with Randall, he takes music, a lifelong interest for Kohut,[11] and notes that the perfect chord is not what makes great music appealing. It is, rather, the "deviation into dissonance" and the complex ways the music returns to consonance. The tunes and harmonies reach out through structures of movements, creating tensions that express the unease, until there is at last a return to balance or at least an illusion of harmony and peace. That process is what Kohut means by the "curve of life."[12] He even ironically thanks God for the scars and traumas of life, for they spur us on to new ways of solving problems. "If life were perfect, man would never have created religion or art or science."

The third specific selfobject need Kohut discusses as being met in religion is what he calls *alter-ego* or *twinship*. Even in theory, the distinction between mirroring and twinship is somewhat blurred. In his first formulation of twinship (1971), Kohut considered it as a subtopic of mirroring, though a decade later, he granted it rather more autonomy.[13] In using this concept, Kohut is trying to explain the dreams and fantasies that often appear in self analysis of a twin or alter, as well as the regressive idea that the analyst is actually quite like the patient. In trying to meet twinship needs, Kohut feels, we often search out others as selfobjects bearing some resemblance to us in reality or in fantasy. Their value lies precisely in their similarity to us. The origin of such self needs appears to lie in our interactions with siblings, peers, and others of our size and insignificance. Twinship is thus a somewhat later emergent self need (later, that is, than mirroring or idealization), and it is often associated with the *period* Freud called "Oedipal," as opposed to the famous complex that Kohut believes is by no means universal or necessary.[14]

Kohut feels that religion satisfies twinship needs in the locale of the church or sacred environment and especially in one's participation in the congregation. Religion, of course, is both a solitary and a communal experience. Much of what religion does in meeting idealizing and mirroring needs is solitary: Something goes on in private between you and your concept of God. But religion is also communal. Church surrounds you with worshippers like yourself who have made common faith commitments. However different your lives might be in other respects, in church you and they are joined in a common spiritual quest before a God you jointly recognize and conceive and to whom you direct your prayers in a shared and utterly familiar liturgy. Week after week, year after year, you return to the same pews and sing the same songs and listen together to the sermons. Such intensely experienced rituals tend to flatten out what might otherwise be felt as significant differences between people in terms of personality, background, wealth, pro-

fession, or even appearance. Within the sacred space of the church, you become more like your neighbor. You abandon the extraneous and emphasize
the essential. The human bonds deepen in this circle of reflected sameness.
And that is enormously reassuring. You become one of God's children in a
powerfully shared experience.

Within these three realms—idealization, mirroring, and twinship—religion meets the deepest needs of the self. The apparent neatness of the distinctions between the three forms of selfobject experience, however, is quite
misleading at both theoretical and applied levels. At the level of theory, as
noted, twinship at best stands in some kind of dependent relationship to
mirroring. But mirroring is itself quite protean in its expression, and it alternates easily between a variety of forms of extension of the grandiose self and
twinship and may blend with forms of idealization. What matters, Kohut
stresses, is not the specific mode of the transference "but the fact that the
transference brings about the (re)establishment of a cohesive and durable
narcissistic object relationship."[15] Furthermore, in actual clinical work, it can
be difficult to distinguish modes of transference. There may be rapid oscilla-
tions between idealization and mirroring and/or the transference may be
mixed.[16] All of this overlap and apparent confusion begins in the earliest self
needs of the baby, which experiences the mother simultaneously as both a
secure and a wonderful figure with which it can merge and as an extension of
its grandiosity that gets reflected back in that gleam.

In terms of religion, Kohut's discursive conversation with Randall conveys just these complications. He never lets his categories of analysis overwhelm and destroy the complexity of his data. He thus emphasizes the importance of idealization in the construction of a God concept and images of
perfection, but in talking about mirroring, he notes that it is the grace of
God that meets this self need. The uplift of religion, which primarily meets
the needs of idealization, is at work just as much in the mirroring experience
of God's grace and in the twinship of choir practice. These kinds of sub-
tleties hardly muddy the waters. There are real differences between the
modes of self experience and the ways in which religion meets them. To sort
out the forms of overlap in the way an individual experiences religion would
require the full-scale work that Kohut challenges theologians sensitive to self
psychology to undertake. He does stress that within a topological scheme,
one can hardly determine, in advance or in theory, the ways in which different individuals will bring their varied self needs into their spiritual life within
an institution as complex as religion.

The Christian Kohut

It is striking how "Christian" a stance Kohut assumes in the Randall interviews. He talks of churches and ministers and the rhythms of the holidays

from Christmas to Easter. At one point, he has a long disquisition on Catholicism, at another on the meaning of the search (especially Albert Schweitzer's search, which he clearly knows well) for the historical Jesus. The whole discourse is Christian. There is no qualification that enlarges the dialogue to include other religions, especially Judaism. In part, this Christian voice with which Kohut speaks reflects the nature of the interview itself. Kohut turns to the historical Jesus because Randall asks him about it. Kohut also knows Randall is a Christian theologian and has granted the interview partly because he knows Randall is concerned with the "soteriological" aspects of self psychology. Kohut holds to Christian themes in part, in other words, out of empathic respect for the person sitting across from him in his study.

But Kohut's Christian discourse may also reflect a much deeper ambivalence about his own Jewishness, which he obscured all his life. There is, in fact, no question that his family—a cultured, well-off, and highly assimilated Viennese family—was Jewish on both sides and had been for generations. And yet, many of his close friends at the University of Vienna during the 1930s had no idea he was Jewish. He never told Jewish jokes or used Yiddish expressions or made any reference to Jewish cultural traditions (and he looked baffled whenever anyone did any of these things in his presence).[17] Kohut's best friend in medical school was still wondering, forty years later when I interviewed him, why Kohut had to leave Vienna after the Anschluss in 1938. In Chicago, colleagues whispered that his mother was Jewish or maybe his father or maybe both or maybe neither. Some wild (and incorrect) rumors floated about that he had crosses on his mantel. One patient, who was himself in psychoanalytic training and concerned about his own ethnicity, asked Kohut directly at the beginning of his treatment if he was Jewish. He was never quite clear about the answer he received.[18]

Kohut's ambivalence about his Jewishness spilled over directly into his work. His interpretation of the case of Mr. A, a Jewish refugee from Poland, for example, is oddly off base in terms of Kohut's refusal to consider the impact of the Holocaust in A's early years. Kohut insisted that what mattered in A's development was his traumatic reaction to his father's repeated business failures after he came to the United States, rather than whatever he experienced as a child in Poland up to eight years of age, the hurried flight from the Nazis and war, exile in South America, and resettlement in the United States in his early adolescence. Kohut enraged some psychoanalytic colleagues in New York when he refused to talk about the case with a study group on second-generation survivors, led by Martin Bergman.[19]

Furthermore, in his last lecture at the self psychology meetings on the Berkeley campus a few days before he died, Kohut said some truly incredible things about the Nazis. The context was a general discussion about empathy. The general point he was making was that empathy in and of itself heals. The mere act of being empathic with someone else has beneficial effects. Empathy is a therapeutic action in the broadest sense, and even if nothing else happens with a patient, if there is empathy from the analyst, healing occurs. Kohut was fully aware of the radical implications of such an idea for someone like himself who was so deeply ingrained in the Freudian tradition. It muddied the waters of inquiry. "I wish I could just simply by-pass it," he said, shrugging. But "since it is true, and I know it is true," it was an aspect of his topic that deserved the closest attention. He had to mention it. During his lecture, Kohut also did not shirk from stating the point in the strongest and most general of terms. "The presence of empathy in the surrounding milieu, whether used for compassionate, well-intentioned therapeutic, and now listen, even for utterly destructive purposes, is still an admixture of something positive."

Kohut's theory of empathy is of the greatest significance for the theory and practice of psychoanalysis, and it was to be elegantly elaborated in the rest of the lecture. But Kohut's first few sentences, which attempted to clarify his challenging thesis, remain the most problematic of all he wrote in his entire life that has survived or of anything he said for attribution (as in this lecture on the Berkeley campus, which he knew was being videotaped by a professional company and, as with previous conferences, would be sold and widely distributed):

> In other words, there is a step beyond an empathy-informed hatred that wants to destroy you; and an empathyless environment that just brushes you off the face of the earth. The dreadful experiences of prolonged stays in concentration camps during the Nazi era in Germany were just that. It was not cruelty on the whole. (The Nazis were not sadistic or cruel in those camps. There were exceptions of course, it couldn't be otherwise, there are always some exceptions; but that was clearly punished, that was clearly frowned on.) They totally disregarded the humaneness of the victims. They were not human, either fully not human, or almost not human (there was a little shift between, I think, the Jews and the Poles, or something like that, in that respect). That was the worst.

It is hard to imagine a more absurd or offensive view of the Nazi concentration camps. Even Paul Ornstein, the editor of *Search* and a longtime friend and colleague of Kohut's, added a footnote after the first passage in parentheses, saying, gratuitously, that neither a "search of the literature" nor "any eye-witness accounts" could validate the idea that the Nazis were not sadistic or that they were regularly punished for breaches of the rules. Should this point even have to be made? Nazi sadism should hardly require scholarly documentation for Heinz Kohut.

Moreover, Kohut's point in this regard is not even clear. His argument about empathy seems to be that there is a sequence or a kind of continuum from an empathic environment to one in which empathy is used for destructive purposes to an empathyless environment. The Nazis, he says, created in their concentration camps empathyless environments in which they "totally disregarded the humaneness of the victims."[20] That is hard to dispute. Kohut's point, it seems, is that the Nazis were psychologically astute and created the most harmful environment imaginable for their victims. But he frames that idea by contrasting it with the notion that the Nazis were "not sadistic or cruel" in the camps and that, in the exceptional cases when they were, "that was clearly punished, that was frowned on."

What is going on here? How could someone of Kohut's background, himself Jewish and driven into exile from his beloved Vienna to escape the Nazis, say such things? There is no question that he knew better and was informed on the nature of Nazi concentration camps. He often read about Nazism and the Third Reich, including the latest German scholarship, which put him well ahead of most U.S. analysts on the subject.[21] He frequently referred to the Nazis to illustrate a point, and he wrote one long piece in the late 1960s, "On Courage," that dealt with the heroic opposition to Nazi tyranny by ordinary people, as well as two other papers at different times that focused on the dynamics of leadership and followership in the Nazi era.[22] Kohut also had access over many years to the most sophisticated forms of witness to Nazi horror, through Anna Ornstein (Paul Ornstein's wife), who was a child survivor of Auschwitz and an outspoken figure in the survivor movement. Anna Ornstein was a devoted follower of Kohut's, was supervised by him, and was the analyst for an important case that both she and he wrote up in different contexts (Mr. M.). Certainly, then, ignorance of the facts is no explanation for Kohut's comments.

Perhaps his physical state absolved him from responsibility for what he said. There were other places in the lecture where Kohut lost the thread of his argument (he became confused about historical method, for example). But briefly losing his way in the rich texture of his digressions was common for him when speaking extemporaneously, which was his favorite style. Indeed, a close textual analysis of transcripts from his various taped presentations reveals many minor rhetorical lapses. His general style was open, informal, discursive, and creative. He lectured with the deceptive familiarity of a Platonic character in the conversational mode of the dialogues, and such a rhetoric of intimacy inevitably left a few loose ends untied. At the same time, as almost anyone who heard him can testify, the lack of formal order in his presentations was more than made up for by the creativity with which he explored ideas with his audience and what can only be described as the charisma of his presence. And both qualities were very much in place at Berkeley. He was in pain and near death, but he was not intellectually confused. He certainly made no other egregious statements in the lecture, and he obviously had thought long and hard about the subject of empathy and was well prepared to discuss it. Indeed, for a talk that was given without notes of any kind, the direct transcript of his actual comments is remarkably clean and coherent. Furthermore, the passage about the Nazis cannot be regarded as a slip in the psychological sense of a mistaken word or phrase that reveals one's truer but unconscious feelings. Kohut's comments on the Nazis were no accident. What he said was too long a passage to be a mere slip. Some psychological truth was being revealed, though its meaning remains unclear.

It is interesting and perhaps enlightening to note that Kohut had specifically discussed the Nazis as a crucial example in his theory of empathy on two other occasions, written or recorded, before the Berkeley lecture (one just a few months prior). The first such comments were contained in his written response to the various papers presented at the first self psychology conference in Chicago in 1978. There, Kohut noted that "the deepest horror man can experience is that of feeling he is exposed to circumstances in which he is no longer regarded as human by others" and that, further, the "deepest horror" of the "Nazi destructiveness—the death of anonymous millions in gas chambers"—was expressed in their concept of "extermination."[23] This passage conveys exactly what Kohut meant, and it introduces no confusing comparisons with other dimensions of empathy used for destructive purposes. It is worth noting that this passage is the written and therefore self-edited version of his actual extemporaneous comments at the conference.

Kohut also turned to the subject of Nazis and empathy in a published interview I conducted with him on January 29, 1981, not long before his comments were made at Berkeley.[24] Kohut first mentioned the Nazis when I asked him about the apparent optimism that pervaded his self psychological formulations. At first, he reacted negatively to the use of the word *optimism*. "After all," he said to me, "I speak about tragic man when I speak about the very dimension you have in mind." After covering some other topics, Kohut then mentioned the parent who uses empathy to hurt the child, which he said was dreadful but not the worst experience. "The worst . . . is to find oneself in a predominantly nonhuman environment," he added. Kohut elaborated on this idea in some of the ways that he later did at Berkeley: For example, he noted that the terror of being shot off into space evoked that empathyless environment, as did the imagery of Mr. K. in Kafka, the "everyman of our times." If Mr. K. (in *The Trial*) could only be found guilty of something, anything, and then be punished, he would be in a human context. Instead, Mr. K. never discovers what he has done wrong and is shot like a dog. In Homer, Kohut added, one finds greatness in killing and being killed because it is human and has meaning. But this is not found in Kafka.[25]

Kohut seemed quite clear in these contexts about the tragic effects of a complete absence of empathy, whether in the family, in the culture, or in history. Empathy as we usually experience it, from mothers to everyone else in our lives who nourishes our vitality, is the essential psychological nutrient of life. Even in situations of cruelty when empathy is being used against us and for destructive purposes, there are beneficial effects on the self. To be engaged but harmed, in other words, is far better than to be ignored. Nothing destroys more than an empathyless environment. In Homeric ballads, he suggested in his 1981 interview with me, you may die cruelly, but you look your enemy in the face as you succumb. Analogously, as he suggested in *Advances*, the intrusive mother who loads guilt onto her children is at least present with them in vital psychological interactions. The problem he got into at Berkeley was that he included in this sequence the Nazis, whose concentration camps were not cruel "on the whole."

Kohut, in other words, was well informed about Nazi Germany and had given plenty of thought to the nuanced way the example of the concentration camps fit into his general theory of empathy. He had even discussed the subject intelligently on more than one occasion. At the same time, he made no simple slip at Berkeley. Something got in the way; some peremptory thought intruded itself.

A Psychology of Religion

Contradictions, however, as Kohut recognized, spur creativity. His own confusions about his Jewish identity led him to think more deeply about the nature of religion itself. He refused to fall back on the secure, if somewhat mindless, rationalism of Freud's view of religion that has always dominated psychoanalysis. He remained concerned with ultimate issues and sought to locate self psychology in the broadest possible sense within human concerns, traditions, and learning. Perhaps if Kohut had been more at ease with himself and his Jewishness, he would not have struggled so intensely with these issues. As Erikson said of Luther, one might say that Kohut lifted his own patienthood to a universal level and solved for all what he could not solve for himself alone.[26]

These "solutions" are richly varied. His is truly a potential psychology of religion. What he left was only a sketch or outline, it is true, but it is there, ready for much larger elaboration. In that work, he clarified the specific needs, in terms of idealization, mirroring, and twinship, that religion meets. Such a perspective captures the most significant psychological purposes of religion, and it shows that uncovering the "illusions" of faith is the beginning, rather than the end, of wisdom.

But I would also note, in conclusion, that Kohut's deeper understanding of religion carried over into his theorizing about the self. His is a psychology with empathy at its core. No aspect of the psychoanalytic encounter makes sense except in terms of empathy. It is a theory about connectedness and the ways in which we seek to recover traumatically disrupted union. That quest can and often does fail miserably; Kohut talked of "Tragic Man" in opposition to Freud's "Guilty Man." And yet, his theory is ultimately full of hope, in contrast to the brooding pessimism of Freud. There is redemption in the selfobject.

There is also an ethical dimension to the very idea of a holistic self. Freud's model divides the self into warring factions that at best work in tandem, if not quite cooperation, to keep a human organism thriving. There are higher and lower functions and an elaborate set of ideas about the transformations of desire from one system to another. Defenses keep the structures apart and clearly demarcate the boundaries. There is no larger unity, and Freud could only sneer with disdain behind his cigar at the idea of life as anything but ultimately a lonely journey by autonomous beings on a detour toward death. According to Freud, we bear no real psychological responsibility for others, who are merely objects in our internalized world. In such a view of human nature, a passionate commitment to help others and become involved in their lives and try to heal their wounds and alter the destructive institutions of society becomes suspect. Psychoanalysis for good reason has fed the solipsism of the contemporary self.

Kohut's ideas move in an entirely different direction. In the end, he completely rejected drive theory as meaningless, while recognizing the psychological experience of feeling driven. His notion of the self is a holistic one, not one built on contending pieces. Everything centers on connection and reconnection, growth from disruption (what he called "optimal frustration"), movement from stasis. We are only human in unities and in union with others. That is what the idea of the selfobject is all about. We are and we become through others. We are never autonomous, though our selfobject involvements may be more or less primitive, more or less mature, and so on. And as we get so much from others, we implicitly carry an obligation to give back. It is a powerful ethics of the self. God is the glue.

Notes

1. *The Curve of Life: Correspondence of Heinz Kohut,* ed. Geoffrey Cocks (Chicago: University of Chicago Press, 1994), 278–286.

2. Ibid., p. 294.

3. Heinz Kohut, *The Restoration of the Self* (New York: International Universities Press, 1977), *Search for the Self: Selected Writings of Heinz Kohut,* ed. Paul Ornstein (New York: International Universities Press, vols. 1 and 2, 1978, vol. 3, 1990, and vol. 4, 1991), *How Does Analysis Cure?,* ed. Arnold Goldberg, with the collaboration of Paul E. Stepansky (Chicago: University of Chicago Press, 1984), and *Self Psychology and the Humanities: Reflections on a New Psychoanalytic Approach,* ed. Charles B. Strozier (New York: W. W. Norton, 1985).

4. On March 22 and April 12, 1981, Robert L. Randall interviewed Kohut about his views of religion, God, theology, and related issues. The interviews were never published, though they are discussed and presented in Randall's as yet unpublished work entitled "Religion and Self Psychology of Heinz Kohut." Randall has gra-

ciously shared with me the original transcripts, from which I quote in this section of the paper. Unless otherwise indicated, Kohut quotes and thoughts on religion are taken from these interviews.

5. At the first self conference in Chicago in 1978, Kohut conceived and participated in a panel on "Self Psychology and the Sciences of Man." See Randall C. Mason, "The Psychology of the Self: Religion and Psychotherapy," in *Advances in Self Psychology*, ed. Arnold Goldberg, with summarizing reflections by Heinz Kohut (New York: International Universities Press, 1980), pp. 407–425. Note also that in the Randall interviews, Kohut returned at one point (2:13) to the value of self psychology for the pastoral work of ministers with the sick and dying.

6. Kohut, *Humanities*, pp. 218–219.

7. Erikson's similar version of this idea is: "We must grudgingly admit that even as we were trying to devise, with scientific determinism, a therapy for the few, we were led to promote an ethical disease among the many." See his *Young Man Luther: A Study in Psychoanalysis and History* (New York: W. W. Norton, 1958), p. 19.

8. Randall, 2:3.

9. Kohut, *Humanities*, pp. 263–269.

10. Kohut, *Analysis*, pp. 116–117. Note also the incredibly important visual aspects of the case of Mr. E. in *The Psychology of the Self: A Casebook*, ed. Arnold Goldberg (New York: International Universities Press, 1978), pp. 263–296.

11. See Kohut's "On the Enjoyment of Listening to Music" (with Siegmund Levarie) and "Observations on the Psychological Functions of Music," *Search*, vol. 1, pp. 13–158 and 233–254.

12. See letter to Roy Menninger, March 3, 1969, in *Curve*, p. 232.

13. Cf. Kohut, *Analysis*, p. 115, and Kohut, *Cure*, pp. 193–199.

14. See chapter 5, "The Oedipus Complex and the Psychology of the Self," in Kohut, *Restoration*, pp. 220–248.

15. Kohut, *Analysis*, p. 123. Note the general discussion in chapter 5, pp. 105–132.

16. Ibid., p. 221.

17. In notes to himself in connection with the visit of Anna Freud to Chicago in December 1966, Kohut recorded a conversation he had with her about their visit to Marshall Field's, the famous department store in Chicago. She was mightily impressed with all the goods. She said it appealed to her. "It's the Jewish in me, isn't it?" Kohut was not amused and said stiffly that it seemed to him a rather general human trait to want material things and that department stores were flourishing everywhere; It was not something specifically Jewish. Anna Freud replied: "No, it's the Jewish in me."

18. Interview with Jerome Beigler, July 10, 1987.

19. I confirmed this in a conversation with Edith Kestenberg of New York, who had been a part of the Bergman seminar.

20. This is the spelling given by Ornstein in *Search*, but it is fairly clear that Kohut said "humanness" in the lecture. That is also what he said in talking about the same subject in *Advances*.

21. In "Courage," Kohut referred on his first page to his friend Alexander Mitscherlich and his work *Society Without the Father*; in notes to the essay, he mentioned Christian Petry, *Studenten aufs Schafott*, and Inge Scholl, *Die Weise Rose*; in "On Leadership," he mentioned Karl Dietrich Bracher, *Die deutsche Diktatur:*

Entstehung, Struktur, Folgen, Des Nationalsocialismus; and in *Advances* (1980), he referred to Matussek's discussion of those heroic survivors of concentration camps who did not lose their humanness during their dehumanizing ordeal, *Die Konzentrationaslagerhaft und ihre Folgen.*

22. Kohut, *Humanities*, pp. 1–72.

23. Kohut, *Advances*, pp. 486–487.

24. Kohut, *Humanities*, pp. 215–223.

25. Kohut concluded his thoughts with some comments on our often desperate strivings for heroes who die for a purpose, like Marie Scholl in Nazi Germany, whom he discussed in "On Courage," *Humanities*, pp. 5–50. In Scholl's dream just before her execution, she puts a baby across a crevice and then dies with her cheeks flushed with excitement. For Kohut, the dream signified that Scholl dies but her ideals live on. And he concluded, with a slight smile: "So is this optimism? Maybe."

26. Erikson, *Young Man Luther.*

10

Creating a New Research Paradigm for the Psychoanalytic Study of Religion

The Pioneering Work of Ana-Maria Rizzuto

John McDargh

How is new knowledge created in the psychoanalytic study of religion? As James Jones's chapter on D. W. Winnicott should make clear, one requisite for new knowledge may be that there be new epistemological paradigms that enable us to understand better the relationships between knower and known, the human subject and his or her objects of religious belief. But fresh understanding also arises with the development of creative new strategies for attending to, as well as interpreting, religious phenomena. Winnicott and the British Independent School of Psychoanalysis have produced theoretical innovations that have given the psychoanalytic study of religious phenomena a new energy and direction. But it was Argentine-born psychiatrist and psychoanalyst Ana-Maria Rizzuto who, in *The Birth of the Living God* (1979), demonstrated the potential of these theoretical innovations to organize new strategies for psychoanalytic investigation into the structure and function of religious beliefs in human psychic life (Rizzuto 1979; see also Rizzuto 1974, 1976, 1982). Clinical psychologist Mary Lou Randour, in her introduction to an edited collection of essays on "religious and spiritual experiences in psychotherapy," expressed this sense of Rizzuto's contribution in these words: "If the symbol of Freud as 'father' of psychoanalysis has been used to explain his historical position, certainly Rizzuto is the 'mother' of all attempts to explicate a developmental and clinical psychoanalytic theory of religious experience" (1993:9). I would suggest, with Randour, that it is indeed the influence of Rizzuto's research that accounts in great measure for the rapid expansion of psychoanalytically informed investigations of religion, particularly outside the traditional social location of such research—the psychoanalytic institutes and their psychiatric constituencies.

The impact of Rizzuto's work cannot be attributed solely to her development of a particular research methodology, however. It must also be related to what the publication of her study represents in the history of the psychoanalytic movement's waxing and waning culture war with Western religion. Here, for the first time, was a fully credentialed psychoanalyst demonstrating in a careful, rigorous fashion the *clinical* utility of taking an individual's idiosyncratic religious beliefs with great seriousness *both* as another "royal road to the unconscious" for the clinical *and* as a resource for the psychic well-being of the patient (and not simply an index of personal pathology). As a major defection from a certain kind of psychoanalytic orthodoxy regarding religion, Ana-Maria Rizzuto's book was greeted either with silence or with critical polemic from within the psychoanalytic establishment. By contrast, the generally appreciative scholarly reception that *The Birth of the Living God* received from psychoanalytically oriented psychotherapists, pastoral counselors, and research psychologists studying religion suggests that it was a work that was particularly timely and responsive to the intellectual needs of that sector. As I shall suggest at greater length, Rizzuto's work has been embraced as significant *not*—as some charge—because it might be recruited to a religious apologetic (a use Rizzuto would have been the first to protest) but rather because it gives clinicians permission to look critically at the psychic functioning of religious images without the a priori assumption that all one will find there is a defensive function in the service of an arrested psychological development. In that sense, Rizzuto's research represents a return to that mode of empiricism that characterized William James's original approach to the psychology of religion—a fascination with the unlimited plurality and variety of religious experiencing and a commitment to investigate the "real work" that is done by an individual's religious beliefs without a need to either attack or defend the ontological status of those beliefs.

In writing this contribution to the volume, I have been interested in a number of questions: (1) How does the research project that eventuated in *The Birth of the Living God* reflect the researcher's own intellectual, including theological, formation? (2) How was the study designed and carried out, and in its published presentation, what are its distinctive contributions to the field? (3) And finally, surveying the range of scholarly responses to this work, what can we say of the future and promise of the trajectory of research and reflection that this work has helped to launch?

Theological and Clinical Background to Rizzuto's Research

A study of the roots of Ana-Maria Rizzuto's research program in her own clinical and theological formation illustrates a general and perhaps unremarkable truism: that one's respective life experiences and philosophy shape the way in which one approaches psychoanalytic thinking as a resource for understanding religion. But her own history as a physician and an analyst makes a more specific and more interesting point. For someone raised and continuing to identify as a Christian believer to take up the deconstructive tools of psychoanalysis to examine religion, perhaps there must be a credible theological warrant that makes that task not only permissible but even necessary. In Rizzuto's own case, as I see it, the path to the psychoanalytic investigation of personal religion tracks along some of the influential intellectual currents in modern Catholic thought that opened the door to consider the historical development of doctrine and the deep and necessary continuities between human psychological growth and spiritual maturation.[1]

Coming of age in Argentina prior to the Second Vatican Council, Ana-Maria Rizzuto identifies as one of the formative personal experiences of her young adult years her pastoral work in a multiclass Roman Catholic parish where she was involved in social work, organizing, and catechetical work with poorer children and their families. With the support and encouragement of the parish priest, Rizzuto delivered social and pastoral services in a role that gave her the rare opportunity to listen to the personal stories and spiritual struggles of parishioners of all ages and classes. One such story that she recalls from those years perhaps illustrates Rizzuto's early awareness of how the individual's religious imagination is organized *relationally*. The child of a deceased prostitute in her town protested to her that she had no desire to "go to heaven." A sensitive listener, Rizzuto also learned that the child rejected the possibility of heaven because she did not want to be separated in death from her mother, whom she imagined was consigned by God to hell. The program of Rizzuto's mature work as a psychoanalytic researcher may be encapsulated in this one small anecdote: how to understand an individual's religious beliefs as a uniquely personal creation that employs the symbolic resources of a religious culture but in a highly idiosyncratic fashion and in the service of constructing a world in which one remains meaningfully connected or related to the "other."

Ana-Maria Rizzuto entered university in the mid-1950s, completing her medical degree at the National University of Córdoba with a specialization in internal medicine and hematology. She also held professorships in child and adolescent psychology at the Catholic University of Córdoba from 1960 to 1965. Meanwhile, however, she continued her involvement as a lay person in the life of the Catholic community, where certain continental and Latin American theologians and philosophers whose work was to be foundational for the Second Vatican Council were beginning to be read. As Rizzuto recounts it, a watershed intellectual experience was her participation in a select year-long study group that focused on the problem of the *evolution of dogma* in the Catholic Church. Working through the writings of such figures as Yves Congar, Gustav Thils, Jacques Leclerq, Henri deLubac, Hans Küng, and Karl Rahner, she encountered for the first time a compelling case for the church as a living and growing social organism, not a static and unchanging institution whose divine constitution inoculated it against the necessity of change or renewal. The organic image of the church that emerged from these thinkers is of a dynamic and constantly developing body. This body is composed of all the faithful, priests and lay persons alike, who are made responsive by the inspiration of the indwelling Spirit to new historical demands and invitations. But if this is true of the church as a collectivity, then mutatis mutandis it must also be the case for individual persons, and the theological door is thrown open to consider human believing as itself a dynamic, continually evolving process. It is a door that Rizzuto walked through with enthusiasm—and not alone.

In the years before and during the Second Vatican Council (1962–1965), there was a growing interest in some sectors of the Argentine church in preparing priests and pastoral workers to work with greater psychological awareness of the human foundations of religious belief. Designated professor of pastoral anthropology at the Pontifical Seminary of Our Lady of Loreto in Córdoba, Rizzuto was invited to design and teach a first-of-its-kind course for clergy and seminarians in Córdoba on the psychology of faith—at a time when the works of Sigmund Freud were still on the *Index of Forbidden Books*. Relevant material on the psychology of religion available in French or Spanish was limited—Roland Dalbeiz, Ignatius Lepp, H. C. Rümke, Carl Jung, and Freud. Rizzuto's response to the invitation, after securing the assurance of the bishop that no topics and no resources would be considered beyond investigation, was to develop an educational strategy that made each course participant an independent investigator. Quite simply, all participants were asked to pay close attention to what they were hearing and seeing in the course of their ordinary pastoral work and then to make that material the substance of their common weekly study. Emphasis was placed on capturing the immediacy of the sharing that had taken place and taking seriously the "data of the details" of each conversation. The approach was inductive, empirical without being positivistic, and certainly radically different from that of the manuals of penitential counsel that had been the stock-in-trade of Roman Catholic seminary education prior to the Second Vatican Council. Again, the conviction emerged that the key to understanding religious faith was a mode of careful, systematic observation of the very particular imagery that persons employ to tell their own life stories and to talk about the God of their understanding. This same general approach to understanding would later characterize Rizzuto's psychological research.

In 1965, when Ana-Maria Rizzuto left Argentina to pursue psychiatric training, she arrived in the United States with a potential research design already in mind, one grounded in her own considerable experience listening to countless conversations with medical professionals, priests, parishioners, and patients. Rizzuto would find the key to interpreting these living human documents in the psychoanalytic training that she began in Boston in 1968, but the basic motivation for her research was already in development prior to her formal analytic training. This, perhaps as much as any other factor, may account for the fresh and original feel of Rizzuto's approach to psychological research: that she began with an immersion in the questions raised by intricate religious experiencing rather than with a set interpretation and methodology defined by psychoanalysis that might subsequently be "applied."

The Research Project: Design

The initial challenge Rizzuto took up was to verify her own intuition that the dynamics of religious believing are the same across normal and clinical populations or, to use Harry Stack Sullivan's fortunate phrasing, that we are "all more simply human than not" when it comes to how we function in this arena of mental life. Rizzuto conducted a year-long pilot study at Boston State Hospital (1966–1967), acquiring along the way the encouragement and support of the late Elvin Semrad, the dean of psychiatric training in the Boston area. Comparing fifteen hospitalized patients with five professional employees at the hospital, she satisfied herself that though the specific *contents* of religious believing may vary, the *process* of believing differed in degree but not in kind between mental patients and persons considered "normal" (Rizzuto 1979:181). This completed, the next stage of her research was conducted at Tufts–New England Medical Center, where she held the position of chief resident and teaching fellow in psychiatry. This three-year project (1967–1970) was the empirical basis for *The Birth of the Living God*.

As chief resident, Rizzuto had permission to utilize the entire inpatient population for her research. For the purpose, she devised a three-part protocol that was administered to 123 inpatients over the period of the study.

1. During the first week of a standard two-week hospitalization, the patient was asked to draw a picture of his or her family and then was given a family questionnaire, reproduced in the appendix of Rizzuto's book

(1979:217–219). The twenty-three-item questionnaire pulled for the patient's identifications (e.g., "Emotionally I resemble my _____ because _____," "The member of the family I admire the most is my _____ because _____"), as well as his or her sense of the lines of loyalty, subgroupings, and patterns of authority in the family (e.g., "The boss in my family was _____ because _____"). Finally, the patient was asked to identify how old he or she was in the family picture that he or she drew and where the family was living that was depicted in the drawing.

2. In the second week of hospitalization, the patient was given a "God Questionnaire" of some forty-five questions (Rizzuto 1979:213–217). The questionnaire allowed the patient to state if he or she believed or did not believe in a personal God and why; regardless of that answer, it inquired into how the patient perceived God, even if he or she did not believe in God (e.g., "What I like the most about God is _____ because _____," or "What I resent most about God is _____ because _____"). As I shall discuss further, Rizzuto found it significant that even those patients who claimed a disbelief in God had some fairly definite notions about what God would or would not want and how they might be related to this God whose existence they denied. The emphasis in the questionnaire was on the patients' affective relationship to the God they imagined and on what the patients themselves saw as the history of that relationship (e.g., "The day I changed my way of thinking about God was _____ because _____"). There were a few questions that tapped into the patient's relationship to other traditional religious imagery, for example, favorite saints or biblical characters and the devil, but the primary focus was on the way in which the patient imagined the actions, desires, intentions, and attitudes of the figure associated with the word-symbol "G-o-d."

3. In the final discharge interview, Rizzuto asked the patient to draw a picture of God and discuss that picture with her. In the course of 123 interviews, apparently only 1 patient ever refused to attempt such a drawing, and interestingly, he was a highly paranoid clergyman.

From the 123 research pictures and questionnaires, Rizzuto selected 20 that spanned all diagnostic categories but included the more articulate and developed questionnaires. She then wrote a painstaking, 30-page formulation of each of these 20 patients, also drawing upon the process notes from over 18 hours of inpatient therapy as well as the social work and nursing notes from the patients' medical records while on the unit. From this extensive array of data on each individual, Rizzuto organized her 20 patients according to a typology of the conscious way in which individuals described themselves as "believing" or "not believing" in God. The 4 cases presented in the second part of her book were selected as particularly rich representations of persons from each of these 4 categories:

(1) those who have a God whose existence they do not doubt;
(2) those wondering whether or not to believe in a God they are not sure exists;
(3) those amazed, angered, or quietly surprised to see others deeply invested in a God that does not interest them;
(4) those who struggle with a demanding, harsh God they would like to get rid of if they were not convinced of his existence and power (Rizzuto 1979:91).

This typology alerts us to a central interest in Rizzuto's work: the exploration and uncovering of the immensely complex, often hidden, and always intensely personal roots of what is, in U.S. culture at least, essentially a social and public action—the declaration of belief or unbelief in "God."[2] Like Freud, then, she begins with a sense of wonder about how it is that people can become fervently committed to and vitally engaged with an object that is invisible and unverifiable. Unlike Freud, however, she recognizes that religious unbelief demands psychological explanation every bit as much as religious belief does. Furthermore, she allows herself to wonder how and why some people maintain an attachment to a God who is punitive and persecutory. Such a God does not appear to provide the kind of compensation and consolation that Freud had held was one of the psychological motivations for the human creation of a deity. The quest for answers leads her where it took Freud: into the vicissitudes of that intricate and lifelong process whereby a human infant, born into a condition of extended dependence on the care of others, becomes a self both separate and related. Her use of Winnicott and post-Freudian psychoanalytic thinking, however, takes her in directions that move in significant ways beyond the Freud of *Future of an Illusion*, even as she remains essentially committed to the psychoanalytic paradigm. In the following section, I shall examine briefly some of the principle features of her findings before considering the range of response her work has provoked from other scholars of the psychology of religion.

The Research Project: Findings

1. *No one coming to awareness in a society where the symbol "God" has any cultural currency is without a conscious or unconscious object representation of God.*

In several places in her book, Rizzuto was quite unequivocal on this point: "In Freud's understanding of the subject, and in my own, *there is no such thing as a person without a God representation*" (1979:47, emphasis added). This is an assertion that has the capacity to make some other psychoanalysts a bit edgy, or so I have personally observed. At an early presentation of her research to a psychoanalytic gathering prior to the publication of her major book, there were several analysts who objected defensively, if not with hostility, that since they had been "fully analyzed," they could not possibly still harbor an object representation of God. What such a response misses, of course, is that Rizzuto was not claiming that her colleagues somehow secretly or unconsciously believed in God but rather that an analytic inquiry into the representations of the God they did *not* believe in would itself yield evidence of its intricate origins in the vicissitudes of a particular family romance.

On the one hand, Rizzuto's claim was based, in part, on her own clinical observation that none of her subjects, regardless of religious upbringing or current conscious philosophical convictions, failed to produce evidence of having some associations to "God" that endured at multiple representational levels. On the other hand, Rizzuto's claim was so sweeping an assertion because it was an extrapolation from an understanding of the early childhood developmental process derived from Freud but read through the work of D. W. Winnicott.

It was Winnicott who held that in the lifelong task of becoming a self, the capacity for "illusory" thinking is an indispensable psychic resource. As Jones has expounded in this book, the child, from a very early age, manages to maintain some basic sense of being a self-in-relationship by means of a process of protosymbolization—the investing of a toy, a blanket corner, a physical practice with the capacity to evoke certain self-states that are at least minimally solacing. This same psychic capacity, enlarged and extended into early childhood, produces the imaginary companions and fantasy figures that populate the child's inner world, and in adulthood, it becomes the sphere of art and religion. Rizzuto maintains, I think rightly, that in the West, "God" is a generally available cultural resource. Even children raised in irreligious or unobservant households hear persons evoke "God" for blessing or curse and notice "In God We Trust" written on currency. They cannot fail to observe that though they and their peers are systematically disillusioned about Santa Claus or the tooth fairy at a certain age, no such intervention is made regarding this suprapersonal figure that seems somehow to hover mysteriously in the background or foreground of other people's lives. Peter Homans has wondered whether Rizzuto has overstated the case, particularly as certain segments of European and U.S. culture become increasingly secular and unchurched (1982:445–446). But that is a question that honestly invites empirical inquiry. Rizzuto herself has urged that her methodology be applied cross-culturally to investigate the cognate psychological function of religious symbols in Hindu, Buddhist, and Muslim societies. The crucial question, Rizzuto would hold, is not whether an individual has a representation of "God" per se. Rather, it is how the representational resources constructed by the child out of his or her creative weaving together of memorialized interpersonal experience and cultural interactions manage to keep pace with the psychological needs of the developing human over the course of the life cycle. To draw the theological analog: What matters is not what dogmas we hold but if and how they are capable of evolution and adaptation to meet the needs of a changing community.

2. *The object representations of God are not simply derived from the child's experience of the historical father, and once fashioned, they do not remain static and unchanging. Rather, they are available for further elaboration, revision, refashioning, or rejection in ways related to the function they are called upon to serve at any given moment.*

There are three significant developments beyond Freud condensed in the previous statement. The first concerns what sort of psychic "raw material" goes into the individual's mental representation of "God." Freud held, of course, that the familial referent for the Judeo-Christian God was the male child's father in the flesh—"a personal God is, psychologically, nothing other than an exalted father" (1910:123).[3] In her four case studies, Rizzuto presents persuasive evidence that a representation of God was more like a composite that could display together features of the pattern of interaction with either or both parents, grandparents, and, in theory, other significant caregivers from the child's earliest life experience.

The second deviation from Freud concerns the fate of these early representations of God, however formed. For Freud, they were necessarily psychological anachronisms that, being frozen in the state of their own primitive developmental origins, had to be surrendered in maturity as the rationally reflective person made his or her own peace with reality. For Rizzuto, it is no more clear that we are wed to the primitive character of our original God representations than that we are sentenced to live forever with the earliest representations formed of our parents. On the contrary, it is possible that these two develop pari pasu. It may also be that the circumstances of an individual's life wall off the God representations from critical psychological elaboration so that they remain arrested and perhaps deeply problematic. As Rizzuto wrote:

> It is a central thesis of this book that no child in the Western world brought up in ordinary circumstances completes the oedipal cycle without forming at least a rudimentary God representation, which he may use for belief or not. The rest of developmental life may leave that representation untouched as the individual continues to revise parent and self representations during the life cycle. If the God representation is not revised to keep pace with changes in self representation, it soon becomes asynchronous and is experienced as ridiculous or irrelevant or, on the contrary, threatening or dangerous (1979:200).

Third, Rizzuto follows the line of Winnicott and other object relations theorists who ascribe to the psychological processes that generate our representations of God an adaptive potential that is not outgrown or superseded in the course of maturation. In his various writings on Western religion,

Freud saw the psychological formation of "God" as serving only a defensive function. With the resolution of the Oedipal conflict,"God" became installed as an aspect of the superego that projects the authority and protective function of the formerly idealized father onto the cosmic screen. God then serves to compensate the individual for the narcissistic injuries inflicted by fate, contingency, and misfortune and for the instinctual renunciation required to live in society. In any case, for Freud, the psychologically adult individual—of which he was willing to grant there might be few specimens—is one who recognizes the illusory (i.e., wish-fulfillment-motivated) character of religious belief and surrenders these beliefs for a view of life informed only by the god *logos,* the still small voice of critical reason (1927).

Rizzuto does not deny that God representations might well serve these needs at a certain stage of development or even that this may remain the dominant function of religious believing for a great many persons. Finally, however, her study persuades her that this is an impoverished, incomplete, and clinically inadequate account of how religious "illusion" serves a human life (see also Pruyser 1974). Her four case studies might be considered "thick descriptions" of the multiple adaptive and defensive functions of the religious imagination. In the same book, she tried to summarize more theoretically and abstractly what those multiple functions are, and they seem to fall into two sorts. There are functions that have to do with *mastery,* and these she described using a language of "integration," "balance," and "equilibrium."[4] Then there are functions that have to do with *meaning making,* and here, her language moved beyond the usual terms of psychoanalytic discourse to sound more existential and even theological. The study of the life-long metamorphosis of the God representations, she wrote, "provide[s] us with a beautiful illustration of the ingenuity and creative symbolic mastery of the human mind in the effort made by the individual to master his present reality, his past, and his contemporary context, *as well as of his need for transcendence and meaning* in the context of the universe at large" (Rizzuto 1979:90, emphasis added). Some of the most creative subsequent work that has been stimulated by Rizzuto's project has used the work of analysts such as Stephen Mitchell, Jessica Benjamin, and Christopher Bollas to show how "mastery" and "meaning making" come together around the problem of maintaining a sense of being a self-in-relation (Shafranske 1992; Jones 1991).

3. *It is important to distinguish the more preconscious, imaginal, primary process dimensions of an individual's "God" from the more public, secondary process, conceptual elaborations of "God."*

Rizzuto's key insight here was illustrated for me in a story told by a colleague, a theologically sophisticated individual who has subjected his own religious formation to intense scrutiny and, he thought, a thoroughgoing critical demythologizing. "God," insofar as he spoke of (or to) a divinity, was something closer to Tillich's existential "Ground of Being." It was with some considerable shock then that he found himself, on one very frightening plane ride, spontaneously and earnestly addressing God in the words of a long-forgotten bedtime prayer that went back to his evangelical childhood. My colleague was surprised; Rizzuto would not have been. The working distinction between the "God of the philosophers/theologians" and the "living God" whose visage is shaped by the individual's whole affective, relational experience is a crucial one for Rizzuto:

> When dealing with the concrete fact of belief, it is important to clarify the conceptual and emotional differences between the concept of God and the images of God which, combined in multiple forms, produce the prevailing God representation in a given individual at a given time. The concept of God is fabricated mostly at the level of secondary-process thinking. This is the God of the theologians, the God whose existence or nonexistence is debated by metaphysical reasoning. But this God leaves us cold. This God is only the result of rigorous thinking about causality and philosophical premises. Even someone who believes intellectually that there *must* be a God may feel no inclination to accept him unless images of previous interpersonal experience have fleshed out a concept with multiple images that can now coalesce in a representation that he can accept emotionally (1979:47–48).

In a more recent talk delivered at the Menninger Clinic, Rizzuto articulated perhaps most clearly this conviction that "believing" must be understood psychologically as an affair of the heart and not simply of the head. "Belief is never only something to be believed *in,* a fact of knowledge or dogma alone. It is an interpersonal disposition that affirms the existence of a *mode of relatedness* between the believer and others, be it people, the universe conceived as a living reality or a divine being. Thus belief as a human act of attribution is always, by its very nature, an affective act of connection" (Rizzuto 1995).

Influence of Rizzuto's Work on Current Research and Theory

At the conclusion of her book, Rizzuto wrote, "If my own research stimulates more scientific investigation in the fields of psychology, sociology, anthropology, comparative religions, mythology and others, I will consider my efforts well rewarded" (1979:211). Some seventeen years after that statement, it is fair to say that Rizzuto's investigative efforts have indeed begun to be rewarded but not necessarily from the intellectual quadrants she might have hoped for as a working analyst.

Though *The Birth of the Living God* was reviewed in over half a dozen national journals of the study of religion or pastoral care and counseling (e.g., *Theological Studies, The Journal of Pastoral Care, The Journal of Religion and Health*), it was reviewed at length in only one psychoanalytic journal, *Psychoanalytic Quarterly*. The author of that single review essay, after praising Rizzuto's "masterful review" of the psychoanalytic literature on religion, quite heatedly charged Rizzuto with having written a "brief for religion" and of having used object relations theory "as a crypto-Jungian basis for a psychoanalytic theology" (Stein 1981:126). The nub of the reviewer's critique is that Rizzuto fails to embrace Freud's ideal of maturity as the relinquishment of all illusions "in favor of mature, post oedipal love and work." To suggest, as Rizzuto does, that even in maturity we never outgrow our need for some form of transitional experiencing is to commit "the error of confusing a persistent group fetish with a true transitional object, that is, an object that is phase-specifically intermediate between lesser and greater self-differentiation and individuation." The reviewer went so far as to intimate that Rizzuto's or anyone else's failure to uphold a thorough, orthodox hermeneutic of suspicion is possible evidence of an incomplete analysis. "There can be no compromise between the pre oedipal and oedipal authoritarian character and the post oedipal human chary of all belief. Any psychoanalysis which admits such a compromise reveals a lacunar resistance, an incompleteness of analysis in the analyst" (Stein 1981:127).

Ironically, Rizzuto's work has also drawn more developed responses that critique her from quite the opposite direction, charging that her search for psychological origins is inherently reductionistic. In other words, it is held that the burden of her research is to make of God "nothing but" the sum of the individual's history of human object relationships as these have been psychologically memorialized, without leaving room for the possibility that the reality of God him/her/itself may be an essential contributor to the representational process. New Haven psychoanalyst Stanley Leavy (1988, 1990) has argued this position, and it is suggested in critiques of Rizzuto's work written from an evangelical Christian perspective (Duvall 1994). The most developed statement of this position, which also attempts to work out a comprehensive theoretical and clinical model of the representational process that incorporates the possibility of a "veridically other" God as a player in mental life, is the work of Orthodox Jewish psychologist Moshe Halevi Spero (1985, 1992).[5]

Between these two critiques—the "orthodox" psychoanalytic and the "orthodox" religious—is a position that finds in Rizzuto's appropriation of Winnicott the beginning of a profound "postmodern" epistemological shift, which judges the adequacy of both the positivism of Freud and the theological positivism of those who must regard "God" as verily an "other" outside and beyond the human knower. James Jones (1991a, 1991b), with an interdisciplinary background in psychology, religious studies, and the philosophy of science, has argued perhaps most persuasively that this challenge to the Cartesian dualisms of subject-object and knower-known has its parallels in developments within the physical sciences, in feminist psychology, and ultimately in postmodern theologizing.

The very positive response to Rizzuto's work from scholars working within the disciplines of pastoral care and counseling reflects the way in which they find in her presentation of psychoanalytic thinking a "tool to think with" about two issues central to their discipline: one clinical and the other theological. It has been argued that, in its essential praxis, Christian and Jewish pastoral care and counsel are processes of helping persons unmask the false gods or idolatries that limit human freedom and compromise the capacity for love (Jordan 1985). Rizzuto models an approach to the individual's religious life that permits a more experience-near investigation of that psychological and spiritual dynamic (Heinrichs 1982). The second issue, which pastoral counseling shares with fundamental theology, is how to find a way to speak meaningfully about two enduring paradoxes: first, that our speech about "God" is simultaneously an imaginative creation of the human mind, yet intends a Reality that exceeds us utterly but to which we essentially and inseparably belong, and second, that human beings, on the one hand, must develop the "capacity to be alone" (Winnicott) and, on the other, are human only insofar as they are in relationship from beginning to end. Rizzuto's particular appropriation of psychoanalytic object relations theory, whether she so intended it or not, alerted those in the pastoral disciplines whose acquaintance with psychoanalysis was largely limited to Freud and ego psychology that contemporary psychoanalytic object relations theory might well be a resource for a kind of theological via media (Meissner 1984, 1987; McDargh 1983, 1986; St. Clair 1994). Pastoral theologian Leroy Howe spoke of this when, with specific reference to Rizzuto, he wrote:

> What is true of transitional objects is quintessentially true of our God representations and of the world coherence we experience by means of them. What we affirm about God is neither an "objectively" valid representation of a real but transcendent entity, nor is it a complex of wish-driven abstractions formed in our minds out of other internal object representations and encounters with "real" objects in an empirical, interpersonal world. It is both, inseparably (1995:110).

In addition to these more theoretical treatments of questions raised by Rizzuto's work, there has been a blossoming of creative empirical work following the publication of *The Birth of the Living God*. European and North American psychologists interested in religion have been researching the psychological dimensions of the individual's "concept" of God for over thirty years. Moreover, many of these studies, influenced by psychoanalysis, have been aimed at understanding how the "concept" of God relates to the individual's associations to parental figures or to idealized notions of father and mother (Vergote et al. 1969). In the main, these research methods have employed adjective checklists (Gorsuch 1968) or semantic differential scales (Benson and Spilka 1973) in order to identify attributional factors of God (loving, controlling, wrathful, etc.), which might then be correlated with other personality variables (e.g., self-esteem, level of ego function, etc.) or with certain religious behaviors (Schaefer and Gorsuch 1992).[6]

Into this vigorous research tradition, *The Birth of the Living God* usefully introduced another order of complexity and opened up a range of questions meant to relate research to its potential value for clinical or therapeutic work. For example, by proposing that our representations of God are conscious, preconscious, and sometimes unconscious, Rizzuto's study challenged researchers to devise new ways of accessing this material (Brokaw 1992; Spear 1994). One way has been for psychologists to work from Rizzuto's clinical findings but develop testing instruments that can be more statistically validated and controlled than Rizzuto's God questionnaire and hence potentially more useful clinically. For example, we have the Spiritual Themes and Religious Responses Test (STARR), which is a projective test inviting responses to a series of photographs of persons at prayer (Saur and Saur 1993). Another instrument under study, which is becoming more psychometrically sophisticated as it is being utilized by other researchers looking at such things as psychotherapy outcomes, is the God Image Inventory (GII) developed at Catholic University by R. T. Lawrence. The God Image Inventory was an attempt to develop scales for the individual's felt sense of who God is for him or her that might correlate with measures of the individual's sense of himself or herself (Lawrence 1991).

A number of other promising lines of investigation can be traced to questions raised in the Rizzuto study. One is to look at the way in which the therapist's own countertransference around religion affects how he or she relates to the religious material of the patient. This is an issue that occupies Moshe Halevi Spero (1981), but it has also been the object of critical study by a number of methods. A suggestive example of these studies is one that looked at how the God representation of the *therapist* and the therapist's own experience of addressing religious issues in his or her own experience of therapy affects his or her ability to respond to religious issues as they arise in the therapeutic context (Sorenson 1994 and in press; see also Kochems 1993 and Kehoe and Guthiel 1993). Other research initiatives have asked how particular traumatic experiences may affect a person's representations of God. Here, Carrie Doehring's (1993) careful empirical investigation of the object representational world of women recovering from sexual abuse is perhaps exemplary. Two edited collections of scholarly articles published in the last four years provide a feel for some of the diverse approaches: Mary Lou Randour's *Exploring Sacred Landscapes* and Mark Finn and John Gartner's

Object Relations Theory and Religion. The latter is remarkable for its extension of religion beyond the Jewish-Christian axis to consider Eastern and in particular Buddhist religious traditions as these have increasingly become part of the religious landscape in the United States (Randour 1993; Finn and Gartner 1993).

Conclusions

A functional approach to the study of our images of God is not new in the history of the psychology of religion. Toward the end of the *Varieties,* William James quoted with approval his colleague James Henry Leuba on this matter:

> The truth of the matter can be put ... in this way: *God is not known, he is not understood; he is used*—sometimes as a meat-purveyor, sometimes as moral support, sometimes as a friend, sometimes as an object of love. If he proves himself useful, the religious consciousness asks for no more than that. Does God really exist? How does he exist? What is he? are so many irrelevant questions. Not God, but life, more life, a larger, richer, more satisfying life, is, in the last analysis, the end of religion (1902:399, emphasis in original).

Ana-Maria Rizzuto's work may be seen as an extended scientific expansion of Leuba's observation, with some significant qualifications. It is psychoanalytic object relations theory that allows a psychological argument (and not simply an assertion) to be made that "a larger, richer, more satisfying life" is the psychological aim of all of our religious imaginings. It is also contemporary psychoanalytic theory as Rizzuto has helped introduce it into the psychology of religion that can trace the ways in which this hunger for more life can go tragically awry and be traced in the representations of God that haunt people's lives. Finally, *pace* Professor Leuba, Rizzuto's research and certainly the critical responses to it that I have considered, show that the question of the existence of "God" is not irrelevant—but may perhaps be discussible in new and more promising ways precisely because of the developments in analytic thought that Rizzuto has promoted and advanced.

Notes

1. In another essay, I have argued that a characteristically "Catholic" concern in psychology has been to maintain the *continuity* between the divine and the human, in other words, to believe their essential interrelatedness out of a conviction that the grace of God builds upon or "perfects" human nature (*gratis perficit naturam*). This loyalty to a unified vision of the human person that looks for the evidence of a "fit" between God and the human person in the unfolding structure of human psychic life is evident, I believe, throughout Rizzuto's work and accounts in part for why she is

clinically unafraid to look in a sustained fashion at human developmental patterns (McDargh 1985). I am indebted to Ana-Maria Rizzuto for generously permitting me to interview her at length about her own professional and religious history as these relate to her research interests.

2. The interest in studying "believing" as both a social and a personal phenomenon is one that Rizzuto shares with a rich tradition of investigation prominent among European psychologists of religion going back to the seminal work of Dutch psychologist H. C. Rümke (1939). See Corveleyn and Hutsebaut (1994).

3. Freud (1913) has a line of phylogenetic argumentation that he set out in *Totem and Taboo* in which he hypothesized that it is the primeval father of a postulated "primal horde" that is the source of the "God" whose memory has somehow been transmitted down through the history of the species.

4. Rizzuto wrote: "Once created, our God, dormant or active, remains a potentially available representation for the continuous process of *psychic integration*"; "we engage in constant dialectical reshaping of our self- and object representations to attain *psychic balance*"; "all these maneuvers serve to maintain *equilibrium* between the relevant objects of the present and their demands, the sense of self at that particular moment, and object representations of the past, God included" (1979:180, 89, emphases added).

5. For a survey of the range of philosophical positions that therapists have taken with respect to the religious material of their clients, see McDargh 1992.

6. For a helpful survey of the major psychological instruments for the study of the religious dimension of human experience, see Hall, Tisdale, and Brokaw 1994.

References

Benson, P., and B. Spilka. 1973. God image as a function of self esteem and locus of control. *Journal for the Scientific Study of Religion* 12: 297–310.

Brokaw, B. F. 1992. The relationship of God image to level of object relations development. Ph.D. diss., Rosemead School of Psychology, Biola University (1991). *Dissertations Abstracts International*, 52, 6077B.

Corveleyn, J., and D. Hutsebaut, eds. 1994. *Belief and Unbelief: Psychological Perspectives.* Amsterdam: Rodopi.

Doehring, C. 1993. *Internal Desecration: Traumatization and God Representations.* Lanham, Md.: University Press of America.

Duvall, N. 1994. Review of M. Finn and J. Gartner, *Object Relations Theory and Religion. Journal of Psychology and Theology* 22: 429–432.

Finn, M., and J. Gartner, eds. 1993. *Object Relations Theory and Religion: Clinical Applications.* New York: Praeger Press.

Freud, S. 1910/1958. *Leonardo Da Vinci and a Memory of His Childhood.* In *Standard Edition* 11, translated by J. Strachey. London: Hogarth Press and the Institute of Psychoanalysis.

_____. 1913. *Totem and Taboo.* New York: W. W. Norton, 1952.

_____. 1927. *The Future of an Illusion* . New York: W. W. Norton, 1961.

Gorsuch, R. 1968. The conceptualization of God as seen in adjective ratings. *Journal for the Scientific Study of Religion* 7: 56–64.

Hall, T. T. Tisdale, and B. Brokaw. 1994. Assessment of religious dimensions in Christian clients: A review of selected instruments for research and clinical use. *Journal of Psychology and Theology* 22: 395–421.

Heinrichs, D. 1982. Our Father which art in heaven: Parataxic distortions in the image of God. *Journal of Psychology and Theology* 10: 120–129.

Homans, P. 1982. Review of *The Birth of the Living God. Journal of Religion* 62: 445–446.

Howe, L. 1995. *The Image of God: A Theology for Pastoral Care and Counseling.* Nashville, Tenn.: Abingdon Press.

James, W. 1902. *The Varieties of Religious Experience.* Cambridge, Mass.: Harvard University Press, 1985.

Jones, J. 1991a. *Contemporary Psychoanalysis and Religion: Transference and Transcendence.* New Haven: Yale University Press.

_____. 1991b. The relational self: Contemporary psychoanalysis reconsiders religion. *Journal of the American Academy of Religion* 59: 119–135.

Jordan, M. 1985. *Taking on the Gods: The Task of the Pastoral Counselor.* Nashville, Tenn.: Abingdon Press.

Kehoe, N., and T. Guthiel. 1993. Ministry or therapy: The role of transference and counter transference in a religious therapist. In M. Randour, ed., *Exploring Sacred Landscapes: Religious and Spiritual Experiences in Psychotherapy.* New York: Columbia University Press, pp. 55–80.

Kochems, T. 1993. Countertransference and transference aspects of religious material in psychotherapy: The isolation or integration of religious material. In M. Randour, ed., *Exploring Sacred Landscapes: Religious and Spiritual Experiences in Psychotherapy.* New York: Columbia University Press, pp. 34–54.

Lawrence, R. T. 1991. The God Image Inventory: The development, validation and standardization of a psychometric instrument for research, pastoral and clinical use in measuring the image of God. Ph.D. diss., Catholic University of America, Washington, D.C.

Leavy, S. 1988. *In the Image of God: A Psychoanalyst's View.* New Haven: Yale University Press.

_____. 1990. Reality in religion and psychoanalysis. In J. H. Smith and S. A. Handelman, eds., *Psychoanalysis and Religion.* Baltimore: Johns Hopkins University Press, pp. 43–55.

McDargh, J. 1983. *Psychoanalytic Object Relations Theory and the Study of Religion.* Lanham, Md.: University Press of America.

_____. 1985. Theological uses of psychology: A retrospective and prospective. *Horizons* 12 (2): 247–264.

_____. 1986. God, mother and me: An object relational perspective on religious material. *Pastoral Psychology* 34: 251–263.

_____. 1992. Concluding clinical postscript: On developing a psycho-theological perspective. In M. Randour, ed., *Exploring Sacred Landscapes: Religious and Spiritual Experiences in Psychotherapy.* New York: Columbia University Press.

Meissner, W. W. 1984. *Psychoanalysis and Religious Experience.* New Haven: Yale University Press.

_____. 1987. *Life and Faith: Psychological Perspectives on Religious Experience.* Washington, D.C.: Georgetown University Press.

_____. 1990. The role of transitional conceptualization in religious thought. In J. H. Smith and S. A. Handelman, eds., *Psychoanalysis and Religion.* Baltimore: Johns Hopkins University Press, pp. 101–127.

Pruyser, P. W. 1974. *Beyond Belief and Unbelief.* New York: Harper & Row.

Randour, M., ed. 1993. *Exploring Sacred Landscapes: Religious and Spiritual Experiences in Psychotherapy.* New York: Columbia University Press.

_____. 1993. *Surveying Sacred Landscapes: Religious and Spiritual Experiences in Psychotherapy.* New York: Columbia University Press.

Rizzuto, A.-M. 1974. Object relations and the formation of the image of God. *British Journal of Medical Psychology* 47: 83–94.

_____. 1976. Freud, God and the devil and the theory of object representation. *International Review of Psychoanalysis* 3: 165–180.

_____. 1979. *The Birth of the Living God: A Psychoanalytic Study.* Chicago: University of Chicago Press.

_____. 1982. The father and the child's representation of God: A developmental approach. In S. Cath, A. Gurwitt, and J. Ross, eds., *Father and Child: Developmental and Clinical Perspectives.* Boston: Little, Brown, pp. 357–381.

_____. 1995. Psychodynamic aspect of religious beliefs. Paper delivered at the Menninger Clinic, March 10, 1995.

Rümke, H. C. 1939. *Karakter en aanleg in verband met het ongeloof.* Amsterdam: Ten Have. Published in English (1952) as *The Psychology of Unbelief.* London: Rockliff.

Saur, M., and W. Saur. 1993. Transitional phenomenon as evidenced in prayer. *Journal of Religion and Health* 32: 55–65.

Schaefer, C. A., and R. L. Gorsuch. 1992. Dimensionality of religion: Belief and motivation as predictors of behavior. *Journal of Psychology and Christianity* 11: 244–254.

Shafranske, E. 1992. God-representation as the transformational object. In M. Finn and J. Gardner, eds., *Object Relations Theory and Religion: Clinical Application.* Westport, Conn.: Praeger, pp. 57–72.

Sorenson, R. L. 1994. Therapists' (and their therapists') God representations in clinical practice. *Journal of Psychology and Theology* 22: 325–344.

_____. In press. Transcendence and intersubjectivity: The patient's experience of the analyst's spirituality. In C. Spezzano, ed., *The Soul on the Couch.* Hillsdale, N.J.: Analytic Press.

Spear, K. 1994. Conscious and pre-conscious God-concepts: An object relations perspective. Ph.D. diss., Fuller Theological Seminary, Pasadena, Calif.

Spero, M. H. 1981. Countertransference in religious therapists of religious patients. *American Journal of Psychoanalysis* 35: 565–576.

_____. 1985. The reality of the image of God in psychotherapy. *American Journal of Psychotherapy* 39: 75–85.

_____. 1992. *Religious Objects as Psychological Structures: A Critical Integration of Object Relations Theory, Psychotherapy and Judaism.* Chicago: University of Chicago Press.

St. Clair, M. 1994. *Human Relationships and the Experience of God: Object Relations and Religion.* Mahwah, N.J.: Paulist Press.

Stein, H. 1981. Review of A.-M. Rizzuto, *The Birth of the Living God. Psychoanalytic Quarterly* 50: 125–130.

Vergote, A., A. Tamayo, L. Pasquali, M. Bonami, M. Pattyn, and A. Clusters. 1969. Concept of God and parental images. *Journal of the Scientific Study of Religion* 8: 79–87.

11

Alice Miller's Insights into Religious Seekership

Marion S. Goldman

Alice Miller, the controversial German-born Swiss psychoanalytic theorist, has never treated religion or religiosity systematically. Aside from passing references, she has not examined religious experience, images, or institutions. Nevertheless, observations about strict German Lutheranism permeate her work, providing the social context for Miller's considerations of childhood socialization and emotional and physical abuse. Moreover, her insights about childhood and narcissistic vulnerability offer valuable strategies for the examination of religious seekership and responses to charismatic leadership in new religious movements.

In this chapter, I will describe Miller and the general development of her theoretical perspectives. Then I will consider her conceptualization of narcissism. Miller's delineation of narcissism as an adaptive response provides a foundation upon which to develop new approaches to religious seekership using object relations perspectives. The concepts of narcissistic vulnerability and narcissistic transferences elucidate the life histories of a small group of individuals who followed the Indian spiritual master Bhagwan Shree Rajneesh. Rajneesh's devotees, called *sannyasins*, gave up their hard-won financial and professional rewards in order to live at his communal city in central Oregon.

Alice Miller's Theories

Like many social theorists, Alice Miller has changed the direction of her work a number of times. She was a practicing psychoanalyst and supervisor for two decades before publishing her first books and shifting from practice to writing. She has published seven books, and she is writing an eighth.

In the first three, *The Drama of the Gifted Child* (1981), *For Your Own Good* (1983), and *Thou Shalt Not Be Aware* (1984), Miller grounded her discussions of parenting and narcissistic symptoms in psychoanalytically oriented self psychology. Her next book, *Pictures of a Childhood* (1986), included Miller's own watercolor paintings, and in it, she began an examination of parental cruelty, childhood experience, and creativity that she continued in *The Untouched Key* (1990). In her most recent works, *Banished Knowledge* (1990) and *Breaking Down the Wall of Silence* (1991), Miller completely severed her ties with psychoanalysis, defining Freud and his followers as the unwitting enemies of children. She has become an advocate for children and is working to develop methods of psychotherapy that permit adults to come to terms with the abused child within themselves.

Throughout her career, Miller has always focused upon the emotional and material injuries that parents inflict upon their children. Until she wrote *Das verbannte Wissen* (1988), later published as *Banished Knowledge* (1990) in the United States, Miller identified herself as part of the broad Freudian tradition. She had even dedicated the first edition of *Thou Shalt Not Be Aware* to Sigmund Freud on the anniversary of his one-hundred-twenty-fifth birthday (1984:VIII).

Although Miller began her work from within the psychoanalytic framework, her theory was always revisionist, drawing from object relations approaches. The theme of developing a sense of self from the first day onward is central to object relations, particularly self psychology within that perspective (Mahler 1968). Self psychology differs crucially from traditional Freudian theory in terms of its orientation toward developmental stages, emphasis on the importance of mothers throughout childhood, and conceptualization of the self. Nevertheless, it is founded on three basic Freudian assumptions: the existence of an unconscious, the importance of infancy and early childhood in personality development, and the probability that unresolved internal conflicts experienced during early childhood will be repeated (Chodorow 1978).

Object relations theorists usually refer to mothering as crucial to self-formation (Winnicott 1964; Chodorow 1978). "Good enough mothering," which is sensitive, responsive, and empathic, is essential to the formation of a child's integrated self. Such mothering does not have to be perfect, and failures of sensitivity are inevitable. However, the effective, nurturing mother must exhibit overall empathy and sensitivity.

Miller, like other self psychologists, assumed that the primary parent was almost inevitably the mother, even when she referred to a general, abstract nurturing parent. She goes beyond individual nurturing, however, to consider both overall family configuration and the historical context of that configuration (Miller 1981, 1983). Long-term, extensive family disruption can create narcissistic children. Thus, it is possible to speak of narcissistic conditions, as well as narcissistic mothers or fathers.

When Miller described young German drug addicts and their parents, she remembered Berlin of 1945 with its poverty, destruction, and enveloping atmosphere of guilt and fear (1983:133–141). Contemporary narcissistic vulnerability among German youth is often a product of parents who experienced the Nazi regime and its aftermath. Although Miller focused on the symbolic and emotional dimensions of narcissism, she was always drawn to its material causes and consequences. This paved the way for her later focus on physical and sexual abuse and her eventual repudiation of Freud and his emphasis on fantasy rather than actual events.

In her recent publications, Miller accused Freud of "dogmatizing the denial of truth" (1990a:58). Like the maverick psychoanalyst Jeffrey Masson (1984), Miller asserts that the sexual abuse that patients recounted to Freud was real and that many neuroses and personality disorders have their roots in some form of childhood sexual exploitation. However, she continues to describe the impact of physical violence and emotional cruelty as well.

Religious themes underlie all of Miller's recent discussions of cruelty to children. She conveys her own absolute values with religious zeal. Moreover, the cases she presents often develop within a social order underlain by a cold, rigid German Lutheran Church. In this context, Miller describes organized religion as both a cause and a legitimization of the exploitation of children.

Miller clearly defined good and evil in her preface to *Banished Knowledge* (1990a:1–9). Evil ranges from absolute abuse to unknowing refusal to respond empathically to a child's distress. Goodness is "unequivocally taking the side of the child and protecting him from power abuse on the part of adults" (Miller 1990a:7). Alice Miller has become an evangelist urging adults to listen and respond appropriately to all children. However, she believes that true empathy is difficult in Western societies where rigid religions reinforce repression and suffering. Miller wrote: "For thousands of years, all religious institutions have exhorted the faithful to respect their parents. These exhortations would be entirely unnecessary if people grew up in an atmosphere of love and respect, for then they would react naturally to all that they received. . . . That this teaching is called moral only magnifies the scandal"(1990a:32).

According to Miller, adults repeat their own religious training in every situation, thus perpetuating the endless cycle of abuse. There is hope for change, however, through recognition, understanding, and the exercise of compassion.

Traditional religious occasions, even the most joyful ceremonies, reinforce the parental authoritarianism that is deadly to the souls of children. Miller finds destruction everywhere, even while wandering through the snowy

Swiss forest in early December. There, young mothers take their small children to light candles and talk with Saint Nicholas. First, however, the mothers speak to the old man about the children's behavior and demeanor over the past year. During individual chats, the Saint Nicholas figure chides the children about activities that interfered with their parents' lives before praising them for compliant behavior. The children who participate in this yearly ritual are publicly shamed and confused, but without intervention, they will perpetuate the ceremony with their own offspring (Miller 1990a:13–20).

For Miller, organized religion opposes spirituality. Religiosity is strict, rigid, and isolating. Spirituality involves faith, compassion, and community. It is part of the ideal society, the ideal family, and the ideal parent. However, in delineating the ideal parent, Miller herself sounds much like a religious devotee, searching for compassionate salvation. She described a good mother whom she had observed in the same way members of new religious movements often idealize their charismatic leader (Jacobs 1989; Goldman 1995). Miller wrote: "She was able to give him plenty of warmth and physical contact, react to him positively, confirm his feelings, sense his needs, pick up his signals, and eventually understand them too. In her arms, the boy learned to show emotions, to experience the anger at what had been done to him in the past, and to discover love" (1990a:52).

The empathic parent knows and understands, as would a loving, omnipotent spiritual leader. Moreover, he or she allows the individual to discover and expand a core identity rooted in true feelings of pain, anger, or love. Empathic responses from an analyst or other authority figure may allow an individual to recapture their authenticity. For Miller, the loving parent, like the leader of a new religious movement, offers support and solace to the seeking self.

Although Miller would never define herself as a religious seeker, her recent work is in zealous pursuit of the ideal parent. Through her exhortations and also by her own example, she seeks to eliminate callous parenting. However, her first two books offer far more insight into the actual processes of religious commitment. *The Drama of the Gifted Child* particularly facilitates a better understanding of the relationships between childhood and religious seekership.

Miller's conception of narcissism includes both familial relationships and the social grounding of those interactions. By expanding the context of narcissism beyond the family itself, she broadens the psychoanalytic construct, while still remaining within the theoretical framework provided by self psychology. The narcissistic vulnerability that Miller delineates may be a key element in intense religious seekership and the desire to devote one's life to a charismatic leader. Because she portrays secondary narcissism as a dynamic set of traits, which are not always pathological or dysfunctional, Miller's conceptual framework has both definitional specificity and also broad applications.

Miller's Conceptions of Narcissism

The Drama of the Gifted Child, originally published in German in 1979 as *Prisoners of Childhood,* was based on several earlier articles in psychoanalytic journals. In *The Drama of the Gifted Child,* Miller articulated and applied psychoanalytic constructs describing narcissism and the unresponsive, self-centered parenting that generates it. Although such parenting is most damaging to individuals during early childhood, Miller's descriptions of cases suggest that destructive parenting through puberty can create and damage an individual's sense of self (1981:30–48).

Narcissistic individuals seek to complete themselves and repair parental damages through finding confirmation in the eyes of others. In the Greek myth, Narcissus, an extraordinarily handsome youth, was much beloved by the nymphs of the forest, whom he treated with callous disregard. To punish him for his lack of empathy, the gods caused Narcissus to fall in love with his own reflection in a mountain pool. But each time he reached out to touch the beautiful image that he so loved, the image fragmented. Eventually, Narcissus pined away because he was unable to love someone real or experience himself as an integrated whole.

There are many different versions of the myth, just as there are many different definitions of narcissism itself. Almost all of the psychoanalytic definitions, however, share at their center the assertion that narcissism is a disturbance involving a fragmented sense of self and the search for self-confirmation in the eyes of others. Miller shares this conceptualization, but she also amplifies traditional psychoanalytic theories of narcissism in two important ways. First, she views narcissism as a continuum rather than as a distinct pathology. According to Miller, very few individuals are without some narcissistic traits, and even those who have damaged, vulnerable senses of self may function well in competitive, postmodern societies. Second, Miller portrays narcissism as the product of sustained family interactions, not merely the result of nonresponsive mothering during infancy and early childhood as most theorists suggest (Winnicott 1964).

The narcissistic traits that Miller describes are often socially adaptive, albeit intrapersonally destructive. First among them is the "false self" that has obliterated an individual's authentic core identity (Miller1981:45). Miller assumes that a core of authenticity does exist, and she does not contemplate the fragmented, histrionic, dependent, or borderline character disorders that are closely related to narcissistic pathology (American Psychiatric Association 1994:657–661). By definition, she describes narcissistic vulnerabilities, not narcissistic pathology.

Other narcissistic traits that Miller lists include fragile self-esteem, high ego ideals, oversensitivity to potential loss of love, aggression, and perfectionism (1981:45). These suggest far more adaptive capacity among narcissistic individuals than the definition supplied by the American Psychiatric Association (1994: 661) in the DSM IV's list of central narcissistic symptoms. The symptoms are a pervasive pattern of grandiosity in behavior and/or fantasy, need for admiration, and absence of empathy for others. This clinical definition includes just 1 percent of the general population (American Psychiatric Association 1994:660). Although Miller never considers quantitative measures of the prevalence of narcissistic predispositions, she clearly believes that many, if not most, people are vulnerable.

Narcissistic vulnerability compels individuals to search for admiration and confirmation from others. They cultivate their abilities and strive for social recognition of their achievements (Miller 1981:40–48). In order to find affirmation, they often work to become different and special. The vulnerable child becomes a talented but anguished adult. Miller described this quest for recognition and self-definition:

> In everything they undertake, they do well and often excellently; they are admired and envied; they are successful whenever they care to be—but all to no avail. Behind all this lurks depression, the feeling of emptiness and self-alienation and a sense that their life has no meaning. These dark feelings will come to the fore as soon as the drug of grandiosity fails, as soon as they are not "on top," not definitely the "superstar," or whenever they suddenly get the feeling they failed to live up to some ideal image and measure they feel they must adhere to. Then they are plagued by anxiety or deep feelings of guilt and shame. What are the reasons for such narcissistic disturbances in such gifted people? (p. 6).

Miller's vivid, detailed delineation of narcissistic vulnerability suggests a broader condition than a clinically diagnosed character disorder. It refers to a set of traits generated by sustained childhood socialization. Narcissistic vulnerability involves long-term childhood experiences of lack of empathy, manipulation, and emotional cruelty within their families. These poisonous families reflect both parents' previous socialization, and they also reflect the disrupted societies that predispose individuals to the fragmentation of self.

Those who are narcissistically vulnerable temporarily develop self-identity through social recognition and applause. However, it is never enough, and they constantly search for some new, healing relationship. Although Miller does not describe seekership, her conception of narcissistic vulnerability allows us to consider symbolic merger with a great cause or charismatic individual as another creative, albeit usually temporary, remedy for the wounded self.

Miller develops a middle range between narcissism as a highly specified clinical diagnosis (Kohut 1984) and narcissism as a generalized cultural broadside (Lasch 1979). Narcissistically vulnerable individuals are sensitive, perfectionistic, envious, and without healthy self-esteem. However, they function well, often superbly, in many social settings. Although their close relationships are shallow and manipulative, the individuals whom Miller describes can initiate and sustain long-term interpersonal ties.

Consideration of middle-range narcissistic vulnerability leads to insights into the personal tension and dissatisfaction that generate religious seekership in some individuals who eventually join intense religious groups led by charismatic figures (Pollock 1975; Jacobs 1989). Narcissistic needs may engender or amplify seekership, although seeking is by no means intrinsically pathological. Miller's conception of narcissism also facilitates examining narcissistic transference as both an impetus toward and a bond within new religious movements. A specific but nonclinical approach toward narcissism opens a large body of theory and research that can be fruitfully applied to the sociology of religion and charisma.

Many sociologists have observed narcissistic vulnerability and its consequences without labeling it. *Predispositions* (Lofland 1981) or *susceptibility* (Barker 1984) to new religious movements are social psychological terms often used to describe seekers and devotees. These social psychological approaches disregard psychoanalytic theory, but they are by no means incompatible with psychoanalytic perspectives. The predisposing personal attitudes and emotions described in a number of conversion and commitment models may be usefully interpreted in terms of self psychology and theories of narcissistic transference discussed in the following section.

Narcissism, Transference, and Seekership

The members of many small, new religious movements re-create family structure in their communal groups, striving for a second chance that provides the emotional sustenance not found in their families of orientation (Jacobs 1989). The charismatic leader "assumes the responsibilities of parenting: love, discipline, guidance, and knowledge" (p. 125). This relationship between leader and devotee promises complete emotional gratification in return for unquestioning subordination. The gratification is much like that Miller describes in terms of the ideal parent, although the subordination of self is precisely what she warns against.

The parent-child relationship between founder and followers that Jacobs (1989) and others portray resembles the process of transference in psychotherapy. In this process, clients re-create intense feelings with their therapists reliving their half-remembered childhood interactions and emotions. Transference, however, can also occur in ordinary, nontherapeutic settings in which there is a parental figure exercising a wide range of authority, such as a supervisor, a priest, or a teacher (Kohut 1984). It is an integral part of all daily life in which people experience ambivalent relationships toward authority, although transference is most often described in terms of the hothouse of psychoanalytically oriented psychotherapy (Coles 1977:192–210).

The transference process is inevitably a mixture of rational, conscious responses and irrational actions and reactions.

There are numerous types of transference within and outside therapeutic situations. Narcissistic transference, reflecting needs for definition and confirmation of the self, is one type (Kohut 1984:192). Narcissistic transference will occur in movements characterized by charismatic leadership, communal settings, and a central goal of self-reconstruction by the followers. Other types of transference may operate in other kinds of groups headed by charismatic leaders (Galanter 1989). A leader emphasizing self-denial and millennialism would attract different types of followers and engender different types of transference than one who promoted self-transformation in which personal perfection was tantamount to saving the world.

Building upon the foundation laid by Miller, we can examine narcissistic transference as an adaptive response within the context of intense commitment to "human divinity" movements and their religious leaders. Miller's conception of narcissistic vulnerability facilitates a better understanding of the behavior of a number of members of those movements in which self-transformation is an immediate, explicit goal. The Rajneesh movement, est, Synanon, and Scientology are but a few of such movements (Goldman 1995; Ofshe 1980; Tipton 1982). Membership in this type of charismatically led religious group may ameliorate individuals' narcissistic vulnerabilities, and their transference relationships with the leader and with other members may permit them to fulfill grandiose narcissistic needs for admiration and self-confirmation.

There are three separate but related forms of narcissistic transference (Kohut 1984:194–210). Within therapeutic contexts, all three forms of narcissistic transference define clients' responses to their therapists. However, in the context of new religious movements, the role of the omnipotent leader encourages two forms of narcissistic transference; the third involves other devotees. Jacobs (1989) noted two sets of bonds within intense marginal religious groups. The most important were those between spiritual teacher and follower, but there are other strong ties among devotees themselves, which intensify and are intensified by their shared relationship to the leader.

The dominant master-disciple transferences are idealization and mirroring. Twinship, the third form of narcissistic transference in psychotherapy, is part of the disciples' relationships with one another. As in psychotherapy, devotees may experience all three types of transference, but generally, at a given time, only one is dominant.

Idealization defines the leader as an omnipotent, powerful, and historically important figure. Interaction with the ideal confirms the devotee's own personal worth, indicating that he or she deserves to be connected with someone who has extraordinary powers. The process of idealization enhances both parties, and it reassures the idealizer that he or she will be protected by someone strong, powerful, and inspiring (Kohut 1984:206). Idealizing transference can even legitimate physical and emotional abuse, as long as the disciple defines abuse as essential to the process of self-discovery and personal transformation. In Miller's words, the devotee may even perceive extreme exploitation as "for their own good."

Mirroring transference, unlike idealization, almost always involves positive interaction and confirmation. In the psychoanalytic context, the therapist offers positive responses whenever possible, becoming an affirming parent as opposed to the parents whom the client originally experienced. Responses are genuine but for the most part hopeful. The therapist becomes a mirror, providing glimpses of the individual's real, best self (Kohut 1984:183–184).

In small new religious movements or when the follower is part of the leader's inner circle, mirroring in new religions resembles the process found within psychotherapy. The leader interacts directly with the devotee. However, in larger movements, surrogates for the leader, such as members of an inner circle, therapists, or team leaders, may initiate mirroring transference. Surrogates must appear to be under the direction of the leader, even if they are not. They are perceived to affirm the follower because of the master's specific directions and general goals. Mirroring and confirmation may be reinforced by leaders' speeches or writings, which followers are encouraged to interpret as personal messages with direct meaning for them.

Twinship transference is closely related to mirroring. In psychotherapy, the therapist becomes an alter ego for the client (Kohut 1984:198–204). In new religions, twinship occurs among followers. Recruits may seek out older, exemplary followers as "twins." Seasoned members may look to the leader's inner circle or to one another in the process. Members share both a quest for self-transformation and a sense of mutual relationship with the idealized leader. Twinship is an intense form of identification that substitutes common goals and interests for genuine empathy. During childhood, the sense of twinship temporarily emerges in mutual participation with parents in enjoyable, adult activities. In communal new religions, twinship transference allows narcissistically vulnerable devotees to develop and cement affective bonds with one another, without fully engaging in empathic understanding. Twinship transference provides the rewards of deep friendship and emotional commitment through the followers' mutual idealization of the leader. Twinship spares them the difficult tasks of developing empathy through emotional identification and self-sacrifice for one another.

Most theories of devotion to charismatic figures are grounded in case studies of male leaders because the majority of visible religious leaders in the United States, Western Europe, and other parts of the world have been men (Camic 1987; Jacobs 1989). George Pollock (1975), however, notes that charismatic figures, either male or female, may symbolize both genders to their devotees. Depending on the type of support that the charismatic leader offers, followers may recapitulate feelings toward either their fathers or their mothers. The leader embodies qualities of the ultimate ego ideal and also the nurturer, supplementing devotees' fragile senses of self. The leader transcends gender either explicitly or implicitly, in terms of the followers' transference emotions. This androgynous view of transference supports Miller's contention that the entire family configuration contributes to narcissistic vulnerability, so the wounded individual will seek confirmation and identity from everyone, regardless of gender.

Neither the concept of narcissistic transference nor narcissistic vulnerability explains religious seekership, affiliation, or disengagement from new religious movements. However, Miller's descriptions of narcissistic vulnerability may add to the understanding of the widespread popularity of small, charismatically led movements that promise self-transformation (Tipton 1982). Theoretical constructs of narcissistic vulnerability and transference also allow us to better consider the ways in which emotional benefits of movement membership may supersede material benefits found in the external world (Iannaccone 1992:11). Even people with many social options and economic resources may affiliate with strict, collective religious groups. In the next section, I will examine narcissistic vulnerability and transference patterns in terms of the highest achieving sannyasins of Bhagwan Shree Rajneesh, in order to demonstrate how those constructs can enrich our understanding of religious behavior.

Some charismatic leaders, such as Bhagwan Shree Rajneesh, Ron Hubbard, or Werner Erhard, speak the language of psychotherapy to their followers, encouraging them to transform themselves in a quest for self-perfection. They address the potential divinity within each individual, thus developing idealization and mirroring transferences. Followers cement their bonds to one another through twinship, as they become brothers and sisters under their leader's direction. Their pursuit of spiritual fulfillment is a search for their autonomous identity and selfhood. It is a quest for validation and appreciation of individuality within the safe context of collective support.

Narcissistic Vulnerability, Transference, and Bhagwan Shree Rajneesh

Although the Rajneesh movement has taken many forms over three decades, therapy and self-actualization have always been among its central goals. The movement began in the mid-1970s in Bombay, when Bhagwan Shree Rajneesh met with a relatively small number of Indians and Westerners. As he attracted increasing numbers of followers from the United States and Western Europe, Bhagwan established a 4-acre ashram in Poona, India, which became a center for many types of group therapy (FitzGerald 1986). At its peak, about 35,000 individuals belonged to the worldwide movement. In the summer of 1981, he moved to the 64,229-acre Big Muddy Ranch in central Oregon, where 2,000 sannyasins relocated in order to build the utopian community of Rajneeshpuram. In late fall 1985, the commune disintegrated amid criminal charges and internal and external political battles. The group reclaimed the Poona ashram, where the movement continues despite Rajneesh's death in 1990.

One of the central themes in Rajneesh's teachings was the creation of an ideal person who would fuse Eastern spirituality with Western materialism. To achieve this ideal, an individual had to engage in symbolic merger with Bhagwan as part of a process of self-transformation and eventual enlightenment. However, individuals did not have to renounce material luxury as part of their spiritual discipline. Rajneesh explicitly promised his affluent followers that "I will be part of your healing process" (1979:238).

Not all of the sannyasins who followed Bhagwan to his Rajneeshpuram commune in central Oregon in the mid-1980s were affluent high achievers seeking a sense of authenticity, but many of them were. As a group, their personal characteristics and achievements contradicted widely held stereotypes about small, new religions attracting either youths temporarily caught in identity crises or older losers who had retreated in defeat from the "real world" (Levine 1984). In 1984, most sannyasins were in their mid-thirties, with a mean age of thirty-four. Most (64 percent) had earned at least a four-year college degree (Latkin et al. 1987). They were children of post–World War II U.S. affluence who had grown up with great expectations for themselves and their society. In Miller's (1981) terms, they had been gifted children, and now they were accomplished adults.

Individuals whose emotional problems rendered them ineffectual were discouraged from remaining at Rajneeshpuram (Strelley 1987). Sannyasins scored well within the normal range on psychological tests such as the California Personality Inventory (Sundberg et al. 1990). The twenty-four high-achieving sannyasins interviewed in this case study also scored well within normative ranges of the Thematic Apperception Test (TAT), while also displaying more creativity and richness of language than a matched comparison group (Sundberg et al. 1992). They did, however, exhibit slightly elevated scores on narcissism. Their scores on these psychological tests suggest that they were not emotionally paralyzed by narcissistic personality disorder as described in the DSM IV (American Psychiatric Association 1994:660). Instead, they may have displayed some of the narcissistic vulnerabilities portrayed by Miller (1981).

Thirteen men and eleven women were interviewed between winter 1983 and the commune's disintegration in late fall 1985. Most held two or more research conversations, and they responded to both the TAT and extensive life-history questions. All met the criteria for high achievement, which were an income of at least $30,000 in 1984 dollars in their last year of full-time labor, an advanced degree, or both. Demographic comparisons indicated that they were representative of the 48 percent of sannyasins who also met these criteria (Latkin et al. 1987). They were articulate, attractive, and successful, but they all portrayed themselves as emotionally battered during their early years.

All of the respondents discussed unpleasant childhood memories. However, all had also completed Rajneesh therapy groups, which encouraged participants to discover their true selves by critiquing their parents and their childhood socialization. Almost everyone who undertook Rajneesh therapy came away with a feeling that they had been wronged by their families. Teertha, the head therapist, often said that there were only two types of dysfunctional people in the world. One type had parents who psychologically abandoned them, and the other had parents who remained too close. Moreover, everyone's parents fit into one of these categories. There was no "good enough parenting" category in the Rajneesh therapy framework.

Clear operational definitions of significant family disruption were developed in order to compensate for the influence of Rajneesh therapy. For this study, I considered empirically verifiable family disruption that would generate the manipulative, unresponsive, and often unintentionally cruel parenting that Miller described (1981). Only one of the respondents' parents had been divorced before their child became an adult and moved on in life. However, most of them had undergone clear, measurable family strains, and most of their families had been subjected to several empirically verifiable difficulties.

Seventeen of the twenty-four respondents had at least one parent whose situation made it unlikely that he/she or the other parent could respond calmly or empathically to the child's emotional needs for confirmation of the self. The disruptive conditions included parent's death (3), parent's extended absence of more than a year (5), clinically diagnosed alcoholism or depression in a parent (6), psychiatric hospitalization of a parent (5), long-term parental physical illness (2), ill or intrusive grandparents living with family (4), and incest (1). Other respondents reported parents who fought constantly or who made fun of their children, but these reports were more subjective and did not involve circumstances that could be verified through documentation other than personal report. Twenty-one of the respondents had been involved with psychotherapy for at least three months before embarking on their spiritual quests. These patterns also suggest narcissistic vulnerability leading to the search for a true, authentic self. In the diverse spiritual marketplace of the 1970s, a number of competing new religious movements offered seekers personal truth and authenticity (Tipton 1982). Rajneesh, however, was extremely effective in recruiting high-achieving individuals who sought to retain material comfort while sustaining a spiritual quest (Clarke 1985).

Sannyasins perceived Bhagwan Shree Rajneesh to be a unique, enlightened leader, creating a new world in the Buddhafield around himself at Rajneeshpuram. They could move closer to ultimate bliss and enlightenment themselves by nonrational, heart-to-heart, silent communication with their master (Clarke 1985). The ultimate actualization of enlightenment lay through self-discovery by means of complete ego surrender to Rajneesh.

Rajneesh encouraged his followers to think of themselves before they considered others, to forego childbearing, and to use intimate relationships as vehicles for self-discovery. These directions complement narcissistic vulnerability, allowing devotees to confirm themselves through other people without requiring mutuality.

Part of the confirmation and construction of a new self in Rajneesh therapy lay with leaders who were assumed to be following Rajneesh's explicit direction with each of their clients. Twelve-hour workdays were also integrated into the ideology of self-transformation. Sannyasins were taught to conceptualize work as a form of worship, to think of their colleagues as fellow travelers on paths toward enlightenment, and to define work as a form of meditation and worship.

Susan Palmer (1987) discussed the integral role of psychotherapy and spiritual healing in the Rajneesh movement. Transference onto Rajneesh was central to devotees' personal growth. Rajneesh therapists, work supervisors, and other sannyasins were there to facilitate the work of psychological merger between master and devotee (Rajneesh 1985:425). Throughout the process of discipleship, Rajneesh *explicitly* took the stance of omnipotent therapist, accepting each sannyasin's unfolding transference. One therapist remarked, "The final attachment, Bhagwan says, is always onto the master" (FitzGerald 1986:297).

In describing his role as a symbolic therapist for all of his sannyasins, Rajneesh developed a classic psychoanalytic role, asserting, "So it is a unique relationship: It is absolutely one sided; from my side there is no relationship" (1985:425). He knew and directed his sannyasins, but they did not understand or affect him!

Transference was at the heart of the process of spiritual growth with Rajneesh, just as it is at the center of the psychoanalytic process. However, transference in psychotherapy is examined in order to facilitate intellectual discovery and emotional recapitulation. Such examination allows the client to leave behind irrational emotional patterns learned in childhood. Methodical termination of the relationship to the therapist is the objective of psychoanalytic psychotherapy. In contrast, the ultimate aim of Rajneesh therapy and devotion to Rajneesh was psychic merger with the master or incorporation of the leader's powers into the devotee's self. The goal of discipleship was interminable transference.

Merger was desirable because Rajneesh represented a perfect master, and devotees could share in his perfection. At Rajneeshpuram, sannyasins gave Rajneesh expensive gifts, disrupted their former relationships and commitments, and donated labor seven days a week, twelve hours each day in order to be close to him and implement his vision of utopia. His image was everywhere in the community. Copies of Rajneesh's signature decorated signs and jewelry. Quotations written in careful calligraphy hung on walls. His face appeared on coffee mugs, key chains, bumper stickers, watches, and, most important, in the lockets sannyasins wore around their necks. He was always with his devotees. Introducing a book of sketches about Rajneesh's childhood, a disciple articulated a theme found throughout written and oral accounts of devotion to the Bhagwan: "Enlightenment is a rare achievement, and only the most sublime people ever achieve it. Bhagwan is enlightened. It happened on March 21, 1953" (Rajneesh 1985:III).

Rajneesh was a strong, powerful, and inspiring figure to his followers (Kohut 1984:206). Commitment to him reassured sannyasins of their own worth and their efficacy as historical actors. The emblem of Rajneeshpuram was a smaller bird soaring in the shadow of a larger one. It symbolized the disciple becoming transcendent under the leader's wing. Rajneesh was both an ideal and a mirror, however. In his writings and discourses and through his surrogates, the commune's many therapists, Rajneesh assured sannyasins of their positive qualities and their own progress toward enlightenment. He spoke explicitly of his role as a mirror within the overall transference relationship: "Certainly my relationship with you is unique. In the first place it is not a relationship, because what relationship can you have with a mirror? You can see your face and be thankful, be grateful—but that is not a relationship" (Rajneesh 1985:424).

Although mirroring transference is closely related to twinship in psychotherapy and in new religious movements, twinship is not the same in both contexts. In psychotherapy, it is an assumed similarity between client and therapist. However, in new religious movements, the leader is usually too much idealized to be a twin. Rajneesh was such a powerful, consummate figure to his sannyasins that they rarely considered themselves to be like him. Instead, they assumed twinship with other followers who shared their admiration for Rajneesh and had similar goals of self-actualization and possible enlightenment. Sannyasins sustained themselves through a sense of communality in the face of negative publicity and internal organizational turmoil (Carter 1990; Goldman and Whalen 1990). They became close to one another through their relationship to Rajneesh and their shared experiences at Rajneeshpuram, without necessarily experiencing long-term empathy or mutuality.

The three areas of self object transference were often intertwined at Rajneeshpuram, as they are in other contexts. Idealization of Rajneesh was the
central transference, grounding his and his surrogates' mirroring functions.
Idealization of Rajneesh also produced a sense of twinship among his followers. Transference bound sannyasins to Rajneesh and to one another, and
the master and his movement organization explicitly encouraged transference. The transferences encouraged at Rajneeshpuram fit the typology developed by Heinz Kohut (1984). They flowered because many sannyasins
experienced the narcissistic vulnerability that Miller conceptualized.

Rajneesh appropriated key themes from psychology and the human potential movement into his teachings and movement organization (Carter
1990). Although he never referred specifically to either Miller or Kohut in
his discourses, he focused on similar issues, often using the same concepts
and terminology, as in the case of mirroring. These issues are central to many
other contemporary groups, fusing self-actualization and personal growth
with religiosity. Attachment to a charismatic leader guides narcissistically
vulnerable individuals in their search for a sense of self. Through participat-
ing in a new religious movement, they may affirm their needs to be protected, while deriving a sense of their own value and importance.

The sannyasins of Bhagwan Shree Rajneesh hoped to shape their own and
the world's futures. They were talented and effective individuals who believed that something important was missing from their lives. Their sense of
authenticity and self had been damaged in childhood, and they sought to repair themselves and create a new, better collective future grounded in Rajneesh's teachings. They were not pathological, but they were narcissistically
vulnerable.

Narcissistic vulnerability is important in understanding why some people
become seekers, particularly in midlife. It is not predictive, but it suggests
propensities. Miller's construct facilitates a better understanding of seekership and of the processes within many new religious movements that fuse
personal growth with spirituality.

Conclusion

Marc Galanter (1989:176–201) and Brock Kilbourne and James T. Richardson (1984) have noted the underlying similarities between new religious
movements and psychotherapy in the contemporary United States. Both
contexts may offer parallel approaches to personal change, attracting similar
seekers. Transference is central to both psychotherapy and new religious
movements centered around charismatic leaders, but it is seldom examined
technically in relationship to religion. The case study of the Rajneesh movement suggests that psychoanalytic constructs of emotional vulnerabilities as
described by Miller and the accompanying transferences discussed by

Kohut may deepen our understanding of religious seekership and engagement.

The narcissistic vulnerabilities and transferences evidenced by Rajneesh and his sannyasins have implications beyond this case study. Charisma is not just a set of personal attributes intrinsic to the leader (Weber 1968:1111–1120). It is, instead, a quality of specialness that is directly, emotionally, and irrationally appealing to responsive individuals. To be effective, charismatic leaders must appeal to extraordinary human needs, and charisma is therefore a two-way process (Camic 1987). The concept of transference focuses on the quality of response, deepening our understanding of religiosity and spirituality in relationship to different kinds of religious movements.

Narcissistic vulnerability is the intense emotional need to be attached to an individual or a group that defines and confirms an individual's identity and self-worth. This vulnerability predisposes individuals to respond to charismatic leaders. When the leader is part of a movement organized around self-transformation, he or she may be particularly appealing to those with narcissistic vulnerability. However, other kinds of movements and leaders may attract different types of followers and engender different kinds of transference.

Alice Miller's concept of narcissistic vulnerability broadens our understanding of religious seekership in contemporary U.S. society. Her research and her interpretations of psychoanalytic theory move narcissism and, by implication, narcissistic transference beyond the clinical context. Her work allows us to view narcissism as a set of predispositions, rather than a sinister pathology. Miller's work suggests that sociologists examine life histories and family configurations in order to better understand religious behaviors. Her work also indicates the wide applicability of psychoanalytic approaches to the study of modern religious phenomena.

Notes

I am grateful for suggestions from Lynn Davidman, Janet Jacobs, and Susan Moseley. Parts of this project were supported by funds from the Center for the Study of Women and Society at the University of Oregon and the University of Oregon Office of Research and Sponsored Programs.

Although Rajneesh changed his name to Osho Shree Rajneesh during his last days in Poona, from 1988 through early 1990, Bhagwan Shree Rajneesh is used in this chapter. Many sannyasins still refer to him as Bhagwan. And throughout the years at Rajneeshpuram, he was known as Bhagwan Shree Rajneesh.

References

American Psychiatric Association. 1994. *Diagnostic and statistical manual of mental disorders.* 4th ed. Washington, D.C.: American Psychiatric Association.

Barker, E. 1984. *The making of a Moonie*. London: Basil Blackwell.

Camic, C. 1987. Charisma: Its varieties, preconditions, and consequences. In J. Rabow, G. Platt, and M. S. Goldman, eds., *Advances in psychoanalytic sociology*. Malabar, Fla.: Krieger, pp. 238–277.

Carter, L. F. 1990. *Charisma and control in Rajneeshpuram*. New York: Cambridge University Press.

Chodorow, N. 1978. *The reproduction of mothering*. Berkeley: University of California Press.

_____. 1989. *Feminism and psychoanalytic theory*. New Haven: Yale University Press.

Clarke, R. O. 1985. The teachings of Bhagwan Shree Rajneesh. *Sweet Reason: A Journal of Ideas, History, and Culture* 4: 27–44.

Coles, R. 1977. *The privileged ones*. Boston: Little Brown.

FitzGerald, F. 1986. *Cities on a hill: A journey through contemporary American cultures*. New York: Simon and Schuster.

Galanter, M. 1989. *Cults: Faith, healing, and coercion*. New York: Oxford University Press.

Goldman, M. S. 1995. Promiscuity to celibacy at Rajneeshpuram: Women and AIDS control. In M. J. Neitz and M. S. Goldman, eds., *Sex, lies, and sanctity: Religion and deviance*. Greenwich, Conn.: JAI Press, pp. 203–219.

Goldman, M. S., and J. Whalen. 1990. From the new left to the new enlightenment: Implications of public attention on private lives. *Qualitative Sociology* 8: 85–107.

Iannaccone, L. 1992. Religious markets and the economics of religion. *Social Compass* 39: 121–131.

Jacobs, J. L. 1989. *Divine disenchantment*. Bloomington: University of Indiana Press.

Kilbourne, B., and J. T. Richardson. 1984. Psychotherapy and new religions in a pluralistic society. *American Psychologist* 39: 237–251.

Kohut, H. 1984. *How does analysis cure?* Chicago: University of Chicago Press.

Lasch, C. 1979. *The culture of narcissism*. New York: W. W. Norton.

Latkin, C. A., R. Hagan, R. Littman, and N. Sundberg. 1987. Who lives in utopia?: A brief report on the Rajneeshpuram research project. *Sociological Analysis* 48: 73–81.

Levine, S. V. 1984. Radical departures. *Psychology Today* 18: 20–27.

Lofland, J. 1981. *Doomsday cult: A study of conversion, proselytization, and maintenance of faith*. New York: Irvington.

Mahler, M. S. 1968. *On human symbiosis and the vicissitudes of individuation*. New York: International Universities Press.

Masson, J. M. 1984. *The assault on truth: Freud's suppression of the seduction theory*. New York: Farrar, Straus and Giroux.

Miller, A. 1981. *The drama of the gifted child*. New York: Basic Books.

_____. 1983. *For your own good: Hidden cruelty in childrearing and the roots of violence*. New York: Farrar, Straus and Giroux.

_____. 1984. *Thou shalt not be aware: Society's betrayal of the child*. New York: Farrar, Straus and Giroux.

_____. 1986. *Pictures of a childhood: Sixty-six watercolors and an essay*. New York: Farrar, Straus and Giroux.

_____. 1990a. *Banished knowledge: Facing childhood injuries.* New York: Doubleday.

_____. 1990b. *The untouched key: Tracing childhood trauma in creativity and destructiveness.* New York: Doubleday.

_____. 1991. *Breaking down the wall of silence: The liberating experience of painful truth.* New York: Dutton.

Ofshe, R. 1980. The social development of the Synanon cult. *Sociological Analysis* 41: 109–127.

Palmer, S. 1987. Therapy, charisma, and social control in Rajneeshpuram. Paper presented at the meeting of the Association for the Sociology of Religion, Chicago.

Pollock, G. H. 1975. On mourning, immortality, and utopia. *Journal of the American Psychoanalytic Association* 23: 334–362.

Rajneesh, Bhagwan Shree. 1979. *The Buddha disease: A darshan diary.* Poona, India: Rajneesh Foundation.

_____. 1985. *Glimpses of a golden childhood.* Edited by Swami Devaraj. Rajneeshpuram, Antelope, Ore.: Rajneesh Foundation International.

Strelley, K. 1987. *The ultimate game: The rise and fall of Bhagwan Shree Rajneesh.* New York: Harper & Row.

Sundberg, N., M. S. Goldman, N. Rotter, and D. Smythe. 1992. Personality and spirituality: Comparative TAT's of high achieving Rajneeshees. *Journal of Personality Assessment* 59: 326–339.

Sundberg, N., C. A. Latkin, R. Littman, and R. Hagan. 1990. Personality in a religious commune: CPI's in Rajneeshpuram. *Journal of Personality Assessment* 55: 7–17.

Tipton, S. M. 1982. *Getting saved from the sixties.* Berkeley: University of California Press.

Weber, M. 1968 [1922]. *Economy and society: An outline of interpretive sociology.* Vol. 3. New York: Bedminster Press.

Winnicott, D. W. 1964. *The child, the family, and the outside world.* London: Penguin.

12

Illusions with Futures:
Jacques Lacan

William James Earle

Jacques Lacan would have a place in cultural history as the premier interpreter of Freud to the French, but he is also an original thinker, famous for having imparted a linguistic spin to the doctrines of his master. In this chapter, I will not attempt a general account of Lacan—there are many available in French and in English[1]—but will try to say something about Lacan's religious views. One question that must be answered is how different, if different at all, he is from Freud. People apparently think that Lacan is more friendly to religion (or at least theology) than Freud. One difficulty in assessing such a claim is that what counts as theology or as religious belief is itself subject to debate. Consider, for example, the following remark from the concluding paragraph of Charles E. Winquist's article, "Lacan and Theological Discourse": "Lacan is an ally of theology because he forces theology to seriously assess the problematic of its own textuality. Reading Lacan helps us understand theology as a formal radicalization of reading" (Wyschogrod, Crownfield, and Raschke 1989:32). Is that what allies do? Is that what theology is? What, for that matter, is a problematic of textuality or a formal radicalization of reading? I hope to show in what follows that there is a less complicated way of speaking of these complex matters and that one can understand, and even make use of, an allusive and subtle genius without being, or even pretending to be, an allusive and subtle genius. One had better believe, at least in writing expository prose, that what can be said at all can be said clearly. Perhaps the texts of geniuses (such as Lacan) show as much— how the unconscious works, for example—as they say. Here, in contrast, showing will be, as far as possible, avoided in favor of explicit statement.

Lacan and Freud

I begin where Lacan begins with Freud. We should, in the first place, notice a contrast in the discursive styles of Freud and Lacan. Freud aims for, and largely achieves, a style of blunt, plain statement, designed to assign misunderstandings to the resistances of readers. Since his purpose is usually persuasive, if not polemical, his texts manage a certain self-contained intelligibility. The arguments and supportive examples are there on the page. Freud is always telling the truth (truth is more important than courtesy), even to people who do not wish to hear it, as in the following remark from "Obsessive Acts and Religious Practices": "I am certainly not the first to be struck by the resemblance between what are called obsessive acts in neurotics and those religious observances by means of which the faithful give expression to their piety" (Freud 1924:25). And the examples of the little ceremonies of the obsessive are, perhaps surprisingly, straightforward: "A woman who was living apart from her husband was subject to a compulsion to leave the best of whatever she ate; for example, she would only take the outside of a piece of roast meat. This renunciation was explained by the date of its origin. It appeared the day after she had refused marital relations with her husband, that is to say, had given up the best" (pp. 28–29). You may not like this style of explanation, Freud is telling us, but that is what is really going on.

What is the contrast with Lacan? I do not want to say that he is obscure, certainly not obscurantist, though Jean-Claude Milner's description, "un auteur cristallin," is probably a trifle hyperbolic (1995:7). *Allusive* may, in fact, be the *mot juste*, though what is alluded to also matters. Freud, in making allusions, tends to use famous figures in world culture such as Moses, Oedipus Rex, and Leonardo da Vinci. The references Lacan makes are often local, figures on the French intellectual scene that you will know about if your intellectual habitus has been formed in the highly standardized, indeed regulated, elite academic institutions that have dominated French intellectual life up to the present and if, after such an education, you land on your feet in the right Parisian milieu. For example, in an important passage on the effect of science on the "position of the subject"—subject of science, subject of psychoanalytic practice—Lacan just said, "Here Koyré is our guide"(1966:856).[2] This is not obscure; one just has to know something of what Alexandre Koyré has said about science. There are also much more oblique instances. For example, when Lacan said (said is the right verb since this comes from a "séminaire" volume), in discussing the companions of Ulysses who were turned into pigs, that "la parole est essentiellement le moyen d'être reconnu [speech is essentially the way to achieve recognition]" (1975:264), the ideal reader will recall the whole context of French Hegelianism, associated (principally) with Alexandre Kojève,[3] Alexandre Koyré,[4] and Jean Hyppolite,[5] in which recognition, indeed the contest for recognition, is so greatly emphasized, and probably also think of the *langue/parole* distinction derived from Ferdinand de Saussure (1983:chap. 4). Fortunately, however, one can construe the main Lacanian themes without total immersion in Lacan's polymathy. Indeed, one thing that differentiates Freud and Lacan (and this is not a matter of allusion or erudition) is the relative simplicity of Freud's view of the relations among science, religion, and psychoanalysis: Science is the one road to truth; psychoanalysis is a science; and religion is a nonstarter.

Psychoanalysis and Religion

Philip Rieff wrote in *Freud: The Mind of the Moralist*: "It is on the subject of religion that the judicious clinician grows vehement and disputatious. Against no other strong-point of repressive culture are the reductive weapons of psycho-analysis deployed in such open hostility." Freudian psychoanalysis, Rieff continued, is "the last great formulation of nineteenth-century secularism" (1961:281). A philosopher would, I think, put it somewhat differently. One has to make up one's mind, qua philosopher, about how knowledge is acquired, and Freud's view, even if one does not accept it, has to be regarded as one of the most plausible basic options: "Scientific work [Freud wrote in *The Future of an Illusion*] is the only road that can lead us to a knowledge of reality outside ourselves. It is once again merely an illusion to expect anything from intuition and introspection; they can give us nothing but particulars about our own mental life, which are hard to interpret, never any information about the questions which religious doctrine finds it so easy to answer"(1989:40). Religious doctrines are "sehr im Widerspruch zu allem, was wir mühselig uber die Realität der Welt erfahren haben [in sharp contradiction with everything we have so laboriously discovered about the reality of the world]" (Freud 1982:165). *Mühselig* is a strong adverb meaning hard, laborious, or toilsome, and it describes the process of scientific discovery in contrast to the easy miracle of religious belief, the quick fix of faith. Freud was proceeding, in *The Future of an Illusion,* as a good epistemologist distinguishing, at the most fundamental level, not true from false beliefs but reliable from unreliable processes of belief formation. "An illusion [Freud wrote] is not the same thing as an error; nor is it necessarily an error." "What is characteristic of illusions is that they are derived from human wishes" (Freud 1989:39). That we wish that something is so is never a reason, a justification, for believing that it is so. Of course, an unreliable process of belief formation can lead to a true belief, but, by definition, the probability of this happening has to be very low. Freud understood this very well: "A middle class girl [ein Bürgermädchen] may have the illusion that a prince will come and marry her. This is possible; and a few such cases have occurred" (Freud 1989:39; 1982:165). He said many harsh things—for example, "Where questions of religion are concerned, people are guilty of every possible sort of dishonesty and intellectual misdemeanour" (Freud 1989:41)—but he was, at least officially, agnostic: "To assess the truth-value of religious doctrines does not lie within the scope of the present enquiry" (p. 42).

Two points should be made about this agnosticism. *First*, Freud was declaring an incompetence because as a scientist he was, and knew he was, competent to make judgments about, and only about, what he had studied. He described psychoanalysis as a "method of research [eine Forschungs-methode]" (Freud 1989:47, 1982:170), but it is a method that has nothing to do with questions of metaphysics or cosmology any more than it has to do with questions of astronomy or physics. Freud's animus against religion was, as much as anything else, animus against what he considered its intellectual irresponsibility. Nor do I think his humility in the following self-characterization was false humility: "A psychologist who does not deceive himself about the difficulty of finding one's bearings in this world, makes an endeavour to assess the development of man, in the light of the small portion of knowledge he has gained through a study of the mental processes of individuals during their development from child to adult" (Freud 1989:67–68). What annoyed him was that other people who should be intellectually modest were not.

Second, it is now more generally understood than it was by Freud's contemporaries and immediately successive critics that possession both of true beliefs and of false beliefs, and not just of false beliefs, needs to be explained.[6] The answer to the question "Why do I believe that p?" cannot be "Because p is true" unless I am claiming omniscience for myself. Even truths get to be believed by me somehow or other if they get to be believed by me at all. Of course, we often think that false beliefs, other people's false beliefs, are especially in need of explanation. And one can read Freud as asking and answering the question "How can you believe that?" where the falsity of "that" gives the question its point. This is not quite accurate. Even if religious beliefs are true, there would be the question of how we come to have them. But Freud was not normatively neutral about processes of belief formation. Beliefs ought to be either "precipitates of experience or end-results of thinking [Niederschläge der Erfahrung oder Endresultate des Denkens]" (Freud 1989:38, 1982:164), but religious beliefs are neither. The religious person can appeal to faith (perhaps definable as a set of beliefs not supported, and frankly not supported, either by ordinary experience or by ordinary thinking), but this would appear to Freud, and indeed to any position outside faith, as massive irrationality. It might once have seemed unlikely that people in general could be so irrational, and at one time, people (or at least religious apologists) took seriously the argument from universal consent: "Everybody believes in God; therefore, God exists." Freud really does help us see why this argument has zero probative value. Psychoanalysis explains both the ubiquity and the strength of religious beliefs in terms of the ubiquity and strength of the desires they may be taken to fulfill. Freud said, of religious ideas, that "the secret of their strength lies in the strength of those wishes" (1989:38), precisely the wishes that compromise processes of belief formation in which they are active.

Do illusions disappear, become unsustainable, in the face of enlightenment? This turns out to be a complex question. In the first place, we may speak about enlightenment globally (Has it begun? Is it over? Should we be glad? Should we be filled with regret?) in discussions of our cultural situation, but psychoanalysis, if it teaches us anything, teaches us that enlightenment is always an individual matter. My analysis makes me, or anyway can make me, more enlightened, more rational, more something than I would be without it, but it does not, and cannot, help my neighbor. Of course, analysts and others can make general pronouncements—*The Future of an Illusion* is a central example—but we may wonder what effect they have on even those, a very small percentage of people, who pay attention to them. Useful, here, is Serge Leclaire's observation—he is a Lacanian analyst—that all his sophisticated Parisian patients know perfectly well, before they enter analysis, that they have Oedipus complexes but that this knowledge has no therapeutic value (Leclaire 1968:14–15) Psychoanalysis, Freudian or Lacanian, has taught us that the mind is not a self-transparent system with instantaneous clearance of cognitive inconsistencies or instantaneous learning, in any operationally effective mode, of newly presented truths. Lacan described Freud as "fundamentally pessimistic," said he "denies any tendency to progress," and placed him "dans une tradition réaliste et tragique" (1981:275–276). This is probably a reasonable overall assessment, though there are remarks in *The Future of an Illusion* that might generate a bit more optimism. "The voice of the intellect is a soft one, but it does not rest till it has gained a hearing." Of course, as Lacan would remind us, none of the other voices rest either, which is why, or one reason why, a human is, in Lacan's view, "the subject in the grip of and tortured by language [le sujet pris et torturé par le langage]" (1981:276). And finally, how optimistic is the following judgment: "The primacy of the intellect lies, it is true, in a distant, distant future, but probably not in an *infinitely* distant one" (Freud 1989:68).

Science and Psychoanalysis

Lacan, as already suggested, has a much more complicated view of the relations among science, psychoanalysis, and religion than Freud. Let us say something first about the status of psychoanalysis. I note in passing that Lacan wrote and lectured over a long period of time and that his views were not static. Writings collected in *Écrits* cover a period from the 1930s to the 1960s; the famous "seminars" stretched from 1953 to 1980 . Nine volumes of seminars, an as yet incomplete and discontinuous record of Lacan's oral instruction, is currently available. There were moments when Lacan closely connected psychoanalysis with the so-called human sciences, sometimes the structuralist linguistics of Saussure, sometimes the structuralist anthropology of Claude Lévi-Strauss. Although the influence of these two thinkers is never absent, Lacan does not, finally, think that psychoanalysis is any kind of science. For example, in the seminar for 1964, Lacan said, "I mistrust the term 'research'. For my part I never considered myself as a researcher [chercheur]. As Picasso once said, scandalizing his entourage, *Je ne cherche pas, je trouve* [I do not search, I find]" (1973:12). This remark obviously needs some interpreting. Is the analyst more like an artist than like a scientist, or at least as much like an artist as a scientist? Various comparisons are possible. Elsewhere, Lacan used Montaigne's expression "un art de conférer [an art of conferring]," specified by the following comparison: "The Socratic art of conferring in the *Meno* consists in teaching the slave to assign true meaning to his own speech" (1975:306). Lacan also said the analyst uses "the techniques of an art of dialogue." "Like the good cook [Lacan continued], we have to know what joints, what resistances, we will encounter" (p. 9).

Part of what Lacan was doing in making these comparisons—this also figures in his attempt to get his readers and auditors back to the texts of Freud[7]—was fighting against "the dominant reading of Freud in France during the 50's," which identified "drive and instinct, desire and need [pulsion et instinct, désir et besoin]" (Dosse 1991:132). Lacan was, in other words, fighting against "la médicalisation de toute forme de pathologie et donc la dissolution de la psychanalyse dans la psychiatrie [the medicalization of every form of pathology and thus the dissolution of psychoanalysis in psychiatry]" (p. 132). If psychoanalysis is not a science and is radically distinct from medicine (seen by Lacan as a mode of normalization à la Michel Foucault), how should it be conceived? The answer is: as something new in the world, as a *sui generis* praxis. (The writings and lectures are then a reflection on this practice[8] and, accordingly, constitute a kind of philosophical discourse.) It is all too easy to suppose, Lacan warned, that the analyst has a kind of knowledge, *Wissen*, *savoir*, but this could amount to nothing more than "un faux savoir"(1975:306–307). Saying "I am an analyst" is, Lacan told us, an extravagance comparable to saying "I am king." "One and the other are entirely legitimate affirmations which nevertheless are justified by nothing in the order of what might be called the measure of capacities." Being an analyst, like being king, is a symbolic matter that, as such, "altogether escapes the register of qualifying capacities [habilitations capacitaire]" (p. 307). We must next consider how this conception of psychoanalysis relates, if it does, to Lacan's attitude, or possibly attitudes, to religion.

French commentators on Lacan have not found this an easy area about which to be definite and have looked for clues outside the texts. On the one hand, we have Michel de Certeau making much of the dedication of Lacan's dissertation "Au R. P. Marc-François Lacan, bénédictin de la Congrégation de France, mon frère en religion" (Certeau 1987:188). (Certeau emphasized "My brother in religion," not just, as he was, biological brother.) On the other hand, we have François Dosse: "Born into a Catholic milieu, Lacan quickly renounced the faith and symbolized this break by abandoning part of his first name, retaining only the Jacques of Jacques-Marie" (1991:121). I nevertheless think, first, that a tolerably definite view can be derived from what Lacan has written and said and, second, that Lacan's view turns out in basic features to be quite similar to Freud's. Nevertheless, the general Lacanian tone is quite different from Freud's.

Religion, Science, and Magic

There is, in the "La science et la vérité" (Lacan 1966:855–877), a stenographic record of a seminar given on December 1, 1965, a number of crucial remarks on science, religion, and magic. We find there, in the first place, a statement of incompetence that parallels the formal, official, or jurisdictional incompetence declared by Freud in *The Future of an Illusion*. In concluding the discussion, Lacan made the following remark: "This exploration does not have as its only aim to give you an elegant take on fields [cadres] which in themselves escape our jurisdiction. That is to say, magic, religion, indeed science" (1966:876). The "our" in "our jurisdiction" refers to actual or potential psychoanalysts, despite the fact that Lacan always had a more than professional audience. This reading is supported by the next sentence: "But to remind you that, in as much as you are subjects of psycho-analytic science, it is to the solicitation of each of these modes of the relation to truth as cause that you must resist" (p. 876). "Subjects of psycho-analytic science" just means "analysts," though two questions need to be addressed. One is why, if psychoanalysis is not supposed by Lacan to be any kind of science, he here spoke of "psycho-analytic science." I think the answer is that Lacan, perhaps not entirely consistently, was thinking psychoanalysis might have something like scientific status. Psychoanalysis, though not a science, could be a science. He said, "The main obstacle to its scientific value is that the relation to truth as cause, in its material aspects, continues to be neglected" (p. 877). Lacan explained another of his concerns as follows: "It is important in the first place to promote, and as a fact to distinguish from the question of knowing if psychoanalysis is a science (if its field is scientific),—the fact precisely that its practice does not imply another subject than that of science" (p. 863). This at the very least suggests compatibility with science.

The second question that needs to be addressed concerns the curious phrase "truth as cause." The concept of truth employed by Freud is pretty much the commonsense concept according to which one might say that a certain historical claim or scientific theory is true and that another claim or theory is false. Lacan's prevalent use of "la vérité" implies a quite different concept. The standard logico-analytic connection between knowledge and truth is suspended. Truth, for Lacan, is always the truth of the unconscious, which contrasts with standing bodies of knowledge. As a general account of truth, this may be unacceptable, but it captures what the process of psychoanalysis is after. Truth, in this special psychoanalytic sense, is supposed to be able to do something, to accomplish something, to be somehow efficacious. This is "truth as cause." Truth, in this sense, has competitors in the form of science, magic, and religion.

There are interesting remarks on magic (an obeyed command is perhaps an instance of magic) and science,[9] but I shall limit myself to those that directly concern religion. Lacan is not attempting anything like a new classification, or objective evaluation, of cultural spheres but confines himself to reflections on the analytic process: "It must be said that, for the subject of science [the scientist], one and the other [magic and religion] are no more than shadows, but not for the suffering subject which is our concern" (1966:870). Religion is important to the suffering subject and is therefore important to the analyst. Freud certainly thought that religion, despite the fact it might save the religious person the trouble of concocting a personal neurosis,[10] was on balance repressive. What does Lacan think? I believe his thinking is the same as Freud's, though it is not going to come out sounding the same for two reasons. First, as already suggested, Freud's contrast between repressive religion and liberating science is abandoned by Lacan. Science, organized bodies of knowledge (and what they say—what they insist on—to the infant, the child, and the adolescent through the medium of parents and teachers) is also repressive in the sense that it has nothing to do with the truth of the unconscious, with truth in Lacan's special, psychoanalytic sense. A particularly obvious example of this repressive potential is psychology or psychologized psychoanalysis, the pseudo-science of "happy egos," which propagates what Lacan referred to, in English and with contempt, as the "american way of life" (1973:116).[11] Second, Lacan is very aware that religion, as an abstract form of hierarchy and dogma, can be given new content, for example, the content of psychoanalysis itself. "As to religion, it must rather serve us as a model not to follow, in the institution of a social hierarchy which conserves a certain rapport to truth as cause. The simulation of the Catholic Church, which is reproduced every time the relation to truth as cause goes social, is particularly grotesque in a certain 'Internationale psychoanalytique'" (Lacan 1966:876–877). This is, for the Lacan who was once expelled from the main French psychoanalytic society, more than a casual comparison.

In thinking about religion, Lacan raised the possibility of "analytic neutrality" only to reject it with the following comment: "We insist upon the principle that to be a friend to all the world does not suffice to preserve a place from which to do our work [nous faisons prévaloir ce principe que d'être ami de tout le monde ne suffit pas à préserver la place d'où l'on a à opérer]" (1966:872). One cannot be—always—either neutral or amiable. One must say things the religious person will not like. So revelation (Lacan was here as elsewhere thinking, or thinking mainly, of the Judeo-Christian tradition) translates, for the analytical subject, into a denial of the very truth that makes him a subject.[12] Lacan went on to say that "the religious person leaves to God the charge of the cause [as in truth-as-cause], but in so doing cuts off his own access to truth. So he makes God the cause of his desire, which is the proper object of sacrifice. He submits his demand to the supposed desire of a God he must then seduce. So enters the play of love" (p. 872). I do not pretend to understand the details of this religious dialectic, though I take it to echo, without reproducing, the master-slave relation in Hegel's famous myth.

What is clear is that Lacan thought this dialectical sequence bad news for the suffering subject, for he commented that "the religious person thereby gives to truth a culpable status" (1966:872). In rough gloss—"d'une façon forcément approximative," as Lacan somewhere said—the religious person feels guilty, and finally needlessly so, because his/her desires do not fit the religious paradigm.

Lacan on Religion

There are many remarks on religion, often quite brief, scattered throughout the volumes of seminars. I shall conclude—or stop, as someplace one has to—by citing three passages of particular interest. (1) "It is not an eccentricity of Freud's, this repudiation, in the field of religious sentiment, of what he called the oceanic aspiration. Our experience is there to reduce this aspiration to a fantasy; we assure ourselves of firm foundations elsewhere, and assign it to what Freud called, a propos religion, the place of illusion" (Lacan 1973:32–33) Here is another passage that supports the reading of Lacan—no more friendly to religion than Freud—that I have been recommending. (2) "But if God is dead for us, that is because he always was dead, and that is just what Freud is telling us. There never was a father except in the mythology of the son, that is, in the commandment which ordains love of the father, and in the drama of a passion which demonstrates resurrection on the far side of death" (Lacan 1986:209). Again, this seems very much in the spirit of Freud where the drama of our ordinary—unavoidable—lives, which are built around fathers and mothers and death, around gratification and renunciation, is variously, and fantastically, elaborated in our civilization's constitutive myths as well as in our own private neuroses. (3) "For the correct formulation of atheism is not *God is dead*—even in basing the origin of the function of the father on his death, Freud protects the father—the correct formulation of atheism is *God is unconscious*" (Lacan 1973:58). This is not an easy passage to interpret. For one thing, we must remember all the things that the unconscious is supposed to be: It is "structured like a language" (Lacan 1973:23); it "escapes totally from the circle of certainties in which the human being recognizes himself as an ego [moi]" (Lacan 1978:16); it is the logical correlative of psychoanalytic practice; it explains why we can be surprised by our own speech.[13] All of these features might be condensed as follows (the formulation is Jean-Claude Milner's): "The unconscious is that which says *no* to consciousness of self as privilege" (Milner 1995:66). As Milner interprets Lacan, *God is unconscious* is part of the denial that there is anything transcendental, anything outside the universe described by modern science. God and the soul die together. It is Lacan's destruction of the soul, more than anything else, that makes him an antireligious thinker. For without a soul, there is nothing to save. Religion loses its object. I suppose that philosophers associate the soul's demise, if that is what they believe, with the triumph of physicalism over any form of psychophysical dualism. Lacan accomplishes the dismissal of the soul much less metaphysically. The soul just loses its point: "Man does not think with his soul as the philosopher [Aristotle] imagines" (Lacan 1974:16).

Conclusion

There is thinking. There are subjects. In Lacan's dispersed and decentered Cartesianism, where there is thinking, there is a subject.[14] Since some thinking is unconscious, as in dreams, there is something for psychoanalysis to be about or, more precisely, something for the analyst to pay attention to, to listen to. People often picture the unconscious as the repository of the primitive, where what is closest to the animal, to the life of instinct, survives to conspire against our higher powers and nobler aims. This was for Freud and is for Lacan a totally false view. The great accomplishment of Lacan is to provide a nonbiological reading of Freud, where the symbolic, the social, the linguistic, the mythological, and, of course, the religious, are given full weight.

Notes

1. For example, Jean-Luc Nancy and Philippe Lacoue-Labarthe, *Le titre de la lettre* (Paris: Éditions Galilée, 1973), and Bice Benvenuto and Roger Kennedy, *The Works of Jacques Lacan* (New York: St. Martin's Press, 1986). The single best book on Lacan, from a philosophical point of view, is Ellie Ragland-Sullivan, *Jacques Lacan and the Philosophy of Psychoanalysis* (Urbana: University of Illinois Press, 1987).

2. This is from an essay, "La science et la vérité," not included among the selections in the English translation of *Écrits*.

3. See Alexandre Kojève, *Introduction à la lecture de Hegel*, ed. by Raymond Queneau (Paris: Gallimard, 1947), based on lectures given from 1933 to 1939. For example: "To desire the Desire of another is in the final analysis to desire that the value which I am or 'represent' be the value desired by that other: I wish that he 'recognize' my value as his value; I wish that he 'recognize' me as an autonomous value" (p. 14). See also the articles by Mikkel Borch-Jacobsen, Pierre Macherey, and Serge Viderman, on Hegel, Kojève, and Lacan, in the collective work *Lacan avec les philosophes* (Paris: Albin Michel, 1991). We know that Lacan attended Kojève's lectures during the thirties; see Elizabeth Roudinesco, *Histoire de la psychanalyse de France* (Paris: Seuil, 1986), p. 155.

4. See Alexandre Koyré, "Hegel à Iéna," "La tèrminologie hégélienne," and "Rapport sur l'état des études hégéliennes en France," in *Études d'histoire de la pensée philosophique* (Paris: Tel/Gallimard, 1981).

5. See Jean Hyppolite, *Genèse et structure de la Phénoménologie de l'Esprit de Hegel* (Paris: Aubier Montaigne, 1946). Hyppolite was a frequent participant in Lacan's seminars.

6. I am appealing here to a principle of explanatory symmetry but not to the principle of symmetry as understood in the "strong (or Edinburgh) program" in the sociology of science.

7. See Malcolm Bowie, *Freud, Proust and Lacan: Theory as Fiction* (Cambridge: Cambridge University Press, 1987), p. 100: "Lacan reads Freud. This is the simplest and most important thing about him."

8. *Praxis* is the word Lacan uses, though it is not clear whether he means anything different from what in English is ordinarily described as a "practice."

9. For example, Lacan, *Écrits*, p. 859: "On sait ma répugnance de toujours pour l'appellation de sciences humaines, que me semble être l'appel même de la servitude [people are aware of my long-standing repugnance for the term 'human sciences,' which seems to me to be an appeal to slavery]."

10. See Freud, *The Future of an Illusion*, p. 56: "It has been repeatedly pointed out (by myself and in particular by Theodor Reik) in how great detail the analogy between religion and obsessional neurosis can be followed out, and how many of the peculiarities and vicissitudes in the formation of religion can be understood in that light. And it tallies well with this that devout believers are safe-guarded in a high degree against the risk of certain neurotic illnesses; their acceptance of the universal neurosis spares them the task of constructing a personal one."

11. Lacan also speaks of "the degradation of psycho-analysis, consequent upon its American transplantation" (*Écrits*, p. 68).

12. This thought is, I believe, contained in the following more complex passage, from which I have tried to abstract it undistortedly: "Si l'on ne peut partir de remarques comme celle-ci: que la fonction qu'y joue la révélation se traduit comme une dénégation de la vérité comme cause, à savoir qu'elle dénie ce qui fonde le sujet à s'y tenir pour partie prenante,—alors il a peu de chance de donner à ce qu'on appelle l'histoire des religions des limites quelconques, c'est-à-dire quelque rigueur" (*Écrits*, p. 872).

13. See Jacques Lacan, *Télévision* (Paris: Seuil, 1974), p. 27: "Il y a des surprises en ces affaires de discours, c'est même là le fait de l'inconscient."

14. This is a paraphrase of Milner, *L'oeuvre claire*, p. 41: "s'il y a du penser, il y a du sujet."

References

Certeau, Michel de. 1987. *Histoire et psychanalyse entre science et fiction*. Paris: Gallimard/Folio.

Dosse, François. 1991. *Histoire du structuralisme*. Vol. 1. *Le champ du signe, 1945–1966*. Paris: Éditions La Découverte.

Freud, Sigmund. 1924. *Collected Papers*. Vol. 2. Authorized translation supervised by Joan Riviere. London: Hogarth Press.

———. 1982. *Die Zukunft einer Illusion* in *Studienausgabe*. Vol. 9. Frankfurt am Main: Fischer Wissenschaft.

———. 1989. *The Future of an Illusion*. Translated by James Strachey. New York: W. W. Norton.

Lacan, Jacques. 1966. *Écrits*. Paris: Seuil.

———. 1973. *Le séminaire*. Vol. 1. *Les quatre concepts fondamentaux de la psychanalyse*. Edited by Jacques-Alain Miller. Paris: Seuil.

———. 1974. *Télévision*. Paris: Seuil.

———. 1975. *Le séminaire*. Vol. 1. *Les écrits techniques de Freud*. Edited by Jacques-Alain Miller. Paris: Seuil.

———. 1978. *Le séminaire*. Vol. 2. *Le moi dans la théorie de Freud and dans la technique de la psychanalyse*. Edited by Jacques-Alain Miller. Paris: Seuil.

———. 1981. *Le séminaire*. Vol. 3. *Les psychoses*. Edited by Jacques-Alain Miller. Paris: Seuil.

———. 1986. *Le séminaire*. Vol. 7. *L'éthique de la psychanalyse*. Edited by Jacques-Alain Miller. Paris: Seuil.

Leclaire, Serge. 1968. *Psychanalyser*. Paris: Seuil.

Milner, Jean-Claude. 1995. *L'oeuvre claire: Lacan, la science, la philosophie*. Paris: Seuil.

Rieff, Philip. 1961. *Freud: The Mind of the Moralist*. New York: Doubleday Anchor.

Saussure, Ferdinand de. 1983. *Cours de linguistique generale*. Edited by Tullio de Mauro. Paris: Payot.

Wyschogrod, Edith, David Crownfield, and Carl A. Raschke, eds. 1989. *Lacan & Theological Discourse*. Albany: State University of New York Press.

13

God and Lacanian Psychoanalysis

Toward a Reconsideration of the
Discipline of Religious Studies

Carl Raschke

In the section of *The Seminar* entitled "On Nonsense and the Structure of God," Jacques Lacan asked the essential theological question of what revealed truth might be. "What is this God, then, who has revealed himself? . . . First, he is presence. And his mode of presence is the speaking mode"(Miller 1988c:125).

Lacan was commenting on the famous case of paranoia of Daniel-Paul Schreber, discussed by Freud in his *Psychoanalytic Notes on an Autobiographical Account of a Case of Paranoia* (1911/1958). Interestingly and ironically, Lacan used Schreber's paranoia to sketch the underpinnings of much of his mature thought, which correlates the origins of language with the concept of God.

Schreber's paranoia is discursively interwoven with his "theological" vision of the world. The strange theological world picture that constitutes the symbolic order of Schreber's psychosis, according to Lacan, arises from the action of the primitive signifier in the formation of the religious unconscious. For Lacan, of course, there is no independent stratum of reference, as Freud and Jung claimed, that we call the unconscious. The psychological construct of "the unconscious" connotes, in Lacan's method, a system of linguistics, a panorama of sign operations and linkages, that can be mapped, ordered, encoded, decoded, and so forth.

By "deconstructing" the quasi-metaphysical topology of conventional psychoanalytical parlance, Lacan moves from the hermeneutics of expressivity that is fundamental to twentieth-century depth psychology to a grammatology of signifying praxis. This signifying praxis constitutes the architecture of the unconscious itself, which Lacan argues is "structured like a language."

The impact of Lacan's linguistic revisionism has been severalfold. First, the now infamous Freudian "hydraulic" of instinct and repression is replaced with a theory of semantic formation that relies upon the insight that the random symbolizing components of desire can be integrated through the analytical process into a decipherable grammar of the unconscious. Second, Lacan draws upon contemporary models of linguistic innovation, including the syntactics of metaphor, to transform psychoanalysis into a flexible dialogical and hermeneutical methodology, as opposed to a sort of crypto-dogmatics, for which it has been criticized repeatedly for generations. Third, Lacan "deconstructs" all forms of metaphysical psychology, including allegedly empirical ones, by showing that such constructions as "ego" and "unconscious" are but chimera generated by what he elsewhere terms the "imaginary" work of language itself.

It is in this context, therefore, that the peculiar Lacanian methodology, which has often been assailed by Anglo-American practitioners as turgid and opaque, can be understood as the royal road to revisioning what traditionally has been called "psychology of religion." The field of religious studies historically has been like central Europe in the eighteenth century—a rich topography of complex, ethnographic contours and divisions artificially segmented and regimented through the theoretical hegemony of the established, "baronial" disciplines. The Lacanian turn, by contrast, allows these baronial dominions to be unmasked for what they truly are, that is, artificial boundaries drawn for the sake of territorial management and control rather than with a sensibility toward the signifying landscape of the subject matter itself.

In the same way that Martin Heidegger ushered in "the end of philosophy" with his profession that the totalizing power of ontological discourse must be stripped away to its horizon of nonrepresentable vocative forms of disclosure (what he calls "poetizing"), so Lacan's writings point toward "the end of psychology" to the extent that they "overcome," in the Heideggerian sense, the hegemonic structures of what might be called the "sciences of mind." Lacan wrote that "the idea of a unilinear, pre-established individual development, made up of stages each appearing in their turn, according to a determined typicity, is purely and simply the giving up the conjuring away, the camouflage, the negation, properly speaking, even the repression of the essential contribution of analysis"(Miller 1988b:13–14). The notion of the "subject" itself is a phantom of the Cartesian world picture. In a word, everything the analysand "ascribes" to himself or herself is a consequence of

"founding speech," the great circuit of discourse that is essentially "everything that has constituted him, his parents, his neighbors, the whole structure of the community, and not only constituted him as symbol, but constituted him in his being"(Miller 1988b:20). If, according to Lacan, Freud had
"shown us that speech must be embodied in the very history of the subject,"
the unmuzzling of speech is the job of psychoanalysis. "Do we not have to
release it, like Sleeping Beauty?"(Miller 1988a:185).

Lacan's de-totalizing of psychology through the application of Saussurian
linguistics, which in other realms has been responsible for the broad integration of cultural and historical research under the descriptor of "cultural
studies," metamorphosizes the field of religious studies from a pale reflection of the once high-riding baronial disciplines into a new style of critical
theory. This new critical theory focuses on what might be termed the "signifying lattices of the 'collective' unconscious."

Before I press this argument too far, however, it is necessary to caution
that the Jungian "collective unconscious" is not a realm of discovery but a
peculiar type of "meta-language" by Lacan's standards. For Lacan, the creation of the "subject" of psychology through language constitutes a gram-
matical articulation of the previously inchoate play of primitive signifiers
that have not been dispatched toward the reflective process of the "mirror
stage." The "unconscious," therefore, is not an order of reference to be discerned but a movement of signifying action that has its genesis in the origi-
nary dynamics of desire and speech. The same would be true of the "collective unconscious," except that in this instance, the signifiers are largely
imaginative "universals" that have arisen over generations and centuries
through phylogenic strata of communication.

The articulation of these "global signifiers" through religious practice and
thought follows essentially the same set of "laws" as the engendering of the
subject of psychology through the mediation of the analyst. The "linguistic
turn" in psychology that Lacanian analysis betokens has powerful ramifications for what in the past has been called the "scientific" study of religion.
The Lacanian project derives from the insight, which is as old as Freud, that
the "material" signified in the therapeutic odyssey is really inchoate speech
of some kind. Because he was heir to the nineteenth-century tradition of ideological analysis, Freud assumed that such material must be "repressed,"
gagged and bound in silence by the force of the supervening "secondary
processes." The metaphor of dominion and subjection, which still inheres in
the residual metapolitics of postmodernist discourse, has blinded both psychological and social researchers to what, for Lacan, was most obvious.

The theory of repression has always been a crypto-metaphysical posture.
It has presupposed that the "dark side" of language is its own counter-dis-
course, a funhouse mirror in which the prevailing speech-world is seen as a

caricature, as an upside-down trick of the eye. The psychoanalytic postulate of the "unconscious" follows this sort of double logic.

Lacan's move from metapsychology to a philosophy of signification parallels Saussure's transformation of historicism into a "linguistic science." For Saussure, the diachrony of linguistic evolution is of little consequence so far as the meaning and structure of speech is concerned. Saussure's famous distinction between *langue* and *parole,* or between formal structure and informal expression, becomes the basis for the contemporary "structuralist" as well as "poststructuralist" understanding of semiosis as a transformation of codes and a shifting relationship among signifiers. The question arises, then, as to how psychology of religion as a semiotic model can play an instrumental part in the revisioning of what we mean by "religious" phenomena as a whole. If the study of religion is indeed the archaeology of "holy" signs, then Lacan's approach serves to unwind the "knots" of primal, collective desire and reveal their entanglement with the fluid vocabulary of the sacred.

The "religious unconscious"—if we can employ such a locution at all—consists in the cultural formation of these networks of global signifiers. The unconscious, according to Lacan, is always a "censored chapter" in the historical record. Yet, he says,

> the truth can be rediscovered; usually it has already been written down elsewhere. Namely: in monuments: this is my body—in archival documents; these are my childhood memories—in semantic evolution: this corresponds to the stock of words and acceptations of my own particular vocabulary, as it does to my style of life and to my character;—in traditions, too, and even in the legends which, in a heroicized form, bear my history;—and, lastly, in the traces that are inevitably preserved by the distortions necessitated by the linking of the adulterated chapter to the chapters surrounding it, and whose meaning will be re-established by my exegesis (Lacan 1977:50).

This "elsewhere" of signification constitutes the essential discovery of Lacanian analysis. Yet it also can become the operative structure of a new religious "hermeneutics" that no longer aims to "read the runes" as if they were straightaway intelligible as discourse but endeavors consistently to rewrite and map anew the nexus of semiotic moments and signifying praxis we comprehend as the experience of the "divine" or "sacred." Religious studies has so idealized and stylized the epigraphy of the sacred that it has lost the sense of the nihility, restlessness, and distortion that is involved in the generation of the global signifier. If the "elsewhere" as the site of semiosis holds valid for the formation of the subject—Lacan's es or S—it also obtains for the creation of those cultural "monuments" and "traditions" that demand constant "exegesis."

Psychology in the Semiotic Register

What would a religious semiotics that shows the significatory relations among the discursive elements throughout a "legacy" or "tradition" consist of? Much of Lacan's strategy of putting psychological terminology within the semiotic register can be traced to his refurbishing of Freud's notions of condensation and displacement. Lacan replaces these pivotal concepts with the "rhetorical" ground plan of metaphorical analysis, including the chains of metonymical substitution that characterize both poetic license and "unconscious" musings. The "laws" that these substitutions follow concern miscommunication and what Lacan calls denegation.

A distinctive trait of unconscious discourse is the absence of internal coherence. But such a "lacuna" becomes the space within which the parade of misappropriated signification can begin to congeal and emerge as language. Speech begins as fractured phonemes, as conflicts of intentionality, as duplicity, as "symptom."

> When Freud realized that it was in the field of dream that he had to find confirmation of what he had learnt from his experience of the hysteric, he began to move forward with truly unprecedented boldness. What does he now tell us about the unconscious? He declares that it is constituted essentially, not by what the consciousness may evoke, extend, locate, bring out of the subliminal, but by which is, essentially, refused (Lacan 1978:43).

The Pygmalion-like re-creation of the symptom as recognizable, meaningful, and "insight"-laden speech act is at the heart of the therapeutic process and can only be attributed to the self-elaboration of language across the entire indicative spectrum, from natural sign to higher-order statements of a "dialectical" type.

In the religious realm, this "fracturing" of the sign at the genetic level corresponds to the cultic process itself whereby the primitive ceremonial, or devotional, language of "experience" is not yet fixed but remains a mobile apparatus of deep and only partially determined significations. Cultic utterance that precedes all narrative, doctrine, catechistics, or theology coincides at the semiotic level with the Freudian primary processes or the inauguration of the Lacanian mirror stage. The metamorphosis of the cultic utterance into what we would generally term a religious "form" is coextensive with the struggle of desire in the psychoanalytical context to become "symbolic," to transform itself into a web of signifiers. The enunciation of a religious "tradition," or discursive systematics, worthy of scholarship and study, is equivalent to the Lacanian order of the "real."

Yet the great Lacanian insight is simply that the coherence, or constellation, of the order of speech has its own strange and enigmatic genealogy in the random patterning of the "instinctualities." In the same way that life can be said to have come from nucleotides in the primordial sea bombarded with radiant energy, so the varieties of religious speech collectivities can be traced back to the formation of durable semomes in the vast, night-shrouded ocean of desire.

The interactions that produce what we glibly, but without understanding, dub "religious consciousness" can be graphed in Lacan's distinction between the "Real," the "Imaginary," and the "Symbolic." In the first section of his *Seminar*, Lacan compared the Real to a six-sided diamond. Although the diamond appears to be an unbroken and seamless entity from a certain angle, when viewed as a refractory gateway for light rays, it is disordered and full of gaps and holes. The totalizing impact of language itself conduces to this illusion of completion and seamlessness.

But the primitive play of body and the expanding world of "otherness" in the psychological development of the infant—the interaction that forms Lacan's *objet a*—opens up chasms of unclarity as well as signifying disjunctions. These disjunctions provide a space for what Freud calls "fantasy," what Lacan refers to as the "Imaginary." It is important to note in this context, however, that Lacan's "imaginary" is not accorded an obvious ontological status as it is in Freud, for whom it connotes the unreal, and in Jung, for whom it designates the ultimately real. The imaginary in Lacan is simply the necessary and ineluctable supplement to the discursive. The symbolizing power of language, which the child acquires early in life, serves to fuse the imaginary and the real and turn the darkness and uncertainty surrounding the objet a into a bright, whole cloth of signification.

For Lacan, then, the notion of the "God of the gaps" in the religious setting is not the same as a Deus otiosus but a central metaphoric construct for the ontological productivity of language itself. What is most distinctive about Schreber's voices, Lacan noted, is that "they tell him that they lack something" (Miller 1988c:133). In a most peculiar fashion, it may be that Jacques Derrida's view of God as the "transcendental signified," which is the semiotic way of talking about Aristotle's First Cause or Heidegger's Being of beings, becomes the key to the Lacanian formation of the "real" through the mediation of the imaginary.

Whereas in both Heidegger and Derrida the transcendental signified manifests as a ghost of the grammatological, in Lacan "God" becomes a kind of global copulative term, a syntactic enzyme that catalyzes the broad connectivity of primal and discursively sophisticated speech acts. The grammar of divinity is the same as that of articulate speech. Lacan made this point decisively in linking the theological "delusions" of Schreber to the genesis of speaking:

> Analysis of the delusion provides us with the subject's fundamental relationship to the register in which all the manifestations of the unconscious are organized

and unfold. Perhaps it will even explain to us, if not the ultimate mechanism of psychosis, at least the subjective relationship to the symbolic order it contains. Perhaps we shall be able to understand how over the course of the evolution of the psychosis, from the time of its origin to its final stage, assuming that there is a final stage in the psychosis, the subject is situated in relation to the whole symbolic, original order—an environment distinct from the real environment and from the imaginary dimension, with which man is always involved, and which is constitutive of human reality (Miller 1988c:120).

Religion is not a discursive formation all its own but a kind of "ur-discursivity" that explodes from the roiling and phatic energies of collective desire that becomes apparent through the merger of the real and imaginary. For Lacan, the "disparity" between science and religion, or between ordinary reality and the religious perspective on matters, is not one of ontological privilege or for that matter of inferiority. Unlike Freud, who dismissed the religious as an ideological by-product to neurosis, Lacan interprets it indirectly as the cipher for the transformation of broad-ranging symbolic processes into the palatial architecture of speech.

The Promise of Lacan

It is in that light that we can understand Lacan's seemingly delphic remark that the formula of "atheism" is not "God is dead" but "God is unconscious" (1978:59). It might be possible to take liberties with Lacan and posit that the logic of his thought was leading toward a fourth sort of "heuristic" order beyond the real, imaginary, and symbolic. We might name this order the "hyperreal" in deference to the terminology of Baudrillard but without his specific applications of the word. Lacan's suggestion of the "hyperreal" arises from what is in many ways the most difficult of his ideas, the so-called name of the father. The *nom de père* is a "law," according to Lacan. In a strict manner, it corresponds to the resolution of the Oedipal complex, which for Freud was the generative structure of human consciousness.[1]

For Lacan, by contrast, the law of the father represents the process of introjected and formative speech, so that the "ego" (Lacan's *moi*) is shaped no longer by the imaginary aims of desire but by the universe of cultural signifiers and "moral" ideals. Lacan sees the Oedipal dilemma as a mythic rendering of the scission between the hegemony of social language and the somatological significations that belong to the heterology of the "unconscious."[2] The "desire" of the child for the (m)Other in Freud's mythic model is really the proclivity of speech toward the imaginary and the substitutional mechanisms of metaphoric discourse that aims for "pleasure" and turns into an indecipherable nexus of intimations and veilings that might be called the romance of the signifier.[3]

The impossibility of producing coherence within this speech, combined with the momentum toward fragmentation of the *moi* that this speech precipitates, leads to a closure of the process of subject formation and its absorption into the "patriarchal" discourse of the culture, merging the alterity of the social domain of signification with the identifying activity of the *moi*. It has been characteristic of all psychoanalysis to regard "father naming" as the enterprise of culture in some immanent sense and to dismiss its religious origins. Yet Lacan opens up a far different prospect. The signifying order of the "name of the father" becomes the chrysalis of language itself.[4]

When drawing on Lacan's insight, it is probably useful to claim that we are not excluding maternal religion or the divine feminine. It is not clear that Lacan is wedded to the gender exclusivity of the concept of "the name of the father" in the way that Freud was. Lacan, after all, is simply redescribing the Oedipal struggle as one of language, not of object preference. The Lacanian m(Other) does not offer a semiotic analog to goddess religions, which consist in the formation of powerful signifying complexes around heavenly female personages. The "name of the father" is simply a stratum of transcendental signification that unifies and agglomerates the different moments of signifying praxis within a mobile field of discourse. It is the *nom* that is also *non* in French. That is, it is the "phallic" name that negates the lush differentiation of metonymical substitutions within an endless chain of signifiers and enforces the coalescence of symbols and images into a regime of communicable speech.

Every "religious" system of communication by this standard, therefore, serves as the ground-"naming" of the structure of meaning that constitutes a culture. Paul Tillich's dictum that religion is the "essence" of culture follows this particular line of argument. But it is a mistake to think that this ground-naming occurs in some historical sense as some sort of integral and finished manner of signifying praxis. The mistake of the "history of religions," or the "study of religion" for that matter, has been to look exclusively at the "real" signifying complexes we erroneously call "traditions" and overlook the skein of spaces, gaps, and disjunctive piecings that belong to their formative genealogy.

The nature of that "dark etiology" of religion itself is the subject of another essay. But it is clear from reading Lacan that this original darkness that is etiologically prior to the emergence of that lattice of significations we would glibly term "religious reality" must become the text for our inspection and analysis.

What, then, would constitute a theory of religion that comprehended the formation of the vocative religious "subject"? If the origins of the religious imagination lie in a kind of cultural "mirror stage," where the tempests of collective desire are tamed and reordered as vastly intricate signifying praxes of myth, ceremony, and doctrine, if the "big ugly ditch" between the language of faith and the helter-skelter of "unconscious" signification has become so great that ordinary scholarship can no longer fathom the yawning, silent spaces beneath the "traditions," then the study of religion no longer retains a system of objects for investigation but is a parallelogram of semiotic analysis and what might be called "psychohistory."

This psychohistory, however, does not amount to explanatory accounts and so-called metanarratives. Such psychohistory is a reconstruction of the signifying process that undergirds the movement and transformation of culture. The signifying process itself can be understood in terms of an archaeology of language that accomplishes what the Romantic philologists of the nineteenth century, who in many ways founded the discipline of religious studies, failed to do, that is, discover the "divine" within the birth pangs of speech, to find "God" in a genuine sense within "grammar."

Lacan's most famous formulation is his reinscription of the Freudian "id" as inchoate subject, of "es" becoming S. This formulation is also the key that unlocks the discursive castle of "religious" talk. For the "es" denotes here the signifying power of the religious unconscious that comes to be "fundamentally structured, woven, chained, meshed by language"(Miller 1988c:5).[5]

The Lacanian turn holds great promise for a recasting of the discipline of the study of religion itself. To quote Lacan himself, it is "by coordinating the paths traced by a discourse, that (although it may proceed merely from the one to the one—that is, from the particular) something new can be conceived, and is able to be transmitted as incontestably by this discourse as in the numerical matheme"(1990:39). Coordinating the paths traced by psychoanalysis and the study of religion no longer has to be an exercise in "reductionism," as the critics would have it. It is the creation of a new, fruitful theoretical discourse that may well unlock both the secrets of the sacred and of the lush potentialities of the whole of human language itself.

Notes

1. For a discussion of Lacan's notion of God and the symbolic order, see Bice Benvenuto and Roger Kennedy (1986:156).

2. See Ellie Ragland-Sullivan (1986:305).

3. The practical application of these concerns in terms of the new science of rhetoric are implied in an interesting work by Ch. Perelman (1979).

4. The aim of psychoanalysis, according to Lacan, is to disclose the "father-naming" that lies beyond the formation of articulate speech. Hence, the discovery of the archaic, paternal other is not so much a recognition of the power of introjected images but a revelation of the general architecture of signifiers. This is why Lacan thought perhaps that, according to Gallop (1985:29), "psychoanalysis is the site of the 'knowledge of meaning.'"

5. See also Lacan's remark in *Television* that "there is no unconscious except for the speaking being" (1990:5).

References

Benvenuto, Bice, and Roger Kennedy. 1986. *The Works of Jacques Lacan: An Introduction.* London: Free Association Books.

Freud, Sigmund. 1911/1958. *Psychoanalytic Notes on an Autobiographical Account of a Case of Paranoia (Dementia Paranoides).* In *Standard Edition* 12, translated by J. Strachey. London: Hogarth Press, pp. 3–82.

Gallop, Jane. 1985. *Reading Lacan.* Ithaca: Cornell University Press.

Lacan, Jacques. 1977. *Écrits: A Selection.* Translated by Alan Sheridan. New York: W. W. Norton.

_____. 1978. *The Four Fundamental Concepts of Psychoanalysis.* Translated by Alan Sheridan. New York: W. W. Norton.

_____. 1990. *Television.* Translated by Denis Hollier, Rosalind Kraus, and Annette Michelson. New York: W. W. Norton.

Miller, Jacques-Alain, ed. 1988a. *The Seminar of Jacques Lacan.* Book 1. Translated by John Forrester. New York: W. W. Norton.

_____. 1988b. *The Seminar of Jacques Lacan.* Book 2. Translated by Sylvia Tomaselli. New York: W. W. Norton.

_____. 1988c. *The Seminar of Jacques Lacan.* Book 3. Translated by Russell Grigg. New York: W. W. Norton.

Perelman, Ch. 1979. *The New Rhetoric and the Humanities.* Dordrecht, the Netherlands: D. Reidel.

Ragland-Sullivan, Ellie. 1986. *Jacques Lacan and the Philosophy of Psychoanalysis.* Urbana: University of Illinois Press.

14

Julia Kristeva and the Psychoanalytic Study of Religion: Rethinking Freud's Cultural Texts

Diane Jonte-Pace

Julia Kristeva's life and career are marked by paradox. She is often called a "French feminist," although she is neither French nor, according to some of her harsher critics, feminist (Nye 1987).[1] A nonbeliever, she has been accused of being an apologist for Christianity (Spivak 1988). A practicing psychoanalyst, she holds a professorship not in psychology but in linguistics. She describes herself as a stranger or foreigner "living in exile, not belonging to a culture or to [a] native language" (in Kurzweil 1986:216). Displacement, negation, exile, and estrangement characterize not only her biography but also her theory. Perhaps more than any other psychoanalyst, Kristeva is a theorist of the divided self or exiled subject, the "subject in process" or the "subject on trial." As human beings, Kristeva argues, we are all "strangers to ourselves" (1991); women in particular live in "eternal exile" (1977:7–8).

In this chapter, I will introduce Kristeva as a psychoanalytic theorist of religion, focusing on this theme of exile, displacement, or division. I will first describe Kristeva's life and career, locating her ideas within an intellectual and historical context—finding a home, as it were, for her theory of exile. Second, I will provide a description of Kristeva's psychoanalytic theory of subjectivity and society, noting briefly the relation of her work to the ideas of Sigmund Freud, Jacques Lacan, and the psychoanalytic object relations theorists. Third, I will discuss Kristeva's theory of religion, arguing that her project has been to retrace Freud's steps—indeed, to rewrite Freud's classic books on religion—from the perspective of her own psychoanalytic and linguistic readings of subjectivity and society.

Life and Career

Born in Bulgaria in 1941, three years before the Soviet takeover in September 1944, Kristeva was raised in a family attentive to music, literature, art, and religion. Because they were not Communist Party members, her family members were denied access to the educational system of the privileged "red bourgeoisie." However, she obtained a "double education" (Clark 1990:172) by attending both the obligatory Bulgarian schools, where she was trained in "Marxist orthodoxy," and the French schools in Bulgaria, where, receiving a "francophile and francophone education," she was trained as "an intellectual in the French sense of the word" (Kristeva 1984:265).

As a graduate student in languages, literature, and linguistics in a Bulgarian literary institute, Kristeva had begun a thesis on the modernist novel when she was offered a doctoral fellowship sponsored by Charles De Gaulle's government in the mid-1960s. She accepted the fellowship, arriving in Paris in the Christmas season of 1965. Enrolling at L'École Practique des Hautes Études in 1966, she began a course of study in linguistics, working with semiotician Roland Barthes, linguist Emile Benveniste, and anthropologist Claude Lévi-Strauss.

Quickly she became part of an avant-garde intellectual and political community associated with the journal *Tel Quel.* In addition to Roland Barthes, the *Tel Quel* group included philosopher and deconstructionist Jacques Derrida, historian of ideas Michel Foucault, literary theorist Tzvetan Todorov (also from Bulgaria), and the writer Philippe Sollers, whom she later married. These were intellectual iconoclasts whose work centered on language and writing understood as subversive practice or production rather than as representation (McCance 1988:18). They emphasized a revolutionary "*écriture limite*" (limit writing) as the focus around which "a new theoretical discourse on language as subjective experience was constituted" (Kristeva 1984:268). Their radical critiques of structuralism and humanism were crucial in initiating the "poststructuralist explosion" in France. Activists as well, they engaged in intense public debate over nationalism, communism, feminism, and the possibilities of revolutionary social change, becoming deeply involved in the Paris demonstrations of May 1968. Thus, Kristeva became a central player not only in the arena of radical political activism but also in the avant-garde literary and academic communities of Paris at a time of intense social and intellectual ferment.

Kristeva's Interest in Psychoanalysis

Even in the early phase of her career in linguistics, psychoanalysis was prominent in Kristeva's work. Her interest in revolutionary forms of speaking and writing led her to seek a theoretical perspective that could attend to subversions of linguistic and social hegemony. Her 1969 publication *Semeiotiké*, for example, offered a method of "semanalysis" involving both psychoanalysis and semiotics, the theory of the meanings of signs. "The psychoanalytic experience," she later stated, "struck me as the only one in which the wildness of the speaking being, and of language, could be heard" (Kristeva 1984:275). Kristeva's doctoral thesis in semiotics, "La Révolution du Langage Poétique," defended in 1973, presented a psychoanalytic theory of the subject through an analysis of poetic texts. She argued that poetic language in the work of Mallarmé and Lautréamont opens to an "Other," which is the corporeal or material body. The publication of the thesis in 1974 led to Kristeva's appointment as professor of linguistics in the Department of Texts and Documents at the University of Paris VII, a position she continues to hold.[2]

Throughout the early seventies, Kristeva was engaged in frequent dialogue with psychoanalytic thinkers and writers, in particular with the French psychoanalyst Jacques Lacan. She attended Lacan's famous seminars until 1974; Lacan soon became a friend and intellectual sparring partner. In an autobiographical essay, "My Memory's Hyperbole," Kristeva acknowledged the significance of Lacan's views during these years for her own work and for the work of others in the *Tel Quel* community: "It was Lacan's insolence in daring to introduce the 'great Other' into the very heart of the speaking structure that propelled us on this course. We were attempting, in our own fashion, to circumscribe the unavoidable necessity of this Other and to analyze its crises, which determine the transformations, the life, and the history of discourses" (1984:270). Thus, in the early and mid-1970s, psychoanalysis became more and more central in Kristeva's thinking. She stated, "Little by little my semiotic mode of thinking . . . expanded to include a truly psychoanalytic approach" (p. 267).

The mid-1970s marked a turning point in Kristeva's life and career, bringing her even more closely into the heart of psychoanalytic theory and practice. After a trip to China in 1974 with Sollers, Barthes, and others (Lacan had hoped to join the group but was unable to do so), Kristeva reevaluated her prior commitment to collective political activism, affirming a continuing commitment to a politicized analysis of intellectual activity but abandoning an activist stance toward revolutionary social change. In 1976, she gave birth to a child. During this period, she began to address the problems of femininity and motherhood, often from a psychoanalytic perspective. And between 1976 and 1979, she trained as a psychoanalyst. Her training was not, as some have claimed, in the school of Jacques Lacan but rather in the Psychoanalytique de France, an association founded in 1964 when its members split from the Lacanian school (Doane and Hodges 1992:87). This group emphasized object relations theory, a branch of psychoanalysis associated with the work of Melanie Klein and D. W. Winnicott, attentive to the interrelationships between self and "object" or "other." Kristeva's publications in the late 1970s, 1980s, and 1990s have become increasingly psychoanalytic; a number of those publications—especially those written during the 1980s—have inquired into the psychological origins and effects of religious ideas and practices. Before examining Kristeva's psychoanalytic theory of religion, I will briefly address her theory of subject and society.

Kristeva's Psychoanalytic Theory of Subjectivity and Society

The "Speaking Being" as "Subject in Process"

Kristeva's background in linguistics provides an important foundation for her psychoanalytic theory of the self: She incorporates semiotics and psychoanalysis, emphasizing language or speech as a crucial component of subjectivity. She refers to the self or subject as the "speaking subject" or the "speaking being." But this "speaking being" is never entirely encompassed by language: affects, drives, and kinesthetic awareness of the physical body, for example, are translinguistic or prelinguistic experiences continuously interruptive of the linguistic order.

The speaking being is also not a unified being. Because of the tension between language and the nonlinguistic realms of affect and sensation at the heart of the speaking being, Kristeva refers to the subject as the *"sujet en procès."* The double meaning of the French term *en procès* (in process or on trial) is significant: In Kristeva's view, all formulations or expressions of the self are tentative for, first, we are constantly changing and, second, we are constantly judged, evaluated, and tested before the structures of language and society that make up the "Law." Thus, our subjectivity, "in process" and "on trial," is never unified or monolithic. Kristeva explained: "As speaking beings, always potentially on the verge of speech, we have always been divided, separated from nature. . . . We are no doubt permanent subjects of a language that holds us in its power. But we are subjects in process, ceaselessly losing our identity, destabilized by fluctuations in our relation to the other, to whom we nevertheless remain bound by a kind of homeostasis" (1987a:8–9).

The Symbolic and the Semiotic

Kristeva describes this destabilization inherent in the "subject in process" in terms of two "orders": the symbolic and the semiotic. The "symbolic order," a term Kristeva borrows from Jacques Lacan, is the space of language, culture, morality, and society. The symbolic describes a social system that requires renunciation of desires and acceptance of cultural and linguistic meanings. In Kristeva's view, the symbolic is constantly disrupted by "the semiotic," "a psychic modality logically and chronologically prior to the sign, to meaning and to the subject" (1987a:5). The semiotic can take many forms: It emerges in art, music, religion, and literature, in rhythm, color, ritual, and poetic language. It emerges in emotion, pain, and pleasure. And it appears in dreams, symptoms, and psychosis. The pre- or translinguistic processes of the semiotic—pre-Oedipal and prelinguistic in origin—are initially structured and directed in relation to the mother's body. They are "archaic traces of the links between our erogenous zones and those of the other, stored as sonorous, visual, tactile, olfactory, or rhythmic traces" (p. 9). Kristeva's ongoing project, evident in her work over three decades, has been to trace the effects of the semiotic upon the symbolic order—the strange or alien upon the familiar—within culture, history, and the individual psyche.

For Kristeva (and Lacan), the symbolic order expresses *le nom du père*, the name of the father. The aural ambiguity of the French word *nom* is significant here. *Le nom* (the name) is aurally indistinguishable from *le non* (the no). The symbolic order is thus a patriarchal social order articulating the name of the father, the law of the father, and the forbidding "no" of the father. The semiotic, by contrast, represents a challenge to the patriarchal symbolic order: The semiotic interrupts and displaces the order of language based on paternal authority by means of ruptures in syntax, rhythm, and semantic coherence.

At times, Kristeva's discussions of the semiotic disruptions of the symbolic order sound like descriptions of gender battles or parental conflicts. The maternally based semiotic disrupts the paternally based symbolic (Kristeva 1986b, 1987a), while feminist expressions of the semiotic challenge the monolithic hegemony of the patriarchal symbolic (Kristeva 1986a, 1986c). Although there is some truth to these formulations, it is important to note that, for Kristeva, the interactions of the semiotic and symbolic occur in the lives and psyches of both men and women. The semiotic and symbolic should not be too quickly identified with female and male. In fact, it is most often in the work of male artists, writers, and poets that Kristeva finds illustrations of creative intrusions of the semiotic into the symbolic (1980, 1987b, 1989).

Does Kristeva idealize the semiotic? Some of her writings portray the semiotic as an enlivening, enriching, transformative, revolutionary realm, somewhat reminiscent of Winnicott's "transitional space" (1971), within which language can open itself to the playful, poetic, or creative. Kristeva's work on the semiotic in the context of avant-garde literature and art, her analysis of the semiotic in religious faith and mystical experience, and her location of the origins of the semiotic in a space "metaphorically suggesting something nourishing and maternal" (1987a:5) exemplify this sense of the semiotic as a benign maternal territory. However, I will show that she also has a clear sense of the other side of the semiotic, that is, its expression in psychopathology, in fascism, in misogyny, and in the "horror" expressed in religious rituals that, through sacrifice, separate the sacred from the profane (1982).

I will first take a brief look at these central Kristevan concepts in relation to the views of Sigmund Freud, Jacques Lacan, and the psychoanalytic object relations theorists in order to locate Kristeva's ideas within an intellectual context.

Freud, Lacan, and Object Relations Theory

Kristeva's psychoanalytic approach to the subject and society builds upon the traditions of Freud, Lacan, and the object relations theorists. In my view, she situates herself as a supportive interpreter of Freud, often defending him against his misinterpreters, pursuing the questions he raised, and extending his insights. In relation to Lacan, she is far more ambivalent. Although Marilyn Edelstein saw Kristeva's approach to Lacan as a "typically non-agonistic . . . revision" (1992:43), I find her stance toward Lacan to be quite argumentative. She is indebted to many of Lacan's insights, but she often poses her arguments oppositionally, challenging his conceptualizations (Kristeva 1983). Her relation to the object relations theorists is more obscure. Kristeva rarely engages the object relations theorists in debate. Instead, these theorists tend to appear in her footnotes rather than her texts: They provide an almost invisible, nearly unacknowledged, structure of support for her theories.

The foundational analytic construct for Freud, of course, is the Oedipus complex: Incestuous desire for the mother and patricidal hostility toward the father—the two central elements of the Oedipal fantasy—provide the structure for psyche and culture. Around the age of three, the child (usually a male child in Freud's texts), feels sexual desire toward the mother and patricidal wishes toward the father. The father forbids the actualization of these incestuous and murderous desires; the father's threats are experienced by the son as threats of castration; and the son renounces his fantasies of incest and patricide, submitting to and identifying with paternal authority. This renunciation and submission is the first moral act: It sets the pattern for the son's future relationships to all paternal structures and father figures in the cultural, religious, moral, and political arenas. Thus for Freud, fantasies of incest and patricide and fear of castration lie at the foundations of subjectivity, culture, and morality.

Although Freud devoted most of his attention to the vicissitudes of the Oedipal period, he did not ignore the period of development prior to the emergence of Oedipal fantasies. He made numerous attempts to theorize the pre-Oedipal in terms of narcissism (Freud 1957, 1961a, 1964a) but was hesitant about making psychoanalytic speculations regarding early phases of human development seemingly impenetrable by analysis. Kristeva, as I will discuss, pursues Freud's unfinished project in a number of ways: She makes a thorough inquiry into the pre-Oedipal and its intrusions into the Oedipal; she broadens Freud's inquiry by exploring the female psyche as well as the male; she posits the mother as well as the father as a central figure in culture and psyche; and she reconceptualizes Freud's schema in terms of the semiotic and symbolic orders.

In her explorations of the semiotic and symbolic, Kristeva is indebted to Jacques Lacan. Lacan was the initiator of the attempt to bring linguistic theory into psychoanalytic discourse. In a series of essays, books, and seminar lectures published between the 1930s and the 1980s, he challenged the psychoanalytic establishment, arguing that the theory of language developed by the great linguist Ferdinand de Saussure complemented and completed Freud's insights into the workings of the unconscious. Lacan argued that Freud's description of the Oedipus complex was not only a description of the construction of subjectivity but also a description of the acquisition of language. In Lacan's view, the Oedipal child's displacement of incestuous and patricidal fantasies into other gratifications recapitulates another set of displacements: the substitutions or displacements involved in the representations of things by words. Thus, the Oedipal conflict marks the initiation into language and "the symbolic order." David Crownfield explained: "Blocked by the father . . . from total possession of mother's desire, the child is forced to substitute other gratifications, other objects of desire. . . . This positional logic of substitution, of representing one thing by another, of displacing desire along a chain of representatives, is the foundation of the formal order of language, of what Lacan calls the symbolic order" (1992a:XIII). Within the logic of Lacan's terminology, then, the "symbolic" originates in the Oedipal encounter with the "law of the father" or the "name of the father," that is, it originates in the displacements imposed by the paternal function of Oedipal interdiction.

If Freud postulated a pre-Oedipal phase prior to the Oedipal, Lacan similarly theorized a presymbolic period prior to the initiation into language: the "imaginary." According to Lacan, at some point between six and eighteen months, the child sees itself in a mirror or is mirrored to itself in the regard of the parent. This reflection, which Lacan described in an important essay on "The Mirror Stage" (1977), provides an image of false unity with which the child comes to identify. This sense of unity is false because the experience of subjectivity is actually an experience of division: The desires of the "other" (the first "other" is, of course, the mother) shape the earliest sensations, both conscious and unconscious. This "imaginary," unified, mirrored, false self is defensively maintained by signification in language within the symbolic order. Behind the symbolic order, then, lies the "imaginary," characterized by nonlinguistic imagery and by an illusory sense of a unified self that disguises earlier sensations of a self that is "other" to itself (Crownfield 1992a:XIII).

Just as Freud's Oedipal phase has primacy in his thought, the symbolic has primacy for Lacan. Language is all—one cannot exist outside of this "symbolic" patriarchal, social order without stepping into psychosis. The symbolic is unavoidable, constant, and all encompassing. Even the unconscious is, for Lacan, "structured like a language" (1977). The "imaginary," like Freud's shadowy, uncharted, pre-Oedipal realm, remains outside of signification, inaccessible.

Kristeva builds upon but radically rethinks Freud's and Lacan's theories. Perhaps most significantly, she engages in an extensive exploration of the territory eschewed by both Freud and Lacan: the pre-Oedipal, presymbolic space. In addition, she transforms Lacan's distinction between the symbolic order and the imaginary and Freud's distinction between the Oedipal and the pre-Oedipal into a distinction between the semiotic and the symbolic. Influenced by psychoanalytic object relations theory, she examines both developmental origins and cultural manifestations of the semiotic, and she attends more carefully than Freud or Lacan to the intrusions of the semiotic into the symbolic. She critiques Lacan's linguistic interpretation of the unconscious and his inattention to affect. In Kristeva's view, Lacan is inattentive to nondiscursive pathological and creative phenomena and to an experiential dimension that eludes the language function (1983). In addition, she brings attention to the androcentrism of Freud's and Lacan's formulations, suggesting that both Freud and Lacan inadequately account for women's thinking and speaking: Freud tends to ignore women in his metapsychological formulations, and Lacan finds "Woman" outside of language entirely (Lacan 1982:144).[3]

Literary theorist Shuli Barzilai offered an Oedipal analysis of the psychological dynamics of the Freud-Lacan-Kristeva triangle: "Kristeva and Lacan are—and will always remain—the children of Freud. From this standpoint, Lacan is . . . the self-appointed son and hero. Kristeva thus enters into a rivalry with Freud's 'French son' [whose] interpretation . . . strips away the full originality of the Freudian insight. Kristeva challenges this appropriation. A defender of the father and his faith, she attempts to resurrect his word" (1991:303). Barzilai's interpretation of the "sibling rivalry" between Kristeva and Lacan is provocative—but it remains incomplete: It ignores the important influence of another of Freud's "children," the object relations theorists.

Barzilai is not alone in focusing on Kristeva and Lacan and ignoring this third sibling. Few have emphasized the prominence of object relations theory in Kristeva's work. Kristeva is usually seen as a Lacanian—or as a thinker close to the Lacanian camp. Theorist Edith Kurzweil asked Kristeva why she chose not to study with the Lacanian school since her theories are so close to his (1986:220); psychoanalyst Otto Kernberg, in the foreword to the translation of Kristeva's *In the Beginning Was Love*, described her as "a thoughtful French Lacanian analyst" (1987:IX); and feminist sociologist Patricia Elliot described Kristeva's thought in terms of "adopting Lacan's definitions" yet "deviating from Lacan" (1991:211). Yet Kristeva often calls upon the work of French object relations theorist André Green (1986) as support for her theoretical claims (Kristeva 1989, 1995), she occasionally refers to Winnicott and other object relations theorists (Kurzweil 1986; Kristeva 1995), and her critiques of Lacan are often framed in terms of concerns important to the object relations theorists (Kristeva 1983; Doane and Hodges 1992). In an interview (although rarely in her own writings), Kristeva acknowledged her interest in object relations theory, defending her functional, pragmatic, psychoanalytic eclecticism. After describing her relationship with Lacanian theory, Kristeva stated, "We (my generation of psychoanalysts) feel that we have to know what all the others have done, even the Kleinians, the Freudians, and the followers of Bion and Winnicott. So we have a sort of psychoanalytic Babylon, but it's useful: you no longer want to be pure, to belong to one and only one group. You want to know what all psychoanalysts have done in the hope of someday hitting upon the pertinent synthesis" (in Kurzweil 1986:221).

Kristeva brings innovative perspectives and fresh insights to Freudian, Lacanian, and object relational discourses. To Freud's and Lacan's Oedipal/symbolic formulations, Kristeva brings attention to the pre-Oedipal/semiotic. To the object relational emphasis on the mother-child relationship, she brings a poststructuralist and linguistic or semiotic interest in the subject as "speaking being." To each of these psychoanalytic perspectives, she brings an interest in gender, maternity, and the problems of women in patriarchal society. And she makes an important contribution to psychoanalytic theory through her attention to the origins and effects of religious practice and discourse in human culture.

Kristeva's Theory of Religion

Neither a critic nor a defender of religion but, in my view, an interpreter of the way religion functions in culture and psyche, Kristeva offers a nuanced reading of religious texts and practices. Her own words provide an indication of the complexity of her experience and evaluation of religion. "I am not a believer," she asserted in *In the Beginning Was Love*. "I recall having been born into a family of believers who tried without excessive enthusiasm perhaps, to transmit their faith to me." In adolescence, she recounted, "I knelt before the icon of the Virgin that sat enthroned above my bed and attempted (unsuccessfully) to gain access to a faith that my secular education did not so much combat as treat ironically or simply ignore" (1987a:23–24). If Kristeva's secular Bulgarian education ignored religion, the larger political structures in Bulgaria nearly negated it. Religion was suppressed throughout Eastern Europe, functioning underground as a realm of possible freedom from totalitarian authority. Kristeva noted, "The experience in Bulgaria permitted me at once to live in an extremely closed environment . . . to understand the weight of social life, and at the same time, to try to find the small spaces of freedom, which include, for example, the arts, the interest in foreign languages, even religion" (in Clark 1990:172; see also Edelstein 1992:47).

Some of her critics attack Kristeva for what they see as a disturbingly sympathetic or "sentimental" stance toward Christianity (Doane and Hodges 1992:73). Feminist deconstructionist Gayatri Spivak, as noted earlier, challenges Kristeva as an "apologist for Christianity" (1988:264), and literary theorist Ann Rosalind Jones critiques Kristeva's interest in religion and romantic love on the grounds that neither religion nor romantic love have "been alternatives to women's subordination; they have been the ideologies through which that subordination was lived" (1984:70). In my view, however, Kristeva takes neither the stance of believer and defender nor the stance of secular critic and attacker. Rather, taking an analytic or hermeneutic stance, she shows how religion functions as a "polylogic" or multivocal discourse in psyche and culture. She reveals the way that, in certain contexts such as the Bulgaria of her youth, religion offers a space of possible freedom. She shows that in other contexts, religion expresses a hegemonic structure of patriarchal monotheism that "represses women and mothers" (Kristeva 1986a:18) or a horror of the "abject" originating in a primal abhorrence of the mother (Kristeva 1982). She is as likely to explore the liberating dimensions of religion as to examine its repressive or oppressive elements; similarly, she is as likely to explore the "semiotic" dimensions of religion as she is to examine the "symbolic" structures of religious and patriarchal law. Her approach to religion is neither apologetic nor critical but analytic. As she put it, "God is analyzable . . . infinitely" (Kristeva 1984:267).

I turn now to a discussion of this "infinitely"—or, to use Freud's term, "interminably"—analyzable phenomenon in Kristeva's revision of Freud's cultural texts. I will show that Kristeva's analysis of religion attempts to retrace Freud's major interpretive texts—*Totem and Taboo, The Future of an Illusion*, and *Civilization and Its Discontents*—rethinking them in terms of her poststructuralist, object relational, and feminist extensions of psychoanalytic theory. Kristeva, in effect, rewrote *Totem and Taboo* in *Powers of Horror*; she rethought the premises of Freud's slender volume *The Future of an Illusion* with her own "pamphlet" *In the Beginning Was Love: Psychoanalysis and Faith*; and she reworked *Civilization and Its Discontents* in *Strangers to Ourselves*. With *Moses and Monotheism*, Freud's fourth major text on religion and culture, written during the final years of his life, I see no Kristevan parallel. Perhaps we are still awaiting a Kristevan rethinking of Freud's great work on the founder of the Jewish tradition of morality and monotheism.[4]

Rewriting Totem and Taboo: *"As Abjection, So the Sacred"*

Underlying Freud's *Totem and Taboo* is the foundational principle that "ontogeny recapitulates phylogeny," the idea that the development of the individual parallels and replicates the development of the species. Fantasies and drives characterizing the childhood of the individual, Freud believed, were analogous to the fantasies and drives characterizing the "childhood" of the human race. He drew parallels among contemporary primitives, young children, and humans in ancient history. Utilizing this principle, Freud constructed an analysis of the origins of human culture, morality, and religion, integrating anthropological data, evolutionary social theory, and psychoanalysis.

Drawing upon the work of the major anthropological and sociological theorists of his day—William Robertson Smith, Émile Durkheim, E. B. Tylor, Edward Westermarck, Andrew Lang, and James Frazer—he described the two primary taboos discovered in "primitive societies." These were the taboo against incest within the clan or tribe—the law of exogamy—and the taboo against killing the tribal totem, or "clan animal." What interested Freud was that the taboos evident in tribal cultures were identical to the prohibitions or renunciations enforced by Oedipal development in the individual: The acceptance of the prohibitions of incest and murder created the post-Oedipal, socialized child, just as the acceptance of the taboos against incest and murder created membership in totemic society.

Freud postulated, following Darwin, that the earliest form of human community was a presocial primal horde ruled by a powerful father who drove away his sons. In Freud's reconstruction of ancient history, the exiled sons rose up against the tyrannical father, killing him in order to have access to the women of the horde, and eating him in an effort to incorporate his strength and power. Remorse and guilt followed the murder, Freud argued, leading to a commemoration of the murdered father as tribal totem (a proto-god in animal form) and to a taboo against killing the totem. This taboo was ritually broken in an annual ceremony in which a collective repetition of the primal murder culminated in a communal meal of the sacrificed totemic animal. The remorse and guilt felt by the fraternal band also led the brothers to establish an incest taboo against sexual relations with the women they had desired.

Thus, the totemic rituals and taboos discovered by late-nineteenth-century anthropologists, the Darwinian theory of a primal horde as the earliest form of social structure, and the Oedipal fantasies Freud had discovered within the unconscious were interwoven in *Totem and Taboo*. The totemic meal, "perhaps mankind's earliest festival," Freud argued, "would be a repetition and a commemoration of this memorable and criminal deed, which was the beginning of so many things—of social organization, of moral restrictions, and of religion" (1955a:142).

Kristeva's project in *Powers of Horror* is nearly identical to Freud's in *Totem and Taboo*. If Freud sought the origins of culture, religion, and morality in a primal murder, Kristeva discovers a primal separation at the heart of individual and cultural development. Just as Freud made the totem meal central to his analysis of the origins of culture and religion, Kristeva makes the sacrificial meal of religious ritual the "meat" of her analysis. And if Freud offered an account of unconscious desires underlying a broad historical span of cultural and religious phenomena, Kristeva similarly constructs an account of unconscious desires and fears underlying cultural and religious developments. Freud traced a historical sequence stretching from primal rites to the Christian Eucharist. Kristeva's historical sequence is similar: She moves from ancient purity rituals to Christian theological notions of sin and defilement. Thus, Freud's foundational principle that "ontogeny recapitulates phylogeny" seems itself to be "recapitulated" in Kristeva's work.

Even Kristeva's methodology recapitulates Freud's: Just as Freud attempted to integrate psychoanalysis with the anthropology of his time, Kristeva applies psychoanalytic theory to the findings of the major anthropological thinkers of the late twentieth century. In fact, Kristeva is quite explicit about her Freudian use of anthropological material: "My reflections will make their way through anthropological domains and analyses in order to aim at a deep psycho-symbolic economy ... such a procedure seems to me to be directly in keeping with Freudian utilization of anthropological data" (1982:68).

Kristeva's reflections begin with a problem posed by Freud in *Totem and Taboo* but incompletely resolved: the problem of the dread of incest. "I shall attempt to question the other side of the religious phenomenon, the one that Freud points to when he brings up dread, incest, and the mother; one that even though it is presented as the second taboo founding religion, nevertheless disappears during the final elucidation of the problem" (1982:57). The dread of incest, in Kristeva's view, can be traced to the repressed and transformed memory of an archaic primal abhorrence or "abjection" of the mother.

This notion of the "abject" provides the foundation for Kristeva's original and insightful analyses of individual, culture, and society. Kristeva finds religious expressions of abjection throughout human history; similarly, she finds psychological expressions of abjection in the prehistory of every subject. What is the abject? Kristeva describes a primitive terror of maternal engulfment that threatens the boundaries of the self almost before those boundaries come into being. Characterized by a sense of nausea, unease, and discomfort, abjection "afflicts a troubled and unformed entity that knows it-self as an I only through the sense of having been thrown out or repulsed from an other" (Kearns 1993:58). The abject can be experienced—or reexpe-rienced—in the loathing one feels for rotting food, filth or excrement, the re-pugnance or retching that "turns me away from defilement, sewage, and muck ... the corpse ... a wound with blood and pus, or the sickly, acrid smell of sweat, of decay" (Kristeva 1982:2–3). In Kristeva's analysis, this ex-perience of abjection is not unrelated to the fear of death: "These bodily flu-ids, this defilement, this shit are what life withstands, hardly, and with diffi-culty, on the part of death. There I am at the border of my condition as a living being" (p. 3).

The abject is what disturbs identity, system, order; it does not respect bor-ders, positions, rules. Kristeva speaks of the abject as the in-between, the ambiguous, that which is not *propre*. The French word *propre* refers to what is "one's own," or one's "self" and to what is "clean" and "proper." For Kristeva's term *corps propre*, her translator used the phrase "one's own clean and proper body" (1982:VII), thoroughly if a bit awkwardly expressing Kristeva's rich linguistic ambiguity. The abject is all that is not propre—all that falls outside the body-boundary of the self, the clean, the law of propri-ety and property. The abject is the horrifying within the semiotic. As Jacque-line Rose pointed out, the abject expresses "the problem which has run right through [Kristeva's] writings—of what can be articulated on this side of cul-ture without breaking its limits" (1986:155). Kristeva's theory of the abject provides the key to her analysis of the xenophobic fear of the other, of anti-Semitism, of racism, of nationalism, and of misogyny in *Powers of Horror* (1982), *Strangers to Ourselves* (1991), and *Nations Without Nationalism* (1993). How does this work?

Within our personal archaeology, the abject confronts us with or reminds us of our "earliest attempts to release the hold of maternal entity even before existing outside of her, thanks to the autonomy of language. It is a violent, clumsy breaking away, with the constant risk of falling back under the sway of a power as securing as it is stifling" (Kristeva 1982:13). The concept of ab-jection shows that "the semiotic is no fun" (Rose 1986:144). If this messy, sticky, violent separation from the mother, this "drastic exclusion of impure elements" (Kearns 1993:60), occasioned by the horror of the mother, charac-terizes the infancy of each individual, and culturally represents the founda-tion of the incest taboo, it also accompanies all religious structures and con-cepts of the sacred: "As abjection, so the sacred" (Kristeva 1982:17).

According to Kristeva, "Abjection accompanies all religious structurings and appears to be worked out in a new guise at the time of their collapse" (1982:17). She offers a chronology of religious attempts to express or control the abject: It appears as a rite of defilement and pollution in paganism; it per-sists as "exclusion or taboo (dietary or other) in monotheistic religions. . . . It finally encounters, with Christian sin, a dialectic elaboration, as it becomes integrated in the Christian Word as a threatening otherness. . . . Various means of purifying the abject—the various catharses—make up the history of religions" (p. 17). In the context of religion, abjection is controlled in two ways: through sacrifice and through taboo. Sacrifice reenacts the violent separation of abjection, establishing the categories of pure and impure. Taboo, on the other hand, "forestalls sacrifice," making it unnecessary by maintaining clear boundaries between pure and impure (p. 94). Cleo Kearns explained: "Religious ritual draws out and defers through language and signification the murderous as well as loving impulses that help to found our identities, both collective and individual" (1993:56).

Kristeva's inquiry into the necessary separation from—indeed the abhorrence of—the mother at the core of individuality and society has evoked critical responses from some feminist theorists. Jennifer Stone (1983) and Marie-Florine Bruneau (1992), for example, complain that Kristeva's analysis makes misogyny universal, biologically determined, and inevitable. If abjection serves to differentiate self from what is not self, they argue, and if abhorrence of the mother provides the psychological paradigm for abjection, then an inescapable fear of the mother (and, by association, an inescapable fear of women) would lie at the very foundations of subjectivity and society. Objecting to these assumptions and conclusions, Stone and Bruneau argue that Kristeva's perspective assumes an antifeminist, biologistic, essentialist, and universalist model of gender and society. Thus, they warn that her analysis supports patriarchy and misogyny as universal and inevitable. In my view, however, Kristeva's analysis of maternal abjection represents not an antifeminist attempt to legitimate patriarchy and misogyny but an important and probing feminist inquiry into unconscious patterns and fantasies that are socially and culturally destructive. Kristeva's discoveries initiate a feminist investigation of the sources and manifestations of maternal abhorrence and misogyny (Jonte-Pace 1992).

In *Powers of Horror*, then, Kristeva asked the questions Freud asked in *Totem and Taboo*, utilized the methodologies Freud utilized in *Totem and Taboo*, and constructed a contemporary revision of *Totem and Taboo*, making significant revisions in his thesis. She made the relationship with the mother foundational for culture and psyche, and she showed that the concept of the abject virtually supplants the primacy of Freud's Oedipal theory. Oedipal fantasies of incest and post-Oedipal renunciations of incestuous fantasies, if Kristeva's analysis is correct, are late experiences overlaid upon a more primal sense of abhorrence of the mother. Kristeva's revision of Freud has important implications not only for the understanding of exogamy and the incest taboo but also for the understanding of deeply embedded patterns of cultural misogyny and, indeed, as she suggests, for the understanding of subjectivity, society, and the history of religion.

Rethinking The Future of an Illusion: *"Images for Even
the Fissures in Our Secret and Fundamental Logic"*

If *Totem and Taboo* pursued the cultural origins of religious belief and social
practice in the earliest periods of human history, *The Future of an Illusion*
mounted a four-part attack on religion. Freud offered an interpretation of
religion as illusion, a critique of religious belief, an analysis of the psychological origins of religious belief, and a manifesto for a religionless utopia.
Freud's interpretation of religion was based on his projection theory: He
showed that religious beliefs are projections or fulfillments of unconscious
wishes and fantasies. His critique grew from this interpretation. In accord
with the enlightenment tradition of skepticism, Freud urged an abandonment of ideas based on fantasy—and he outlined what he saw as the individual and cultural pathologies produced by religion. Freud's analysis of religion brought psychoanalytic attention to familial and Oedipal patterns
underlying religious beliefs, while his manifesto outlined a utopian vision of
a glorious future based on science rather than religion.

Kristeva's text *In the Beginning Was Love* raises the same issues Freud addressed in *The Future of an Illusion*. In her rethinking of Freud, she accepts
Freud's interpretation of religion as wish but rejects his enlightenment critique. She extends Freud's analysis of religion, arguing that religion embodies
not only Oedipal but also, as she suggested in *Powers of Horror*, pre-Oedipal
fantasies, some of which provide creedal and visual representations of developmental moves into language from pre-Oedipal, prelinguistic states. Finally,
she offers a manifesto of her own, articulating a utopian vision of a psychoanalytic—rather than a scientific—future. I will look more closely at this
Freudian assessment of religion and this Kristevan revision of Freud.

Religion, in Freud's interpretation, is a projection or fulfillment of three
human wishes: the wish for a loving, protective, omnipotent, parental figure;
the wish for immortality; and the wish for a just and moral universe. These
three wishes are "fulfilled" quite directly by religious claims for the existence of a loving and omnipotent God, a blissful afterlife, and a system of divine reward and punishment (Freud 1961b:30). Illusions are thoughts based
on wishes. Because these religious notions are direct fulfillments of human
wishes, these ideas are "illusions." They are not necessarily "delusions,"
wishes for which there is clear negative evidence, but unless their truth can
be demonstrated, illusions should be treated with suspicion, for they fail to
provide solid foundations for morality or culture.

In his critique of religion, Freud turned his attention from the epistemological weakness of religious belief to the negative consequences of the acceptance of these religious illusions. The consolatory belief in a protective
deity obstructs a mature and resigned acknowledgment of our status as in-
significant beings in the universe. The belief in a heavenly afterlife inhibits an

effort to improve the quality of life on earth, and it discourages an encounter with life as a unique, richly meaningful, and transitory moment.

Freud acknowledged that his critique was in many ways a traditional one. As he put it, "I have said nothing which other and better men have not said before me. All I have done . . . is to add some psychological foundation to the criticisms of my great predecessors" (Freud 1961b:35). These "psychological foundations" represent his *analytic* contribution to the understanding of religion. In his analysis, God and morality are products of Oedipal structures: The belief in God is a projection of the helpless child's need for the father's protection, and the religious demand for morality is a projection of the father's demand for the son's renunciation of Oedipal fantasies. Linking critique with analysis, he argued that the belief in divine reward and retribution contributes to an immature form of morality where fear of punishment remains the primary motivating factor and an internalized, independent sense of conscience is suppressed.

Freud ended *The Future of an Illusion* with a deeply optimistic vision of a religionless world, a golden age characterized by "primacy of the intellect" and "education to reality" (1961b:53, 49). "You must admit," he proclaimed, "that here we are justified in having a hope for the future—that perhaps there is a treasure to be dug up capable of enriching civilization and that it is worth making the experiment of an irreligious education" (p. 49). He proposed a new foundation for morality through conscious, rational control over the instincts rather than fearful submission to Oedipal authority, and he outlined an illusionless, resigned engagement with the realities of human finitude. New generations of humans will "have to admit to themselves the full extent of their helplessness and their insignificance in the machinery of the universe; they can no longer be the center of creation, no longer the object of tender care on the part of a beneficent Providence" (p. 49).

Freud's optimism and enthusiasm about this religionless future affected even his style: Near the end of his book, he became witty and playful, inverting his own terms to proclaim devotion to "Our God Logos" (1961b:54). His words echo theological notions of Christ as the Logos, the Word of God, and acknowledge Freud's fantasy that psychoanalysis or science will replace religion as a cultural ideology or worldview. His hope for a better world may be "illusion" according to his definition, but he insisted that "science is no illusion" and its "future" is not in doubt (pp. 54–56). Thus, both his reference to "Our God Logos" and his title, *The Future of an Illusion*, are beautifully ambiguous: The future of the religious illusion of divine providence and justice is thrown into question, while the future of the scientific illusion of increasing justice and reason on this earth is affirmed as a realizable dream or illusion.

Kristeva's *In the Beginning Was Love: Psychoanalysis and Faith* seems to me to represent a clear rewriting of *The Future of an Illusion*. Allusions to

The Future of an Illusion, although rarely noted explicitly with footnotes, fill Kristeva's book, and Kristeva systematically addresses each of Freud's four arguments, agreeing with some and (nonagonistically) disagreeing with others. Even the structure of her book recapitulates Freud's. Freud's ten chapters are nearly matched by Kristeva's nine; Freud's "punch line" chapters defining illusion and outlining the illusions fulfilled by religion are exactly in the center of his book (chapters 5 and 6), and Kristeva's analysis of the fantasies fulfilled by religious belief is located just at the midpoint of hers (chapter 5).

Kristeva referred directly to *The Future of an Illusion* near the outset of *In the Beginning*. In a chapter entitled "The Unshakable Illusion," she stated that Freud "saw religion as nothing less than an illusion, albeit a glorious one . . . a rather unrealistic construct which nevertheless gives an accurate representation of the reality of its subject's desires" (Kristeva 1987a:11). Taking up the Freudian project, she initiated an inquiry into those desires, exploring not the Oedipal fantasies Freud uncovered but a rather different set of desires. Whereas Freud sought the fantasies underlying the belief in God, the belief in the afterlife, and the belief in salvation and judgment, Kristeva focused on the "Almighty Father" and the "Virgin Mother" in the Nicene Creed. Almighty Father and virgin mother, she suggested, are transparent expressions of desires. We all fantasize a powerful father and a mother who belongs to us alone: "The Credo embodies basic fantasies that I encounter every day in the psychic lives of my patients. The almighty father? Patients miss one, want one, or suffer from one. Consubstantiality with the father and symbolic identification with his name? Patients aspire to nothing else. . . . A virgin mother? We want our mothers to be virgins, so that we can love them better or allow ourselves to be loved by them without fear of a rival" (Kristeva 1987a:40–42). Thus, although her project is identical to Freud's, the specific content of her interpretation differs.

Kristeva's revision of Freud led her to a stance toward religion and illusion that is far less critical than Freud's. For Freud, illusion provided a weak epistemological foundation for thought, but Kristeva emphasizes the enlivening, creative effect of illusion: "Fantasy returns to our psychic life, but no longer as cause for complaint or source of dogma. Now it provides the energy for a kind of artifice, for the art of living" (1987a:9). She argues that the goal of psychoanalysis is, in fact, to make possible a self-reflexive engagement with the illusions produced by the unconscious, to enact a resurrection of the imagination: "The function of the psychoanalyst is to reawaken the imagination and to permit illusions to exist" (p. 18).

Freud's epistemological critique of religious belief as illusion was accompanied by a critique of the negative effects of religious belief—the obstruction of intellectual development and the discouragement of efforts at enacting social change. Kristeva's assessment, however, differs substantially. In her view, religion provides valuable support for our vulnerable, fragmented subjectivities. Christianity "supplies images for even the fissures in our secret and fundamental logic" (Kristeva 1987a:42), she argued, suggesting that religion can be effective, valuable, even therapeutic.

However, Kristeva's affirmation of the efficacy of religion does not imply an affirmation of religious faith. She proposes a nondefensive affirmation of illusion accompanied by a nonrepressive renunciation of faith: "What today's analyst must do, I think, is restore to illusion its full therapeutic and epistemological value. Does this mean restoring value to religion as well? Not altogether. . . . [R]epression can be atheist; atheism is repressive whereas the experience of psychoanalysis can lead to renunciation of faith with clear understanding" (Kristeva 1987a:21–26). Although she and Freud both renounce faith, her "renunciation with clear understanding" is perhaps less "repressive" than Freud's strident atheism.

Turning to Kristeva's *analysis* of religion, we find that she incorporates Freud's Oedipal reading of religious ideas but seeks other factors as well, factors visible to her through recent developments in psychoanalysis in both Winnicottian object relations theory and Lacanian poststructuralist theory. In a discussion of the powerful symbolism of the crucifixion, for example, she acknowledges an Oedipal fantasy but also explores more "primitive layers of the psyche" involving the relation of child to mother and the trauma of the entry into language: "The crucifixion of God-made-man reveals to the analyst, always attentive to murderous desires with regard to the father, that the representation of Christ's passion signifies a guilt that is visited upon the son, who is himself put to death. Freud interprets this expiation as an avowal of the oedipal murder that every human being unconsciously desires." But she argues that "Christ's Passion brings into play even more primitive layers of the psyche; it thus reveals a fundamental depression (a narcissistic wound or reversed hatred) that conditions access to human language" (Kristeva 1987a:40). In her reading, the crucifixion provides an image or a visual representation for an experience all humans share—the death or loss of union with the mother that is essential for the birth of the self as a speaking being: "The child must abandon its mother and be abandoned by her in order to be accepted by the father and begin talking. . . . language begins in mourning inherent in the evolution of subjectivity" (p. 41).

Thus, the crucifixion embodies the deep sense of division we experience as we are torn from a prelinguistic, edenic state. Kristeva described this in terms of an "essential alienation that conditions our access to language, in the mourning that accompanies the dawn of psychic life . . . the death that marks our psychic inception" (Kristeva 1987a:41). The powerful story of Christ's crucifixion, so central to Christian theology, doctrine, and liturgy, becomes, in Kristeva's analysis, an expression of the division, loss, and sacrifice marking the developmental shift from preverbal immersion in the maternally linked semiotic to initiation into the symbolic order of the "Father."

Christology thus has a positive and even necessary function. With this, Kristeva has moved far beyond Freud's hermeneutic of suspicion.

"What about the future, as we grapple also with the future of—tenacious—illusions?" (Kristeva 1987a:57) Kristeva asked. Her question here not only echoed the title of Freud's book[5] but also provided an introduction to her own discussion of the future of our firmly held illusions. Like Freud, Kristeva painted a glowing picture of the future of those illusions: If the conclusion of *The Future of an Illusion* offered a utopian vision of a religionless future guided by science, Kristeva's conclusion projected a similarly utopian vision of a better future. In her case, however, the utopia was guided not by science but by Freud's psychoanalysis. Acknowledging the desiccating possibilities of an objectifying scientism, she asked whether psychoanalysis is, in the final analysis, a form of nihilism. She answered cautiously: "In a sense it is not incorrect to argue that Freud represents the culmination of the nihilist program. Psychoanalytic theory, viewed as a theory of knowledge of psychic objects . . . is part of the nihilist effort to objectify man's being. Nevertheless . . . the analytic process is first and foremost an unfolding of language prior to and beyond all unification, distantiation, and objectification" (p. 60). Thus, psychoanalysis is not a cold, nihilistic science, in Kristeva's view. Rather, it constructs a pathway to the realm of imagination and meaning. Through psychoanalysis, the analysand "learns to know himself, submerged though he is in the immanence of a significance that transcends him. That significance can be given a name: the unconscious" (Kristeva 1987a:61).

Psychoanalysis in Kristeva's reading creates not only the possibility of playful illusion, imagination, and meaning, it also provides a foundation for ethics. Again, Kristeva poses a Freudian question here about the foundations of morality. She responds with a psychoanalytic answer that honors Freud but differs from the answer Freud himself proffered. Though Freud sought a new foundation for morality in science and rationality rather than in Oedipal submission to religiously formulated paternal authorities, Kristeva finds the source of morality in the awareness of the Other, of meaning, of drives, and of death made possible through psychoanalysis. She made this claim in the eloquent last paragraph of her book: "No restrictive, prohibitive, or punitive legislation can possibly restrain my desires for objects, values, life, or death. Only the meaning that my desire may have for an other and hence for me can control its expansion, hence serve as the unique, if tenuous basis of morality. In my opinion, therefore, psychoanalysis is the modest if tenacious antidote to nihilism in its most courageously and insolently scientific and vitalist forms" (Kristeva 1987a:63). Thus, through an affirmation of psychoanalysis as a via regia to imagination, meaning, and morality, Kristeva affirms, revises, and extends Freud's utopian vision.

Even Freud's playful, ironic, and ambiguous reference to "Our God Logos" reappears in Kristeva's text. She interprets Freud's "famous remark" as an expression of the healing effects of the "logos" or the "word" in psychoanalytic discourse and as a paean both to relationality and to the biblical God: "This mobilization of two people's minds and bodies by the sole agency of the words that pass between them sheds light on Freud's famous remark in *The Future of an Illusion* that the foundation of the cure is 'Our God Logos.' It also recalls the words of the Gospels 'In the beginning was the Word' and 'God is love'" (Kristeva 1987a:3). Kristeva's title *In the Beginning Was Love* offers a similarly ambiguous reference to the biblical "in the beginning," and her emphasis on the foundational qualities of love—for psychoanalysis and faith—underlines her radical revisioning of Freud's assumptions.

Thus, *In the Beginning Was Love* revises Freud's *The Future of an Illusion*. Kristeva offers an *interpretation* of religion that affirms Freud's definition of religion as illusion, but she goes further than Freud in her embrace of illusion as beneficial. She reevaluates Freud's *critique*, showing that his own attitude toward fantasy and the unconscious was far more tolerant of illusion than he admitted in *The Future of an Illusion*—establishing the possibility of a more benign psychoanalytic reading of religion. In her *analysis* of religion, though she notes Oedipal fantasies involving fathers and sons, she emphasizes narcissistic fantasies involving relationships with the mother as well. And, like Freud, she ended her book with great optimism for the future—Freud's hope that science could create a better world is transformed in Kristeva's volume into a hope that psychoanalysis can create a better world.

Reworking Civilization and Its Discontents: *"A Journey into the Strangeness of the Other and the Self"*

If Kristeva constructed revisions of *Totem and Taboo* and *The Future of an Illusion* in *Powers of Horror* and *In the Beginning Was Love*, she constructed, in my view, a revision of another Freudian classic in her award-winning book *Strangers to Ourselves*. Recipient of the 1989 Prix Henri Hertz, an award given by the Chancellerie des Universités de Paris to the best book of the year by a faculty member, *Strangers to Ourselves* is a rewriting of *Civilization and Its Discontents*. Freud's central concern in *Civilization and Its Discontents* was the difficulty of living in civilization; Kristeva's concern in *Strangers* is the difficulty of living in civilization "as an other" and "among others." Both Freud and Kristeva address the problem of aggression and intolerance; both investigate religious attempts to solve these problems. Kristeva's approach is more historical and political than Freud's: She brings Freud's abstract concerns into a localized context.

In *Civilization and Its Discontents*, Freud examined the unhappiness, malaise, or discontent inevitably generated by life within the human community and the unavoidable hostility we feel toward each other. The "fateful question for the human species," he dramatically proclaimed, is "whether and to what extent their cultural development will succeed in mastering the disturbance of their communal life by the human instinct of aggression and self-destruction" (Freud 1961c:111). This "fateful question" leads Freud to direct his attention to religious discourses promoting universal love as a moral mandate: "We are especially interested in what is probably the most recent of the cultural commands of the superego, the commandment to love one's neighbor as oneself" (p. 108). Developing a complex analysis and critique of the Christian "love commandment"—and its extension in the mandate to "love one's enemy"—he traces it through biblical formulations and contemporary political manifestations, arguing that the human instinctual inheritance makes such a commandment impossible to follow. Although we might love some of our neighbors, we cannot love them all, nor are we capable of loving our enemies (pp. 108–116).

The universalism of the love commandment, Freud argued, is paradoxically self-defeating: The stronger the demand for universal love, the more extreme will be the hostility toward those who fall outside of the community. The teachings of Saint Paul exemplify this pattern: "When once the Apostle Paul had posited universal love between men as the foundation of his Christian community, extreme intolerance on the part of Christendom towards those who remained outside it became the inevitable consequence" (Freud 1961c:114). Love and aggression work together, he argued, in creating bonds among some only if there are others available to hate: "It is always possible to bind together a considerable number of people in love, so long as there are other people left over to receive the manifestation of their aggressiveness" (p. 114). He gives this phenomenon the name "narcissism of minor differences," ironically noting the "useful services" rendered by the Jewish people throughout history to the "civilizations of the countries that have been their hosts" (p. 114).

The inevitable opposition between Eros and Thanatos, Love and Aggression, in Freud's view, creates further problems: The tension between them, amplified by civilization's demands, leads to a situation of nearly unbearable conflict and to the emergence of a heavy burden of guilt. "As a result of the inborn conflict arising from ambivalence, of the external struggle between the trends of love and death, there is inextricably bound up with it an increase of the sense of guilt which will perhaps reach heights that the individual finds hard to tolerate" (Freud 1961c:132). This guilt, he worried, had generated widespread cultural pathology: "May we not be justified in reaching the diagnosis that under the influence of cultural urges, some civilizations, or some epochs of civilization—possibly the whole of mankind—have become neurotic?" (p. 144).

Although Freud remained deeply concerned about the bleak future for civilization, he concluded *Civilization and Its Discontents* on a cautiously optimistic note, suggesting that in spite of the apparent hegemony of the "death drive," evident in the twentieth-century proliferation of wars and weaponry, the other great human drive, Eros (or Love), might yet reemerge: "The present time deserves a special interest. Men ... would have no difficulty in exterminating one another to the last man. They know this, and hence comes a large part of their current unrest, their unhappiness and their mood of anxiety. And now it is to be expected that the other of the two 'Heavenly Powers,' eternal Eros, will make an effort to assert himself in the struggle with his equally immortal adversary." A year after writing these lines, he added a far less optimistic final sentence: "But who can foresee with what success and with what result?" (Freud 1961c:145).

Published in 1930, *Civilization and Its Discontents* remains relevant today as a profound and prophetic exploration of the difficulties inherent in living in the human community, difficulties associated with tensions between aggression and love, tensions between civilization and instinct. Kristeva, I believe, intentionally revisited this text in *Strangers to Ourselves*, offering a rereading of Freud's "fateful question for the human species" and a solution to that question.

Kristeva's formulation of the "fateful question" is not far from Freud's, although her analysis updates the question by bringing it into European political and regional contexts of the 1980s. Citing recent political and economic crises—especially problematic in contemporary France—in which foreigners, immigrants, and "natives" constantly cross paths, often in tension and conflict, she asks how we can live with the other, the immigrant, the foreigner, *l'étranger*. Again, the French is richly ambiguous: *L'étranger* means stranger, foreigner, other, and alien. "Can the 'foreigner,'" Kristeva asked, "who was the 'enemy' in primitive societies, disappear from modern societies? ... As a still and perhaps ever utopic matter, the question is again before us today as we confront an economic and political integration on the scale of the planet: shall we be, intimately and subjectively, able to live with the other, to live as others?" (1991:1–2).

Allusions to *Civilization and Its Discontents* can be found throughout *Strangers to Ourselves*. Kristeva stated, for example, echoing Freud's title, "My discontent in living with the other—my strangeness, his strangeness—rests on the perturbed logic that governs this strange bundle of drives and language, of nature and symbol, constituted by the unconscious, always already shaped by the other" (1991:181–182). Evoking Freud's discussion of the forces that unite groups through an exclusionary stance—Freud's "narcissism of minor differences"—she described the ostracism of the other inevitable among the marginalized: "Foreigners of the world unite? Things are not so simple. For one must take into consideration the domination/exclusion fantasy. ... Just because one is a foreigner does not mean that one is without one's own foreigner ... as enclave of the other within the other, otherness becomes crystallized as pure ostracism: the foreigner excludes before being excluded" (Kristeva 1991:24).

Like Freud's, her analysis spans religion, culture, and history. Freud finds evidence of "discontent," intolerance, and aggression—and demands for their renunciation—in both biblical texts and twentieth-century politics. In a sequence of analyses far more precise and detailed than Freud attempts, Kristeva finds examples of xenophobia, rejection of the foreigner, and cultural discontent—as well as a variety of unsuccessful attempts to control them—in historical contexts spanning more than two thousand years of Western religious and secular history. She examines attitudes toward the foreigner in ancient Greece, biblical Judaism, Pauline Christianity, Augustinian Christianity, Renaissance Europe, Enlightenment France, and the modern era. Moving beyond Freud's broad psychological inquiries, she investigates the specific and particular forms of relationship to the stranger, the foreigner, and the immigrant.

Kristeva often frames apparent differences from Freud as connections with him. She suggests that an unspoken concern with psychological foreignness underlies Freud's texts: "Delicately, analytically, Freud does not speak of foreigners: he teaches us how to detect foreignness in ourselves" (Kristeva 1991:191). In actuality, Kristeva errs: Freud did speak of strangers. In challenging the "love commandment," for example, he argued "this stranger in general (is) unworthy of my love . . . he has more claim to my hostility and even my hatred" (Freud 1961c:110). Kristeva here overlooks a close connection to Freud. Nevertheless, her larger point is valid. Whether or not Freud actually and explicitly wrote about foreigners or strangers, he did, in fact, expose the foreignness within the psyche. His theory as a whole represents a charting of the unknown, a cartography for the journey into the strangeness or foreignness of the psyche.

Although Freud ended *Civilization and Its Discontents* with a note of cautious optimism, hopeful that "Eternal Eros" would reemerge to transform Thanatos's hegemonic hold over civilization, Kristeva modified Freud's conclusion, offering an unambiguously optimistic vision of the future, a vision that reiterates and extends the conclusions she drew in *In the Beginning Was Love*. To the fateful questions she and Freud asked, she suggests, psychoanalysis provides the solution—and psychoanalysis *is* that solution. If religion and culture were previously unable to find answers to the problems of civilization's aliens and discontents, Freud, in Kristeva's view, has found those answers. She proclaims the dramatic political and ethical effects of Freud's discoveries, arguing that psychoanalysis enacts a major transition in the human ability to accept new modalities of otherness. She describes "the political and ethical impact of the Freudian breakthrough," claiming that only through psychoanalysis "do we know that we are foreigners to ourselves and it is with the help of that sole support that we can attempt to live with others" (Kristeva 1991:182).

Kristeva's contention, then, is that the unconscious is a partially unchartable territory within the psyche of each individual. When, through psychoanalysis, we become aware of this otherness within, it becomes the foundation for the ability to encounter—and perhaps even to love—the other, the stranger, or the foreigner: "With the Freudian notion of the unconscious, the involution of the strange in the psyche loses its pathological aspect and integrates within the assumed unity of human beings an otherness that is both biological and symbolic" (1991:181). Thus, psychoanalysis is a "journey into the strangeness of the other and of oneself, toward an ethics of respect for the irreconcilable" (p. 182). Only as strangers to ourselves can we live among other strangers. Our own internal otherness makes possible the encounter with the external other. Kristeva offers, in effect, an ethics of exile: a foundation for morality in a world in which all are strangers (McCance 1990; Nickolchina 1991; Young 1990).

Perhaps most significantly, Kristeva takes up the challenge with which Freud ended his book. Freud expressed the hope that someone might complete the diagnosis and treatment of cultural pathology that he had begun: "An analytic dissection of such (cultural) neuroses might lead to therapeutic recommendations which could lay claim to great practical interest. I would not say that an attempt of this kind to carry psychoanalysis over to the cultural community was absurd or doomed. . . . We may expect that one day someone will venture to embark upon a pathology of cultural communities" (1961c:144). Freud refused the prophet's mantle, saying, "I have not the courage to rise up before my fellow-men as a prophet" (p. 145). But Kristeva takes up the prophet's mantle, offering a diagnosis and a solution to the problem of civilizational "discontent." She recapitulates and extends Freud's hesitant diagnosis of cultural pathology ("some civilizations, or some epochs of civilization—possibly the whole of mankind—have become neurotic"), diagnosing "negative narcissisms" and "new maladies of the soul" as the contemporary pathologies of Western culture (Kristeva 1991 and 1995:30, 227). And she prescribes psychoanalysis as the solution to this cultural pathology.

Conclusion

Julia Kristeva brings an integrative and nuanced approach to the psychoanalytic study of religion. Moving gracefully among the discourses of literature, semiotics, anthropology, gender theory, and psychoanalysis, she constructs complex analyses of psyche, society, and religion, focusing on "speaking beings" as "subjects in process." Her approach is significant in its integration of Freudian, poststructuralist and object relational forms of psychoanalysis, in its attention to the terrain of the pre-Oedipal and presymbolic; in its linguistic focus on the "speaking being" and the semiotic forces that interrupt the symbolic order; in its attention to women, maternity, and gender; in its attention to broad social, cultural, and economic concerns; and in its attention to the experience of exile, strangeness, or self-division. Rereading Freud's texts, reconsidering Freud's questions, she enacts a major move beyond Freud himself.

Kristeva's theory of religion, most clearly expressed in three volumes originally published in the 1980s, *Powers of Horror, In the Beginning,* and *Strangers to Ourselves,* represents a rewriting of Freud's major cultural texts from this position of exile, strangeness, or self-division. *Powers of Horror* revises *Totem and Taboo* by introducing the concept of the "abject"—that which we exile from ourselves—as the foundation of ritual, sacrifice, impurity, and sin. *In the Beginning* revises *The Future of an Illusion* by interpreting religious faith and imagery in terms of the penetration of the exiled semiotic into the culturally affirmed symbolic order. And *Strangers to Ourselves* revises *Civilization and Its Discontents* by finding a solution to the problem of our "discontent" in the exile, otherness, division, or "subjectivity in process" we encounter in our own unconscious. "Eternal exile" (1977:8–9) becomes Kristeva's vantage point for a new hermeneutics of religion and a new formulation of ethics, politics, and psychoanalysis.

Notes

I'd like to thank my colleague Marilyn Edelstein of Santa Clara University for her comments on an earlier draft of this paper.

1. Feminist critics of Kristeva include, in addition to Nye 1987: Stone 1983; Bruneau 1992; Butler 1989; Doane and Hodges 1992; Myers 1992; Smith 1989; Lowe 1991; and Spivak 1981, 1988. Feminist theorists who, by contrast, defend Kristeva's work include, among many others: Chopp 1993; Moi 1985; Elliott 1991; Jardine 1986; Rose 1986; Young 1990; and Zepp 1982.

2. Kristeva also is a regular visiting professor in comparative literature at Columbia University in New York.

3. For further analyses of Kristeva's differences from Lacan, see Oliver 1991; Chase 1989; Brandt 1991; Barzilai 1991; and Huffer 1991. For Lacan's third term, "the real," see Lacan 1977.

4. For some of Kristeva's other essays and books on religion, see Kristeva 1980, 1986a, 1986b, 1986c, 1987b, 1987c, 1989, and 1995. For discussions and applications of Kristeva's theory of religion, see Chopp 1993; Crownfield 1992; Edelstein 1992, 1993; Fisher 1992; Graybeal 1992; Jonte-Pace 1992; Kavanagh 1992; Kearns 1992, 1993; Reineke 1988, 1990, 1992; and Richardson 1992.

5. There is further evidence that Kristeva's inspiration was Freud's text: She introduced a case study of her own by recounting Freud's psychoanalytic interpretation of

the religious crisis of a U.S. doctor. She erroneously located Freud's interpretive essay on the doctor "in one chapter of *The Future of an Illusion*" (Kristeva 1987a:11). Freud's analysis of the religious crisis of the U.S. doctor, "A Religious Experience," a short essay written in 1928, is in the same volume of the Standard Edition as *The Future of an Illusion* (Vol. 21), but it is not part of that text. Enacting a "repetition compulsion" of sorts, Kristeva thinks she is recapitulating Freud's book, even when she is not.

References

Barzilai, Shuli. 1991. Borders of language: Kristeva's critique of Lacan. *PMLA Journal* 106: 294–305.

Brandt, Joan. 1991. The power and horror of love: Kristeva on narcissism. *Romantic Review* 82: 89–104.

Bruneau, Marie-Florine. 1992. Psychoanalysis and its abject: What lurks behind the fear of the "mother." *Studies in Psychoanalytic Theory* 1: 24–38.

Butler, Judith. 1989. The body politics of Julia Kristeva. *Hypatia* 3: 104–118.

Chase, Cynthia. 1989. Desire and identification in Lacan and Kristeva. In Richard Feldstein and Judith Roof, eds., *Feminism and Psychoanalysis*. Ithaca: Cornell University Press, pp. 65–83.

Chopp, Rebecca. 1993. From patriarchy into freedom: A conversation between American feminist theology and French feminism. In C. W. Maggie Kim, Susan M. St. Ville, and Susan M. Simonaitis, eds., *Transfigurations: Theology and the French Feminists*. Minneapolis: Fortress Press, pp. 31–48.

Clark, Suzanne, with Kathleen Hulley. 1990. An interview with Julia Kristeva: Cultural strangeness and the subject in crisis. *Discourse* 13: 49–180.

Crownfield, David. 1992a. Pre-text. In David Crownfield, ed., *Body/Text in Julia Kristeva: Religion, Women, and Psychoanalysis*. Albany: State University of New York Press, pp. IX–XX.

_____. 1992b. The sublimation of narcissism in Christian love and faith. In David Crownfield, ed., *Body/Text in Julia Kristeva: Religion, Women, and Psychoanalysis*. Albany: State University of New York Press, pp. 57–66.

Doane, Janice, and Devon Hodges. 1992. *From Klein to Kristeva: Psychoanalytic Feminism and the Search for the Good Enough Mother*. Ann Arbor: University of Michigan Press.

Edelstein, Marilyn. 1992. Metaphor, meta-narrative, and mater-narrative in Kristeva's "Stabat mater." In David Crownfield, ed., *Body/Text in Julia Kristeva: Religion, Women, and Psychoanalysis*, Albany: State University of New York Press, pp. 27–52.

_____. 1993. Toward a feminist postmodern poléthique: Kristeva on ethics and politics. In Kelly Oliver, ed., *Ethics, Politics, and Difference in Julia Kristeva's Writing*. New York: Routledge, pp. 196–214.

Elliot, Patricia. 1991. *From Mastery to Analysis: Theories of Gender in Psychoanalytic Feminism*. Ithaca: Cornell University Press.

Fisher, David. 1992. Kristeva's Chora and the subject of postmodern ethics. In David Crownfield, ed., *Body/Text in Julia Kristeva: Religion, Women, and Psychoanalysis*. Albany: State University of New York Press, pp. 91–104.

Fletcher, John, and Andrew Benjamin, eds. 1990. *Abjection, Melancholia and Love: The Work of Julia Kristeva*. New York: Routledge.

Fraser, Nancy. 1992. The uses and abuses of French discourse theories for feminist politics. In Nancy Fraser and Sandra Lee Bartky, eds., *Revaluing French Feminism: Critical Essays on Difference, Agency, and Culture*. Indianapolis: Indiana University Press, pp. 177–194.

Freud, Sigmund. 1955a. Totem and taboo. In James Strachey, trans. and ed., *The Standard Edition of the Complete Psychological Works of Sigmund Freud* (hereafter *SE*). Vol. 13. London: Hogarth, pp. 1–161.

_____. 1955b. The uncanny. In James Strachey, trans. and ed., *SE* 17 (pp. 217–252). London: Hogarth.

_____. 1957. On narcissism: An introduction. In James Strachey, trans. and ed., *SE* 14 (pp. 67–104). London: Hogarth.

_____. 1961a. The ego and the id. In James Strachey, trans. and ed., *SE* 19 (pp. 3–66). London: Hogarth.

_____. 1961b. The future of an illusion. In James Strachey, trans. and ed., *SE* 21 (pp. 5–58). London: Hogarth.

_____. 1961c. Civilization and its discontents. In James Strachey, trans. and ed., *SE* 21 (pp. 64–148). London: Hogarth.

_____. 1961d. A religious experience. In James Strachey, trans. and ed., *SE* 21 (pp. 167–172). London: Hogarth.

_____. 1964a. New introductory lectures on psychoanalysis. In James Strachey, trans. and ed., *SE* 22 (pp. 1–182). London: Hogarth.

_____. 1964b. Moses and monotheism. In James Strachey, trans. and ed., *SE* 23 (pp. 1–138). London: Hogarth.

Graybeal, Jean. 1992. Joying in the truth of self-division. In David Crownfield, ed., *Body/Text in Julia Kristeva: Religion, Women, and Psychoanalysis*. Albany: State University of New York Press, pp. 129–138.

Green, André. 1986. *On Private Madness*. Madison, Conn.: International Universities Press.

Huffer, Lynne. 1991. Julia Kristeva (1941–). In Eva Martin Satori and Dorothy Wynne Zimmerman, eds., *French Women Writers: A Bio-Bibliographic Sourcebook*. New York: Greenwood, pp. 244–252.

Jardine, Alice. 1986. Opaque texts and transparent contexts: The political difference of Julia Kristeva. In Nancy K. Miller, ed., *The Poetics of Gender*. New York: Columbia University Press, pp. 96–116.

Jones, Ann Rosalind. 1984. Julia Kristeva on femininity: The limits of a semiotic politics. *Feminist Review* 18: 56–73.

Jonte-Pace, Diane. 1992. Situating Kristeva differently. In David Crownfield, ed., *Body/Text in Julia Kristeva: Religion, Women, and Psychoanalysis*. Albany: State University of New York Press, pp. 1–22.

Kavanagh, Graham. 1992. Love and the beginning: Psychoanalysis and religion: Discussion. *Contemporary Psychoanalysis* 28: 442–449.

Kearns, Cleo McNelly. 1992. Art and religious discourse in Aquinas and Kristeva. In David Crownfield, ed., *Body/Text in Julia Kristeva: Religion, Women, and Psychoanalysis*. Albany: State University of New York Press, pp. 111–124.

_____. 1993. Kristeva and feminist theology. In C. W. Maggie Kim, Susan M. St. Ville, and Susan M. Simonaitis, eds., *Transfigurations: Theology and the French Feminists*. Minneapolis: Fortress Press, pp. 49–80.

Kristeva, Julia. 1969. *Semeiotiké: Recherches pour une semanalyse*. Paris: Seuil.

_____. 1977. *Polylogue*. Paris: Seuil. (Parts translated into English as *Desire in language*, 1980.)

_____. 1980. *Desire in Language: A Semiotic Approach to Literature and Art*. Edited by Leon S. Roudiez and translated by Thomas Gora, Alice Jardine, and Leon S. Roudiez. New York: Columbia University Press.

_____. 1982. *Powers of Horror: An Essay on Abjection*. Translated by Leon S. Roudiez. New York: Columbia University Press.

_____. 1983. Within the microcosm of "The talking cure." In Joseph Smith and W. Kerrigan, eds., *Interpreting Lacan, Psychiatry and the Humanities*. New Haven: Yale University Press, pp. 33–48.

_____. 1984. My memory's hyperbole. Translated by Athena Viscusi. In Donna C. Stanton, ed., *The Female Autograph*, special issue of *New York Literary Forum* 12–13: 261–276.

_____. 1986a. *About Chinese Women*. Translated by Anita Barrows. New York: Marion Boyars Publishers.

_____. 1986b. Stabat mater. Translated by Leon S. Roudiez. In Toril Moi, ed., *The Kristeva Reader*. New York: Columbia University Press, pp. 160–186.

_____. 1986c. Women's time. Translated by Alice Jardine and Harry Blake. In Toril Moi, ed., *The Kristeva Reader*. New York: Columbia University Press, pp. 188–213.

_____. 1987a. *In the Beginning Was Love: Psychoanalysis and Faith*. Translated by Arthur Goldhammer. New York: Columbia University Press.

_____. 1987b. *Tales of Love*. Translated by Leon S. Roudiez. New York: Columbia University Press.

_____. 1987c. La vierge de Freud. *L'Infini* 18: 23–30.

_____. 1989. *Black Sun: Depression and Melancholia*. Translated by Leon S. Roudiez. New York: Columbia University Press.

_____. 1991. *Strangers to Ourselves*. Translated by Leon S. Roudiez. New York: Columbia University Press.

_____. 1993. *Nations Without Nationalism*. Translated by Leon S. Roudiez. New York: Columbia University Press.

_____. 1995. *New Maladies of the Soul*. Translated by Ross Guberman. New York: Columbia University Press.

Kurzweil, Edith. 1986. An interview with Julia Kristeva. *Partisan Review* 53: 216–229.

Lacan, Jacques. 1977. *Écrits: A Selection*. Translated by Alan Sheridan. New York: W. W. Norton.

_____. 1982. God and the jouissance of the woman. In Jacqueline Rose and Juliet Mitchell, eds. and trans., *Feminine Sexuality: Jacques Lacan and the École Freudienne*. New York: W. W. Norton, pp. 137–161.

Lechte, John. 1990. *Julia Kristeva*. New York: Routledge.

Lowe, Lisa. 1991. *Critical Terrains: French and British Orientalisms*. Ithaca: Cornell University Press.

McCance, Dawne. 1988. Kristeva and the subject of ethics. *RFR (Resources for Feminist Research)/DRF* 17: 18–22.

_____. 1990. Julia Kristeva and the ethics of exile. *Tessera: Dialogue, conversation, une écriture à deux* 8: 23–39.

Moi, Toril. 1985. *Sexual/Textual Politics: Feminist Literary Theory.* London: Methuen.

Myers, Diana T. 1992. The subversion of women's agency in psychoanalytic feminism: Chodorow, Flax, Kristeva. In Nancy Fraser and Sandra Lee Bartky, eds., *Revaluing French Feminism: Critical Essays on Difference, Agency, and Culture.* Indianapolis: Indiana University Press.

Nickolchina, Miglena. 1991. The lost territory: Parables of exile in Julia Kristeva. *Semiotica* 86: 231–246.

Nye, Andrea. 1987. Woman clothed with the sun: Julia Kristeva and the escape from/to language. *Signs* 12: 664–686.

Oliver, Kelly. 1991. Kristeva's imaginary father and the crisis in the paternal function. *Diacritics* 21: 43–63.

Reineke, Martha. 1988. Life sentences: Kristeva and the limits of modernity. *Soundings* 71: 439–461.

_____. 1990. This is my body: Reflections on abjection, anorexia, and medieval women mystics. *Journal of the American Academy of Religion* 58: 245–266.

_____. 1992. The mother in mimesis: Kristeva and Girard on violence and the sacred. In David Crownfield, ed., *Body/Text in Julia Kristeva: Religion, Women, and Psychoanalysis.* Albany: State University of New York Press, pp. 67–68.

Richardson, Herbert. 1992. Love and the beginning: Psychoanalysis and religion. *Contemporary Psychoanalysis* 28: 420–442.

Rose, Jacqueline. 1986. *Sexuality in the Field of Vision.* New York: Verso.

Smith, Paul. 1989. Julia Kristeva et al.; or, Take three or more. In Richard Feldstein and Judith Roof, eds., *Feminism and Psychoanalysis.* Ithaca: Cornell University Press, pp. 84–104.

Spivak, Gayatri Chakravorty. 1981. French feminism in an international frame. *Yale French Studies* 62: 154–184.

_____. 1988. *In Other Worlds: Essays in Cultural Politics.* New York: Routledge.

Stone, Jennifer. 1983. The horrors of power: A critique of "Kristeva." In Francis Barker, Peter Hulme, Margaret Iversen, and Diana Loxley, eds., *The Politics of Theory: Proceedings of the Essex Conference on the Sociology of Literature.* Colchester, England: University of Essex, pp. 38–48.

Winnicott, D. W. 1971. *Playing and Reality.* New York: Basic Books.

Young, Iris Marion. 1990. *Justice and the Politics of Difference.* Princeton: Princeton University Press.

Zepp, Evelyn H. 1982. The criticism of Julia Kristeva: A new mode of critical thought. *Romantic Review* 73: 80–97.

About the Book and Editors

Religion clearly remains a powerful social and political force in Western society. Freudian-based theory continues to inform psychoanalytic investigations into personality development, gender relations, and traumatic disorders. Using a historical framework, this collection of new essays brings together contemporary scholarship on religion and psychoanalysis. These various yet related psychoanalytic interpretations of religious symbolism and commitment offer a unique social analysis on the meaning of religion.

Beginning with Freud's views on religion and mystical experience and continuing with those of Horney, Winnicott, Kristeva, Miller, and others, this volume surveys the work of three generations of psychoanalytic theorists. Special attention is given to object relations theory and ego psychology as well as to the recent work from the European tradition. Distinguished contributors provide a basic overview of a given theorist's scholarship and discuss its place in the evolution of psychoanalytic thought as it relates to the role that religion plays in modern culture.

Religion, Society, and Psychoanalysis marks a major, interdisciplinary step forward in filling the void in the social-psychology of religion. It is an extremely useful handbook for students and scholars of psychology and religion.

Janet Liebman Jacobs is associate professor of women studies at the University of Colorado, Boulder. She is author of *Victimized Daughters: Incest and the Development of the Female Self* and *Divine Disenchantment: Deconverting from New Religions.* She is co-editor, with Donald Capps, of *William James: The Struggle for Life.* She has also published numerous articles in the *Journal for the Scientific Study of Religion, Signs,* and *Sociological Analysis.*

Donald Capps is professor of pastoral theology at Princeton Theological Seminary. He received his doctorate from the University of Chicago and holds an honorary doctorate in theology from the University of Uppsala in Sweden. He is the author of several books, including *The Depleted Self: Sin in a Narcissistic Age, The Child's Song: The Religious Abuse of Children,* and *Men, Religion, and Melancholy,* a book on classic texts in the psychology of religion. He has been editor of the *Journal for the Scientific Study of Religion* and president of the Society for the Scientific Study of Religion.

About the Contributors

David Bakan is professor emeritus and senior scholar at York University and continues to teach one course on the thought of Maimonides and Freud. He has written numerous articles and books, including *Sigmund Freud and the Jewish Mystical Tradition*. His most recent book is *Maimonides on Prophecy* (1992).

Patricia H. Davis is assistant professor of pastoral theology at Perkins School of Theology, Southern Methodist University. She received her Ph.D. at Princeton Theological Seminary. She is author of several articles on empathy and women's religious experience and *Counseling Adolescent Girls*. She is currently studying the spiritualities of adolescent girls.

William James Earle is professor of philosophy at the City University of New York, Baruch College and the Graduate Center. A former Woodrow Wilson Fellow and National Endowment for the Humanities Fellow, he has written many scholarly articles, including one on William James in the *Encyclopedia of Philosophy*. He is associate editor of the quarterly *Philosophical Forum*.

Marion S. Goldman is professor of sociology and religious studies at the University of Oregon. She has done research on the former Jesus People, who belonged to the Shiloh Youth Revival Movement, and on the devotees of the Bhagwan Shree Rajneesh. She is completing a book to be titled *The Women of Rajneeshpuram*. Her publications include articles using psychoanalytic frameworks and others from a rational choice perspective.

Ralph W. Hood Jr. is professor of psychology at the University of Tennessee at Chattanooga. He is past president of the Division of Psychology of Religion of the American Psychological Association and a recipient of the Willliam James award for research in the psychology of religion given by that division. He is a former editor of the *International Journal for the Psychology of Religion* and current editor of the *Journal for the Scientific Study of Religion*. He is editor of *The Handbook of Religious Experience* (1996) and the senior author of *The Psychology of Religion: An Empirical Approach*, 2nd edition (1996).

James W. Jones holds doctorates in both religious studies and clinical psychology, is professor of religion and adjunct professor of clinical psychology at Rutgers University, and is a clinical psychologist in private practice in New York. He is the author of twelve articles and eight books, including *Religion and Psychology in Transition: Psychoanalysis, Feminism, and Theology; Contemporary Psychoanalysis and Religion;* and *In the Middle of This Road We Call Our Life*. He serves as cochair of the religion and social sciences section of the American Academy of Religion. In 1993, he was given the William J. Bier Award by Division 36 of the American Psychological Association for outstanding contributions to the psychology of religion.

Diane Jonte-Pace is associate professor of religious studies at Santa Clara University. She has published numerous articles on psychoanalysis, feminism, and religion, including "At Home in the Uncanny: Freudian Representations of Death, Mothers, and the Afterlife" in the *Journal of the American Academy of Religion* (1996). She is currently writing a book on Freud, gender, religion, and modernity. She serves as chair of the editorial board of the *Religious Studies Review*.

John McDargh is associate professor of religion and psychology in the Department of Theology at Boston College. A graduate of the Harvard University program in religious studies, he is the author of *Psychoanalytic Object Relations Theory and the Study of Religion: On Faith and the Imaging of God* and numerous articles on religious development and the integration of psychology and spirituality, particularly in the practice of psychotherapy. In 1995, he was awarded the William Biers Award by the Division of the Psychology of Religion of the American Psychological Association for his contributions to the field.

Dan Merkur is research reader in the study of religion at the University of Toronto, Canada. He trained in the history of religions at the University of Stockholm, Sweden, and conducted postdoctoral research at the Hebrew University of Jerusalem. He has taught at Syracuse, McMaster, and York Universities, and the University of Toronto. His books include *Powers Which We Do Not Know: Gods and Spirits of the Inuit* (1991); *Becoming Half Hidden: Shamanism and Initiation Among the Inuit* (2nd ed., 1992); *Gnosis: An Esoteric Tradition of Mystical Visions and Unions* (1993); and *The Ecstatic Imagination: Psychedelic Experiences and the Psychoanalysis of Self-Actualization* (1997).

Carl A. Raschke is professor of religious studies at the University of Denver, where he has taught since 1972. He is the author of numerous books and hundreds of articles on subjects ranging from philosophical theology to the study of popular culture. His most well-known works are *Theological Thinking* (1988); *Fire and Roses: Postmodernity and the Thought of the Body* (1995); and *Painted Black* (1990). He is also coeditor of the volume *Jacques Lacan and Theology* (1987). He holds a Ph.D. from Harvard University.

Charles B. Strozier is professor of history at John Jay College and the Graduate Center, City University of New York, and a senior faculty member and practicing psychoanalyst at the Training and Research Institute in Self Psychology in New York City. He is author of *Lincoln's Quest for Union* (1982), editor of *Heinz Kohut, Self Psychology and the Humanities* (1985); and coeditor of a variety of works, including *The Leader: Psychohistorical Essays* (1986); *Apocalypse: On the Psychology of Fundamentalism in America* (1994); *Trauma and Self* (1996); and *Genocide, War, and Human Survival* (1996). He is currently working on a psychological biography of Heinz Kohut.

Marcia Westkott is professor of women studies and sociology at the University of Colorado, Boulder. She is author of *The Feminist Legacy of Karen Horney* (1986) and numerous papers on the psychology of women. Her current work includes an interpretation of the concepts of self and other from both Buddhist and Western philosophical and psychological perspectives.

Index